TRUE SPEED

TONY STEWART
TRUE SPEED
MY RACING LIFE

with
Bones Bourcier

HarperEntertainment
An Imprint of HarperCollins*Publishers*

FOR MOM AND DAD, WHO GAVE ME A GREAT START
IN RACING AND IN LIFE, AND FOR EVERY CAR OWNER
WHO TOOK A CHANCE ON ME ALONG THE WAY,
ESPECIALLY THE LATE GLEN NIEBEL

❰ CONTENTS ❱

THERE HAVE BEEN TIMES WHEN I'VE WANTED TO STRANGLE TONY STEWART.

His occasional four-letter outbursts during live interviews and temper tantrums directed at fans, the media, and other drivers have made me cringe. I've wanted to remind him where he is, how he got there, and that, given his status in the racing world, he really has nothing to complain about.

But I've never had that talk with Tony, because I know that he already realizes those things.

Besides, I know exactly why he has these outbursts. It's because the guy has more competitive juices flowing within him than any race driver I've seen in a long time.

Stewart refuses to accept defeat. Winning is everything to him, whether

(© Mike Adaskaveg)

it's on the track, or with a rod and reel in his hand, hoping to catch the largest fish on one of the farm ponds for which Indiana is famous, or at a poker table. I can testify to the latter, having played a few hands against him myself.

Understanding his competitive spirit may require a look back at where he came from.

Tony and I grew up in the same general neck of the woods. I'm from Liberty, Indiana, about seventy miles east of Indianapolis, and Tony originally hails from Columbus, which is located about forty-five miles south of the capital city. Both are county seats, and therefore each proudly displays one of the Hoosier State's stately courthouses. And both locales also frequently see their young men and women marrying classmates and staying in the area to carry on the family business, often on the farm. If reproduction follows—and it usually does, sometimes faster than hoped for—the child is welcomed warmly. If the child is male, it is viewed as the ultimate gift from God.

In Indiana, a male offspring is important for a couple of reasons. To carry on the family name, for one; but just as important is the hope that the child might somehow become a hometown hero on the basketball court.

Indiana, of course, is renowned for its devotion to hoops, and throughout the state parents dream of their son being the high-point man on the high school team. If the boy were to duplicate the accomplishment of the legendary Bobby Plump, the youngster whose last-second shot in the 1954 state tournament propelled his small-town Milan team to victory over a big-city rival and is documented in the movie *Hoosiers*, that would be the ultimate thrill of a lifetime for a mom and a dad. And for the player, it would mean being the instant envy of all other male athletes in the area, and the object of the cutest cheerleader's affection.

Well, thankfully, not every young Hoosier shoots baskets in the driveway or beside the barn every night after school. Some spend their spare hours in the family garage, trying to figure out how to make a go-kart or quarter-midget run faster.

No, Tony Stewart was never the hero of the hardwood for the Columbus North Bulldogs. Rather than fantasizing about making the buzzer-beating shot in the big state tournament game, Tony's desire was to make a last-lap move for the lead, with the checkered flag in sight.

Those of us who enjoy auto racing, and especially watching fellow Hoosiers succeed, are glad he had that dream. Because today, this eldest male child born in the heart of basketball country is showing the world of sports that not all of Indiana's athletic heroes perform in gymnasiums and arenas. And Tony's parents, like all of those basketball moms and dads, are rightfully bursting with pride.

Watching Stewart mature and move through the ranks of his profession has been a fascinating experience for me. I've watched him as a broadcaster, having covered virtually every step of his career through my work with the ABC and ESPN networks, and I've watched him as a fan seeing a local boy make good.

Although Indiana is known as the capital of American auto racing, primarily but not solely because of the Indianapolis 500, few drivers born in the Hoosier State have actually risen to superstardom. In fact, until Stewart won the points title in the Indy Racing League in 1997, Indiana had not produced a national driving champion since Wilber Shaw in 1939. (Bear in mind that although Jeff Gordon claims Pittsboro, Indiana, as home—and I'm happy he does—Jeff was actually born in California.) But from Tony's first race in the United States Auto Club's midget division in 1991 at age nineteen to his first USAC championship in that division in 1994, it was apparent to me that Indiana had on its hands the first born-and-bred auto racing hero it had seen in a long time.

That belief was confirmed for good the following year.

USAC sanctions races in three Midwest-based open-wheel divisions: midgets, sprint cars, and the similar-looking but larger and heavier Silver Crown machines. In 1995, Tony Stewart won the championship in all three of those divisions.

Consider the difficulty of that accomplishment. He competed in fifty-eight combined USAC national events that year, juggling the schedules of the three classes; in fact, he won the midget championship despite missing one event in favor of racing in a competing sprint car program. There seems little doubt that Tony's effort in that ten-month period will never be duplicated.

His progression through the open-cockpit ranks next led to the Indianapolis 500, where in his freshman year he was the second-fastest qualifier at over 233 miles per hour, but was placed on the pole position for the race when his teammate Scott Brayton was killed in a practice crash after earning the inside front row starting spot. Stewart's Indianapolis speed was a hint of things to come in the IRL, and his '97 title showed that he had mastered the art of driving the fast Indy cars.

Then came what might have been the biggest dilemma of Tony's young life: to stay with the open-wheel Indy cars, or to follow the lead of so many other young drivers—including fellow USAC graduates like Jeff

Gordon and Kenny Irwin—and point his career toward NASCAR and its popular Winston Cup series.

By now, we all know what his choice was. We also know that the winning did not stop when he went south.

Stewart turned a lot of heads when he unexpectedly won the outside front row starting spot for the '99 Daytona 500. That same year, Tony became the first Winston Cup rookie driver since Davey Allison to win more than one race—Tony won three times—and was also the first rookie to finish in the top five in points since 1966. And since that rookie season, his stock car performances have only gotten better.

In just over ten years of racing at the professional level, Stewart has compiled an impressive record. But I think his true character was best displayed in a place just a bit out of the national limelight, at the Irwindale Speedway near Los Angeles. It was there, on Thanksgiving night in the year 2000, that Stewart stood in victory lane with tears streaming down his cheeks, having achieved a longtime personal goal by driving a USAC midget car to a convincing win in the Turkey Night Grand Prix. We covered that race on ESPN, and I thought that scene perfectly captured the real Tony Stewart. A casual fan might think that after all the guy had accomplished at the highest levels of racing, one more midget win would not be all that important to him, or result in such an emotional display. But that's Tony. Winning is everything, regardless of where the race happens to be, or what the reward is.

And it's that side of Stewart's personality that makes folks like me overlook the outbursts, the tantrums, and the occasional cuss. It's that side of his personality that keeps me from having that little talk with my old friend.

I think you'll enjoy reading the chapters that follow, and hearing, in Tony's own words, about his life in racing. I can only say that as a Hoosier, and a lifelong auto racing enthusiast, I'm awfully proud of the kid from Columbus. And I'm glad to see someone from Indiana making national sports headlines dressed in a firesuit and a helmet, instead of a tank top and shorts.

BOB JENKINS
ESPN motorsports anchor

IF PEOPLE LEARN ANYTHING FROM THIS BOOK, I HOPE IT'S THAT I'M NOT such a bad guy.

Really.

I don't enjoy being in the middle of controversy, and I don't like being "NASCAR's bad boy," which is a term I hear a lot. My problem is, I'm honest. Some people have said that I'm *too* honest. I guess what they

(© Mike Adaskaveg)

mean is that I'm too blunt, because I don't think there's such a thing as being too honest. But I was brought up by two great parents who always preached to me that you can never go wrong by telling the truth.

I still believe that. But now I believe this, too: in this sport, honesty can get you in a lot of trouble.

I've gotten in more hot water with race fans over things I've said than over things I've done on the track. See, when I'm upset, especially when I feel like I've been done wrong—by a competitor, by an official, it doesn't matter—I don't hide the way I feel.

The only problem is, sometimes things get lost in the translation.

With our sport as big as it is, the primary connection between the participants and the public is the media. For the race fan, that's the pipeline: the newspapers, the magazines, the TV motorsports shows. Now, I'm not one of those people who blames everything bad on the press, like some athletes and politicians do; I actually have a lot of friends in the media. But I think what happens sometimes is that there are so many sources of information, and so many media outlets sharing that information, that what comes out the other end of the pipe isn't always accurate. It's distorted. Something you say gets taken the wrong way, and by the time it gets re-reported ten more times, the level of distortion is magnified.

For example, I've done interviews in which I've talked about how unpleasant it can be to deal with certain types of fans, the pushy ones who are just plain inconsiderate, and five days later my quotes are reprinted by some columnist who says, "Stewart doesn't like race fans."

What kind of reaction do you think that gets me at the track on Sunday?

It's enough to make honesty look a lot less appealing. I mean, I'm at the point where whenever somebody mentions that there's a big story about me in the paper, I flinch.

Just today, I had a long, face-to-face interview with a newspaperman. He seemed like a nice guy, and I felt comfortable enough to open up about a lot of different things. Well, after he left I caught myself wondering if I had let my guard down too much. Did I say something in a joking way that he thought was serious? If I said something sarcastic, would it read funny, or would I just come off like a wise guy? And if some other reporter sees those quotes and borrows them for a story of his own, is he going to understand their meaning as well as the fellow who was sitting three feet away from me? Or does everything end up getting distorted, and does something come back to haunt me again?

What I've tried to do in this book is to tell my own story. It's a look at my career and my personality, for better or worse, through my eyes, rather than somebody else's.

In a lot of ways, it has been a fun process. For one thing, it provided me with opportunities to reflect on things that had been lying dormant in the back of my mind. My life seems to move so fast these days that I rarely get a chance to sit down and sift through my old memories. I don't have time to say, "Gee, 1993 was a really neat year," and then run through all the things I did that season. But as we were putting this book together, it was like one good memory led to another, and another.

And it was fun working with my co-author, Bones Bourcier. We've known each other for several years, because through his magazine work he's covered me in just about every form of racing I've participated in. He shares the same love of this sport that I do; he could follow the Winston Cup series everywhere we go, or he could just as easily chase the entire Indy car circuit, but instead he'll mix in some USAC midget races and World of Outlaws sprint car races and NASCAR modified races because he enjoys grassroots racing and the people in it. I appreciate that, because I'm the same way. I think Bones understands me, because he knows where I come from and what I've been through.

It's not realistic of me to expect *every* media member to know the smallest details of my background, or to know about every little struggle I've seen. But, at the same time, it's not realistic of them to portray me as some loudmouthed spoiled brat just because they happen to disagree with my version of the truth.

That's another description I've heard in the past couple of seasons— "spoiled"—and that drives me crazy. Nobody in this sport ever *gave* me anything. I was not a rich kid. I didn't have a single door open up for me because I was a famous driver's son, or a famous driver's brother. Any opportunity that came my way, I earned. Every ride I was ever offered was based on my performance, my reputation, or both.

Even when the rides got better and better, it wasn't an easy life in those short-track days. I slept in the backseat of my car more than once, too broke to even think about a motel room. I went to racetracks praying I'd win enough gas money to get back home. I had months where things on the track didn't go so well, and the rent only got paid because my fans bought enough of the T-shirts I'd had printed up.

So show me when I was spoiled. Show me when I asked racing to give me something I didn't have coming to me. Show me when I got something I didn't fight for, or didn't deserve.

I believe this in my heart: I've worked as hard, and gone through as much, and made as many sacrifices, as anybody in Winston Cup racing today. That's why I am the way I am, and that's why I say the things I say.

I think I've earned that right.

Hope you enjoy the book.

TONY STEWART

FIRST, THE OBVIOUS: WHY *TRUE SPEED*? WELL, IT'S SIMPLE, REALLY. *TRUE GRIT* was already taken. Too bad, because it would have been perfect; hands down, Tony Stewart is the grittiest race driver of his generation.

In an age in which so many racers have been homogenized by corporate sponsors and PR handlers, Stewart remains as raw as raw gets. He wears his heart on the sleeve of his flameproof uniform, right out there for all to see. Whatever he feels at a given moment—joy, anger, sorrow, rage—comes through unfiltered. The result has been a raucous young career marked as much by personality as by performance.

That's not an easy thing to say, because Stewart's on-track performances in everything from dirt-track cars to Indianapolis 500 machines to NASCAR Winston Cup stockers have been brilliant. But it is the way he has carried himself outside of his race cars—fiery, cocksure, and absolutely driven—that has set him apart, marked him as special.

Already, in just half a dozen seasons of top-level racing, he has left us with some indelible Tony Stewart moments. My personal favorite, not for the shock value but for the passion it laid bare, came in 1998, when Stewart's car failed him just a single lap after he had taken the lead in the one race he prizes most but has never won, the Indianapolis 500. A network television reporter did what network television reporters are supposed to do in such situations: he stuck his microphone in Stewart's face and asked him how he felt. And Stewart did what, in this day and age, anyway, race drivers are not supposed to do: he replied as directly as he could, not giving an ounce of weight to the uproar he must have known his candor would produce.

"This is the only thing I've ever wanted to do in my life," he said in a sad, even tone. "This has been my number-one goal."

Now Stewart paused. "And every year, I get shit on doing it."

Then he stalked back to his team's headquarters in Indy's fabled Gasoline Alley garage complex, and sat with his head in his hands for the rest of the afternoon. He refused to so much as acknowledge the pack of print and electronic media folks camped outside the door.

I was there that day, scribbling down notes about this young kid—he had just turned twenty-seven—so devastated in his moment of defeat that nothing else in the world seemed to exist, let alone matter. I saw all of this as gripping human drama.

Within a day or two, it was clear that lots of other folks in my line of work saw it differently. For weeks to come, Stewart took a beating from columnists and commentators enraged not just by his use of profanity, but also by his refusal to heed their beckoning notebooks and cameras. I guess I should have seen that coming; by '98, the motorsports press in general had grown so accustomed to being spoon-fed meaningless, saccharine-laced quotes from winners and losers alike—"I had a great car, the guys in the pits did a wonderful job, and God bless my sponsors"— that it had forgotten how to deal with genuine emotion.

My, how times—not to mention journalists—had changed. In 1952, when another amazing phenom, Bill Vukovich, fell out just short of victory in the Indianapolis race and then sequestered himself in his garage, writer Ross R. Olney served up this colorful word picture: "Vukovich was blistering mad. Gracious in defeat? He was a terror. He brooded, then ranted and raved, then brooded some more."

Forty-six years later, that sort of imagination had apparently gone out of fashion. It was easier to paint Stewart as a spoiled brat who didn't know how to play the media game.

Once, this was a sport that embraced characters. Today, it prefers to embrace corporate spokesmen.

Well, to hell with all that. One of the things that drew me to racing, as a fan and later as a writer, was that its participants were, well, different from the rest of us: not just braver—that was obvious—but also more brash, more open, more confident in themselves. Today, that has all changed; the thought of offending a sponsor or jeopardizing an endorsement deal causes too many drivers to live in fear of their own opinions.

And then there is Tony Stewart.

For the life of me, I cannot figure out why anybody in the racing media would have a problem with the guy. I look at it like this: putting aside personal tastes in language, anybody bold enough to curse on network TV should be viewed as a gift by reporters used to a diet of bland PR fluff. And even when he's *not* speaking, you can fill up a notebook page or two just recording Stewart's facial expressions and his body language. If your job is to portray racing as a sport of people rather than of machines, Stewart is gold.

I believe that part of the problem is that there is a tendency among the media and some fans—particularly those who have only seen the last few years of his act—to view Stewart as a kid who got to the top of his game and then turned into this monster, combative and bombastic and confrontational. But you can forget that notion. Because the Tony Stewart you see today is no different from the Tony Stewart who in 1995, having been punted out of the lead in a nationally televised midget division race by an overaggressive rival, emerged from his damaged car to flash an obscene gesture—okay, he flipped the bird—to the driver who had just taken him out.

It was a telling moment. By that point, Stewart was clearly poised on the brink of *something*: he had won a United States Auto Club championship the previous year, was in the midst of a season in which he would win three more, and was getting as much ink as any short-track racer in America. Many a driver in his position, mindful of the extra scrutiny, would have climbed from the wreckage, gathered his composure, grinned a phony grin, and offered up some politically correct version of what had happened.

But not Stewart. He had been crashed, damn it. The last thing on his mind was to worry about how things looked. To worry about an *image*.

I had to chuckle in September of 2000 when, through sheer coincidence, Stewart ended up in a brief prerace handshake with Ted Williams, the baseball legend who was serving as grand marshal for that weekend's Winston Cup event at the New Hampshire International Speedway. Williams, of course, was his era's and his sport's Tony Stewart: obsessed with his own pursuit of perfection, constantly feuding with anybody he saw as getting in the way of that pursuit—chiefly the sportswriters of the day—and not giving a damn about his public image.

Stewart knows little of baseball history, and one night at his home in North Carolina I found myself explaining the man known as Teddy Ballgame. There was no way to do this without repeating the famous line that summed up Williams's philosophy about how others saw him: "All I want out of life is that, when I walk down the street, folks will say, 'There goes the greatest hitter who ever lived.'"

I pointed out to Stewart that Williams wasn't saying, and in fact has *never* said, that he was baseball's best hitter, only that he *wanted* to be the best. Then, just sort of fishing, I asked Stewart if he could relate to that.

"Absolutely," he said, and then he paused for a long while. When he spoke again, his words came quietly. "I mean, all I want is for people to respect what I can do with a race car."

The smart ones do. Listen to A. J. Foyt, a man not given to complimenting other race drivers but also a man who, having won four Indy 500s, the Daytona 500, the 24 Hours of LeMans, and, oh, a couple hundred other major and minor races, knows a thing or two about talent.

"In my lifetime, there's probably been only two or three guys I've known who could drive just about anything they sat down in," says Foyt. "And Tony Stewart is one of 'em."

I don't know that history will one day view Stewart as the best race driver who ever lived. Nor can I say, with certainty, that he is the best I have ever seen; I suppose I've seen stock car racers as good, Indy car racers as good, midget racers as good. But you know something? I don't believe I've ever seen one better.

And I know I've never known one more honest.

He is true to himself, true to his code. He is true speed.

Watching him race has been a privilege. Covering him as a journalist has been a challenge. Collaborating with him on this book has been both. Just as I'd figured.

BONES BOURCIER

TRUE SPEED

I HAVE BEEN TO THE TOP OF THE WORLD.

Well, the NASCAR world, anyway.

It happened in February of 2001, after I'd won the Budweiser Shootout at Daytona, which is an all-star race for Winston Cup drivers held a week before the season officially opens with the Daytona 500. To be eligible, you have to have won a pole position in qualifying for one of the previous year's races. Obviously, there are no slow cars and no bad drivers in the Shootout, so it's a difficult race to win. The day I did it, it was extra difficult, because the guy I beat, the late Dale Earnhardt, had always been considered the master of that place.

Actually, Earnhardt was the master of just about every track, but at Daytona he was the boss. He had won more races there—thirty-four, in a number of different divisions—than any other driver.

When you win a race at Daytona, you go through the usual TV and radio interviews in victory lane, and then they load you into a van and drive you outside the track, to the base of the grandstands. From there, you jump into an elevator and ride up to the press box level for a much longer round of interviews. The press box sits so high, just towering over the racetrack, and it gives you a perspective of that place that you can't appreciate until you see it.

The thrill of the ride is felt from all sides. (© 2000 Phil Cavali/Winston Cup Scene)

Like I said, it's like being on top of the stock car world.

From the time I was eight years old and racing go-karts, I have seen a hundred different tracks from ground level, looking over the steering wheel. And I've been lucky enough to see a bunch of them from higher up, being interviewed in other press boxes and celebrating with sponsors in the VIP suites. Most of the time, it's just part of the job; a good part, yes, because you're usually up there for the right reasons, but part of the job anyway. You hang out for a while, and then you're anxious to get back down to the pit area to be with your guys, your teammates.

But Daytona was different. I looked out at that famous old speedway, and I thought about all it has meant to stock car racing—just to auto racing, period—and I felt like I'd been crowned king for a day. I could have stayed there forever.

Any win at Daytona is an accomplishment to cherish, but to beat Earnhardt there was an amazing feeling. The Shootout doesn't pay a million bucks to win, like the 500 does, but the fact that Dale ran second was something that couldn't be measured in dollars. In some ways it was sweeter to beat him in a race like this one—a short sprint, where there's no holding back—than to do it in a full Winston Cup event. In the Daytona 500, so much comes down to strategy and luck. In the Shootout, the only way to win is to just plain outrun 'em. And, obviously, Earnhardt wasn't an easy man to outrun.

It's ironic: that day is so special to me because of who I beat, and yet during the final few laps I had mixed emotions about having to battle with Earnhardt. On the one hand, the guy had so much talent and experience—hell, he'd won seven Winston Cup championships—that you never worried about him getting you into trouble. On the other hand, all that talent and experience was lined up against me.

At Daytona and Talladega, the biggest tracks in the series, NASCAR keeps the speeds down by reducing horsepower with restrictor plates that limit the air flowing through the carburetor. It's a safety thing; once these cars start crashing at over two hundred miles per hour, it's hard to figure out where they're going to land. What we end up with are 190-mph cars that feel extremely *underpowered*, like the go-karts at your local recreation center. We run around those two tracks wide open, holding the throttle down for the entire lap. The only way to gain speed is by drafting, taking advantage of the aerodynamic wake; the lead car punches a hole in the air, and the cars behind him kind of tag along, getting a free ride because they're essentially rolling through still air. You can follow a guy—ride in his draft—all day long, or you can use the draft as a passing tool: lay back a bit, then close on him until you sense that you've got enough momentum to swing out and pass him. It sounds simple, but it's not; drafting is a tricky, mysterious game.

It takes awhile to learn exactly how the air moves: where the calm spots are, and where the wind will swirl and buffet your car, slowing you down. Some guys never figure it out. But Earnhardt elevated drafting to an art. Around the garage area, they used to claim that Dale could *see* the air.

All I was seeing, when I found myself leading with three laps to go, was the black hood of his number 3 car in my mirror. Getting closer.

He passed me as we got to turn three, like I knew he would, and I'm sure most of the people in the grandstands figured, Well, that's that. Once Earnhardt had the lead at Daytona, it was supposed to be impossible to get it away from him.

But, you know, if I had backed down and surrendered every time somebody told me something was impossible, I'd still be back in Indiana, working a dead-end job and maybe racing part-time, and no one outside my hometown would even know my name. Because, see, I heard that it was impossible to get anywhere in this sport without big money behind you, and my family never even had *medium* money. I heard that it was impossible to win three major USAC championships in the same season. I heard that it was impossible in this day and age to jump from dirt tracks to the Indianapolis 500. I heard that it was impossible to run stock cars one week and Indy cars the next, and to be competitive in both.

But I'd *done* all that stuff.

And so when Earnhardt passed me, I did the only thing I knew: I went right back after him. I drafted up to his bumper, the same as he'd done to me, and rode there for a lap, sizing him up. And then, as we were coming around to get the white flag, I passed him back.

I did it in almost exactly the same spot where he'd passed me.

He came at me again, of course. Earnhardt never learned to back off, either, right up until the moment he was killed on the last lap of the Daytona 500 a week later. But he wasn't going to beat me that day. *Nobody* was going to beat me that day. I won the Shootout by 0.145 seconds.

Here's how small that margin is: you can't even *say* 0.145 seconds in 0.145 seconds.

Half an hour later, there I was, on top of the world, looking out from above that racetrack. Looking toward turn three, mostly, and thinking about that winning pass. I really enjoyed the view.

I answered a ton of questions from the reporters in that press box, but, to tell you the truth, I really don't remember much of what I said.

What I do remember is the feeling that for that one Sunday, I was the best guy there. And on any given day, in any given race, that's all I've ever wanted to be.

One thing about racing: it'll take you from hero to zero in a heartbeat. Five months after that great win in the Bud Shootout, I was back at Daytona. But this time, instead of crowning me king for a day, it felt like stock car racing was trying to kick me to the curb.

NASCAR had put a rule in place for the July four-hundred-miler which said, basically, that any driver who crossed over the yellow line marking the extreme inside boundary of the track would be subject to getting black-flagged. The intent of the rule was a good one, because a lot of guys were really abusing the track aprons at Daytona and Talladega. See, with the restrictor plates, anytime you get some momentum going your instinct is to take full advantage of it, even if it means running clear off the track to find a passing lane. But that's risky, because when the pack gets down to the next corner you've got cars swerving out of the infield, trying to blend in with the traffic that's already clogging all the usable lanes. We'd seen some close calls at both tracks, and with everybody jittery about safety anyway—this was our first trip back to Daytona since Earnhardt's death—I think NASCAR was just trying to keep a lid on some of the more overaggressive driving.

Well, leave it to me to find the bad points of a good rule.

I was running fourth, and heading forward, with five laps to go. Coming out of turn four, I had built up a great head of steam, which we call "getting a run" on the car ahead. It didn't hurt that my teammate, Bobby Labonte, was drafting right along behind me, pushing me toward the front. As we entered the tri-oval area of the frontstretch, I swung to the low side of Johnny Benson, who was third, and I was going to blow right by him; the speed differential was that big. But Johnny moved left to block and shut off the inside lane, which I had already committed to.

I couldn't just back off, because I had Bobby on my rear bumper, and God knows who behind Bobby. Jumping out of the throttle would have caught them all off guard and stacked up a dozen cars, I was sure of that. And I couldn't just hold my line, or I'd have spun out Benson and wiped out those same dozen cars. So I did the one thing left for me to do, the one thing that would get us all through that tri-oval: I dipped down into the only clear lane left, which happened to be just below that yellow line.

My car wiggled a bit when it transitioned from the banking to the flat apron, but I held on, and by the time I eased it back up into the groove I'd actually passed Johnny. But the main thing, to me, was that we'd all made it. Instead of a horrendous crash, it was just one more near miss. Or so I thought.

The next time we got back to the start-finish line, I got black-flagged.

I had violated the yellow-line rule.

Well, it takes a lot to surprise me, but I was absolutely stunned. Diving below the line wasn't an overtaking move on my part; it was an *evasive* move. Anyone who understood racing should have seen that.

I was sure that given the circumstances, the officials would reconsider. You see cases all the time in other sports where the referees discuss a call, maybe even look at an instant replay, and reverse themselves if they were wrong. And in my mind, then and now, whoever made that call against me at Daytona *was* wrong.

I had a decision to make. If I heeded the black flag by pulling onto pit road for a stop-and-go penalty, our shot at a decent finish was done, because I'd be two miles behind the leader by the time I got out of the pits. On the other hand, if I stayed out there and kept racing, maybe over the course of the last four laps NASCAR might review the incident and withdraw the black flag. So I stayed out there.

> **GREG ZIPADELLI**, crew chief, Joe Gibbs Racing: "Tony didn't intentionally go down there to pass [Benson], but we did go below the line, and that's what the rule says. It doesn't say, 'It depends how you get there,' it says, 'If you go below the yellow line . . .'"

We took the checkered flag in sixth spot, but NASCAR stuck to its guns. As a penalty, they dropped us to twenty-sixth, the last car running on the lead lap, which is where they figured I'd have finished had I obeyed the black flag.

If you remember, this was the night when Dale Earnhardt Jr. won at the track where his father had died, and needless to say the place was going crazy for him. I was going a little crazy myself. I did a lot of venting in the team transporter, then headed to my motorhome to change out of my firesuit. One of the regular reporters who covers our series, Mike Mulhern, was walking beside me, following up on the black-flag issue. Mike was just doing his job, I understand that, but, man, he caught me at the worst possible moment. When he held out his tape recorder, looking for a quote, I slapped it out of his hand and kicked it under a truck.

Don't bother trying to tell me that this was the wrong thing to do. I *know* that. But it happened, and once you do something like that, you can't undo it until you've got a clear head. Mine wasn't clear just yet.

As soon as I changed clothes, I went to the NASCAR trailer. Greg Zipadelli and my team owner, Joe Gibbs, were involved in a heated discussion with NASCAR's Gary Nelson, and I immediately heated it up some more. I admit, my end of the discussion wasn't exactly PG-rated. What bothered me most was this: all I wanted was a rationale for this decision that had ruined our race, and Gary wouldn't—or couldn't—give me one.

NASCAR ended up fining me ten thousand dollars for my outburst, and extended a probation I'd been on since March for *another* outburst we'll get into later on. It's not that I'm a slow learner, it's just that I've got a quick fuse when it comes to things like this.

I can live with getting outrun, but getting robbed—by a competitor or an official, it doesn't matter—is something else altogether. And maybe I don't always handle that in the most graceful way, but, damn it, this is my career, my life.

> **GREG ZIPADELLI:** "There's a fine line that we've talked about with Tony. We encourage him to think about what he's doing, to try to control himself so there aren't any repercussions later on when these things happen. And yet, you don't want him to lose his passion or his desire. I wouldn't ever want to suggest that he lose that passion."

I got crucified for a while in the press, which I expected. Every reporter in the country had either seen the video of me hollering at Gary Nelson, or heard about how I'd treated Mike Mulhern. It was suggested to me that before the next race at Chicago, I ought to issue some kind of a statement, just to quiet the uproar. That made sense to me because, if nothing else, it might stop the press from hounding me once I got to the track. So I got together with Mike Arning, our team's public relations guy, and we printed out something that said, in a nutshell, "While I still disagree with the black-flag penalty . . . I accept the fine and probation that NASCAR has issued to me as a result of my post-race conduct. Specifically, my treatment of reporter Mike Mulhern and Gary Nelson of NASCAR was inappropriate, and for that I apologize . . ."

I was satisfied with that, because it dealt with the things I'd done wrong and yet restated my feelings about that lousy call. Which, incidentally, nobody ever apologized to me for.

I also met with Mulhern privately when we got to Chicago, because I wanted him to understand that what I'd done wasn't personal. I'd probably have slapped that tape recorder out of the pope's hand in that same situation.

And, yes, I bought Mike a new recorder. Hey, I've got a soft side.

I've been in Winston Cup racing since 1999, and for that entire run I've had the same people around me: same owner, same crew chief, same pit crew. Any team gets stronger the longer it remains stable, and we've proved that. Still, it amazes me sometimes to think of what we've done together.

The Winston Cup series runs on a pretty good variety of tracks: there are small half-mile ovals like Martinsville and Bristol; one-mile tracks like Dover, Phoenix, and New Hampshire; the "intermediate tracks"—anything between one and two miles around—like Michigan, Charlotte, Texas, and Atlanta; the road courses at Watkins Glen in New York and Sears Point in California; and, of course, the two giant superspeedways, Daytona and Talladega.

I was fortunate enough to come into Winston Cup racing with a great team owner, Joe Gibbs. May 22, 1999. (© 1999 Phil Cavali/Winston Cup Scene)

In my first three years with Joe Gibbs Racing, we managed to win on every basic layout in that mix. That says a lot for our program, obviously, because even the best driver can't win without a good car. But it's satisfying for me from an ego point of view, too. I mean, anytime you conquer something new, you think, Okay, that's done, but there's always that little bit of doubt: What about the *next* thing? Well, I feel like I've proven, most importantly to myself but also to my team and my peers, that I can handle this stuff.

> **JOE GIBBS,** team owner: "I think everybody felt all along like Tony had real talent, and that he would run up front at some point in Winston Cup. But I don't think anybody guessed that he'd have done what he's done this quickly. He amazes me."

Knowing that we've won at every discipline NASCAR throws at us is a real confidence booster. I can't imagine going to a particular type of track thinking, Boy, this is going to be a tough weekend, because we always struggle at places like this. That's not the attitude you want to have on Friday morning when you show up for the first practice session, and I'm sure there are a lot of drivers who do feel that way.

But even if you're successful, this business won't let you rest on your laurels. If anything, the racers who are on top—and by racers, I mean drivers and crew chiefs and mechanics—work even harder once they *get*

to the top, because there isn't a form of racing anywhere as tough as Winston Cup. From top to bottom, it's got the closest competition. One little slip, and you're not just knocked from the peak, you're sliding down the side of a mountain.

All the variables that are merely important in every form of racing are *critical* here. You need great equipment and solid backing, which goes without saying. You need a level of communication between a driver and

Right from the start of our Winston Cup program, there wasn't a single type of track where we weren't competitive. In a series as diverse as ours, that's important. (© 2000 Phil Cavali/Winston Cup Scene)

crew chief that can overcome any problem that comes up, because in any race four or five hundred miles long, problems *will* come up. You need a pit crew at least as quick as everybody else's, because giving up two seconds on a tire stop can mean giving up fifteen positions. You need cars that, in addition to being fast, never break down. And you need a driver who will strap into that seat and drive the wheels off the car every weekend.

We've got all of that stuff.

Which is why, when everybody in the world was wondering how we could possibly top the three races we won in 1999, my rookie season, we were able to go out and lead the series with six victories in 2000. And it's why we kept winning in 2001, and why I believe we'll keep winning as we go down the road.

When we reached the double-digit mark in victories in May of 2001, it was amazing to me to think that we'd done that in just seventy-nine starts. But I didn't have long to reflect on that, because the next thing I knew we were at eleven wins, and we never looked back. We were too busy searching for number twelve, and then number thirteen, and on down the line.

BOBBY ALLISON, 1983 Winston Cup champion: "Tony has been very impressive. I've really enjoyed his performance, and it has absolutely been that: a special performance. There's been a really good chemistry with that whole team—the car owner, the crew chief, the engine builder, right through the jack man and the gas man and the tire changers—but there's also been a lot of input from the driver himself. Like I said, it has been a great performance."

The thing everybody gets wrong about my first few years in Winston Cup is that they say we've made it look easy. I don't understand that, because from where I sit, even in retrospect, it looks unbelievably hard.

I've done a lot of racing in my life. I've been fortunate enough to win a lot of things, and I've suffered some serious losses, too, personally and professionally. But never have I encountered anything that presents the highs and lows you get in this league. I mean, the emotional spikes just wear me out some days, and lately it seems like those days have come along more and more frequently.

But you know what keeps me coming back? Every now and then, there comes a day like I had that time at Daytona, beating Dale Earnhardt. When that happens, you're reminded just how nice the view is from the top of this world. And you want to do all you can to get back there.

MY FIRST WINSTON CUP VICTORY CAME ON SEPTEMBER 11, 1999, IN A
Saturday-night race at Richmond. It was only my twenty-fifth start in
the series, so it came quicker than most first wins do. In victory lane I
climbed out of my car and stood on the roof, and I had so much adrenaline running through me that I grabbed everything with reach—drink
bottles, sponsor props, everything—and threw it about a mile.

I've seen the footage of that celebration a hundred times, and every
time I watch it it's like I'm looking at somebody else. Because when I
remember that night, I still see the whole scene from *my* viewpoint.
I see the crowd going nuts, waving. I see the TV crew closing in for
an interview. I see Earnhardt and Dale Jarrett walking up to congratulate me. I see Greg and Joe and the rest of my guys grinning and
hugging.

That's a night I will never forget.

Actually, that entire weekend is pretty memorable. We lost the pole
by only a tiny margin, and by the time we got through the final practice
session our car was driving beautifully. I remember telling Greg that the
competition was going to have to come up with something really special
to beat what we had.

Generally, drivers don't talk that way. Most mechanics will tell you

*We began 1999 just hoping we could qualify for every Winston Cup race. We ended up in victory lane
three times, including here at Phoenix. November 7, 1999. (© 1999 Phil Cavali/Winston Cup Scene)*

that we're never happy with our cars. But Richmond was one of those days when you can sense that things are going your way.

Now, I'd had that feeling a couple of times already in 1999 only to have one thing or another go wrong, so I tried not to be overly optimistic. But at Richmond I knew, in my heart, that barring any crazy disasters we were *not* going to be beaten.

And I was right. The only guy who was anywhere near me at the end of the race was Bobby Labonte, which was nice because it gave Joe Gibbs his first one-two finish as a Winston Cup team owner.

Just knowing Bobby was back there made me relax. I knew that if he caught me he was going to race me hard, because that's Bobby, but I also knew that he's not the kind of driver who would lay a bumper on my car if he caught me on the white-flag lap. That's not to say another driver *wouldn't* have raced me clean, but with some guys you can't be sure.

The way it turned out, we were quick enough that it really didn't matter who was second. Bobby got close, but not *that* close. I ended up leading 333 of the 400 laps, and yet I never beat up the engine, never abused the brakes, never hurt the tires. We weren't up front because the driver was charging hard; we were there because we had a perfect car.

The only thing that wasn't perfect was the victory lane ceremony, with me throwing all that stuff around. I looked like a guy who had never won a thing, and didn't think he'd ever win again. But, God, I was just so relieved.

I had won a bunch of races in my life, and, deep down, I believed I could win at the Winston Cup level. But believing and knowing are two different things. The higher up you get in this sport, the truer that gets.

Our objectives heading into 1999 were pretty basic: to qualify for every race and to log as many laps as we could, building experience. For a team as green as ours—I had never driven a Winston Cup race, and Greg had never been a Winston Cup crew chief—that experience was going to be the most important thing in the world.

We hoped that if everyone on the team did his job, we might be able to finish some races in the top fifteen. If we did that enough, it stood to reason that we might end up in the top fifteen in the points standings, too. That was the goal.

GREG ZIPADELLI: "It's kind of funny, looking back. There were no real big expectations on us. It was easy, it was fun, it was exciting."

Well, things went a little better than that. We won twice more after Richmond, in back-to-back races at Phoenix and Homestead. No rookie had ever won three Winston Cup races in what NASCAR calls its modern era, going back to 1972. In fact, not since Davey Allison in 1987 had a rookie won even twice. And none of our victories were flukes; we were in the picture all race long, every time.

I have loved Phoenix International Raceway from the first time I went there in 1993, and I'd had a lot of great days there in Indy cars, midgets, and Silver Crown cars. I was eager to run Phoenix with the Winston Cup car, because I felt like I wouldn't be giving anything away to the competition. In the course of the '99 season we had gone to several tracks I had never even *seen*, let alone driven. That's spotting a lot of knowledge to the NASCAR veterans, and knowledge always translates to speed. Those guys had all been to Phoenix, but I felt like I knew that place as well as any of them. I could pinpoint every bump, every ripple, and every usable inch of that track.

For most of that race, I had the same feeling I'd experienced at Richmond; I *knew* we had a winning car. But toward the end, Mark Martin was lurking in second, and Mark is one of those guys who always finds a way to chisel away a hundredth of a second here and a tenth of a second there, and next thing you know he's on your bumper. Thankfully, my guys did a great job on our last pit stop, and that gave us the cushion we needed.

Richmond had been a victory for our entire team, our first win together. This one, on the other hand, was a personal victory for me. Phoenix is probably fifteen hundred miles from the places around Indiana where I cut my racing teeth, but in a lot of ways it feels like my home track. I'd been out there eight or ten times, and I had developed nice relationships with the folks who run the place. On top of that, my mom and my sister had flown out there for the race. Nobody from my family had been at Richmond, so this was the first time we got to celebrate a Winston Cup win together.

PAM BOAS, mother: "It's hard to even describe the feeling I had. To be able to share that joy with Tony was a real thrill."

NATALIE STEWART, sister: "That was incredible. It was a totally different feeling than I'd ever had after any of Tony's wins in different forms of racing. I was so excited for him, and so proud of him."

Just one week later, we went to Florida for the first-ever Winston Cup race at Homestead, and won again. This time, it wasn't exactly a dominant performance; we struggled quite a bit. NASCAR opened practice a day early because this was a new venue, but the extra laps didn't seem to help my car much. We finally got it going pretty good with lots of help from Bobby Labonte and his crew chief, Jimmy Makar, who got a handle on the place a lot quicker than we did.

There came a point late in the race when Bobby and Jimmy probably wished they hadn't straightened us out. It was clear that one of us was going to win; our cars were pretty equal, with Bobby's just a tiny bit faster. He made his final pit stop, and then I came in a lap or two later, and as I got back up to speed we were neck-and-neck on the backstretch, with him inching ahead as we reached turn three. I knew my only chance to win was to beat Bobby into that corner, and I took that chance. But my tires hadn't heated up enough to build the grip I needed; my car slipped, and I hit Bobby's car just hard enough to knock us both out of control for an instant.

I came away from that bump with the lead, while Bobby slid up into all the sand and spent rubber that builds up outside the racing lanes. Fortunately, he didn't crash, which is a testimony to his skill. He kept his car out of the wall, and together we gave Joe Gibbs Racing another one-two finish.

It was not the prettiest performance I'd ever had, but it was another Winston Cup victory.

We ended 1999 on a high note, celebrating three wins, but we'd started one, too. Right out of the box we set the second-fastest time for the Daytona 500, which wasn't a bad Winston Cup debut at all. When I walked into the media center for the front-row press conference and sat down beside Jeff Gordon, who had won the pole, that seemed to give instant credibility to our whole team: me, Greg, all the guys, and even our sponsor. The Home Depot had never been involved in NASCAR racing, and right away they had their rookie driver sitting alongside a three-time Winston Cup champion.

Still, I wasn't about to get overly optimistic. You've probably heard other drivers say this, but running a fast lap at Daytona is not a particularly hard thing to do. The driver's only job is to be smooth and not scrub off any speed. The whole ball game is having the right car: a strong engine, a sleek body, the perfect chassis. So even though it was great to be on the front row for my first Cup race, I knew in my heart that any number of drivers could have gone as fast as I did.

And I knew that, fast or not, I was still a rookie in the eyes of everybody in the garage area, especially the veteran drivers. But just in case I had forgotten that, they were quick to remind me.

The qualifying procedure for the Daytona 500 is the most complicated on the circuit. After time trials, the field is divided in half, then everybody lines up for two 125-mile heat races. The odd-number qualifiers run the first 125, and the even-number qualifiers run the second, which meant that I started on the pole in our 125.

I jumped out front and led the first seven laps, with Earnhardt on my bumper. I knew it was only a matter of time before he decided to put the rookie in his place, but I wasn't sure what I ought to do when that moment came. I had watched a lot of Daytona races on television and seen plenty of guys, including Dale, do some pretty blatant blocking. But would that be the right thing for a newcomer to do? Would that be following the proper rookie etiquette?

There was only one way to find out, I figured. So when Earnhardt made his move, out of turn two, I threw him a block. It worked. It also upset him, I guess, because he gave me a tap. That was my warning: *Don't do that again!* On the next lap he made a run on the frontstretch, and this time I didn't defend my position. Earnhardt went by, with a long freight train of cars drafting along behind him. I dropped from first to fourteenth, but to be honest that was something of a relief. Now, instead of worrying about my lead and about

Earnhardt, I could concentrate on learning the draft better myself.

If you're going to race with these guys, you'd better know what *they* know, and that 125-miler was like one long study hall for me. I tried a few moves that worked and a few that didn't, and by the end I had climbed back up to sixth.

It wasn't a great first run, but it was a good one. In fact, it was a better run than we had three days later, in the 500; our engine went sour early, so all I could do was limp around for the rest of the race. We finished twenty-eighth. Still, between our qualifying run and our effort in the 125-miler, we could hold our heads up leaving Daytona. Everybody certainly knew we were there.

We were on a pretty good roll, and we stayed on it for a while. In the next race, at Rockingham, we finished a lap down in twelfth; that's not normally a finish to brag about, but Rockingham is a tricky place. A lot of guys never get the hang of it, and yet we were just out of the top ten, so we were close. Then we got caught up in a wreck at Las Vegas, but we were competitive while we were running, so I didn't let it get me down too badly.

Already, I could see some potential. Across the next couple of months, that feeling just grew.

In the seven races after Las Vegas, we either started

There came a point early in 1999 when our team's potential became obvious. Every week we were somewhere near the top of the time sheets. (© 1999 Phil Cavali/2000 Winston Cup Scene)

in the top ten or finished there, including a great run at Bristol where we had a shot to win until we got tangled up in somebody else's crash. What that stretch showed me, and showed everybody else, too, was that we were capable of being in the hunt on a weekly basis. We were always in the picture somewhere: maybe we started near the front, maybe we finished near the front, but at *some* point we were near the front.

Little by little, our outlook changed. We didn't *talk* about it much, but I think every member of the organization, from Joe and Greg right on down, started thinking of himself as part of a team that was now a proven threat to run in the top five.

And once you convince yourself that you're a top-five team, it's not a big jump to think about winning. It's like the idea slowly sank in: "We can *do* this."

> **SCOTT DIEHL,** chief mechanic, Joe Gibbs Racing: "The thing about Tony is, he's a racer. How do you tell somebody is a racer? That's hard to explain. But you either are, or you aren't. The way I like to say it is, you're either a talker or a doer, and he's obviously a doer. You could see that right away."

Other people began to see that, too. I'm not one of those drivers who says he never reads the newspapers and the magazines, or says he doesn't watch the racing shows on TV. I see *all* that stuff, and early in 1999 I sensed a change in the way the media looked at our team. At first we had been the object of a lot of curiosity; every commentator asked if we were, to use their cliché, "the real deal." But by the time the season was just a few months old, they had ditched that question. We were qualifying great, we were leading races, and we were hovering between fifth and seventh in the points standings. As a Winston Cup team—not just a rookie team, but a Cup team, period—we were about as real as it gets.

Remember that goal of maybe finishing some races in the top fifteen? Well, we had one stretch—from the ninth race at Talladega to the twenty-eighth at Dover—when we never finished *out* of the top fifteen. That's twenty consecutive races!

Better still, eleven of those finishes were top-fives.

There were actually times in that period when we'd finish seventh or ninth, and it would feel like a bad day. I'd get out of the car dejected that we'd missed out on a top-five. Then I'd think, Dude, look at the big picture. You had a better finish today than you ever hoped to have when the year started. What is there to feel bad about?

Of course, there *were* a couple of days when I was justified in feeling bad. At New Hampshire in July, we were leading with three laps to go when we ran out of gas. Instead of getting my first Winston Cup win, I was lucky to end up tenth. And in the Brickyard 400 at Indianapolis, where I had hoped to do well in front of my home crowd, we never really got going and finished a boring seventh.

But Indy and New Hampshire were rare letdowns that summer. We finished sixth and fourth in the two Pocono races, ran a strong sixth in the four-hundred-miler at Daytona, and climbed all the way from thirty-seventh—our worst start all year—to finish third at Michigan.

And, of course, there was that Richmond win.

All those good finishes just kept pushing us higher in the Winston Cup standings. Just like we'd adjusted our thinking regarding our race finishes, we started to look more closely at our potential in the points, too. By April we were tenth, and I told myself I'd be happy just to stay there because a top-ten gets you onto the stage at the televised NASCAR banquet and is a huge perk for the sponsors. But then we climbed to eighth, and then sixth, and then fifth, and then fourth.

We backslid a bit in October, finishing forty-first at Martinsville—after a wreck I'll tell you more about later—and then running nineteenth at Charlotte, sixth at Talladega, and twelfth at Rockingham. It wouldn't be fair to call that a slump, but we were definitely scratching our heads, trying to figure out what we needed to do to get back on track.

As it turned out, all we needed was to go to the next two races.

At Phoenix and Homestead.

Those two wins locked us into fourth place in the final standings. It was the highest finish by a rookie in better than thirty years.

We ended that season with twenty-four top-ten finishes, sixteen of them top-fives. And here's something to think about: in thirty-four starts, our *average* finish was tenth.

GREG ZIPADELLI: "We were so caught up in trying to not make those rookie mistakes that I'm not sure it dawned on us how good we were doing. But when you look back at it now—winning three races, leading all those laps—I'm still waiting for somebody to wake me up and tell me it was a dream."

JOE GIBBS: "Tony's first year was phenomenal. I mean, it raised the bar for all these new guys coming along."

It seemed pretty sure that I was going to be named Winston Cup Rookie of the Year, but I wasn't taking anything for granted because the award is based on more than statistics; there's a panel that considers everything from your off-track behavior to your relations with the media. When NASCAR made it official, it was almost like graduating from high school, like saying, "Well, that's behind me now, but it sure was fun."

I figured our 1999 results would get everybody on our team jacked up for 2000, and I was right. What I hadn't counted on was that the rest of the world would have big plans for us, too.

Over the winter, a bunch of reporters and columnists picked me to win the Winston Cup championship in just my second year. Earnhardt had won his first title in 1980, *his* sophomore year, and a lot of these people figured that since I'd been the hottest rookie they'd seen since Dale in '79, it was only logical that I'd follow up with a championship, just like he had.

Even *Sports Illustrated* had us down as the favorite.

All of that was flattering, but I'm a realist. Sure, if we took the speed and consistency we'd shown in the second half of '99 and stretched it across an entire season, maybe a championship was possible. But in this sport, you can't ever count on maybes.

So I had a choice heading into the 2000 season: I could buy into the hype and start clearing a spot on my shelf for the Winston Cup, or I could climb into the car like I hadn't done a damn thing the previous year, or any year before that. I chose the second option.

— — — — —

Obviously, we proved a lot of the experts wrong by missing the championship by a mile, ending up sixth in the standings, but we had a pretty spectacular 2000 anyway. We led the league with six Winston Cup victories: two at Dover, and one each at Michigan, New Hampshire, Martinsville, and Homestead. There were three drivers with four wins each—Rusty Wallace, Jeff Burton, Bobby Labonte, who won the championship—and to beat that bunch as handily as we did was a major deal for us.

The most satisfying win came late in the year, at Martinsville. I had never been fond of that track, and I'm still not. Oh, the people who run the place are nice, and the fans there really get into the race; the grandstands are so close that you can literally look the spectators in the eyes, whether they're cheering or flipping you off, and I've seen both. But Martinsville, with its long straights and tight, flat turns, is the toughest track in the world to negotiate with a Winston Cup stock car. You find yourself wearing out the brakes trying to slow down, and spinning the rear wheels trying to speed up.

SCOTT DIEHL: "You've got to be smart at Martinsville. It's not like you can go out there and race balls-to-the-wall, like you can at Dover or someplace like that. Martinsville is a finesse place."

In my sophomore season, we led the league with six Winston Cup victories, including two at Dover. (© Phil Cavali/Winston Cup Scene)

And yet we swept the weekend, setting a new track record in qualifying and then winning the race. But it sure wasn't easy. Jeff Burton had the fastest car for most of the day, but toward the end my guys made some adjustments and gave me the best car I'd ever driven at Martinsville, maybe the best car *anyone* had ever driven there. We took the lead just twenty-six laps from the end, and I figured we were going to just run off and hide. Then there was a yellow flag for a crash, and when the race restarted with eleven laps to go, I had Dale Earnhardt glued to my back bumper.

Now, it's tough enough to get the best of Martinsville Speedway, and even in your worst nightmare you couldn't dream up an opponent more fierce than Dale Earnhardt. So I'm sure that it's the combination of those two ingredients—beating that man at that track—that makes that win so special.

People talk about how great Earnhardt was at Daytona and Talladega, and he really *was* magic there. But don't forget, his whole "Intimidator" reputation was built at bump-and-grind places like Martinsville. If he was in second place in the closing laps of a short-track race, he had a better-than-average shot at the victory. He had a way of making things happen; he might drive deeper into the corner than you, or he might beat you back onto the throttle coming *out* of the corner. If all that failed, he might roughhouse you a bit. Even then, it was not so much a physical game with Earnhardt as a mental game; he'd get you so focused on what he was doing back there that you'd lose track of what *you* were doing. Just by his presence, that man forced a lot of good drivers into making mistakes.

All I wanted from those last eleven laps was not to become one of those guys.

I got the restart exactly right and built a nice gap by the time we reached turn one, so Dale never even got a chance to rattle me. From there until the end, I ran a series of textbook laps: perfect braking, perfect entry, perfect exit, perfect acceleration.

It was, and is, one of the best victories of my life.

Our Dover wins were pretty satisfying, too. The strange thing was, I didn't qualify well either time. But Dover is a place I just love to race. Even though it's got a concrete surface, it takes me back to my dirt-track roots. See, on dirt you have to search around for the fast groove, the lane where your car works best, and that groove is always moving. In four hundred miles at Dover, it can change a dozen times, and some drivers don't recognize that.

Our Homestead victory in the next-to-last race of the year was pretty straightforward. We had the best car, and we were able to sustain our pace all day. There's no such thing as a boring win, but this wasn't exactly the most exciting race I'd ever had. Nobody else was fast enough to give us much of a fight, and I wasn't about to drop back just to give *them* one.

> **DALE EARNHARDT JR.,** Winston Cup driver: "It's like this: You're at Homestead. You're sitting there wrestling your car, busting your ass, trying so hard not to spin out. Then there's Tony. You see that guy cruise on by you and just drive away, and you say to yourself, 'Man, that dude right there is gooooood.'"

The only problem I had at Homestead, really, was the Florida heat. I've always been claustrophobic, which, as far as I know, makes me pretty unique among race drivers. I can't predict when my claustrophobia will kick in, but whenever I feel like I'm trapped in a small space— an elevator, a tight crowd of people, whatever—it trips a wire in my brain. When that wire trips, it's like the walls are closing in, and I want out of there, fast. For some reason, heat exaggerates the process, and that can be a problem on a hot day in the interior of a stock car, which is a pretty tight space to start with.

Anyway, as soon as I started to feel the heat at Homestead I radioed my guys to get some ice ready. They stuffed it into my firesuit, right onto my chest, on the next pit stop. That chilled me down enough to ward off any claustrophobic attacks, I guess, and from there we cruised home with the win.

But what was even cooler than the ice was the victory lap. Bobby Labonte clinched the Winston Cup title by finishing fourth, and the two of us toured the speedway at half-speed for an extra lap. That's a big endorsement for the strength of a team: one car wins the race, the other wins the championship. Days like that don't come around often, and Bobby and I both wanted to savor the moment. I was as happy about him winning that championship—happy for Bobby, for Joe, for Jimmy Makar, all of 'em—as I was about the ninth Winston Cup victory of my career.

GREG ZIPADELLI: "That day meant so much to both teams. From our side, we had dominated the race, and we could also say that we had a hand in helping Bobby's team win the championship. It was just a special thing. I mean, it was easy for us, me and Tony and the guys on our team, to look over there and say, 'Hey, we could do that, too.' It was the kind of thing that gets you motivated."

But my most emotional win of 2000 came in July, at New Hampshire. Two days earlier, at the start of the opening Friday practice, Kenny Irwin had been killed in a one-car crash. Kenny was still so young, just thirty, and his Winston Cup career was really just getting started. His death was a devastating thing for everybody who knew him, me included.

I had been around racing long enough that I'd seen this sort of thing before—too many times, in fact—but I'm not sure I'd ever had anything hit me as close to home as Kenny's crash. For ten seasons, all the way back to 1991 when we both broke into USAC as rookies, our two careers had run almost parallel: up through midgets and sprints and the Silver Crown series, then onward from there. I went to Indy cars, and Kenny went to NASCAR, first in the Craftsman Truck series and then in Winston Cup, where he was Rookie of the Year in 1998. Sometimes we were friendly and sometimes we weren't, because each of us was usually trying to take something from the

This was an emotional moment. I'd just learned that I'd been declared the winner at New Hampshire in July of 2000. That weekend, Kenny Irwin had lost his life in a practice crash. July 9, 2000.
(© 2000 Phil Cavali/Winston Cup Scene)

other one, whether it was a midget trophy or a single position in a Cup race. But we were always sort of linked together, at least in my mind, and now Kenny was gone.

That Sunday, we dominated the race. Rain shortened the distance from 300 laps to 273, and I led 156 of those. They set up a makeshift victory lane in one of the garages to keep us dry, and when I was standing there with the trophy I didn't know whether to smile or cry. So I did a little bit of both.

If those were the races when things went right, we also had plenty in 2000 when things went wrong. In fact, the single biggest reason we did so poorly in the points standings—compared to '99, anyway—was that we had too many stupid things knock us out of contention, and sometimes out of races altogether.

In March at Atlanta, I messed up and hit the wall. Just when I thought the wreck was over, here came Robert Pressley, sliding into me at warp speed. We were done for the day, with a thirty-sixth-place finish. That same month at Bristol, something flew up off the track—a rock or a small piece of debris—and knocked off the belt that drives the oil pump. When the oil doesn't pump, the engine doesn't survive. We finished forty-second.

At Pocono in July, we won the pole, but I never led a single lap of the race. We cut a tire, lost a lap, and finished twenty-sixth. And in October at Talladega, we fell a lap behind again because of a tire problem and ended up twenty-seventh.

All of those days were frustrating. Others were just kind of silly.

At Talladega in April, both Bobby and I had engine trouble in qualifying. He started thirty-seventh, with me thirty-ninth. Well, it's common knowledge that the tight drafting packs in restrictor-plate races often lead to big wrecks that can involve fifteen or twenty cars; you always hear drivers say, "Our game plan today is to avoid the Big Wreck, and hopefully get us a good finish." So we had a little team meeting and decided that the two of us were going to outsmart the world: we'd draft around at the back, avoid the Big Wreck by not being in the middle of the pack, and then chase down the leaders at the end.

The only problem was, as we got into the last third of the race, the

TRUE SPEED

crash hadn't happened yet, and the leaders were literally out of sight. So Bobby and I got serious, and we began to reel in the front pack, lap by lap. We had just about pulled ourselves up into contention when all hell broke loose.

It began the way the Big Wreck always begins: somebody wiggled and hit somebody else. This one tangled up sixteen cars, and Bobby and I, charging from behind, were about the last two men in.

If it wasn't for the fact that there's a lot at stake in crashing at 190 miles per hour, it would have been funny.

But I think our worst day came at New Hampshire in the fall. NASCAR had reacted to Kenny Irwin's death by making us run restrictor plates in the second race there. The thinking was that slowing the cars down was a quick temporary fix. Well, none of the Cup teams had any experience with restricted engines on one-mile tracks, and with so little horsepower most guys found it impossible to pass. Jeff Burton led all three hundred laps.

We qualified sixteenth, and in the race I seemed to be one of the few guys able to do any passing at all. But anything that could go wrong *did* go wrong that day. Three times we pitted under green-flag conditions for scheduled stops, only to have the yellow flag come almost immediately, costing us a lap each time. At the end of the race, we were three laps behind, in the twenty-third spot.

> **GREG ZIPADELLI:** "That was probably our worst day together, because we had a car good enough to win and yet there was nothing we could do about it. Neither one of us was in a talkative mood that day."

The best thing about that weekend was lifting off the runway on Sunday evening and seeing New Hampshire disappear as we passed through the clouds.

But you know what might be even worse than a race where you're never in contention? A race where you *think* you're in contention, only to have some weird circumstance change all that. We had several days like that in 2000.

In the Daytona 500 we were quick, but I ran into a stray tire on pit road and caved in the nose of our car. My crew fixed it as best they could, but you don't spend all winter fabricating the perfect, slippery nose, and then replicate it in the pits with hammers and duct tape. Our car handled like a truck after that. Then, just to make a bad day worse, I ran into one of my crewmen, Mike Lingerfelt, on a later stop; he had jumped out to retrieve another runaway tire just as I was accelerating out of the pits, and I never saw him. Poor Mikey broke his leg and was out of action for several months.

At the Sears Point road course in June, I was the one who was hurting. I had a stomach flu, but still we managed to qualify fourth, and even though I was pretty weak on race day I passed Jeff Gordon for the lead just past halfway. Then Scott Pruett, who had fresher tires than Jeff and I, got into the mix. We had a fun little battle, but then Scott's car slipped and nudged me out into the dirt, and the whole field passed me. That was enough; I didn't think I was physically strong enough to get the car back to the front, so I came down pit road and handed the car over to John Andretti, whose own car had dropped out earlier. John did a terrific job, charging all the way back up to tenth at the finish, but tenth was less than I thought we deserved that weekend.

We also had too many days when the car was good for parts of a race, but we just couldn't get it to run right for the *whole* race. At Rockingham in the spring, I abused the tires toward the end of the race, trying to catch Bobby Labonte, who won, and Dale Earnhardt, who finished second. I ended up slipping and sliding so badly that Ward Burton passed me for third with three laps to go. Yet when we went back to that same track for the fall race, the exact opposite scenario occurred: as other drivers fell back on worn tires, my car handled better. In the last forty laps, we went from battling for a top-twenty spot to finishing seventh.

Go figure.

> **GREG ZIPADELLI:** "It's all just part of the learning process. If we have a day where I don't understand exactly what Tony's saying about the car, or how much we need to change it, there might be a little gap between us and some of the guys who know more about these Winston Cup cars. And at this level, that little gap can turn into a big one."

But, you know, most of that stuff is at least explainable. What I couldn't figure was why, when I was tracking down Jeff Burton for the lead at Las Vegas, it rained so hard that they called the race official after just 148 of 267 laps.

Isn't Las Vegas in the *desert*?

Looking back, the general pattern of our 2000 season wasn't a whole lot different from our rookie year: we came out of the box slower than I'd have liked, but once we hit our stride we were usually in the picture. I mean, just from the point when we won our first race, we went six for twenty-two in the victory column, which is really strong.

> **GREG ZIPADELLI:** "We had an up-and-down year, but to come back and perform so well, after all the hype and pressure we were facing early on, said a lot for this team."

Incidentally, we weren't the only young team putting up good numbers. Matt Kenseth, the 2000 Rookie of the Year, won the Coca-Cola 600 at Charlotte, and Dale Earnhardt Jr., another rookie, won at Texas and Richmond.

All year long, the media kept asking me—as the reigning rookie, I guess—what I thought about how well those guys were running. I kept saying that it wouldn't have surprised me if one of those guys had a better rookie season than I'd had. After all, they were both great drivers, and in a lot of ways their backgrounds prepared them for Winston Cup racing better than mine did. Besides, I liked Junior and Matt both, so I was happy they were doing well.

But was I happy that neither one of them got to three wins, like we'd done the year before? Hell, yeah. Anytime somebody does something special, like those guys were doing in 2000, it's nice to be able to grin and say, "Been there, done that. Actually, done it *better*."

It's a pride thing.

Speaking of pride, there's probably nothing more humbling to a race driver than a couple years in Winston Cup.

All of us, right from the time we're kids, have parents and coaches and teachers drilling into our heads the idea that you can't win 'em all.

Well, somewhere during the 2000 season I finally began to accept that. I can't pinpoint exactly when it happened, because it's not like I woke up one day after a tough loss and caught myself smiling. But I slowly came to realize that in a series stacked with so many good drivers, good mechanics, and good teams, I'd have to take the bad with the good.

As long as the bad didn't come too often.

There was a time back in my short-track days when I'd be upset about running second. If I finished third, I was *really* down. Anything past third, don't even talk to me. But at the Winston Cup level, you learn to get over that. You *have* to. The idea that you're never going to come up short to Jeff Gordon or Dale Jarrett or Rusty Wallace or Mark Martin or Dale Earnhardt Jr. is ridiculous, and if one of those guys doesn't get you, his teammates might. Or *your* teammate might.

Don't get me wrong, I will never be completely satisfied unless I win. But I've come to understand that a top-five finish in a Cup race is a pretty good day. It's a reason to celebrate. No, you may not have that wild, ecstatic feeling after running third that you do after a victory, but you still deserve to feel an enormous sense of achievement.

I guess it's like being in the Olympics. When you're on that podium, holding your bronze medal, you might not be as happy as the guy with the gold. But when it comes right down to it, the bronze isn't such a bad thing. You're an Olympic medal winner. You've accomplished something worthwhile at the highest level of your sport.

It's the same deal in Winston Cup, and if you don't understand that, you're going to be one sad race driver. Even in his best years, Richard Petty lost a lot more than he won. So did Dale Earnhardt. So has Jeff Gordon. And so will I.

As long as we manage to put up decent numbers even on our bad days—top fives, top tens—I can deal with getting outrun.

What I *can't* deal with is getting things taken from me. I had that feeling a couple of times in 2001—most notably that yellow-line/black-flag incident at Daytona—and it didn't exactly make for a calm season. I guess I've never been one to walk away quietly if I feel like we've been done wrong.

RONNY CROOKS, chassis specialist, Joe Gibbs Racing: "You know what? When I see Tony get mad like he's done a few times, it's pretty cool to me, because I can see how nuts it drives him when something goes wrong. I look at it like, No fire, no desire."

We had an infamous incident with Jeff Gordon at Bristol, where he spun me out on the last corner of the last lap and knocked me from fourth to twenty-fifth. I was disappointed enough in Jeff that I spun him out on pit road after the race, and ended up getting fined ten thousand dollars and put on my first NASCAR probation of the season.

And I got a little bit hot under the collar at Pocono, after what was called a "miscommunication" between NASCAR and our team. What happened was, we were fourth when a yellow flag waved on lap 12, and Greg called me in for tires. Pocono had been very tough on tires that weekend, and Greg's logic was that as the other cars started to slip and slide, we'd gain ground on our fresher rubber. It was a good strategy, but it blew up in our faces. See, NASCAR had scheduled a caution on lap 25 to check tire wear, but the official on pit road never passed that information to Greg. Had we known, we'd have waited to pit with everybody else. As it was, when that scheduled caution came out, we couldn't afford to spot those guys the extra laps we had on our tires, so we pitted again, but instead of ducking in with the leaders we were deep in the pack. We fought our way back to finish seventh, but we'd have been higher if we hadn't had to climb out of that hole.

Now, I understand that people make mistakes. I've already admitted to a few, and you'll find lots more before we get to the last page of this book. Most times, when I make a mistake, I'll do my best to set things right. But when a bad call goes against you, no matter what organization you're racing with, you're expected to take your lumps. You're lucky if you even get an explanation.

I look at it like, my race team lost positions, points, and money at Pocono. Who do I fine for that?

Controversy might have kept us in the headlines, but we managed to get into the news for some good things in 2001, too.

In August we went to Bristol for the night race, which is a huge hit with fans and maybe the toughest ticket in NASCAR, and won the show. And at Richmond in June, I won maybe the best Winston Cup race I have ever driven. For most of the night we chased Rusty Wallace; I had the feeling that my car might be better than his on a long run, but caution flags kept interrupting the flow of the race. We also had some pit-stop problems that cost us a few positions. Anyway, with one hundred laps to go we were running fifth, and our chance at another Richmond victory looked slim.

Then, just when we needed it most, I got the long run I had hoped for, and it confirmed every good thought I'd had about that race car. We worked up into fourth, then third, and I had to wrestle for about twenty laps with Ricky Rudd before he gave up second.

I caught Rusty with fifty laps to go.

I mentioned earlier what a thrill it was to race with Dale Earnhardt at Daytona. Well, anytime Rusty Wallace is on top of his game at a short track, fighting with him gives you a similar sensation. At Richmond, we had one heck of a fight. They told me later in the press room that he and I ran side by side for six consecutive laps before I took the lead for good.

I said, "Six? It felt more like sixty!"

Rusty was quoted in the papers as saying, "I really hated giving up that victory," and I can tell you that he wasn't lying. He drove me hard, but he drove me fair. It was the kind of battle I love to be a part of.

GREG ZIPADELLI: "Tony drove a real good race that night. We got behind on a couple of pit stops; it's not that they were bad stops, it's just that you're not always going to beat the best of these teams. But every time that happened, Tony showed a lot of maturity. It would have been easy for him to get upset, but he had confidence in his car and in himself. He used his head, wore the other guys out, and took the lead."

We had another thrill-a-minute win at Sears Point. For a while, it looked like third was as good a finish as we could expect. Jeff Gordon was awfully strong, like he always is on road courses, and Robby Gordon, who was between steady rides and just filling in for a team that needed a good road racer, was doing a great job. Between them, Jeff and

Robby—who aren't related, by the way—led the first two-thirds of the race.

Then Jeff slipped a couple of times in the hairpin turn, which was rare; that guy doesn't slip twice in most seasons, let alone twice in the same corner in the same race. But those mistakes moved Robby into the lead, and me into second. Then Robby got into a long scrap with Kevin Harvick, who was a lap down but had just gotten fresh tires and was pretty quick. That ended up being the worst thing that happened to Robby Gordon that day, and the best thing that happened to me.

There's a reason why you should never give up, even when you don't have the best car. If you're not clear on that, all you need to do is pop in that Sears Point video and watch the last fifteen laps.

If I had given up and accepted that Robby was going to win, I wouldn't have been so close to him and Harvick. I wouldn't have had the great view I had of their duel, which was getting more heated, corner by corner. And I wouldn't have been able to slip past Robby and into the lead when the two of them finally tangled with eleven laps to go.

In other words, I wouldn't have won the race.

The absolute best part of that win was hearing everybody say later that Robby and Kevin should have shown the same kind of patience I used. That's something I hadn't heard often in my three Winston Cup seasons.

And there were some other bright spots. I finished second twice at Talladega, once to Bobby Hamilton and once to Dale Earnhardt Jr., and second to Sterling Marlin at Charlotte in the fall. We were third in the Coca-Cola 600 just a few hours after I'd run sixth in the Indianapolis 500, and third again at Pocono, which was a satisfying team result because Bobby Labonte won the race.

Of course, we had our bad days in 2001, too.

The worst was in February, in the Daytona 500. Actually, that was *everybody's* worst day, because it was the day Dale Earnhardt died. It was hard to come to grips with the fact that the next time we went racing, Dale wouldn't be there. I had never seen a Winston Cup race, on television or from the driver's seat, that didn't have Dale in it. I was eight years old when he was Rookie of the Year in 1979, so he had always been a part of my NASCAR picture. His loss, like Kenny Irwin's, was a big jolt to me, and we'll get into that some more a bit later.

I had gone into the Daytona 500 full of optimism, which is unusual because I hate restrictor-plate racing. But we'd tested well there in January, we'd won the Bud Shootout, and we'd had a great run in our 125-mile qualifying race until I got loose and spun on the backstretch. Even after the spin, which bent the bodywork a bit, our car was fast; we came from twenty-third to eleventh in the last ten laps.

I might not have been as good at this restrictor-plate stuff as some guys, but I knew I was better than I'd ever been.

> **GREG ZIPADELLI:** "Tony had a ton of confidence all week. I know I've only been to a few Daytona 500s as a crew chief, but I went to the track that day telling myself that this was our race."

My guys and I had decided that if we could run up front all day long, we'd do that, but if we got shuffled to the middle of the pack I'd just drop all the way back until it was time to go for the win.

I know, I know: we had tried this before, in 2000 at Talladega, and that time it worked just well enough to get Bobby and I wrecked. But our belief again was that if we couldn't hang in the top six or eight, we'd be better off watching all that chaos from behind.

I still think that's a great plan, but it didn't work any better this time around. The only difference was, I got a little bit farther up before the Big Wreck, so I didn't just slide in at the tail end of the carnage. This time, I *was* the carnage.

I had driven from the tail right up to the lead pack, and I honestly think we had as good a car that day as Michael Waltrip, who ended up winning. But with twenty-five laps to go, somebody zigged, somebody else zagged, and the Big Wreck was on.

> **GREG ZIPADELLI:** "We went from somewhere around thirtieth right up into the top five in just a few laps. I'm thinking, Okay, we're in a good position, we've got an awesome car, and the driver's doing a great job. Our plan has worked. Then I look

at the television monitor on our toolbox, and Tony's flipping down the backstretch. I mean, my heart just stopped."

I remember being turned into the wall, but that's *all* I remember, because the impact knocked me out. But everybody's seen the film: my car went rolling down the track, end over end, and behind me something like eighteen other cars stacked up. Running as tightly as we all were, they had no way out.

Plenty of people mentioned this, but it's worth pointing out again: when the accident started, I was running fifth, and Bobby Labonte

Here's what's left of my car after the Big Wreck at Daytona in February 2001. I ended up with a concussion and a badly bruised shoulder, but I felt like I'd been lucky. (© Mike Adaskaveg)

was twenty-fifth. Yet when my car came down out of the sky after its last flip, it landed on Bobby's hood. Now, Bobby is as good as anybody at avoiding an accident, but even though he was twenty cars behind the lead car in this wreck, he didn't have the time or the room to miss it. *That's* why most Winston Cup drivers hate restrictor-plate racing.

I left Daytona with a concussion, a bruised shoulder, and, in view of what happened to Earnhardt later on, a heavy heart. My guys left there with a torn-up Pontiac and not much else to show for a winter's worth of hard work.

> **GREG ZIPADELLI:** "We had the best car we'd ever had in the three Daytona 500s we had run, and we ended up coming home with the biggest piece of junk we'd ever had."

We had a similar letdown in the Brickyard 400, although both the car and the driver ended up in better condition. We ran in the top three for most of the day, even led a few laps, and I thought we were in good shape when a caution flag waved just under thirty laps from the finish. I was running second to Steve Park when all the lead cars ducked onto pit road.

That's where everything fell apart for us. We changed four tires, and my guys had a great stop. Our problem was, several guys opted for two-tire stops, so they beat us out, and we were seventh when the race restarted.

Now, seventh isn't horrible, especially if your car is as good as mine was. But when you factor in NASCAR's double-file restarts, with all of the lapped cars filling up the inside line, running seventh means you line up fourteenth. And because Indianapolis is such a tough place to pass anyway, lining up fourteenth is like lining up in Fort Wayne. Coming through turn two, trying to get around some lapped cars whose drivers were more eager to race than they'd been all day, I slid wide and glanced off the wall.

It wasn't a hard hit, but it knocked our suspension out of whack and from there I was a lame duck. All things considered, we were probably fortunate to hang on for seventeenth.

When the reporters asked me to sum things up, I gave them two words—"Bad day"—and then headed for the gate.

If the Daytona 500 is the biggest NASCAR race of the year, then the Brickyard 400 is probably second. We were good enough to win at least one of them in 2001, and maybe both, but in the end we didn't come close in either.

— — — — —

In the end, 2001 was a season of mixed feelings. On the one hand, if somebody had told me five years earlier that someday I'd be less than thrilled with winning three Winston Cup races and finishing second in the standings, I'd have told them they were nuts. From that standpoint, I suppose I ought to look at my numbers and feel satisfied.

On the other hand, just being satisfied has never been enough for me. That's not what got me here.

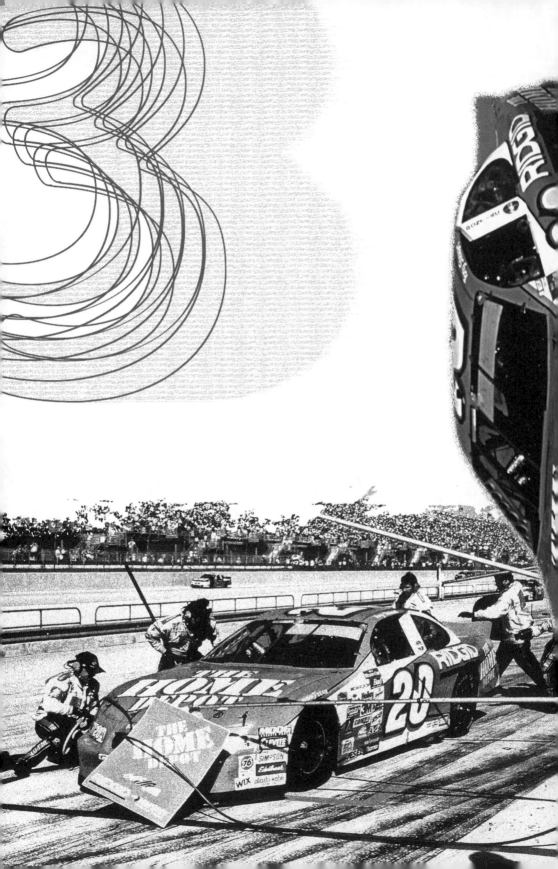

A LOT OF PEOPLE HAVE ASKED ME, AS I'M SURE THEY DO EVERY SUCCESSFUL NASCAR driver, how I knew I was ready for Winston Cup. Well, in my case, I *didn't* know. Joe Gibbs figured that out a lot sooner than I did, and, to be honest, I wasn't sure it was the right move just then.

By that point—which was in '98, when I was driving Busch Series cars for Joe—I was pretty sure that Winston Cup cars would figure into my future at some point. I'd had a good apprenticeship in the Busch division, and by then I'd already won an Indy Racing League championship, two USAC midget championships, USAC Silver Crown and sprint car championships, and a ton of races. I believed, in my heart, that I had the ability to drive a Cup car.

But the thing is, Winston Cup is *the* top rung of the racing ladder in the United States. It draws the largest attendance, gets the highest TV ratings, and attracts the biggest sponsorships, and no other series comes close in any of those categories. Obviously, it's the place every young driver wants to be these days, and I was feeling that way, too. It just felt strange to be planning this one last step up a ladder I'd been climbing so long.

I mean, I never aimed my career in this direction, or *any* direction. I wasn't one of those kids who tries to follow a map to the big time. Sure,

These guys saw me through to Winston Cup. Here they are at Homestead helping me get a move on.
(© 1999 Phil Cavali/Winston Cup Scene)

when I was a teenager racing go-karts, I had dreams of bigger things, the same way every kid who picks up a basketball fantasizes about playing in the NBA. Me, I thought about the Indianapolis 500. But, man, that was just a daydream.

My everyday hopes were much more realistic. Even after I'd moved from karts to three-quarter midgets—everybody in racing calls them TQs—all I knew was that maybe, if I impressed the right people, someone might eventually hire me to drive their midget or sprint car. There were lots of guys who made a living in sprints and midgets, and I envied every last one of them. The way I saw it, if I managed to get to their level, that was going to be a successful career for a kid who grew up where I did, when I did, and the way I did.

And you know something? I don't think any of the guys I competed against thought any differently. The idea of running an Indy car or a Winston Cup car just wasn't a realistic option in our world.

So I just kept on racing, up through the TQs and into USAC, and before long I really *was* making a living. It wasn't a great living, and it sure wasn't easy; there were a lot of all-night drives, a lot of little dirt tracks most NASCAR fans never heard of, and a lot of tough races.

But I was winning, and the winning led me to better things: nicer rides, bigger paydays, more and more calls from car owners looking to hire me. I didn't *plan* any of it. It just sort of happened.

> **PARNELLI JONES,** 1963 Indianapolis 500 winner: "Tony came up the hard way. He didn't have any real financing behind him, but his talent and his desire began to show early on. It's no different than baseball; if you're watching a Little League game, you can tell the kids who are going to excel in that sport from the ones who won't."

Before I knew it, I had climbed further up that ladder than I'd ever imagined was possible. And now, here was Joe Gibbs telling me it was time to take that last step.

The biggest reservation I had was that a lot of people suggested that none of the racing I had done before—meaning the USAC stuff and the

Indy cars—had prepared me for Winston Cup. Looking back, in a lot of ways they were right, because a Winston Cup stock car is unlike anything else in the world. But they hadn't considered this: if I had learned one thing from all the other racing I had done, I had learned how to win. I think that's what Joe saw in me.

In the end, agreeing to Joe's offer was a gut-instinct decision. That's how I had made every key decision in my racing life to that point, and things had usually turned out fairly well.

Meanwhile, Joe was making some decisions of his own. Normally, a team owner with a rookie driver on his hands will pair him up with a veteran crew chief. The idea, of course, is that the veteran can guide the kid along, show him the ropes, give him guidance about everything from driving techniques to the strategies that work best at each track. But Jimmy Makar, who in addition to being Bobby Labonte's crew chief was kind of overseeing the formation of this second Gibbs team, was urging Joe to go in a different direction. Obviously, it was important to Jimmy that the other crew chief be somebody he could work closely with, and he saw some potential in a guy who probably hadn't been on the radar screens of most team owners.

> **JOE GIBBS:** "I said to Jimmy Makar all along, 'We need a veteran crew chief. Go out and find a veteran to help us bring along this rookie driver.' But Jimmy said, 'There's this young guy out there who I think will do us a good job . . . '"

Greg Zipadelli—Zippy is what his friends call him—is a few years older than I am. He had only been around the Charlotte area for a couple of years, but he had been involved with racing for most of his life. His family had run short-track cars for years in New England, so he'd grown up in garages. As a crew chief he'd won a NASCAR modified championship with Mike McLaughlin and a Busch North title with Mike Stefanik. Later on, he'd worked for Jeff Burton's Winston Cup team, which was where he'd attracted Jimmy's attention.

But ultimately it was Joe's call. To his credit, he told Jimmy that if Greg was the guy he wanted, Greg was the guy we'd get.

So we headed into 1999 with a rookie driver and a rookie crew chief who hadn't even met until this new team got off the ground.

GREG ZIPADELLI: "Honestly, I knew nothing about Tony before we started this deal. I mean, I knew he had run IRL cars and run really good, I knew about some of the short-track stuff he had done, and I had watched him run some Busch races. But it's not like I was a Tony Stewart fan. After I took the job, I called him and we chatted a little bit. He wasn't hard to talk to, and we got along right off the bat. I think it's partly because we both grew up in similar ways; we were in different parts of the country, but we had both been around racing all our lives."

For a couple of guys who came into Winston Cup Racing as rookies, my crew chief, Greg Zipadelli, and I have done all right. (© 2000 Phil Cavali)

Jimmy and Greg put together a team which, like the driver and crew chief, was mostly young guys. That was good thinking, because right from the start we had an open-minded approach that I think was a nice contrast to the other Gibbs team; Bobby and Jimmy had been together for four years by then, and they had established their own way of doing things. The beauty of a situation like this is that if the new kids stumble onto something new it helps both cars, and if they get too far lost they can always return to the baseline setups developed by the veteran team.

It also helped that we were lucky enough to hire a fellow named Ronny Crooks, who had worked with Dale Earnhardt, Ward Burton, and a bunch of other folks, and who had a reputation for being one of the sharpest guys in the garage when it came to shocks, springs, and stuff like that. Right from our first test, I could see that Ronny was going to shorten up the learning curve considerably for both Greg and me.

RONNY CROOKS: "I had never really paid Tony too much attention. I had heard something about him when he won those three USAC championships in the same [1995] season, and I had never known about anybody doing something like that, so I thought, 'Man, that kid must be good.' But, see, in this deal you're pretty busy doing what you're doing, and you don't have time to look around a whole lot, so I just didn't know much about him. Then I talked to Joe, and in five minutes he had me pretty impressed over what Tony had accomplished. In fact, I was actually cranked up about working with him."

That's how this whole thing started: with all of us pumped up and ready to go.

And, you know, we haven't ever really felt any differently.

If anything helped establish us as a solid Winston Cup team, at least in our own minds, it was this: every time we heard that a particular race or a certain track was going to be a real test for us, we passed that test with flying colors.

That happened a lot. Early in '99, once we had put in a few good runs, everybody in the garage area was looking for the track that would trip us up. First it was Bristol, because that place is normally hell on rookies, but we started in the second row and led a bunch of laps. Then everybody figured Martinsville would be our downfall, but we ended up qualifying on the pole. Then it was Sears Point that was going to bite us, because I hadn't done any serious road racing since I'd gotten past go-karts; well, I started outside the front row, and had it not been for a flat tire we were a lock for a top-three finish.

Anytime anybody took it upon themselves to build a hurdle in our path, we jumped it, and our confidence just grew. We were going to all these tracks that required widely different disciplines, and we were holding our own. As rookies.

> **SCOTT DIEHL:** "Tony exceeded my expectations long before we won a race. I'd say it was about three races into that first season that we realized we had somebody special driving for us."

If you tell me I can't do something, I'll do anything to prove you wrong. When I hear the words "You can't," I just say to myself, "Watch me."

So when I heard all that stuff about Bristol and Martinsville and Sears Point, I took it as a personal challenge. We tested for two days at Martinsville, and that went so badly that I wouldn't have cared if a tornado went through there and blew Martinsville off the map. But we obviously learned something, because, come race weekend, the car ran better and I drove it better. Same with Sears Point: I was so determined to do well there that I went to two different road-racing schools, and I didn't take those lessons lightly. I put in every ounce of effort I had, and it paid off.

Don't let anybody convince you that you're beaten. Ever.

> **RONNY CROOKS:** "Tony does not like to lose. Now, I don't hunt and I don't fish and I don't have any hobbies; no boat, no motorcycle. So if something good doesn't happen to me on Sunday, it's gonna be a bad week. Well, when I see Tony trying as hard as he does, I know he's putting out every possible ounce of effort, and I appreciate it."

I'm not trying to make it sound like life as part of a championship-level race team is all peaches and cream. *Nothing* in life is all peaches and cream. Probably the worst thing about being involved in a multicar team is that there are days when your teammate is also your primary opponent. That's happened to me in midgets, it's happened to me in Indy cars, and it was inevitable that sooner or later it would happen to me in Winston Cup.

When I ran into Bobby Labonte's car and shoved him out of the lead at Homestead in '99, it was the one nightmare in a dream rookie season. I didn't *want* to knock Bobby out of my way, and he knew that. But he sure wasn't happy with me, and I can't say I blamed him.

We never got a chance to talk after that race, because by the time I finished the media interviews the garage area was just about deserted; probably 90 percent of the drivers and crews were long gone, Bobby included. But I didn't need to see him to know he was upset. Nobody who is the least bit competitive wants to lose because of somebody else's mistake, and Bobby is one of the most competitive people you will ever meet. On top of that, he had lost because of his *teammate's* mistake.

Not being able to explain myself to Bobby at the track took some of the shine off the trip home. But I caught up with him on Monday morning, and did my best to clear the air between us.

BOBBY LABONTE, 2000 Winston Cup champion: "Tony called me at home, and he said, 'Hey, I think I screwed up.' Actually, he didn't say, 'I think,' he said, 'I screwed up.' I said, 'Yup. But don't worry about it now. Let's just go on from here.' It wouldn't have been a good situation for him to go to the next race being nervous about how I felt. Anyway, he said what was on his mind, and I said what was on my mind, and in a matter of two and a half minutes, it was over with."

JOE GIBBS: "I try to let my guys resolve things like that by themselves, and Bobby and Tony did that."

Bobby was still unhappy, but it was important to me that he knew, by hearing it straight from me, that I hadn't run into him on purpose. It was important for me to let him know that although I want to win just as badly as he does, I'd never want to do it unfairly. It ended up being a productive conversation, and I think we came out of it with a greater mutual respect than we'd had before.

JOE GIBBS: "They both know that when the race starts, it's every man for himself. I mean, we'd all like for them to help each other whenever that's possible. But that's not always going to happen."

And, you know, despite the fact that Homestead didn't go as smoothly as we all would have liked, the day did have one positive outcome: I think every employee of Joe Gibbs Racing, whether they wore my orange Home Depot colors or Bobby's green Interstate Battery colors, came away from that race convinced that they had two drivers who were committed to winning races.

There was a team meeting at the shop on the Tuesday following the race—Bobby and I weren't there—and there was still some leftover tension. But Joe and Jimmy Makar allowed everybody to talk things out, and by the time the meeting ended everybody realized that it wasn't such a bad thing that Bobby and I cared so much about getting them all to victory lane.

> **JIMMY MAKAR**, general manager, Joe Gibbs Racing: "The way our shop is set up is such that it doesn't let things like that go on for long. Everybody works side by side, and that forces them to see each other, talk to each other, be around each other. That's good for mending fences when things happen. So after that Homestead incident, we all got over it pretty quickly. Obviously, it was something we'd rather not have had happen, but it did. You have to move on. You don't need to dwell on it."

From that point on, we've never had another serious in-house problem. In fact, I think that whole episode helped us end 1999 on a high note. We all went to Atlanta for the season finale with a renewed sense of unity, and even though I had trouble that day—we jammed a lug nut on a pit stop and ended up finishing fifteenth—my guys left there happy, because Bobby won the race. A Gibbs car was in victory lane, and that was a reason to celebrate.

It's kind of ironic that our biggest celebration so far, on the day I won my sixth race of the 2000 season and Bobby wrapped up the Winston Cup title, happened right back at Homestead. It was like we had come full circle, as a team, in the space of that year.

> **BOBBY ALLISON:** "I ran several times for teams that had more than one car, and my lifelong feeling has been that when you've got teammates together, one of those teammates has to lose. And I never wanted that to be me. But, you know, Joe Gibbs

> seems to have figured that deal out, because in the same season
> he had the guy who won the most races and the guy who won
> the championship. So everybody was happy."

One thing I'm sure about: my relationship with my team is stronger than ever. I'm including the entire organization, from the sponsors to the mechanics to the people who work in the office.

But the most important thing is that I've got really solid bonds with the people I need to work most closely with as a driver.

I never had anything but the highest respect for Joe Gibbs, but I've come to appreciate him more with each passing season. Lately I've seen a different side of him, a more competitive side, and it's made me understand how good a match we are.

I've always been aware of my own intensity, but it didn't register with me for a while that Joe is a pretty intense guy himself. I'm not sure how I missed that, because you don't win three Super Bowls as an NFL coach without being a highly driven individual. But all through our early meetings, and right on through our first couple of seasons together in Winston Cup, I saw Joe as someone who was so proper, so gentlemanly, that I must have overlooked the fighter in him.

What changed all that was the way he jumped in to defend me after my problems with NASCAR in 2001 at Bristol and Daytona. Joe had his nose right in there both times, arguing my point—arguing *our* point— and he was every bit as passionate as I was. We had different methods of explaining ourselves, sure, but Joe made it very clear to the officials that he thought we had been treated unfairly, and that he wasn't pleased about it. It was like we went to war together, and Joe Gibbs was as determined to win those battles as I was.

An outsider might not look back on those two incidents as high points in the history of our race team, but, trust me, they took an owner and a driver who were already close and brought them even closer.

On the other hand, it would probably be impossible for Greg Zipadelli and I to get any closer. Early in our rookie season, way before we managed to win a race, I knew that the two of us had the potential to compete with the best driver–crew chief combinations in the sport. At that time, Jeff Gordon and Ray Evernham were the standard, and the other great examples people pointed to were Bobby Labonte and Jimmy Makar, and Mark Martin and Jimmy Fennig. Well, as early as May of '99, I could see that on our best days we could match wits and speed with any of them.

The great thing was that I knew our personal connection would only get stronger with time, and it has. When we teamed up, Greg and I were tied in the Winston Cup win column, with zero. Well, we're still tied, but thanks to the communication between us—my ability to explain myself to Greg, and his ability to understand what I need from our car—our numbers look a lot better now.

I'll bet Zippy and I spend as much time together as any other driver and crew chief in this series. We go to dinner fairly often, we go fishing together, we do all kinds of things. We just enjoy each other's company. Most of the time when we're out like that, we don't even talk about Winston Cup racing. We're teammates *and* friends, and that's pretty cool.

> **GREG ZIPADELLI:** "We're still going through some growing pains, me and Tony both, and I think we'll continue to do that for a couple years. I mean, we're racing against a lot of people who have tons of experience at this stuff compared to us. And, you know, we're both competitive people, so there are days when we get mad at each other. But I know, deep down in my heart, that there's nobody I'd trade him for."

Bobby Labonte and I have been strong teammates from the start, and I think our partnership has only grown deeper as we've gone along. (© 2000 Phil Cavali/Winston Cup Scene)

Bobby Labonte and I are another example of a good relationship that has only changed for the better. Don't get me wrong, we've been friendly right from the day he and Joe Gibbs asked me about doing some Busch races for them back in 1997. But for a long time, I kind of felt like we were on different levels: Bobby was a guy who had won Winston Cup races, and I was a new kid trying to break into NASCAR from the outside. Even after I started to win in Winston Cup, in my mind he was still the teacher, and I was still the student.

It's been only recently, probably in 2001, that I've gotten comfortable seeing the two of us as true teammates. And it's not as if he's suddenly treating me differently, or talking to me differently; maybe now I just feel established enough that I don't look at it like Bobby is the varsity quarterback and I'm the second-string. There's more of a two-way-street feeling to our conversations than there has ever been, and that's only going to make us both better.

> **JOE GIBBS:** "Tony and Bobby have really teamed up. I honestly believe that they have helped each other's careers. I don't think Bobby would have won his championship if Tony and his team hadn't helped him, and I don't think Tony would have had the first two seasons he had if he hadn't stepped into a team that Bobby helped build."

> **JIMMY MAKAR:** "Bobby and Tony are different people by nature. They're both fiercely competitive, but the way they go about things is different; Bobby is a quiet, laid-back guy, where Tony has an outspoken, up-front personality. I sometimes think they might complement each other, similar to the way a husband and wife with different personalities complement each other. And in watching them grow together; I think they've migrated closer. They have a lot more respect for each other, and they talk a lot more than they did in the beginning. It's just a better relationship."

> **BOBBY LABONTE:** "Hey, we're all in this together. Hopefully, I'll win my share and Tony will win his share. But we're still working for the same team."

I'll tell you how cool Bobby Labonte is. When I was half a lap away from my first Cup victory back in '99 at Richmond, I heard this strange voice through my helmet radio. I say "strange" only because I knew it wasn't Greg, and it wasn't my spotter watching from the top of the press box, warning me about something up ahead. Normally, those are the only two voices I'll hear during the course of a race. What happened was, Bobby had turned his radio to my frequency; our radios are set up in such a way that, just by flipping a switch, he and I can talk to each other if we need to. But that's pretty rare, so I was caught completely off guard when his voice came booming into my ear.

"Hey, Tony."

"Yeah?"

"Good job. You're buying lunch this week."

I was so surprised, I almost missed my entry point for turn three. I mean, lunch is not usually a topic you discuss on the last lap of a race, or *any* lap. But Bobby wasn't trying to distract me, of course. He was congratulating me in his own way, a way that was just between us, away from the TV cameras and the microphones.

If I'd been as cool that night as he was, I'd have told him how thankful I was for everything he had done for me, and how that win wouldn't have been possible without all the help he had given me along the way. But I wasn't very cool at that moment, so I just went ahead and finished out the race, and gave Bobby a wave on my slow-down lap.

> **BOBBY LABONTE:** "I didn't feel like I had done any big tutoring job with Tony, or anything like that. But it was exciting to me to know that, yeah, I had a hand in that win."

At that point, I was only about seven months into my Winston Cup career, but victory seemed like it had been a long time coming. And now that it had arrived, you know what I felt most? I felt like I was part of something.

I was part of a great race team, and I had paid enough dues to be a part—a *winning* part—of the top racing series in the country.

I felt like I belonged.

I'll never forget my first trip to New York City, for the Winston Cup awards dinner in 1999. They hold the ceremony at the Waldorf-Astoria, but because I'd won the rookie title I had several other obligations around Manhattan in the days leading up to the banquet. It was a neat chance to see a place I'd heard about all my life.

But, I'll tell you, it was an enormous culture shock for me. Just a few years earlier I was struggling to pay rent in an apartment back in Indiana, and now here I was, being driven by limo from appearance to appearance, getting a guided tour of the city. And this was no casual deal; we spent almost a week there, and I think I put on a pair of blue jeans only once. I was constantly changing into dress pants, dress shirts, dress shoes, even a tuxedo on the night of the dinner. It was probably one of the most uncomfortable weeks of my life, just from the standpoint of feeling like I didn't fit in. For me, slacks and blazers and black-tie dinners were never supposed to be part of the game. I guess I had more of an old-school outlook when I was coming up.

> **PARNELLI JONES:** "In 1959 I ran the old IMCA sprint car circuit, and I traveled a lot with [fellow driver] Jim Hurtubise. We raced all over the Midwest. We'd run a state fair someplace, then we'd have to be six hundred miles away for another race the next day. We'd take off down the highway, and in the morning we'd stop on the side of the road and take a bath in some lake. For dinner, we'd tie a can of beans to the exhaust manifold to heat it up. That's how we lived. And Tony would have fit right in with us, I think. Because, see, he's got that same hunger to compete. He'll do whatever it takes."

There's one thing that blows me away every time we go back to New York City. I'll be sitting in a hotel suite bigger than some of the places I've lived in, or walking down Park Avenue with all its fancy stores and elegant restaurants, and it will hit me all at once: *I got here by driving race cars. Wow.*

FOUR ☰ TRAINING WHEELS

OFFICIALLY, COLUMBUS, INDIANA, IS A CITY. JUST UNDER FORTY THOUSAND people live there today, and when I came into the world, on May 20, 1971, its population was something like twenty-seven thousand. They can call it a city if they want to, but when I think of a city I see lots of tall buildings. The nearest place like that was Indianapolis, which is about forty-five miles up I-65. Columbus felt like a town, with quiet neighborhoods, like the one I grew up in.

Both my parents worked regular jobs—my dad as a traveling salesman, my mom as a receptionist in a doctor's office—and we lived in a middle-class subdivision. Our street was mostly one-story ranch houses; ours had a backyard garage, and my dad was always out there tinkering. From everything I remember, I had your average happy childhood. We weren't a rich family by any means, which meant that like most kids I didn't get everything I wanted, but I got everything I needed.

My sister Natalie is two and a half years younger than me, and like most brothers and sisters we had our little spats.

> **NATALIE STEWART:** "We fought all the time. The only really fun times we had together—although I'm sure we fought then, too—were when we played Ping-Pong or played video games.

I've pretty much been on wheels since the day I was born. This is my mom and dad letting me try on my dad's go-kart. This was in July of 1971, so I was two months old. (Courtesy of Pam Boas)

We fought over everything: who got the remote control for the TV, what we watched, who got to sit in the front seat of the car on the way to school."

I did the things all normal kids do. In Indiana that means playing basketball, of course, but I'd also get together with my buddies and we'd ride our bikes to the park and just sort of hang around. To me, the riding part was more fun than the hanging-around part, because my bicycle had wheels, and, from what my parents have told me, I was drawn to anything with wheels from the day I was born.

NELSON STEWART, father: "We had an old half-bushel basket that I'd painted green, and we used it for a magazine rack. Before Tony was big enough to walk, he would crawl over there and pull every magazine out. He'd throw anything that resembled a car magazine into one pile, and everything else into another pile. He'd go through the car magazines, pick out two or three, crawl over to the couch and throw 'em into my lap. Then he'd climb up and sit there while we went through the car magazines."

PAM BOAS: "We used to buy him Matchbox cars, and he'd play with them on a little oval-shaped braided rug. To him, the different braids made lanes; that was his racetrack. We'd haul that rug wherever we went, because that thing kept Tony busy for hours. As long as he had his little racetrack with him—or, if we didn't have it, as long as he could go outside and make a racetrack in the dirt—he was one happy little boy."

Somewhere between the Matchbox cars and the bicycle, my most precious possession was one of those Big Wheel–type tricycles, although mine was a generic off-brand instead of the authentic Big Wheel. In a way, mine was better than the real thing, because while the Big Wheel had three plastic wheels, I had a front tire made of rubber. That gave me a huge advantage over the other kids when we raced; see, if you tried to take off fast with a Big Wheel, all your pedaling just spun the front wheel, but my rubber tire would give me plenty of traction.

The other bad thing about a Big Wheel was that eventually, all that spinning wore a hole in the plastic. I never could wear out my big rubber front tire, but, man, I was hell on those plastic rears, sliding them around.

Everybody knows what a racket those little trikes make. I'd pedal around for hours in the carport next to the house, and it would drive my mom so crazy that she'd ship me out to my dad's garage. I'd ride right there in the shop; Dad would be working, and I'd be turning laps. Whenever I got bored, I'd cut the wheel just as I got near the garage doors. The front end would turn on a dime, thanks to that rubber tire, but the rear end would kick out and slam into the doors. That made a lot of noise, which amused me quite a bit but didn't have the same effect on my dad.

From what I remember and what I'm told, I had a pretty good handle on that little three-wheeler.

> **NELSON STEWART:** "One night I was facing my workbench, with my back to him, and I noticed that the noise had changed. It didn't go away completely, but it changed. I looked over at Tony, and here he was, riding that tricycle around on two wheels! He rode it that way for two or three rounds before he put it back down. Then he turned around, headed in the other direction, and jacked it up on the other two wheels."

I did so much riding around in that garage that eventually my dad was able to tune out the fuss I made. He has told people that the only time he'd even bother to check on me was when the noise stopped, because the silence sounded strange. That's the kind of kid I was: if I *wasn't* making a lot of noise, you knew something was up.

People talk about the day they saw their first race, but I honestly can't remember mine. Racing has always just *been there*, because my father was involved in the sport before I was born. He did some stock car racing on the local tracks, and by the time I came along he was involved on a hobby level with the Sports Car Club of America. He was also a big fan of the Indiana short-track scene. I remember him taking us to Salem Speedway and Winchester Speedway, two famous old high-banked ovals. I remember going to the indoor midget races on winter nights in Fort Wayne and Indianapolis.

But when I was five years old, my perspective on racing changed dramatically. My dad bought me a go-kart—not a racing kart, just a yard kart—and I fell in love with that thing. All I wanted to do was drive it faster and harder. I tore the hell out of every bush, small tree, and blade of grass in our yard before my mom put a stop to it.

As it turned out, that was the best thing that could have happened to me.

> **PAM BOAS:** "Tony carved a definite oval into our backyard, and he would just go around and around on that go-kart. It wasn't long before we decided he needed to be out on a real track someplace."

The summer I turned seven, my dad took us to a little dirt oval in Westport, about a half-hour east of Columbus. It was my first exposure to organized karting, and I was amazed by the number of kids who were out there sliding around. Then my dad introduced me to a friend of his named Johnny Johnson, whose son Eric was racing that day. The next thing I knew, the Johnsons invited me to take a few laps.

> **NELSON STEWART:** "Johnny had told me that his boy was running a go-kart. Eric and Tony were about the same age, although Eric might have been a year older. Anyway, I said, 'Gosh, I'd love to let Tony try one of those things sometime, just to see how he'd like it.' Johnny said, 'Well, bring him over to Westport. He can try ours.' So that's what we did."

You could say my career started right there at Westport, with that ride in Eric's kart. The next week, my dad made me an offer I couldn't refuse: he'd buy me a racing kart and keep it running, as long as I did my part by keeping it neat and clean. That sounded like a better deal for me than it turned out to be; at that age, wiping down a go-kart after school isn't nearly as much fun as running off to play with your friends. But this was my dad's way of making sure I developed a good work ethic, and that I learned the value of being prepared.

> **NELSON STEWART:** "I bought a used kart that was really outdated, threw away everything but the frame, and started adding pieces over the winter. That next summer, when Tony was eight, we started him out right there at Westport."

It's funny, but I don't remember much about racing that kart. I do remember getting my first trophy, which was for a second-place finish. I also remember being confused when I got my next trophy, which was for a win. See, the track presented different types of trophies—one week it might be a statue, another week it might be a cup—and my first-place trophy was smaller than the second-place trophy I'd won earlier. That didn't make sense to me. Still, I was really happy about the win.

My dad and I made a heck of a go-kart team. He did the upkeep and I kept it clean. We won an awful lot of races around home between 1979 and 1982. (© Images Unlimited/Jack Wart)

I ran the last six races of 1979 in what was called the four-cycle rookie junior class—for ages eight through twelve—and in that time we had a win and two runner-up finishes. The following year, they moved the races from Westport to the fairgrounds in Columbus, not far from our home. I won a bunch of races, and ended up being the class champion. In '81 we expanded our team a bit; we hung on to that old kart and kept running the four-cycle rookie juniors, but my dad was so pumped up that he bought a state-of-the-art piece for me to run in the next class, the two-cycle rookie juniors. The coolest thing about this new kart was that it had a formed fiberglass racing seat; on the older kart, I sat in a box-style seat made of aluminum panels.

For a while I raced in both classes, and then from '82 on we concentrated on the two-cycle. But no matter what I was running, we won our share.

People talk about getting bitten by the racing bug. With me, that bug was about the size of a hawk.

There were two major karting organizations: the International Karting Federation (IKF) and the World Karting Association (WKA). Their power was basically divided by geography; the IKF had the West, the WKA was an eastern group.

In 1983, when I was twelve, my dad thought we were ready to enter the IKF's biggest race, the Grand Nationals in Oskaloosa, Iowa. Looking back, that was awfully ambitious. The Grand Nationals, which hosts all the various IKF classes, is the karting world's Indianapolis 500. All the top kart racers in the country—most sponsored by the karting equipment manufacturers—focused their attention on that race, and we were just a little backyard team. I guess we didn't know enough about it to be scared off, so we loaded up and headed to Iowa.

We must have been quite a sight, rumbling down the road in my dad's Toyota pickup truck with all our stuff piled under a tarp on a two-wheel wooden trailer. I'll bet we stopped every hundred miles to retie that tarp, because the wind kept catching it, and eventually it shredded.

We thought we were in great shape. We had brought along a few extra wheels and tires borrowed from friends, and some spare parts courtesy of the only sponsor we had, Comet Kart Sales. Comet is owned by the Dismore family out of Greenfield, Indiana, and all the Dismores—including Mark Dismore, the Indy Racing League driver—were great to us. They gave us a break here and there on parts, and always made sure we were ready for anything big that came up, like the Grand Nationals.

MARK DISMORE, Indy Racing League driver: "It wasn't like I went to the racetrack, saw Tony, and said, 'Man, this kid's got a lot of talent,' and decided to sponsor him. It's just that Tony's dad, Nelson, is such a great guy. Nelson and me are about as far apart in age in one direction as Tony and me are in the other direction, so I kinda felt like Tony's big brother and Nelson's oldest son. But I established a relationship with Nelson first, because Tony was still just a little kid."

When we got to Oskaloosa, it was like we had driven into a different world. Mark Dismore had arranged for us to share pit space with some of Comet's bigger clients, and they turned out to be nice people. But I could see right away that they were much better prepared than we were. Hell, *everybody* was much better prepared than we were.

At Westport and Columbus, the tracks I came from, everybody had pretty much the same equipment. You never felt like the kid pitted next door had any real advantage. Well, it wasn't that way at Oskaloosa.

There was one team there with a big yellow truck, an ex-Ryder rental that somebody had outfitted. I snuck a look inside that thing, and there were *fourteen* go-karts standing on end around the three walls of that truck. Above the karts was a shelf that had *twenty-three* engines on it. All this stuff belonged to Mike Berg, a kid from California who had won everything in karting: the dirt Grand Nationals, the pavement Grand Nationals, even the Grand Nationals for road-racing enduro karts. Mike Berg had a giant reputation.

I was overwhelmed. It wasn't so much jealousy; it was obvious to me even then that Berg had to be a great driver, because he didn't win all those races on equipment alone. But the fact that he had this kind of support floored me. I glanced over at our little wooden trailer and said, "We don't stand a chance."

NELSON STEWART: "You could see that Berg was in a class of his own. But I told Tony, 'You've got to keep one thing in mind: all these guys might have extra motors and extra karts, but they can only drive one at a time.'"

We struggled through the preliminaries, because we were simply outgunned. But little by little, through his own knowledge and what he was able to pick up, my dad got our kart fast at exactly the right time: just prior to our class's feature race.

Oskaloosa was a terrific track, maybe a fifth-mile around with a fair amount of banking, and it was prepared about as nicely as any full-size dirt track I've ever seen. I can't remember exactly where I started, but right away I moved up into second, behind Mike Berg. Then we had a restart, and I got past him. From there, it was between the two of us. I pulled out a gap once we started to lap the slower karts, and drove away.

My dad had been right: sure, Berg had a lot of equipment, but right now it was just him and his kart against me and my kart.

NELSON STEWART: "Right from the start, all those other kids were running clear down on the bottom; they just didn't know any better. They were down there fighting it out among themselves, and Tony ran up high, cruising. He won that thing by a full straightaway."

This was a huge moment in my life when I was twelve years old, and it's still huge. That's me getting the trophy for winning the IKF Grand Nationals at Oskaloosa, Iowa, in 1983. (Courtesy of Pam Boas)

A magazine called *Karter News* pointed out something really cool that happened after the race, something I've never forgotten: "Berg peeled off the number one that he had so proudly worn into combat . . . walked quietly over to Stewart's kart and stuck the number over the number four that Tony had displayed. He reached over and shook Stewart's hand and said, 'Congratulations, Champ!' "

To the victors go the spoils: after we won the IKF Grand Nationals, we became sort of an official house team for Comet Kart Sales. It wasn't an all-out factory effort like some of the bigger national teams, but the Dismores did everything they could for us.

> **MARK DISMORE:** "Tony had a lot of heart and a lot of desire, and Nelson was a working-class guy who put in an incredible amount of hours so his son could continue racing. When you see something like that—you know, the sacrifices people make for their kids—it makes a soft spot in your heart, so we tried to help them."

My dad and I were a great little race team. The only hitch was that he was still pretty big into his work-ethic thing, and I was finding it increasingly hard to give up hanging out with my buddies. I think every teenaged boy goes through that goof-around phase; maybe I just took my goofing around more seriously than most.

I've got to admit, my behavior strained things from time to time. When I was about fifteen, my dad and I had a major blow-up. One Saturday, he and my mom went off to visit some relatives, and he left me with one specific instruction: mow the yard. Naturally, I didn't get it done. When they rolled back into the driveway, my dad went tilt. He told me he'd had enough of my laziness; he was going to get rid of the go-kart. That got me on the mower pretty quickly, and I figured the storm had blown over.

Wrong.

> **NELSON STEWART:** "When we pulled in, I saw Tony and half a dozen other kids in the backyard, playing baseball. I looked around, and the grass wasn't mowed. I pulled straight back to the garage, and Pam went into the house. We hadn't been home ten minutes, and the phone rang. It was a guy I knew from go-karting. He said, 'Hey, Nelson, do you know of anybody who's got a kart for sale?' I said, 'Yep. I've got Tony's kart for sale.' He said he'd be there in fifteen minutes, and he was."

While I was speeding around on that riding mower, I glanced up and saw a pickup truck backing down our driveway. The driver climbed out and walked into the garage. When he came out, he was holding one end of a kart—*my* kart!—and my dad was holding the other end. They loaded the kart into the bed of that pickup, and the guy drove away.

Seeing that kart disappear down the street absolutely destroyed me. I finished mowing the yard, but I was literally crying my eyes out the whole time.

This whole thing caused a civil war in the Stewart household, with my dad on one side, me on the other, and my mom and sister in the middle. It lasted about two weeks, until a fellow named Don Williams—"Jumbo" was what everybody called him—asked my dad if he thought I'd be interested in driving his enduro kart. My dad, figuring I'd learned my lesson, said yes.

Jumbo hauled all his equipment over to our place and dropped it inside my dad's shop. Then my father got busy with his wrenches, and I got busy making sure that enduro kart—and the lawn—stayed nice and neat. We were a team again.

I spent a couple of years running enduro karts with the WKA, and that was really an educational process. Until then, most of my racing had been on short dirt ovals; the enduro karts—also called "laydown" karts because the driver lies almost flat on his back—ran primarily on road courses. The series included places that were pretty eye-catching for a teenager: Charlotte, Talladega, Rockingham, Pocono, and Road America up in Elkhart Lake, Wisconsin.

My debut in a laydown kart came at the Daytona International Speedway, and my memory of first seeing that place is exactly like everybody else's: I couldn't get over looking up and seeing those big banked corners.

I'm sure most fans are familiar with the Daytona road course: you go through the superspeedway's tri-oval, make a hard left, run through a few kinks and hairpins in the infield, and reenter the superspeedway just prior to the turn one banking. It was a fast place in a go-kart—over one hundred miles per hour for long stretches—but, in all honesty, it wasn't very exciting.

I guess what I disliked most was that we didn't get to use the banking in the turns; the karts were agile enough that you could stay right down on the flat apron. But one of my buddies told me that the previous year, he'd wandered onto the banking and his kart handled so well up there that he was able to take his hands completely off the steering wheel. Well, that sounded like fun; at fifteen years old I wasn't scared of anything. So instead of turn-

My racing kind of branched out when I started running enduro karts at sixteen. At a place like Daytona, these things went over a hundred miles per hour, so it was a great high-speed experience. (Courtesy of Pam Boas)

ing into the road course after the checkered flag I just kept right on trucking. I drove flat-out around that entire track at what must have been 110 miles per hour, with no hands on the wheel in the turns. That was pretty cool.

Enduro karting exposed me to a lot of nice tracks and a lot of nice people. I also got to see a great deal of the country—one year, we drove seventeen thousand miles just traveling to the races on weekends—and that was a terrific educational experience.

It didn't hurt my racing résumé, either: in 1987, I won a WKA national championship.

When I was in high school, my parents divorced. This isn't something I've discussed a whole lot elsewhere, and I won't here, either, because that's their business. But I will say this: obviously, that's not an easy thing for any family, and it was no different with us. I had a hard time dealing with it.

Maybe that's because, contrary to the image I've helped create by blowing up in public from time to time, I don't like conflict. I have never liked being in situations where people are angry, or where arguments are going on. Generally, my response is either to walk away or to block out whatever is causing the commotion. When you're a teenager you can't just walk away, so I blocked it out, or at least I tried to.

> **PAM BOAS:** "When Nelson and I were going through our divorce, Tony would not talk about it. He refused to. To this day, he still doesn't really talk about it, but he's accepted it, and since Nelson and I are such good friends today it's not a big problem anyway. But that was a difficult time for him, and for us as a family."

I guess what got me through that period was that somehow I knew that this separation was the best thing for everybody involved. I'm not sure how I reached that conclusion at such a young age, but I did, and it helped keep me level through the whole thing. Sure, I was upset, because my dad was leaving and that's hard on a son. At the same time, I thought everybody would eventually be happier this way.

I lived with my mom, but I still went racing with my dad, which was nice. In so many situations like ours, you see the kids gradually pull away from one parent or the other, but that never happened with us.

> **NELSON STEWART:** "Tony never drifted away from me, and I was glad about that."

Then, a little at a time, all the success we'd had in go-karts seemed to start working against my dad and me. Every step up the ladder meant more exotic equipment and more travel, and even at the karting level that's expensive. By the time I was sixteen, we were out of our league, financially. My parents had spent everything they could, together and individually, but they couldn't go dollar-for-dollar with some of the wealthy people we competed with.

Any racer can tell you what a struggle that is. You're out there trying to beat teams that are buying new tires every week, and you're bolting on the tires they threw away. It's a losing battle, no matter how hard you work.

From the moment he brought home that first kart, my father had told me that the day racing ceased to be fun, we'd stop. That day came in 1988. I told him I didn't see any sense in racing if we couldn't do it right, so we sat out the last two-thirds of the season. That was the right thing to do, I know, but it killed both of us. It probably killed him even more than it did me, because I'm sure he kept racing after the divorce mostly as a way of maintaining our relationship.

MARK DISMORE: "Everything Nelson did, he did for Tony. There's no doubt about that. He was Tony's biggest supporter, and he deserves all the credit in the world, as far as I'm concerned."

One more time, though, things worked themselves out. For the next couple of years I drove karts here and there for other people, and my dad and I still raced our own kart occasionally. It wasn't the grinding halt we had feared it would be.

I ended up running go-karts until I was eighteen, and in retrospect it was a great training ground. Kart racing is bigger in the Midwest than in many parts of the country, so right from the beginning I was in an ultracompetitive environment. And because we couldn't match equipment with the leading teams, I learned to make the most of what I had, which meant making my kart work better than the next guy's.

And karting gave me something else: early on, maybe as soon as that 1983 win at Oskaloosa, I got a taste of what it meant to be one of the top guys. My picture was in all the karting magazines. Wherever we raced, the other teams would stop by our pit, checking out our operation. I was *somebody*.

Back home, I wasn't nearly as big a deal. Oh, I had lots of friends, and I did the normal adolescent-male things: developed a serious addiction to radio-controlled cars (which I have to this day), played trombone in the high school band, went to my senior prom (Columbus North High, class of '89). But racing was *it*. Racing gave me my identity.

I was a race driver, and that was what I wanted to be for the rest of my life.

The problem was, I had no idea how to make this happen. There was a time when putting together a race car was a cheap deal, something anybody could do if he had access to a junkyard, but those days were long gone by the eighties. And if karting was too rich for our budget, anything beyond that seemed impossible.

Then my dad and I found TQ midgets.

A three-quarter midget is just about what it sounds like: it looks like a midget race car, but it's a little bit smaller and a little bit less powerful. All around the United States, there are pockets where TQ racing thrives. One of them, luckily for me, was right there in Indiana.

If you look into the résumés of most of the top USAC stars of the last ten or fifteen years, you'll find a bunch of TQ midget victories. It's a fierce division, and it seemed like the perfect step for us to make.

PAT SULLIVAN, veteran race announcer: "The TQs are an interesting group. They have their own legends, guys who have run with them for twenty years and have won a lot of races, and then you have all these young guys who are trying to cut their teeth. Well, the older guys aren't about to give those kids any slack, so it becomes a great proving ground."

We couldn't afford to go TQ racing on our own, but I thought that if I got a chance to run a car a couple of times, I might persuade someone to take a shot at hiring me. The odds were against that, and we knew it;

most of the TQs were owned either by the guys who drove them or by someone related to the driver. But my dad kept checking around, operating on the idea that it never hurts to ask.

> **NELSON STEWART:** "A guy named Bill Grider, who worked at a parts store in Columbus, knew a bunch of those TQ folks, and one day I asked if he knew anybody who might be willing to let a young kid run a little bit. Bill told me about a fellow named Roy Barker, who was building a brand-new car, and said I ought to talk to him. I said, 'Hell, I don't even know the guy,' but Bill told me he'd introduce me to him."

> **ROY BARKER,** TQ midget veteran: "I had raced myself, back in the fifties, but once I got out I stayed away from it for years. Then my son Brian got interested and bought an old car that he ran in 1988, but he got married and decided he wasn't going to race anymore. Well, by then I had gotten the bug again. I decided I could build a better mousetrap than anybody else had. I had this new car pretty well finished, and I guess Tony and his dad heard about it. I didn't know them at all, but they came to see me about Tony driving for me. I made a couple of phone calls and asked some people what they knew about this kid, and I found out he had done a heck of a lot in go-karts. And I just decided, Well, I'll give him a try."

Roy had put together a really nice car, but he ran into the same problem my dad and I had faced in the go-karts: money. He had himself a car, but owning one and racing one are two different things. Roy needed wheels, he needed tires, he needed all the little things you always need when it's time to go to the track. My dad gave him five hundred dollars to finish up the car, with the stipulation that I'd drive it through at least five races.

To this day, that's the only time I've ever bought a ride.

My first TQ race came on July 1, 1989, at a quarter-mile dirt track in Greensburg, Indiana. I still remember saying hello to the driver pitted next to us. I didn't know at the time that he would play a big role in my life; all I knew was that his name was Larry Martz, and that he seemed like a good guy. We hit it off immediately.

> **LARRY MARTZ**, longtime friend: "I remember this like it was yesterday. I looked over at him and I thought, Aw, look at that scrawny little kid. I had seen tons of people come and go in TQ racing, and I figured this was just one more kid trying to make a name for himself."

It was with a fellow named Roy Barker that I moved up into TQ midgets. We ran—and won—at dirt tracks all over Indiana. (Courtesy of Pam Boas)

I'd like to say I took to the TQs right away, but I didn't. The car steered a lot slower than the karts did; I thought it steered *too* slowly, but I figured that was something I'd have to get used to. I also had to get used to the fact that you really had to manipulate the throttle, easing it on and off as you found traction, where in a kart you were either *on* the gas or *off* the gas. I did qualify for the Greensburg feature, which I was pretty proud of, but we had problems with the fuel pump and my big debut only lasted a few laps.

Still, it was a thrill. A TQ midget is small, but it was the biggest, most powerful thing I had ever raced, and it felt so *different*. You sat upright, as opposed to reclining, and the car kept you incredibly busy: sawing the wheel, reacting to the ruts and bumps, swiping away the plastic tear-off lenses you stack on your helmet shield and discard once they get too muddied up to see through.

I had a ball.

My second race was on the Fourth of July in Rushville. Now, the Rushville track doesn't look like much—it's just a flat little oval, one-fifth of a mile around—but every summer, when they hold two races in conjunction with the Rush County Fair, it becomes Mecca to the TQ fraternity. Folks from all over the area show up, and they fill that joint to standing room only.

> **PAT SULLIVAN:** "Rushville is a phenomenon. One of the hallmarks of that place is that, from about turn one and all the way down the backstretch, people back their pickup trucks as close to the fence as they can, and they sit in their lawn chairs and watch the races. Some of them build scaffolding to get a better view. They're avid, very dedicated race fans."

A Rushville fair event was *the* race to win if you ran a TQ midget, so the competition was extremely tough. That first night, it was especially tough on me. I started up front in my heat race and led it for a while, but the track had dried out; on a dry-slick track you slide around quite a bit, and the slow steering made things extratreacherous for me. It was only a matter of time until I crashed.

> **ROY BARKER:** "He was leading the heat race by half a lap, but he just kept running wider and wider. I said, 'He's going to wreck it,' and in the next lap or two he did. He hit the wall, and it flipped him. Bent the heck out of that car."

> **NELSON STEWART:** "What happened was, they had a pitman arm on that thing that was just too short; what that does is, it takes about forty turns to steer it from lock to lock. Tony

came off turn two sideways, and, shit, he couldn't keep up with the steering."

I was pretty upset, but not as upset as Roy was; I mean, here's his brand-new race car, and this kid has put it on its head. He was pretty distraught. But he brought the car home and straightened it out, and while he was fixing it we bolted on a longer steering arm to quicken the response.

Ten days later—July 14, 1989—the TQs were back at Rushville for the second fair race. I qualified tenth, which was a good break because it just so happened that they inverted the top ten for the feature. I took off with the lead, and I never looked back. We led that race from the green flag to the checkered flag.

It was unbelievable. Just our third time out, and we had won a TQ feature. A *Rushville* TQ feature.

ROY BARKER: "They couldn't touch him. At the start, and then every time they had a restart, he'd just run off and hide. He was just amazing."

NELSON STEWART. "Oh, I was so proud of him. I'll bet that night I had a hat size about five times bigger than normal."

The Fair Queen was a local girl named Amanda Keaton, and her big responsibility was to present the trophy to the winner of the race. We talked later on in the midway at the fair, and she ended up being my steady girlfriend for about the next five years. I thought it was pretty cool that we actually had our photo taken the moment we met, right there in victory lane.

Four days after my Rushville win, we raced in Madison, Indiana, down along the Ohio River. I won the feature again, but this time I really had to work for it, because I started a few rows back. I had to fight my way to the front, doing most of my passing on the outside.

One of the challenging things about dirt racing is that there's not one particular groove that's always the quickest. On most asphalt tracks, there's a line through each corner that is ideal, and you don't normally budge from that line unless traffic dictates you run someplace else. Dirt is different: the track changes tremendously, sometimes drying out and sometimes blackening with tire rubber and sometimes building what's called a cushion, which is really a curb of dirt that's been pushed from the lower grooves. You run where your car works best, even if it's not where *you'd* prefer to run.

If you're running fast down low, stay low. If you're fast in the middle, run the middle. The most fun situation, to me, is when I'm fast up top, when I can bounce my right rear tire off that cushion and use it to launch my car forward. It's a feeling every good dirt-tracker knows, and I discovered it early on at places like Madison.

It was also at Madison that I met one of the first people aside from my parents who really believed I would make it as a race driver.

Everybody in the Midwest knows Crocky Wright. He's a former motorcycle racer and midget driver who later became a writer, and who, even though he was in his late sixties by the time I met him, religiously followed midgets and TQs.

CROCKY WRIGHT, racing writer: "Jack Gladback, a friend of mine who was a racing photographer, said, 'Crocky, there's a new kid running TQs, and I think you might like him.' I asked him for the kid's name, and Jack said, 'Tony Stewart. He won the feature last night at Rushville.' Well, I went to the next TQ race at Madison to check him out. I noticed this kid standing beside Roy Barker's 81. I watched him prepare the car for a while, but I didn't say anything. When it came time for warm-ups, I saw the 81 go up near the outside guardrail and put on a spectacular display of broadsliding, throwing rooster-tails of dirt. I was very impressed. I walked over to the car and stood a short distance away, but I didn't talk to the kid. As I recall, he was in the third heat race, and we stood about fifteen feet apart as we watched the first two heats, but I still hadn't spoken to him. Well, he made it into the feature, and he didn't appear to have much trouble going through the field to win it. After the race, I walked through the crowd around his car and said, 'Congratulations. You looked terrific.' He smiled and said, 'Thanks, Crocky.' I wondered how he knew my name. I figured he must have asked somebody about the old guy who had been eyeing him all evening."

One of my first real supporters was Crocky Wright, an ex-racer who later became a writer. Crocky started following me in the TQ midget days, and he's never stopped. Here we are at my surprise birthday party in 1994. (© John Mahoney)

From that day on, and for the rest of my active open-wheel career, I ran into Crocky Wright everywhere. Talking to him before the races was something I always enjoyed. I came to find out that he was doing quite a bit of talking behind my back, too; I can't count the number of people who have told me that the first time they ever heard my name was when Crocky bragged up something I had done in a midget or a TQ.

JOHN MAHONEY, veteran racing photographer: "I always say that it was Crocky who discovered Tony."

CROCKY WRIGHT: "In all my years, I had acquired a number of heroes and idols, especially Johnny Thomson. Johnny was a great midget racer who made it all the way to the Indianapolis 500 before he was killed at Allentown, Pennsylvania, in 1960, and I still consider him the most outstanding and fearless driver of all time. But most of those idols were drivers I had watched when I was a teenager sitting in the grandstands; now, with Tony, the roles were reversed. For the first time, I began to idolize a teenager."

I drove Roy Barker's TQ for the rest of 1989 and all of '90, and had a wonderful time. The sanctioning body, the United Midget Racing Association—UMRA—didn't have a home base; in the spring and the fall we'd visit the local tracks, and in the summer we'd hit all the county fairs.

Nobody makes a living running TQs, so I supplemented my racing income with a couple of different jobs. For a while, I worked at a McDonald's in Columbus. I did every job there was, from salting the fries to cleaning the milk-shake machine. The best part of that deal was that my hours were flexible; my managers knew how badly I loved to race, and that I wanted to make it my life. I guess they saw me as a kid with a goal, and they were very understanding about that, which I'm still thankful for.

I also spent some time in 1990 working for Gary Irvin, a sprint car racer who ran a brick-and-block plant. My job description was simple: I was a gofer, chasing parts for the trucks and forklifts. When there were no parts to fetch, I did a lot of floor-sweeping.

Both of those gigs left me plenty of time for daydreaming, and mostly I dreamed about the coming weekend's TQ race.

Actually, that's not quite true. I dreamed about *winning* the coming weekend's TQ race. I was a very enthusiastic racer.

> **ROY BARKER:** "We won some. But, don't forget, Tony was still very young and not very experienced. He thought he could put a four-foot-wide car through a two-foot hole. So for us, it was either win or wreck, and we did our share of wrecking."

> **NELSON STEWART:** "I think the maddest I've ever been at Tony was one night at a TQ race up in Rochester, Indiana. He was ungodly fast: set a track record, won his heat race going away. Well, in the feature he jumped the start, so they threw the caution flag as a warning. He jumped again on the restart, and they put him to the tail. That's bad enough, but when they threw the green a third time, he jumped that start, too, and they threw him out of the race. I didn't talk to him the rest of the night. I mean, he was so fast that he could have started half a lap behind and he'd have won anyway, but he had to jump that third start."

In the winter of 1990–91, I hooked up with Larry Dwenger, a TQ owner from Greensburg. Larry, who has since passed away, was one of the big dogs on the Indiana TQ midget scene; he had the best equipment, and with his father, Dick, driving he won multiple UMRA championships. When I got together with Larry, I moved in with him and his wife, Dawn, for about six months, and they were wonderful to me. We won some races early in that '91 season, and we'd have won more had it not been for the fact that something totally unexpected came along: a USAC midget ride.

It was Mark Dismore who put together that first midget deal. He was friendly with Chuck Leary, a driver whose family fielded a multicar midget team. The Learys owned a water-tower business, and Chuck had gotten hurt on the job. With the first midwestern race of the USAC national season coming up at Winchester on April 7, 1991, Dismore suggested that they enter me in Chuck's car.

I was still a month shy of turning twenty.

> **MARK DISMORE:** "I had driven midgets a little bit, and I always believed that a midget and a go-kart parallel each other. Sure, with a midget the center of gravity is higher, so the thing rolls more, and it has a tendency to lift up the inside front wheel when you're cornering. But a kart does that a little bit, too, even though it's not as noticeable a transition. Anyway, the seat-of-the-pants feel is similar, and Tony had been such a natural in the karts that I thought, Man, this is a great opportunity for this kid. I just wanted to see him get a break, because he deserved one."

I was absolutely awed by the idea of racing at Winchester. I mean, it's the fastest half-mile oval in the world, with turns banked as steeply as Daytona's. A week or so before the race, the Learys took me there and let me run some test laps. Their mechanic, Steve Brummet, did a really smart thing: he knew how scary Winchester could be, so Steve set the throttle to utilize only about three-quarters of its travel. That let me learn both the car and the track without having enough speed to frighten myself to death.

I guess I did all right in the test, because Steve gave me full throttle when we went back for the race. Even so, I couldn't keep up with the fastest guys that day. Don Schilling and Doug Kalitta were teammates, and they had these high-dollar Pontiac engines that had all kinds of horsepower. I never saw them until the end of the thirty-lap feature, when they lapped me. The only real fun I had was racing hard with Tyce Carlson,

The day this photo was taken, I didn't think life could get any better: I'm just about to make my USAC midget debut at Winchester, Indiana, April 1991. (© John Mahoney)

but "fun" might be the wrong word, because we were both struggling. In the end, I finished tenth, and Tyce ran eleventh.

CROCKY WRIGHT: "Initially, Tony was credited with eleventh. He told me he had passed the tenth-place car, and asked me who the USAC scorer was. I told him, and Tony said, 'Show me where he is.' I took him up to the scoring area, and they went through the lap sheets with him. Tony was right: he did place tenth. The scorer said, 'You know, Tony, we're only talking about five or ten dollars difference,' and Tony said it wasn't the money. He wanted to be able to say he finished in the top ten in his USAC midget debut."

That was the only USAC national midget feature we ran that season, although later that summer I raced the Leary car in some USAC regional events at the Indianapolis Speedrome.

The Speedrome is a tricky little place. It's a flat, paved oval, just a fifth-mile, and inside the corners there are marker tires that are actually bolted to the ground. Those tires can trip up a midget in a heartbeat if you aren't careful. But if you use your head, a place like that can teach you a lot about patience, because you have to race both the track and your competitors an inch at a time, a turn at a time, a lap at a time.

I had stepped into an excellent situation, because the Learys and Steve Brummet had a great Speedrome setup. In our second outing there, we ran sixth; in our third, we won the fifty-lap feature, beating Ted Hines, the defending track champion.

Two races later we won again, this time in a one-hundred-lapper.

Winning at the Speedrome was a major high for me. That place had been the home track for televised midget racing in the 1980s, when ESPN launched its *Thunder* series. By the time I came along, ESPN had moved on to the bigger tracks like Indianapolis Raceway Park and Winchester, but it still meant something to me to win at a place where I had watched guys like Rich Vogler win those early TV races. Besides, the Speedrome was the place where I became an official USAC winner, and, let's face it, USAC was—and is—at the top of the heap when it came to midget groups.

I just didn't think life could get any better than that.

But it did. Just north of Columbus sits a little town called Flat Rock, and that's where a USAC sprint car owner named Steve Chrisman had his shop. I'd gotten to know him a little bit, and anytime I was in the neighborhood I'd visit Steve, mostly because it was a chance to get close to that sprinter and daydream about driving it. Anytime Steve needed somebody to sit in the cockpit for one reason or another, I'd jump right in before anyone else had a chance to volunteer.

STEVE CHRISMAN, USAC sprint car owner: "Tony was just an eager young kid who wanted to drive a sprint car. If I was fitting brake pedals or throttles or steering gear, he'd always want to be the one to get in there. Sometimes he'd come in and sit down in that car just for the heck of it."

When Steve asked me in July if I'd like to drive for him at Salem, I couldn't say yes fast enough.

Before the Salem race, Steve took me up to Winchester for my initial practice laps in a sprint car. The biggest single thing I remember was feeling, for the first time, the brute horsepower. I just couldn't believe how fast that thing wanted to go on the straightaways.

On my second fast lap, I saw a quick flash of color dart into my field of vision; a bird had flown directly into my path. Bad decision on the bird's part. It clipped the hood of the car and then bounced up into the roll cage, and when it hit that steel tubing the bird's body just exploded. I don't tell this story to gross anyone out, but to illustrate just how quickly you are traveling at a place like that.

Salem happened to be an ESPN race. That was cool, because it meant that my first sprint car start was on TV. Unfortunately, I missed the qualifying cut by one spot in my heat race, and by one spot again in the last-chance semi-feature. But I guess I made a decent impression, because they interviewed me on the broadcast.

TARA ARMSTRONG, wife of USAC driver Brad Armstrong: "We used to tape all the races back then, and watch 'em as soon as we got home from the track. Well, Tony got more coverage that night at Salem than anybody but the winner, and he missed the feature! I remember thinking at the time that this seemed crazy, but I think now that a lot of people saw something in him early on."

LARRY MARTZ: "There was just something about this kid. He had charisma."

I went to eight more USAC sprint races with Chrisman in 1991, and qualified for all of them. We actually put together a string of pretty fair finishes: seventh and sixth on successive nights at Winchester, eighth back at Salem, sixth at Indianapolis Raceway Park, fourth at Lakeside Speedway in Kansas City, fifth at the I-44 Speedway in Lebanon, Missouri.

All in all, it was a pretty nice sprint car debut.

For the first time, 1991 had me in a position where I was juggling different schedules and different cars. I had a sprint car deal and a midget ride, and whenever I got the chance I was sneaking back to Rushville or

Columbus to run a TQ. It was impossible not to get caught up in the fun of it all.

I was also getting an education in racing that you couldn't have bought at any price. All these rides took me to every sort of short track there is: dirt tracks, paved tracks, flat tracks, banked tracks, fast tracks, slow tracks. Because of that, I never fell into the common trap that snags so many young drivers: they develop a fixed style which helps them go fast at one type of track, but hurts them at another.

There are guys who excel on pavement but seem lost on dirt, and vice versa. Other guys fly on the small bullrings, but don't do well on high-speed tracks. I never really felt like I've been better or worse on any one type of track, and that all goes back to the fact that I jumped around so much in my formative years. Anytime we'd pull into a new track, I'd look at it and say, "Okay, this is what I think I need to do to go fast here." Then I'd get in the car and go do it.

> **IRISH SAUNDERS**, product manager, Hoosier Tire Company: "Back when he first started driving for Steve Chrisman, I took Tony to a Silver Crown race at the Indy Fairgrounds. He didn't have enough money for a pit pass; back then, he was so broke he couldn't pay attention. So I snuck him in by hiding him under a stack of tires in my truck. I remember pointing him out to a bunch of car owners, telling them, 'Hey, this kid has some talent. You need to keep an eye on him.' One of them said, 'Right, Irish, he's going to be another Jeff Gordon.' I said, 'I'll tell you what: this kid might be better than Jeff Gordon.'"

One winter day, a month or so after the 1991 season ended, I stopped at Steve Chrisman's house. As soon as I walked in the door, he grabbed a liquor bottle, poured some into a glass, and handed it to me. I didn't know what was going on, because we both knew I was too young to drink. But he told me that on this day, that wasn't an issue; I *had* to take a sip, because we had something to celebrate.

"I want you to hear this from me," Chrisman said. "You're the USAC sprint car Rookie of the Year."

To this day, I can recall the warm feeling of pride that came over me at that moment.

Not long after that, I learned that I'd also won the Speedrome rookie award.

Up until then, every trophy I'd ever had signaled the *end* of something: a race I'd won, a championship I'd earned. These rookie titles, on the other hand, drove home the point that maybe I was just getting started.

Started on what, I wasn't sure. All I knew was that everything up to that point—my little plastic trike, the karts, the TQs, everything—now seemed like it had been part of a learning process. I never planned on any of that stuff taking me anywhere, but it had happened. Now here I was, maybe on the edge of something big.

I felt like, Okay, the training wheels are off. Time to ride.

▌FIVE ▌ BUSTING OUT, BREAKING THROUGH ▐

MY PRIMARY FOCUS IN 1992 WAS CHRISMAN'S SPRINT CAR. WE PLANNED TO hit all the USAC pavement events, and maybe mix in a few dirt races if things went well. And things did go well, right from the start. In our third race of the season, at Indianapolis Raceway Park, I set the fast time; it was the first time I'd ever done that in a USAC national event.

In June we went on a weekend swing through Missouri, running one night at Lakeside Speedway and the next night at the I-44 Speedway. It ended up being a hell of a weekend: we ran fourth the first night, and won the second.

I-44, a paved three-eighths, was a place I took to in a hurry; the previous September I had run fifth there. This time around, I remember the track being fairly slick and the weather being unseasonably cool; not freezing by any means, but chilly. I also recall the support division being the local stock car class, and their feature was an extradistance deal.

USAC was always big on running quick, professional shows, particularly at places we didn't visit much, like I-44. They wanted to leave a good impression on the local folks, I guess. So when there were about fifteen laps left to run in that stock car race, the officials started urging all the sprint drivers to climb into our cars. That was fine with Steve

This was a great night for me, but not a great moment. I won my first USAC sprint car feature at Lebanon, Missouri, in June 1992 . . . but the night was not exactly accident free! (Kevin Horcher Photo)

Chrisman, because he wanted me to fire off early so we could bring the whole car—the engine oil, the gear lube, the tires—up to temperature. That's always something to consider when you're racing on a cool day.

I jumped into the seat, strapped in, and waited to go. But after a few minutes of sitting there, I thought, "Gee, I think I might need to go to the bathroom." Here's another thing to think about on chilly days: if you load up on liquids as usual before a race, but you're not sweating like you would in the heat, all those liquids will seek an outlet sooner or later.

I told Chrisman I was going to run to the men's room, and he said, "Forget it. There's no time."

> **STEVE CHRISMAN:** "Hell, we were gridded and ready to go. You can't just get out."

Steve was the boss, so I sat there hoping we'd push off at any second. Well, it took *forty-five minutes* just to run the last fifteen laps of that stock car feature. They had yellow flags, they had red flags, they had a cleanup for somebody losing oil. And still I was afraid to jump out, because I had gotten my orders from Chrisman.

So I sat there dying, feeling like my kidneys were about to burst. Finally, the stock car fiasco ended, and we pushed off. All I could think as I rolled out of the pits was, Can I hang on? Can I hold it? I've got to run thirty laps, maybe fourteen seconds a lap, that's . . .

The least embarrassing way to finish this story is just to tell you that we won the feature, and I was thrilled beyond belief to be in victory lane after a USAC sprint race.

The honest way is a lot more humbling.

> **PAT SULLIVAN:** "I was the pit announcer at I-44 back then. Tony rolls to a stop at the start–finish line, and I walk over there to interview him. Right away, he says, 'Hey, man, I can't get out of this car.' I said, 'What do you mean, you can't get out of the car? I've got to interview you.' And he says, 'Uh, I peed my pants on the parade lap.'"

STEVE CHRISMAN: "I told him, 'Aw, don't worry about a thing. Climb out of there, and when they hand you the plaque, just hold it down low in front of you. Nobody will ever know.' And they didn't."

Aside from that little humiliation—and, trust me, the same thing has happened to more drivers than you'd ever believe—that was an awesome day. To get the win, I'd had to chase Robbie Stanley, the defending USAC sprint car champion, but little by little I was able to reel him in. We had a great battle, and as we came down for the white flag I nosed ahead. The lead was mine, and so was the victory.

USAC had an eighteen-race sprint car series that year, and we made fourteen of them. Aside from the Lebanon win, our best results were that fourth at Lakeside, another fourth at Berlin Raceway in Michigan, and fifths at both Salem and Winchester. Those were some pretty fair showings, but they were all on asphalt.

We weren't nearly as impressive on dirt. Chrisman and I made only three dirt starts, and we didn't have much to show for it. I worried that people would look at me as a pavement-only racer; all my midget racing the previous season had been on asphalt, too. In USAC, if you get labeled as a specialist on one surface, people tend to translate that as meaning that you aren't so tough on the other.

In 1992, I ran a pretty busy schedule with Steve Chrisman's sprint car. Most of our races were on pavement, but we did run a few dirt tracks. This is me at Eldora Speedway in Ohio, October 1992.(© John Mahoney)

CROCKY WRIGHT: "When Tony started getting midget and sprint rides, they were always pavement cars. I couldn't understand

> why the owners who had good dirt-track cars never gave him
> a ride. In my mind, I considered Tony a dirt-track driver."

In the TQ midgets, dirt had been my specialty. I believed in my heart that I could get out there and run dirt in a sprint car or a midget just as well as I'd done it in my TQ days, but I wasn't getting the chance to prove that.

Come September, I was going through some serious dirt withdrawal. When I went to the Terre Haute Action Track to watch the Hut Hundred midget race, I brought along my helmet bag, hoping I might be able to beg my way into something.

The Hut Hundred was one of the country's most prestigious midget races. It had an Indy-style start—thirty-three cars, eleven rows of three—and it brought in the best guys from all the major clubs: USAC, the Badger association from Wisconsin, and the rest of the midget racing alphabet soup: UMARA, NAMARS, AAMS, you name it.

I walked around the pits, making a note of which teams had spare cars, and I stopped to check out Randy Koch's team. I had never met Randy, but I knew he was one of the top drivers at Sun Prairie, Wisconsin, a great midget track. He had two cars, and I asked one of his guys about my chances of running the second one. He didn't know me from Adam, and he gave me one of those looks: *Don't bother me, kid.*

I told him my name, said that I had been running USAC sprints and that I'd had a lot of success on dirt in the TQs. He walked off to talk it over with the rest of the team. I'm not sure if any of them recognized my name, but they looked like they were mulling it over. What clinched the deal was me telling them, "Look, I'll drive it for nothing."

Nobody likes working cheap, but I'm awfully glad I did it that day. I qualified twentieth, stayed out of trouble, and worked my way toward the front. I was seventh when we got the white flag, and on the last corner of the last lap I caught and passed the sixth-place driver: Randy Koch.

It wasn't a win, but it seemed to turn a few heads. The next weekend the midgets were scheduled to run at Lakeside and I-44, and I was invited to run a backup car for Ralph Potter. Ralph and his sons had been a force in midget racing for as long as I could remember, so driving for them was an honor.

TRACY POTTER, chief mechanic, Potter Racing: "I had heard about Tony for a long time, how he'd always come from the back of the pack at the Speedrome. Anyway, my dad was looking for somebody to run, and I said, 'Let's give this Stewart kid a shot.'"

RALPH POTTER, championship USAC midget owner: "We thought we'd try him and see how he did."

At Lakeside I ran second to my teammate, Tony Elliott, a solid open-wheel racer who was really starting to come into his own. It was my best finish ever in a USAC national midget race. The next night I matched it, finishing just behind Stevie Reeves, who went on to win the 1992 USAC championship.

It was also in '92 that I made my first start in the USAC Silver Crown division, driving for the late Ben Leyba. That was a thrill for me, because Ben was a highly regarded guy; Sheldon Kinser, Ken Schrader, Steve Chassey, Rich Vogler, and other great racers had driven for him.

My first outing in the Leyba car was at Indianapolis Raceway Park in June. I liked IRP, but I was a little bit anxious about going there with a Silver Crown car because I wasn't sure exactly how the thing was going to feel.

A Silver Crown car looks like a slightly longer, slightly heavier sprint car, and that's what everybody told me it would drive like. Benny and his mechanic, Jack Steck, said it would give the same type of feedback, but not as quickly or violently as a sprint car might. They were right: in practice, it felt like a lazy sprinter. It took longer to accelerate, it was harder to stop, and it didn't turn as well. And because it wasn't as responsive, you couldn't *carry* a Silver Crown car like you could a midget or a sprint car. You could run it to its limits, but you couldn't ease it beyond that limit and get away with it. I qualified fifth, which thrilled me.

The big challenge in Silver Crown racing is adjusting to how the car changes in the course of an event. Those cars don't make pit stops, so you load 'em up with as much fuel as it takes to go the distance. In some cases, you'll fill the seventy-gallon tail tank right to the brim. Methanol weighs roughly seven pounds per gallon, so you're adding almost five hundred pounds to the rear of the car, and that's weight that won't be there when the race ends. When you figure that the *total* weight of the car without fuel is only 1,550 pounds, you get an idea of the huge shift in the car's balance. That really takes some getting used to.

At IRP we had what I thought was a respectable result: sixth, one lap down.

The next race was on the dirt mile at the Illinois State Fairgrounds in Springfield, where we struggled, finishing fourteenth. Still, I liked Silver Crown racing; I thought that once I got used to the car, and once Benny and Jack got used to me, we'd have better results.

And that didn't take long. On Labor Day of 1992, we went to DuQuoin, Illinois, another great mile, and had an outstanding day. I qualified ninth and spent the entire race battling with George Snider as the two of us worked our way toward the front. Snider was a guy who had been around—he had qualified for twenty-three consecutive Indy 500s—and his ability on dirt was legendary. For a guy with no more experience than I had, it was a thrill just to be on the same track with George, and a huge achievement to actually duke it out with him. Right at the end, I edged him out to take fourth.

> **GEORGE SNIDER,** former USAC Silver Crown champion: "The first I really noticed Tony was that day at DuQuoin. For a guy who was so young, he was great to run with. He and I went back and forth all day, and after the race he came over and said, 'I learned a lot today, racing with you.' At the time, I didn't think much about that, but today it makes me feel pretty good."

We finished out the Silver Crown season by running fourth again, this time at Eldora. It was another great day in a great season in one of the most interesting periods of my life.

All of this was in the middle of what you might call my gypsy phase. Back then, I slept on half the sofas and in half the spare bedrooms in the state of Indiana. It started when I ran TQs for Larry Dwenger and bunked at his home. That set a pattern: if you noticed me hanging around on a regular basis, it was only a matter of time until you were tossing me a pillow. This was especially true if I either worked for you or drove your race car.

One afternoon in May of '91, I stopped to see Mark Dismore at Comet Kart, and Brad Armstrong happened to be in there. Brad was a little older than me, and he had been a Comet driver, too, but now he was racing sprint cars on the weekends and running a towing service in New Palestine, southeast of Indianapolis. He was looking to hire a wrecker driver on a temporary basis, and asked if I was interested. It sounded like the job would give me everything I wanted, which at that age—I turned twenty that month—meant a few dollars in my pocket and weekends off.

And, of course, free room and board. I moved in with Brad and his family, which worked out well because I was technically on call twenty-four hours a day.

BRAD ARMSTRONG, USAC sprint car driver: "We set him up in our living room. Tony would get out of bed whenever the first wrecker call came in; if that was at noon he'd be okay, but if it was at seven o'clock in the morning we'd have to get him up and shove him out the door. He was a little tough to get going."

I also lived for a while in Bloomington, where Amanda was attending Indiana University, and shared a three-room apartment with her and a friend.

It was a carefree period for me, and almost everything I did was fun. Even the wrecker job, which could sometimes be hard work, was cool, because I'd just truck along and think about racing.

I found a terrific way to *combine* racing and work when I lucked into a job at a family fun center in Nashville, Indiana. This place had an alpine slide, batting cages, bumper boats, and a go-kart track. I did a little bit of everything—shagged baseballs, looked after the alpine slide, all the grunt work—but mostly I ran the go-kart track. It was a nice oval with a little bit of banking, and of course I'd get out there and play whenever I could. These were just normal rental karts, pretty tame compared to the racing karts I had run but still a lot of fun.

Well, it was only a matter of time before I talked the owners of the facility into letting me organize races. We had ten karts, and I signed up forty participants, so we had to whittle down the field with qualifying heats. It was a pretty big success; just a couple of weeks into it, we were filling our Saturday rosters by Tuesday night. As things went along, we came up with some extra challenges: I set up a garden hose at the top of each corner, with its stream flowing down the banking, and when those karts hit the water they'd get nice and sideways, like they were on a dirt track.

Everybody was happy with the arrangement, except the guy who did the maintenance on the karts. He felt like they got a little too much abuse, and in hindsight I guess he was right. My career as a go-kart promoter ended right there.

My next gypsy move came in September of 1992, and this one lasted awhile.

I had known Larry Martz for a few years, right from the night of my TQ debut in '89. I had even driven for him a few times; the first night I ever sat in his car, we won at Columbus. After I stepped away from the TQs, Larry and I remained friends, and by '92 we were very close. He and his wife, Tutti, lived in Rushville, where Larry owned a used-car lot, and I'd stop to see them when I was in the area. Well, we got along so well that before long I found myself making excuses to *be* in the area. I went from stopping in, to staying overnight, to staying three or four nights a week.

Finally, Larry and Tutti said, "Look, why don't you just move in?"

The Martzes had three sons, Brian, Brad, and Brady, but from day one I knew them by their nicknames: Fuze, Buck, and Tate. Fuze had left home for college in August, which created some empty sleeping space. I was happy to fill it.

TUTTI MARTZ, longtime friend: "It all came about gradually. Tony began calling and talking to Larry, then he began coming around, and his stays just got a little longer each time. At first he might be here for an afternoon, then he'd be here for two or three days at a time. I always say that eventually I got tired of tripping over his suitcase, so we gave him some drawer and closet space."

LARRY MARTZ: "By that point, our kids and Tony had kind of bonded, and Tutti and I liked him. It just made sense."

They told me to make myself at home, and I did. I ate there, slept there, and talked my way out of doing chores there, just like I had done as a kid in Columbus. I'm tempted to say that it put me back into a calm, stable living environment, but that would be fibbing; with three sons—four, if you counted me—things never stayed calm or stable for long at the Martz household.

I never had a brother, although as a kid I had sometimes treated my sister, Natalie, like one. Now, it was like I had three.

> **LARRY MARTZ:** "Our three boys are each four years apart. Well, when Tony was with Fuze, he acted Fuze's age. When he was with Buck, he acted Buck's age. When he was with Tate, he acted Tate's age. He had that kind of personality. He'd race Hot Wheels cars on the floor with Tate when Tate was ten or eleven, and they'd do that all day long."

Larry had a minibike, a Honda Spree, and we put that thing to good use. There was a concrete area, maybe fifteen feet by thirty feet, between the back of the house and the front of Larry's shop. We turned that patch into a little oval—the house was the frontstretch wall, and the shop was the backstretch wall—and ride that Spree around and around. Naturally, it's always more fun to *race* than to just ride around, so we'd haul out a bicycle and have ourselves a battle. I'd ride the Spree, and either Tate or Buck would ride the bike. It probably sounds like that gave me a lopsided advantage, but in that tiny space those kids could accelerate as fast by pedaling as I could with the minibike.

We were pretty organized. We'd actually count off our laps—one hundred, two hundred, however long the race was—and sometimes we even had the neighbor's daughter be our flagman. But a little bit of organization doesn't mean that a typical race was a nice, civil contest. It wasn't. It was chaos.

> **LARRY MARTZ:** "Those races were intense. Tate and Tony would be out there, and neither one of 'em would give an inch. It used to make me mad, the way they'd beat my garage up. They'd bang into it, and they dented the aluminum siding. They'd beat on each other, and there would be wrestling and name-calling.

> Tate would be screaming, 'You jumped the start!' and Tony would be screaming right back at him. Oh, it was war."

I lived with the Martz family for a year and a half, and in that time Rushville became a second hometown to me. Even at the races, they stopped announcing "from Columbus, Indiana," before my name; now they referred to me as being from Rushville, because that's where I lived. It was only a matter of time until I picked up the "Rushville Rocket" nickname that has stuck with me ever since.

Today, when you drive in and out of Rushville, you see signs declaring the town as the "Home of Racing Champion Tony Stewart." I like that.

As for the Martzes, we developed a strong relationship during my time there. I grew very close to Larry and Tutti and the boys, and in some ways I feel even closer to them today. They taught me a lot of lessons that didn't seem like lessons at the time; it was only later, somewhere down the road, that I understood.

Living with that family was one of the best experiences of my life.

> **LARRY MARTZ:** "I think that as a kid, Tony had a good family life, and when his parents got divorced I'm sure he missed that. I think he had a hard time for a while. That must have been the connection he felt: here, he had a good, enjoyable family-type atmosphere."

> **TUTTI MARTZ:** "I really think he needed someplace to call home."

I don't want to create the impression that I had gotten away from my parents, because I hadn't. Far from it. My mom had gotten remarried to a great guy named Mike Boas, and they were living in Lafayette, an hour or so northwest of Indianapolis. My dad was still a regular at my races, so we spent a lot of time together. Their divorce never stopped either of them from being a strong presence in my life. Together or separately, they always provided the right amount of discipline for me, and I'm sure for Natalie, too.

And that's good, because at the age we're talking about here—late teens and early twenties—things can get really tricky for a young guy, especially when he's juggling homes and making new friends every day. A lot of kids in that position get swayed by the temptations you read about every day, but I never did. I didn't want to know about drinking; I didn't want to know about drugs. And I believe that the reason I never got in trouble with any of that stuff was plain old fear. I was scared that my father would beat the hell out of me, and I was even more scared of disappointing my mother. So I walked a pretty straight line.

PAT SULLIVAN: "It's funny to me that Tony gets slapped with the 'immature' label so often today, because in a lot of ways he was obviously very mature, and very smart, as a kid. He was incredibly centered for someone of that age."

I'm sure it also helped that I was generally in the company of guys—car owners, mechanics, officials—much older than me. That helped me grow up a lot quicker than I would have if I'd passed that time hanging out at the local playground.

As things went along, a lot of those older people became my friends. Maybe that's because I was never a party animal who wanted to hit the bars five nights a week. I just found it easier to hang out with guys who had gotten past that stage.

It didn't matter to me what someone's age was, or what he did. I met a lot of people in that period who had been around the sport a long time, and we'd spend hours talking about racing in general. I appreciated their insight and their advice, and the fact that, whether they knew it or not, they helped keep me pointed in the right direction.

DICK JORDAN, USAC director of communications: "Early in his career, I began to see Tony as a friend more than anything else. I mean, I knew he was a good racer; everybody could see that. But he was just a neat guy to be around, and we did a lot of things together: played pool, golfed, played cards."

JOHN MAHONEY: "If I'm not mistaken, the first time Tony ever played poker was after a race at the Speedrome. Jordan and I were playing that night with some friends, and Dick said to Stewart, 'You want to come along?' Tony said, 'I don't know how to play.' But he came with us, and he learned. In fact, he learned fast."

PAT SULLIVAN: "When you deal with any young person, it's easy to get hung up on all the superficial stuff—maybe they've got an earring, or it's the color of their hair, or they're really cocky—and miss really connecting with the person. Well, it was easy to connect with Tony, even for those of us who were much older. Yes, he was cocky at times, but he also embodied everything about this sport that all of us treasured. We gravitated to him because we liked his spirit."

The Copper World Classic at Phoenix is one of the neatest events in all of open-wheel racing, teaming the Silver Crown cars and midgets with the wild offset supermodifieds that run out on the West Coast. It's the first outdoor race of the USAC season, and after being cooped up all winter everybody loves hanging out in the Arizona sun. I had heard about that race for years, but my first one came in 1993, when Ben Leyba took me out there to run the Silver Crown opener.

I had never been on a one-mile paved track, but I qualified second, next to Davey Hamilton. Today Davey is best known as an Indy car driver, but in those days he was the young king of supermodified racing on the West Coast; he had already won the supermod end of the Copper World twice. We were both relatively new to Silver Crown racing, but he was a hot name, and it was neat to share the front row with him.

DAVEY HAMILTON, Indy Racing League veteran: "Up until that race at Phoenix, I honestly hadn't heard of Tony, but there he was, qualifying second. I was thinking, 'Well, sure, this kid qualified good, but he shouldn't be a factor in the race. I'll just jump him on the start, and he won't be a problem.' Well, it wasn't that easy."

I chased Mike Bliss all race long in the 1993 Copper Classic feature for Silver Crown
cars at Phoenix. Mike won, but it was still a big day for me: it was that February afternoon that
I decided to race for a living. (© John Mahoney)

The Silver Crown feature was fifty laps long. I took the lead at the
green flag, and stayed out front for thirty-one laps before Mike Bliss got
past me. Bliss was another guy who was just starting to make his mark,
and since then he's since made a name for himself in NASCAR. In our
USAC days he was always about a year ahead of me, and on a couple of
occasions I ended up in his old rides after he moved on. But that day at
Phoenix, we had a nice duel. I stayed close to him after he passed me,
and with a few laps to go I snuck back around him. For an instant, I was
sure I had the race won. But a yellow flag came out and the scoring
reverted to the previous lap, which put Mike back in front. Once we got
rolling again, Mike just pulled away.

Still, second place in the Copper Classic, especially my *first* Copper
Classic, was a better result than I'd ever dreamed about on my way out
there.

DAVEY HAMILTON: "I knew after that day that Tony was going to
be a good one, and his career went straight up from there. Looking back, it reminds me of the first time I ever raced against Jeff
Gordon. You always look at the young, up-and-coming guys,
and he and Tony were two guys who really stuck out."

But my best memory of that weekend isn't of the race. It's of just being out there in Phoenix at all. I mean, I was just a kid, twenty-one years old, living in Rushville and working odd jobs: I sold cars for Larry Martz; I worked for Gene Crucean and Jeff Jones at Beast Karts in Indianapolis; I even did a stint as a maintenance man at a joint called the Covered Bridge Motel. At the time of the Copper Classic, I was earning five dollars an hour working in a machine shop. The shop was in a pole barn, and to keep the place warm we had one space heater, which didn't even take the chill out of the air. For eight hours a day, I'd have my hands either on cold steel or in a cold bucket of solvent.

Now I'm standing in the warm Phoenix sunshine, and somebody is telling me that the second-place purse is $8,600. I was racing for 40 percent, and a quick calculation told me that my end came to almost $3,500. I was in heaven. I kept thinking, How many eight-hour days at five bucks an hour would I have to work to make $3,500?

And the wheels in my head started turning: *Maybe I can make a living driving race cars . . . No, not all the events pay as good as Phoenix does, but if I can keep this ride in Leyba's Silver Crown car, run all the midget shows I can find, and squeeze in some extra sprint car races . . .*

I came home, quit my job at the machine shop, and became a full-time racer.

Filling up my 1993 schedule was easy: I'd run the Silver Crown races with Leyba, that was a given. Benny had a sprinter, too, so I penciled in a bunch of races with that car. And I was in excellent shape for the midget season, thanks to a telephone call I got.

There's an old saying that you can chart a driver's career by the size of his phone bill. If it's high, he's calling around to look for rides; if it's low, he's answering his phone more than he's dialing it, so he's in demand.

I knew I was on the right track when Larry Martz walked into the room one day and told me Rollie Helmling was on the line.

LARRY MARTZ: "Rollie Helmling was, like, the Roger Penske of midget racing. Anybody who was a really talented driver got to

drive for Rollie. Well, one day my phone rang, and the voice on the other end said, 'Hello, this is Rollie Helmling. May I talk to Tony Stewart?' I was absolutely speechless. I went upstairs, where Tony and my son Tate were playing a video game. I covered up the mouthpiece and said, 'Tony, it's Rollie Helmling, and he wants to talk to you.' Tony said, 'I'll be done in just a minute. Tell him to hold on.' I said, 'Tony, it's Rollie Helmling! I can't tell Rollie Helmling to hold on!' Finally, I got him off the video game and gave him the phone."

Being asked to drive Rollie's midget was probably the biggest break I had gotten to that point. He'd always had terrific drivers—Chuck Gurney, Larry Rice, Mel Kenyon, John Andretti—and in 1990 Jeff Gordon had driven Rollie's car to the USAC title. Every division has a couple of cars any driver would be honored to steer, and Rollie's midget was of that caliber. Just sitting in that thing pushed my career to another level.

Every division has a car owner or two who every guy in the pits would love to drive for. In the USAC midgets in 1993, Rollie Helmling was one of those guys. Just sitting in his car was a huge honor for me. (© John Mahoney)

ROLLIE HELMLING, champion USAC midget owner: "The thing about Tony, like Jeff and John before him, was that you could see in him this desire to succeed. You just knew that he'd get the bit in his mouth, and he'd be off and running. I've always liked to say that when the face shield goes down and the ignition switch goes to the 'on' position, there arc guys you just know are going to take that car to the front. Tony was one of those guys."

The Midwestern USAC midget season opened in April at Winchester, where we ran second to Stevie Reeves. I remember thinking that was a pretty good start; Stevie was the defending national champ, and he was driving for Steve Lewis and Bob East, whose team was on a par with Rollie's.

Well, that Winchester finish was the closest we would get to the front for a while.

Rollie was trying a new engine, a Scat V4 he was really high on. He felt like the Pontiacs that had dominated the division were at the end of their development curve, and he wanted to be on the leading edge of the next wave of technology. Unfortunately, we didn't yet have the raw horsepower it took to beat a lot of the guys we were up against.

LARRY MARTZ: "I was still running my TQ, but I used to go to the midget races and Rollie let me help with the car. Because Rollie was developing that engine, it was just underpowered. As long as you could run it wide open—keep it on the upper end of the torque band—it was good. But if you had to get out of the throttle, like in traffic, you were done."

Rollie is a brilliant guy when it comes to setting up a car, and I felt like I was doing a good job of driving, but most of the time we went home from the track without a whole lot to show for our efforts.

What kept us from getting totally discouraged was that when things went right, we were really quick. In June we were set to win a USAC feature at Lawrenceburg, Indiana, until we broke a bolt in the rear suspension and I had to back off to keep from crashing; we still finished third. The next afternoon we went to Terre Haute for an All-American Midget Series event, and scored an amazing win.

ROLLIE HELMLING: "Terre Haute was in the best shape I've ever seen for a daytime race. Normally it gets too dry, but on this day there was a good cushion and you could run wherever you wanted. Well, that was one of the greatest midget races I've ever seen. Tony was running up on top, with Page Jones, driving for Rusty Kunz, down on the bottom. I'll bet the lead changed

> twenty times in twenty-five laps. Going down the backstretch one of them would lead, and the other would lead down the frontstretch. I mean, it was just a great show. In the end, we won it and Page ran second."

In the summer of '93, Page Jones was one of the hottest young prospects in all of racing. He was the son of Parnelli Jones, who won the Indy 500 in 1963, and Page and his older brother P.J. were following in Parnelli's footsteps. Both of them had won a bunch of midget races on the West Coast, and now P.J. was racing sports cars and Page was racing everything: midgets, sprints, Silver Crown cars, even some NASCAR stock cars. Beating him that Sunday at Terre Haute was a real feather in my cap.

I was still kind of scratching out a nickel-and-dime living, like a lot of open-wheel guys do. If your sole income is your percentage of the winnings, it's in your best interest to race as often as you can, so whenever I wasn't committed to a USAC event with Rollie or Ben Leyba, I'd figure out where else I could pick up some extra money.

It was a hectic lifestyle, but it made me a few dollars, and left me with more than a few great stories.

On the last weekend of July in '93, USAC held a doubleheader for midgets and Silver Crown cars at Milwaukee. Well, I found out that the Badger group was racing that Friday night at a third-mile dirt track in Hales Corners, Wisconsin. Rollie wasn't too keen on me running there because he wanted me to be fresh for Milwaukee, but from my point of view, it was another payday.

Somebody mentioned that the Kunz car might be open, because Page Jones would be off racing a stock car someplace. Now, like Rollie Helmling, Rusty Kunz and his brother Keith had hired a who's-who list of midget drivers over the years; even though I had beaten their car at Terre Haute, I still felt a little shy about asking to drive it.

Finally, I got up the nerve.

> **RUSTY KUNZ,** veteran midget owner and mechanic: "With the Silver Crown cars running at Milwaukee, there were going to be a lot of good drivers in the area. We tried a lot of guys, but for one

reason or another they weren't available. Then, just a couple days before the race, the phone rang. Keith picked it up, and he hollered across the garage, 'Hey, you remember that Tony Stewart kid from Terre Haute? He wants to go up to Hales Corners and run that race.' We thought it over and figured, You know, we can't get anybody else. Let's take him up there."

I was pleasantly surprised how easily that phone call went. I didn't have to beg for the ride, didn't have to offer to drive for nothing. Keith and Rusty just said, "Sure. Come up and drive."

The morning of the race, I left Rushville in my Ford Escort, with my girlfriend Amanda as my co-pilot for the six-hour ride. Like most of my road trips back then, this was a low-dollar deal. I knew that most of my cash would be eaten up by pit passes, so when the gas gauge hit empty I pumped in only as much as we'd need to get the rest of the way; I always counted on earning enough money at the track to get back home.

Amanda and I were starving, so we stopped at a McDonald's and ordered the best lunch I could afford: one cheeseburger, one small order of fries, one child-sized Coke. For both of us. Thank God, Amanda didn't eat much; I think she took a bite of that cheeseburger, ate a few fries, and left the rest to me.

When we finally made it to Hales Corners, the price of a pit pass was higher than I had counted on. In fact, between Amanda and I, we had just enough money for one. Luckily, Crocky Wright happened to be standing there, and while I signed in he drove off with Amanda to find an ATM machine. She pulled the last few dollars out of her checking account, came back to the track, and bought her own pit pass.

RUSTY KUNZ: "If I remember it right, Tony didn't even have enough money left to buy tear-offs for his helmet, so he borrowed five bucks from us."

I figured this was a typical midget feature: thirty laps, maybe forty. Well, when I climbed in to check out the seat, they told me, "Make sure you're comfortable. You know, one hundred laps is a long race."

Now, one hundred laps on a third-mile track might not sound like a great distance, but midget racing on dirt is a physical thing; you're slamming off the cushion, you're bouncing through the holes. It can drain you every bit as much as a Winston Cup five-hundred-miler. All I could think about was Rollie Helmling telling me he would prefer that I skip Hales Corners; he kept stressing that Milwaukee was a big deal, and that I'd need to be in good shape to run his midget and Leyba's Silver Crown car.

I tried to convince myself that it wouldn't be so bad. The previous fall, when I ran the Hut Hundred, I think we only had sixty or so green-flag laps, with the rest under yellow, so it wasn't too tiring. Then, when it was time to line up the Hales Corners feature, I watched Rusty and Keith pour in so much fuel that the tank almost overflowed.

I said, "Gosh, do you really think we'll need that much fuel for one hundred laps?"

They said, "Well, you never know how many *total* laps we'll have. Don't forget, this is one hundred green-flag laps. They don't count yellows."

My heart sank, and I'm sure my jaw dropped.

Thankfully, the race actually went by pretty quickly, and it couldn't have gone better for me. With about ten laps to go I was running second to Kevin Doty, one of the Badger club's top drivers. Then I noticed Doty's car stumbling in the corners; he was running out of fuel. I caught him, passed him, and we won the race.

At the time, the standard winner's purse for a midget race topped out at around $2,000. I nearly fainted when I found out that this one paid $7,000. And the Kunz brothers had made me a great deal: I was in for 50 percent. The track paid us in cash, all in the small bills they'd taken in at the ticket windows. I promise you, $3,500 in small bills makes a *big* pile of money.

A week earlier I had bought a briefcase, the first one I'd ever owned. I brought it with me to Wisconsin—trying to look like a professional racer, I guess—but all I had inside was a notepad and a couple of pens. Well, we stuffed that thing full of cash, and when we got done it looked like something out of a gangster movie.

RUSTY KUNZ: "Tony was standing there holding his three thousand five hundred dollars and you could tell he had never seen that much money. His eyes were bigger than silver dollars."

Just before I closed the briefcase, I pulled out a hundred bucks and tucked it into my pocket. Then I put the briefcase in the trunk of the Escort, and vowed not to open it until we got home. I was scared to death that I'd get robbed.

As soon as we left the track, we stopped for a late-night meal. Yes, it was another fast-food joint, because nothing else was open, but this time I bought dinner for everybody with me. Then I literally threw away the tennis shoes I was wearing—I'd worn them all summer, too broke to buy new ones, so they smelled pretty funky—and gave Amanda some money to pick up another pair the next day while I was qualifying at Milwaukee.

The rest of the weekend didn't go so well: we burned a piston in Rollie's midget, and lost the magneto in the Silver Crown race. But on the ride home, I had new sneakers and a full tank of gas.

We had some other crazy adventures just trying to make ends meet. One Saturday I was set to drive Leyba's Silver Crown car at Springfield in the afternoon, and Rollie's midget at Indianapolis Raceway Park at night. The two tracks are three hours apart, driving time, if you're really on the gas. That was going to make things tight if Springfield ran long.

I thought I had that problem solved when a friend of a friend hooked me up with somebody who owned a plane. The guy said he'd meet me at the Springfield airport and fly me back to Indianapolis. Larry Martz drove out to Illinois with me, and we lined up a buddy of ours to bring the car back home. As things turned out, I dropped out early at Springfield, which was disappointing, but on the bright side I figured we'd get to IRP in plenty of time.

We headed to the airport and met the fellow who was going to fly us back. He had a buddy with him. We walked out to the ramp, and I was checking out the nice Cessnas and Beechcrafts, thinking that this was definitely the way to travel. But the pilot walked straight past all those planes, and over to this old military airplane. It was a single-engine,

World War II–era thing with a sliding canopy over the cockpit and two big fuel tanks, one on the end of each wingtip.

Larry and I didn't know what to think, but we climbed in. The thing seated four, but barely; we had the pilot and his buddy up front, Larry and me shoulder-to-shoulder in the back. We rolled down the runway and took off, and between the engine and the air rushing in through the canopy it was ridiculously loud. But after what happened several minutes later, I decided all this noise wasn't so bad.

First I heard the engine sputter once, then sputter again, and then— *bbbrrrrrrr*—it quit altogether. Silence. To me, it acted the way a race car acts when it runs out of fuel. Then, much to my relief and Larry's, the engine restarted, but in another minute or so the cycle repeated: sputter, silence, restart.

> **LARRY MARTZ:** "It wasn't that we didn't have enough fuel on board. We had plenty of fuel in one tank, but when the first tank started to run low, it wouldn't switch to the full tank. I remember the pilot trying to switch the tanks; he was actually rocking the plane, which I guess he thought might help."

The pilot began to look around for an airport where he could land to check things out, but the only place he could find was an unmanned strip in the middle of a cornfield; no fuel sales, no repair facilities, just a strip. As we made our approach, you could see that there was just a country road going past the place, and nobody in sight. The pilot made a nice landing, then we all analyzed the situation: we had one tank which was full but not functional, and another that was functional but not full. The working tank had a small amount of fuel in it, but we weren't sure exactly how much.

> **LARRY MARTZ:** "I remember the pilot getting his map out. He figured out that we were eighteen miles north of Charleston, Illinois. He said, 'If we can make it eighteen miles, we can get more fuel there.' So, off we went. Why I got back on that airplane, I'll never know. But I'll tell you this: that eighteen-mile flight was just the most intense thing. You know, this is some-

> thing I don't usually talk about; it's one of those events I've tried to put out of my mind, because I thought we were going to die, I really did. I remember Tony squeezing my hand, just squeezing so hard. I've never been as relieved in my life as when those wheels touched down in Charleston."

Those wingtip tanks, the pilot told us, were each supposed to hold thirty-nine gallons. Well, at Charleston they pumped 39.5 into the one we'd been using.

Then we flew on, landing at Speedway Airport just a couple of miles from IRP. That brought up another problem: we had never lined up a ride to the track, because we figured we'd be there so early that we could call any number of friends to come and get us. By now, however, all our pals were already at IRP, and this was in the days when you didn't see many cell phones in the pits at a midget race.

> **LARRY MARTZ:** "There was one guy working at the airport, and he was a really nice man. He had an old station wagon, and he took us over to the track. He actually left the airport unattended and drove us right to the pit gate."

We had missed all the practice sessions, and qualifying was about to start. Well, the pit gate at IRP is located way out beyond turn two, and the crossover tunnel to the infield pit area is over by turn four. Larry and I picked up my gear—my new briefcase, of course, and a couple of heavy bags loaded with helmets and firesuits—and took off running. By the time we made it to the frontstretch, we were absolutely whipped, so we slowed up for a second to catch our breath. Wouldn't you know it, that's the exact moment Rollie Helmling happened to look across the track.

Now, Rollie had no idea what we had gone through. All he knew was that they were lining up the time trials, and his driver was still missing. When he saw me loafing, or so he thought, it was more than he could take. I could hear Rollie screaming, "Don't you *walk*! You *run*!"

I'll tell you exactly how late we were: when I got to the car, Mike Fedorcak, a real good pavement racer from Fort Wayne, was in the seat.

Rollie growled, "You've got five minutes to get your ass in that car, or Fedorcak's qualifying it!"

I didn't have the energy to tell him how close he had come to needing a replacement driver for *all* the races.

I got changed as quick as I could, hopped in the car, and actually qualified the thing fifth. I've never felt more exhausted after time trials. We ended up sixth in the feature, then I went home and got a good night's sleep.

I found out later that there were a bunch of people who stayed at Springfield until that race was over, then *drove* to IRP and beat us there. For years, Larry and I called that trip the Flight from Hell.

In that summer of 1993, I had some great races with Benny Leyba's sprinter, winning twice, and some decent Silver Crown runs. But it was in the midgets that I seemed to be attracting the most attention. I still hadn't won a USAC national midget race, and yet that was where most of my notoriety was coming from.

Looking back, I'm not sure I was driving better in the midgets than I was in anything else, but I guess I *looked* better. I think it just so happened that my midget rides were the best in the business, while Leyba's cars were just a tick behind the competition. Benny had a solid team in terms of the people involved; the trouble was, all the USAC divisions were getting overrun by "specialty" cars, built to run either pavement or dirt, and we were running our sprint and Silver Crown cars on both surfaces. It was getting harder all the time to keep up.

Anyway, I was really geared up to bring Rollie Helmling's midget back to Terre Haute for the Hut Hundred. Even though Terre Haute is a fast track that generally rewards cars with big horsepower, we had learned in June—when I'd beaten Page Jones—that if it was dry enough we could hold our own.

All the normal invaders turned out for the Hut, including Stan Fox, who had been phasing out his short-track starts and trying to get his Indy car career going. Fox was in the Steve Lewis car, which made him an automatic threat. And Page was back with the Kunz brothers, so we knew he'd be tough.

But I felt pretty tough myself. In qualifying I set the quick time, smashing the old track record. That put me on the pole, with Page next to me. He took off with the lead at the start, but not very far into the race something broke in his car, and Page's day was done. That left things to me and Fox, and we had ourselves a hell of a battle.

Terre Haute's surface was glazed over, slick, and full of holes. It was one of those days where, as the car owners love to say, you have to stand up in the seat and just *drive* the thing. Fox was all over me, but I wasn't sure whether he was just sizing me up or really struggling to get past me. Rollie was flashing me hand signals from the infield—you don't run radios in midgets and sprint cars—but all he could tell me was what I already knew: that Fox was on my tail.

ROLLIE HELMLING: "There was a red-flag stop with about twenty laps to go, and Tony kept asking, 'What do I need to do? What do I need to do?' I said, 'Just keep doing what you've been doing, and don't make any mistakes. You're going to win this race.'"

My first USAC national midget win was a beauty—I won the Hut Hundred at Terre Haute, and I had to fight off Stan Fox to do it. (© John Mahoney)

I listened to what Rollie told me, and concentrated on running my own line from the restart to the end of the race. Fox took a look at passing me from time to time, but that's all I ever gave him: just a look.

The 1993 Hut Hundred became my first USAC national midget victory.

To see the excitement and relief that was on Rollie's face, after all the trials and tribulations we had been through that season, was gratifying. Not only had he gotten his new engine into victory lane, he'd done it in one of the biggest events of the year.

ROLLIE HELMLING: "I had already won the Hut Hundred in '90, with Jeff Gordon. But I'm from Vincennes, fifty miles from Terre Haute, and I had been going there from the time I was a kid. I watched Jim Hurtubise and Parnelli Jones race sprint cars there, and I had seen a lot of Hut Hundreds. I saw Don Branson win it, and I was there in '61 when A. J. Foyt came from last to win. So to me, the Hut Hundred was always the race to win."

I was on cloud nine that day, but I think that win means even more today than it did in September of '93. See, just a couple of years later, Stan Fox suffered a serious head injury in a crash at the start of the 1995 Indianapolis 500, and he never raced again. In December of 2000, just before Christmas, he was killed in a highway accident. Stan was a neat guy and a great racer, and to have beaten him on a real driver's track, like Terre Haute was that day, is something I'll always be proud of.

As the '93 season wound down, Rollie came to the conclusion that he needed to get out of racing for a while. He had a growing retail business to look after, and, besides, he had climbed just about every mountain a man could climb in his division. I hated to see him go, first because I really enjoyed racing with him and second because I knew I'd need to line up another midget ride for 1994.

Fortunately, we got that problem solved early when Ralph Potter asked me to run his car in the final three USAC events of '93. All three were in Southern California: there was Ventura on the Saturday before Thanksgiving, then the Turkey Night Grand Prix at the Oildale track in Bakersfield, and the season finale back at Ventura on the Saturday after Thanksgiving. I think Ralph and I had sort of made up our minds that we wanted to team up for '94, and these races would give us a chance to get acquainted.

Just having the opportunity to run Turkey Night was awesome to me. They've been running that race since 1934 at a variety of California tracks, and the list of the guys who have won it is incredible: Bill Vukovich, A. J. Foyt, Parnelli Jones, Mel Kenyon, Gary Bettenhausen, Bubby Jones, Ron Shuman, Kevin Olson, and Stan Fox, just to name a handful.

Actually, to a kid from Indiana, the whole idea of going to California, race or no race, was wild. To me, that had always seemed like a magical place. You know, for your whole life you hear all those songs about the beaches and the pretty girls and the hot rods, and now I had the chance to see it all for myself.

I'll always remember riding out there in Ralph Potter's truck, me and Bryan Potter and Jerry Riley. It was a two-thousand-mile haul from Indianapolis, but I didn't mind. It was a chance to see parts of the country I'd never been to, and it was a hell of a lot cheaper than an airline ticket. My nickel-and-dime days were far from over.

> **TRACY POTTER:** "Tony left home with probably twenty bucks in his pocket. We ran the first race, and USAC paid by check. Well, Tony hadn't counted on that, so he had to hit my old man up for some money."

It was pretty neat to show up at those California tracks with one of the best midget rides in the country. And we did okay, all things considered: at Ventura the first time around, we ran thirteenth; at Turkey Night we finished a respectable seventh; and back at Ventura, I set quick time and finished third.

> **RALPH POTTER:** "Tony had a lot of talent, I knew that. But then we got to run him a little bit, and we found out how good he really was."

Looking at it now, the end of 1993 was like the close of a chapter, a real turning point for me. Back home, the gypsy phase of my life was coming to a halt. In the off-season I did some apartment hunting, said good-bye and thank you to the Martz family, and moved into my own place in Indianapolis. It was a good way to be close to the hub of things.

LARRY MARTZ: "It was extremely difficult to see him leave. It was like watching a son go off to college, or go off to join the army."

I had pretty much completed a stage every driver goes through: that period of trying to establish himself. I still had a long way to go to get where I wanted to be, but in those couple of years—1992, '93, right in there—I think I turned that corner. That's evident just by the people and teams I was now associating with; I was getting the kinds of rides that could win a guy lots of races.

It was a period of breaking through, and it laid the groundwork for all the good things that were yet to come.

PAT SULLIVAN: "There was a point when you began to hear some other drivers grouse a little bit about Tony. They'd say, 'Oh, sure he's winning, but it's because he got the right breaks, the right equipment.' Well, okay, he did have the right equipment, but the car owners he was attracting—the Ben Leybas and the Rollie Helmlings—had watched a lot of drivers over the years, and they could see what everyone else saw. It didn't take a genius to see that Tony had that little extra something."

STEVE LEWIS, champion USAC midget owner: "You could see an exuberance in his driving. When Tony got into a car, that car would come alive; it would almost look like a different machine. It was obvious that there was something special going on here."

I BELIEVE THERE COMES A POINT IN THE LIFE OF EVERY SUCCESSFUL person— every winning athlete, every man or woman who excels at his or her job—when they come to understand that they have something that separates them from most of the pack, that places them among the winners.

It's a point when all doubts go away, and you say to yourself, "I can do this."

For me, that point was 1994. It wasn't just because I won my first USAC championship that year, or because I got my first real TV exposure by winning a couple of ESPN races. It was a matter of noticing a confidence in my driving that hadn't been there before. I think maybe other people saw it before I did—as I mentioned earlier, all the right car owners were calling—but now I could see it for myself: I really *could* do this.

The season opened pretty quietly, with a so-so Copper Classic. We had a mechanical problem with the Potter car and dropped out of the midget race, but I finished third in the Silver Crown feature driving for Gene Nolen. (Ben Leyba had taken ill and cut back on his racing, and he died a short while later, which was a big loss to open-wheel racing.) Still, I came home from Phoenix pumped up about my prospects; Potter's

Right from the start of the 1994 season, my biggest rival for the USAC national midget title was Andy Michner. That's him chasing me at Winchester, April 24, 1994. (© John Mahoney)

team was definitely championship material, as long as the driver was.

I was feeling racy, anxious for the rest of the season to get going. I didn't have to wait long.

A week or two after Phoenix, I got a call from a midget mechanic named Larry Howard. The first thing he asked was if I knew who he was, and I sure did. For several years he had taken care of the cars raced by P.J. and Page Jones, and helped mold those guys into winners. But long before he hooked up with the Joneses, Larry Howard had a huge reputation in midget racing.

Every form of motorsports has its legendary mechanics: NASCAR has Junior Johnson and the Wood Brothers; Indy car racing has George Bignotti and A. J. Watson; the World of Outlaws sprint car series has Karl Kinser. Well, West Coast midget racing has Larry Howard.

He said he'd gotten hooked up with Larry Brown, a California chassis builder and part-time driver. They wondered if I'd be interested in driving for them in USAC's Western States midget division, which runs independently of the national midget series.

LARRY HOWARD, veteran midget mechanic: "I had basically retired from working on race cars. P.J. had already moved on, and Page was heading to the Midwest, so I was going to quit. Then Larry Brown called and said, 'Would you at least talk with me about working for me?' So we agreed to have dinner. My wife said, 'What are you going to tell him? You keep saying you don't want to do this anymore.' Well, I figured I'd just do whatever I could to discourage him. We had dinner, and one of the things I said—again, trying to discourage him—was, 'I absolutely have to pick the driver. If we can't get the guy I want, I don't want to do this.' Larry asked me who I wanted, and I said, 'Tony Stewart.' And Larry said, 'Who's that?' So I told him about something I'd seen at the last race of '93, at Ventura. Tony was there with the Potters, and I was working with Page. Tony had a good starting spot, but right at the beginning of the feature he fell back to about twelfth. Page won the race, but the thing that attracted my attention was that Tony had gotten back up to third at the finish. Now, we're talking about a forty-lap race on a fifth-mile track where you can hardly pass. I couldn't get that race out of my mind; there was something about this kid. Larry Brown said, 'Do you think we can get him?' I said, 'Well, I've never talked to him. In fact, I'm not sure I'd recognize him if he walked in the door.' Anyway, later on I called Tony and said, 'Hey, do you think you'd like to come out and run for us?'"

It didn't seem smart to pass up a shot at driving for Larry Howard, so I packed up everything I owned and flew out there to spend seven weeks in California. I was standing at the baggage claim at LAX with all my gear piled on one of those rented carts, and here came this fellow with a racing T-shirt.

He said, "You must be Tony Stewart."

I said, "You must be Larry Howard."

Except for that one phone call, we were total strangers. But on the ride to Bakersfield, where I'd be staying at Larry Brown's home, I felt instantly at ease. Just from talking with Larry Howard, I could sense that I was in a situation that was going to be really good for me.

LARRY HOWARD: "You couldn't help but like him. I mean, we've got all his stuff loaded in my truck, and he sat there with my dog on his lap the whole way, and we talked. He was just a kid, really."

At first, my plan for the Brown car was to run six Western States races in the early spring, which would keep me busy right up until the USAC national season kicked into high gear at the end of April. But we did so well in that trial period—we won three times and finished second twice—that we were all happy with the arrangement. I liked Larry Brown's car and the guys I was working with, and they seemed to like me.

On top of that, we had built a nice lead in the USAC regional standings. Because of all that, we extended our deal a bit: we decided I would fly out there and run the Western States series whenever I didn't have a conflict with a USAC national race back home. Larry Brown would pick up the airfare, which was okay with me.

Once I got looking at our new schedule, it hit me that running for both the national midget championship *and* the Western States crown was not out of the question. Sure, I would miss a handful of California races that clashed with national dates, but if we could keep up the speed and consistency we established in the spring, it could happen. That was good enough for me.

Looking back, that was pretty optimistic. There was a tendency, I think, for the national midget guys to underrate the Western States series, but that was one tough circuit.

One of the things that made it so tough was a kid from Phoenix by the name of Billy Boat. Billy is now an Indy car regular, but in '94 he was still on his way up. He had switched his focus from sprint cars to midgets and had a great ride with John Lawson, and he was just entering a phase when he was *the* guy to beat in West Coast midget racing. Instantly, we developed a real rivalry.

> **BILLY BOAT,** Indy Racing League veteran: "Tony was the guy we wanted to outrun. See, he was the young big-shot USAC guy from back east coming out to the West Coast, and we wanted to show him that we were for real."

I absolutely loved racing against Boat. We ran close so many times when I first went out there that we quickly developed a mutual trust. There's only one way that happens: you see how the other guy reacts when the two of you are in a tight spot. If he leaves you enough racing room—you're not asking for a lot of room, but *just enough* room—you come to trust him.

Normally, that sort of on-track relationship can take months to build, but it took Billy and me maybe two or three races. And because that trust existed, we felt free to push each other to the limit. We might bang wheels a dozen times in a thirty-lap feature, and yet we knew that none of that contact was intentional. It was just the product of tight tracks, thick traffic, and hard competition.

One of my fondest racing memories involves Billy Boat. We were at Ventura for an ESPN race, our second TV race that spring; I had won the first one a week earlier. On this night, Billy and I battled wheel-to-wheel for the lead for the entire feature. I'd dive under him getting into a corner, slide up because I'd carried too much speed, and watch him drive right back under me. A lap or two later, the roles would be reversed: he'd put a big slider on me, and I'd turn underneath him and take the lead back. And despite all that fierce racing, we were pulling away from the rest of the field, just checking out.

Of all the photos he's taken of me over the years, John Mahoney says this is one of his favorites. Don't I look like I'm enjoying myself? (© 1994 John Mahoney)

As it turned out, Billy made the last good pass that night. He won, and I finished second. Still, it was the kind of a race a driver lives for. When the two of us crawled out of our cars, we were absolutely worn out.

BILLY BOAT: "I remember that race vividly. Ventura tended to have two grooves; you could run the bottom or the top. On that particular night, either one of us could have won, but I guess I just had the right position at the right time. But what I remember most is being totally exhausted, physically and mentally, because of how hard we ran. Actually, that was pretty typical of most of the races I had with Tony. We both wanted to win, and we were giving it 100 percent, all the time, to do that."

I'll tell you how much respect I had for Billy, even at that early stage of our rivalry. At one point in that Ventura race, he hit a slick spot and his car jumped sideways exiting turn two. If I had given him even the most gentle nudge, he'd have spun into the infield and I'd have cruised to an easy win. But when I saw him get crossed up, I jumped on the brakes and almost spun my own car just to keep from bumping him. Later, Larry Howard asked me, "Why didn't you just go ahead and tap him out of the way?"

I said, "Man, I was having too much fun, and I didn't want it to end." Besides, in a moment like that you react according to racing's version of the Golden Rule: you do unto the other driver as you believe he would do unto you. And I knew somehow that Billy would have showed me the same respect.

> **BILLY BOAT:** "It was a lot of fun racing with Tony. We'd swap the lead back and forth, bang into each other a little bit, rub nerf bars. But, you know, as many times as we've raced hard together, I don't think we've ever crashed. Nobody ever took the other guy out."

Most of our early races were at Ventura, but we also ran at Bakersfield and at King's Speedway in Hanford, near Fresno. The Western States guys had an edge on me at those places, because I'd never even seen them before. That's more important than you might realize, especially if you're heading to a dirt track. Some people, I'm sure, hear those words—*dirt track*—and think, Well, dirt is dirt. But it's not; the composition of the surface is different everywhere you go, so every dirt track has its own personality. Some stay moist and tacky all night, some are known for building extra high cushions, and some harden up and behave almost like pavement.

Dirt isn't just dirt. Dirt is strange.

For instance, Calistoga Speedway, a half-mile track in the California wine country, had the weirdest dirt I've ever seen. I picked up a handful, just checking it out. It was nice and heavy, real moist, but when I squeezed it I noticed something crazy: it packed into a nice ball, but when I turned that ball ninety degrees and squeezed it again, it crumbled. The dirt packed just one time, in one direction, and that was it. I had never seen dirt do that before, and I've never seen dirt do that anywhere else.

> **LARRY HOWARD:** "The dirt is definitely different out here. Like, a tacky track in Indiana is a whole lot different from a tacky track in California. I think that's what's always made it hard for guys from the Midwest to come out here and do well."

But if the Western States drivers had local knowledge on their side, I had Larry Howard. He and I would walk the tracks wherever we went, and he would tell me things about each particular place. I listened, and I learned. What started out as a great rapport grew stronger as we went. Larry learned how I liked my cars to feel, and I learned to explain the car's behavior in a way that helped him figure out what adjustments we needed to make.

You know that driver-to-driver trust I mentioned? Well, drivers and mechanics develop that, too. Larry Howard and I saw eye-to-eye when it came to setting up cars, reading tracks, just about everything.

We were great teammates and great friends, and we had some special times. One night at Ventura—it was a television race—our car was unbelievably fast, and I guess I did a good job with it; we ended up winning by about half a lap. Now, Larry never really got overly excited by winning, probably because he'd done so much of it. If he was really excited, he might just crack a smile. But that night at Ventura, he actually ran up and kissed me.

Later, I said, "Why are you so thrilled tonight? We've won before."

And Larry said, "Yeah, but tonight you didn't just win. You won *big*."

On the way home, he told me what he meant. He said that it's one thing to just beat a guy, and something else to dominate. And that night, we—the driver and the car—dominated.

> **LARRY HOWARD:** "I'm not sure Tony knew this at the time, but that was my 150th career win. I got up on the left-rear tire as he was climbing out of the car, and I hugged him and kissed him

> on the cheek. I remember [ESPN's] Dave Despain asking me, 'What about this guy?' And my words were something like, 'This is probably the best race car driver I've ever had.' That got me in a little bit of trouble; it upset some of the guys who had driven for me in the past. But, you know, I meant it."

When you run like we did, it's hard not to become a more confident racer. I found myself doing things with Larry Brown's midget that woke me up as a driver, things I never thought I could do. To this day, I can't say exactly what they were, even though I can still sense the *feeling* they gave me.

The best way to explain it is to say that I had grown self-assured enough to try moves that would have seemed too bold before. But now, time after time, those moves worked.

By the time the Midwest season fired up, I had my confidence set on kill. I had already run eight or ten races, and I'd been competitive in just about all of them. Meanwhile, most of my rivals in the USAC national series had basically been sitting idle.

On the last weekend in April, I beat Boat at Ventura on Saturday night and stuck around just long enough for the victory lane photos. Then I made a mad dash to the airport to catch the red-eye flight to Indianapolis, so I could be at Winchester for a USAC national event on Sunday afternoon. Luckily, I'm pretty good at sleeping on airplanes; I snoozed for about four hours. Then I stopped at my apartment long enough to grab a shower and a fresh uniform, and headed to Winchester, where I met up with the Potters.

It would have been a dream to sweep the weekend, but we weren't even close; we had problems at Winchester and finished only thirteenth. Mike Bliss won the race driving for Steve Lewis, and Andy Michner ran second.

Michner's finish concerned me more than Bliss's, because I saw Andy and Kenny Irwin as our biggest rivals for the championship. Bliss was an excellent racer, but the Lewis team was kind of divided between Mike and Page Jones; since neither of them ran all the races, that took both of them out of the hunt for the title. Michner and Irwin, on the other hand, seemed as intent on winning the championship as we were, and both of their teams were very well-rounded.

I felt like ours was, too. We were running a Stealth chassis, which had a bigger reputation on dirt than it did on pavement, but it was plenty quick on either surface. And Ralph Potter, who had come up with a homemade V6 engine, had the horsepower end covered.

We rebounded from Winchester with a win at Indianapolis Raceway Park, where we beat Bliss and Jones, and came right back to IRP and ran second to Brian Gerster the following week. By the end of May, we were leading the points. But Michner hung tough; he won at IRP in June, and finished on my tail when I won at a little dirt bullring in Lima, Ohio. Then I got hot: after Lima I ran second at Bloomington, Indiana, won at North Vernon, Indiana, and won again at IRP. In fact, I should have won four in a row, but Russ Gamester ruined my chances at Bloomington by pulling off one of the cagiest tricks I ever saw.

Bloomington, a quarter-mile dirt track with a great surface and no outer wall, had built a nice cushion around the top lane, and that's where I was running. I passed Gamester for the lead, and I had everybody covered until a caution flag late in the race. Unbeknownst to me, as we idled around under yellow, Russ ran lap after lap right atop the cushion, packing it down with his tires. I never noticed it disappearing—my mistake—until the green flag flew and I aimed for the cushion in turn one. It was gone, and so was I. I sailed over the bank, and gave Gamester the win.

> **RALPH POTTER:** "You know, Stewart never gave up at Bloomington. When he slid off the track, we were about three or four laps from the end, and he fell all the way back to fifth. Well, in those three or four laps he got back up to second. In fact, he almost won it. That's where he's different than a lot of 'em: he just won't give up."

Michner made things interesting—a little too interesting—when he won twice in July and made a real scrap out of the points battle. But, generally, we stayed fast, and, more important, we stayed consistent:

fourth at IRP, second at Kokomo, Indiana, fourth at Portsmouth, Ohio, third at Louisville, third at IRP, first at Bloomington, second in the Hut Hundred at Terre Haute, fifth at Eldora.

We went to Winchester in October with a healthy lead on Michner. Bliss had moved up into third, despite missing a race, while Irwin had slipped a fair distance behind. Personally, I couldn't have arrived at Winchester on a greater high, because the previous night I'd won a Western States feature out at Ventura.

The Winchester feature was thirty-three laps, and we absolutely ran away with it. The car was perfect, the engine was great, and the driver had finally beaten Winchester. That old track meant a lot to me; it was the first place I'd ever raced a midget, and the first place I'd ever tested a sprint car. To take home a Winchester trophy would have been a big enough reward, but the victory also all but clinched the 1994 USAC midget crown.

Before and after: Me posing with Ralph Potter's midget . . .
(© John Mahoney)

There were two races left on the schedule: Ventura on the third weekend in November, and then, of course, Turkey Night at Bakersfield. On paper, Andy Michner still had a shot at the championship, but it was a slim one. USAC awards each driver a token number of points just for showing up at an event, and all I needed to do was keep breathing for another three weeks, walk up to the Ventura pit shack, and throw my money on the counter.

I managed that, and, lo and behold, I was a national champion.

The Potters and I had put together a heck of a season. In twenty-two

... and then with Ralph himself, on the day we all but wrapped up my first
USAC championship, October 23, 1994. (© Jim Haines)

starts we won six times—tops in the series—and had a total of twelve
finishes in the top three. There were guys who were faster occasionally, but none who were faster than us regularly. That was the difference.

I did come up short on my other goal for '94: I ended up fourth in the
Western States standings behind Johnny Cofer, Billy Boat, and Jay
Drake. That was still awfully good, considering that the conflicting
schedules kept me away from seven races. I was proud that I tied
Cofer, the champion, for the most feature victories with six. And
when we weren't winning, we were still strong: I ran second three
times—twice to Boat, once to Page Jones—and had a few other
top-fives.

So, even if I didn't end up at the top of the Western States points
sheet, I felt like everybody knew we'd been out there.

In July at Calistoga, I broke the track record on the first night of a two-day show, missed the preliminary feature because a tire exploded in my heat race, then came back on the second night and won the big thirty-lap finale. I remember starting five rows back, hounding Johnny Cofer for the lead, and then stealing the win on the last corner of the last lap with a perfect slide job. I can still hear the ovation from the crowd when I got out of that car; they were going berserk. Memories like that will keep 1994 special to me.

> **LARRY HOWARD:** "Calistoga was a magical, magical night. Everybody in the grandstands was on their feet for the last ten laps, watching Tony. Everybody."

It seemed like I spent half my summer in airports and the rest on the highway. Because, see, I had more than the USAC midget stuff going on:

I ran a bunch of midget races for Jay McKinnie and the Kunz brothers, winning three; I finished second three times at IRP in Darryl Guiducci's sprint car; I drove from twenty-sixth to third at DuQuoin in Nolen's Silver Crown car; and ran a strong second in the Silver Crown finale at Mesa Marin Speedway in California subbing for George Snider, who had broken some ribs.

It was a long year, and a hard year, but it was worth every hour of sleep I lost and every last drop of sweat.

1994 was a hectic year. If I wasn't racing or traveling to a race, I was trying to catch naps in the infields of various racetracks. But, boy, those were fun days. (© John Mahoney)

After '94, I never again doubted my ability. I had shown myself what I could do with a race car.

PAT SULLIVAN: "To me, it was clear when he was driving for Rollie Helmling in '93 that Tony was as talented as anybody. But because the results weren't always there, maybe he didn't feel that way. In '94, he was winning more, and I think his talent became clear to him, mentally."

TRACY POTTER: "You know what it was? I think he'd won enough that now he hated not winning."

SEVEN ICING ON THE CAKE: THE TRIPLE CROWN

IN 1995, I WON CHAMPIONSHIPS IN ALL THREE USAC DIVISIONS: SILVER Crown, sprint cars, midgets. Obviously, winning those three titles changed my life.

But, you know, it wasn't like the realization of some big dream, even though that's how it gets written up from time to time. The first time it even occurred to me that it might just be possible to chase all three championships, all I remember thinking was that if anyone could ever pull off that hat trick, it would be one hell of an accomplishment.

And it was.

But in the winter of 1994–95, I just did what I had always done: I tried to line up the best rides I could. That meant driving midgets again for Ralph Potter, and hooking up with Glen Niebel, who had fielded winning race cars for years, to run a Silver Crown car and a sprinter. Only then, once I started dealing with the logistics, did I take a good look at the entire USAC schedule and discover that if everything went exactly right, a driver could contend for all three championships.

The only other guy who had won all three titles in his *career* was Pancho Carter, who is an icon in open-wheel racing, and he won his over a six-year span. Winning three in a season was almost too big to think about.

First off, although USAC gave its ten Silver Crown events preferred status—meaning there were no other national events scheduled on those dates—that wasn't the case in the other two divisions. With the sprint cars booked for twenty-six races and the midgets twenty-four, there were bound to be a couple of conflicts. Second, I knew from our midget effort in '94 how many things had to go just right to win just one title, let alone *three*.

Obviously, I figured the Potters and I had a good shot at repeating our midget championship. I thought we'd be in decent shape with the sprinter, too, because, although Niebel had never been a points-chaser, his sprint cars were awesome; he was on the leading edge of the movement toward V6 engines in that division in the late eighties and early nineties. On the other hand, Glen had never run his own Silver Crown team, so I took a wait-and-see attitude into that program.

All I knew was, it was going to be an interesting season.

One thing I had going for me, I figured, was that even though I had three rides, I only had to answer to two owners. Anytime you're juggling schedules, keeping all your bosses happy is a job in itself. Having Niebel in charge of both the sprint and Silver Crown efforts took away some worries in that department.

I first met Glen back in 1991, when I was driving Steve Chrisman's sprint car. Glen had an engine shop in Mount Auburn, Indiana, not far from Chrisman, so it was only natural that they had a bit of a rivalry. I remember Steve always wanting to beat Niebel; that was because Steve looked up to Glen an awful lot, and as time went along I came to look up to him, too.

I got to know Glen better when I drove Gene Nolen's Silver Crown car in '94, because he built our engines. Glen was friendly, easy to approach, always willing to help if you had a question. Right up until the day he died in December of 1999, he was a special person: half of him was this country guy who had an easygoing temperament, and the other half was a fierce competitor. I liked hanging out with the country guy, but the fierce competitor was the guy I wanted to drive for. That man was a hell of a racer.

Glen really had his act together for 1995. He had a great partner in Willie Boles, whose auto dealerships have sponsored winning open-wheel cars for years, and a terrific right-hand man in Bernie Hallisky, a fabricator and mechanic who had migrated up from Florida. Basically, Bernie dealt with the cars themselves while Glen handled the engines.

I guess the least confusing way to reflect on that season is to look at it one division at a time, in the order in which the championships came. I mean, when I try to recall it chronologically—night by night, race by race—all the jumping around I did almost makes me dizzy. And I was there.

SPRINT CARS

USAC's sprint division has always been hard to get a handle on. There are teams that run only the pavement races, teams that run only the dirt races, and teams that run both surfaces but only manage to be competitive on one. I'll give you a couple of examples: in '95, Jack Hewitt ended up winning six races, all of them on dirt, and Kenny Irwin won four times, all on pavement. So you find yourself focusing on different rivals every week: Are we going to Winchester, where I have to worry about Irwin, or is this the week we go to Terre Haute, where Hewitt is the guy to beat?

On the other hand, running against those specialists can make you a better driver. Think about it: to win a USAC sprint race on pavement, you've got to beat the best pavement guys; on dirt, same story. And if you want to be the champion, you can't afford to give up anything on either type of track, because the schedule is usually divided pretty evenly. In '95, it was an exact split: thirteen asphalt races, thirteen dirt races.

As a driver, I felt like I had both the dirt and pavement figured out, but I thought our team would be stronger on the pavement side. Niebel had focused on asphalt for years, running a famous homebuilt car he had raced since 1978. I knew firsthand how tough that car was, because I ran second to it three times at IRP in '94, when Mike Bliss drove for Glen.

But what really made me optimistic about the asphalt races was that, as dominant as that old car had been, Niebel was building a new pavement sprinter for '95. Anybody who parks the toughest car in its class because he thinks he can build something even faster is a guy I want on my side.

> **BERNIE HALLISKY,** veteran sprint car mechanic: "Originally, we built that new car with a different driver in mind. Then Glen and I sat down one day, and he said, 'What do you think about Tony Stewart?' Well, I had no doubt the kid could drive, because he had waxed everybody's ass in the midgets in '94. I guess Glen had started watching him early, way back when he was in Chrisman's car."

Our dirt program was more of a question mark. I had no doubts about the dirt sprinter itself—we had an ex-Hewitt car, a wreck that Glen and Bernie had repaired and tweaked a little bit—but on dirt the V6 was still an unproven product. Niebel was stubborn about using it, but the same characteristics that made it such a great engine for pavement looked like they might work against you sometimes at the dirt tracks.

On pavement, where your goal is to transfer as much power as you can directly to the track, the six-cylinder engine was perfect. A typical V8-powered sprint car is actually *over*powered; if you stomp on the throttle, you just get a lot of wheelspin. Well, because the V6 was down on power, it obviously produced less wheelspin. You could get traction earlier than the V8 guys could, which is always an edge coming off the corners.

It's not so simple when it comes to dirt, where you're dealing with more variables: the consistency of the surface, the wider range of tire and gear choices, even the weather. It might sound crazy to a casual fan, but a good dirt racer has to be a part-time meteorologist, because the weather has a huge impact on conditions.

Early in the year the soil has a lot of moisture near the surface, thanks to the spring rain and the melting snow. Come summer, the tracks dry out considerably because of the sun and the heat, and they *stay* dry through autumn. Most track owners try to fight this natural drying by laying down thousands of gallons of water, but the ground soaks it in from below as fast as the sun evaporates it from above. The surface itself doesn't ever fully recover until winter sets in and starts the cycle again.

Every dirt track is naturally tackier in April than it will be in July or August, and we knew this would work against us initially. See, a dry track can be like pavement: you're fighting wheelspin, searching for bite, and too much horsepower can be your enemy. But on a tacky surface you need lots of power, because you *want* to keep the rear tires spinning as you blast through the ruts and holes. Without that wheelspin, the soft dirt will grab at the tires and try to tip the car over. Even if you don't flip, all that excess bite will bog the engine down, which was definitely a problem for our little V6.

USAC opened up in April at Eldora and Terre Haute, two dirt tracks which are rarely dry in the springtime. Not surprisingly, we were terrible at both of them: eighth at Eldora, eleventh at Terre Haute.

The good news was that between those dirt races came two strong runs on pavement. We had a great second-place behind Kenny Irwin at Winchester, in what turned out to be the last race for Glen's antique car. It would have been nice to win, but at least I could say I gave the ol' girl one last good run. Then we brought out the new car at Salem, and it was a rocket: I was running second to Irwin when the rear-end gear broke. The pavement program, obviously, was good.

That was fine with me, because after Terre Haute we ran two straight races at Indianapolis Raceway Park. Glen had a way of making his cars get around IRP better than anybody else's; then, once the competition caught up, he'd change a few things and get going better still. Well, we didn't need to change much at those two races. We beat Michner and Irwin to win the first one, and Irwin and Eric Gordon to win the second.

In that early part of the season, Gordon turned into our toughest rival in the points battle. That made sense, because Eric was always in the hunt on both dirt and pavement. But Doug Kalitta, the defending USAC sprint car champion, was hanging right there, too. By early July, the three of us were tied for the points lead.

I still felt like the wet dirt tracks were killing us. It was always the same story: we just didn't have the horsepower to overcome a sticky track, no matter what sort of tricks we pulled out of our hats.

BERNIE HALLISKY: "Tony and I sometimes had to white-lie it a bit with Glen. See, that V6 would run really good if you ran it at a lot of RPMs; if you didn't, it would bog down real bad, and just kill your momentum. So Tony would always say, 'Let's turn it up a little.' But Glen didn't like to run his motors very hard, so Tony and I had to sneak around him a bit. Let's say Glen wanted to turn the motor 7200 or 7400 RPMs, and a 5:96 gear would do that. Well, instead I'd put a 6:15 gear in there, and let it run up to 7800 or so. Tony and I had to conspire on that."

One of the biggest challenges I've ever faced was getting Glen Niebel's V6 sprinter to work on a dirt track. But by the end of the season, we had won three races with it. (© John Mahoney)

Our speed on pavement kept us in the ball game, but if we were going to win the championship, we *had* to get better on the dirt tracks.

Little by little, that did happen. Mother Nature came over to our side, and as the tracks dried out we found ourselves on more equal footing with the V8 cars. We were also helped by the fact that Glen and I had a special relationship with the folks at Hoosier Tire. We did a bunch of testing for them, working directly with Irish Saunders and Neil Cowman, Hoosier's product managers, and indirectly with Bob Newton, the company president. When we got together, they were struggling as badly as we were on dirt, but that test program seemed to help us all out.

> **IRISH SAUNDERS:** "For a while, we had to be real careful when we tested with Tony. See, he was so good at compensating for the car's behavior; he'd change his line just a little bit from lap to lap, and figure out a way to get the car working. I had to drill it into his mind: 'Tony, this is a tire test. We need you to run every lap the same way, time after time. Don't change your line according to what the tires are or aren't doing.' Once he figured that out, he was a great test driver. I really believe that between Tony and Glen Niebel, they helped turn our dirt program around."

It seemed like all these ingredients—our setups, the tires, the weather—had come together by the end of July, just in time for a race at the Santa Fe Speedway in Hinsdale, Illinois. When I first saw the place, it looked like the worst possible configuration for us: a half-mile dirt oval shaped like a paper clip, with long straights and hairpin corners. In other words, a horsepower track. But the corners were nice and slick, and while everyone else spun their tires I could really put the power down. We ended up winning the feature, and we did it in style, beating Dave Darland, Tony Elliott, and Jack Hewitt, three of the best dirt racers USAC ever produced.

That win lifted a huge weight off our shoulders, and it seemed to signal that our dirt-track turnaround was complete.

> **BERNIE HALLISKY:** "At Santa Fe, we made one torsion bar change and one shock change; I still remember that. Tony won the race, and it was like we'd found the right combination."

The next night I ran second to Hewitt at the I-96 Speedway up in Michigan, another half-mile dirt track. We hadn't became a dominant force on the dirt, by any means, but at least now we had a fighting chance.

The asphalt car was still a bullet, winning at Salem and running second to Chet Fillip, one of the real pavement specialists, at Winchester. All these consistent finishes put us into the lead in the USAC sprint car standings; Gordon had slipped a bit, but Kalitta was still hanging tough.

Then, in September, we caught a huge break. We won ourselves another dirt-track feature at Granite City, Illinois, on a night when Kalitta had a problem and finished dead last. It had a huge impact on the battle for the championship, and obviously Glen and his guys were on cloud nine.

I was ecstatic, too. It wasn't because we won, but because of *how* we won.

I don't remember where I started that feature, but I do recall that by the time I got up into second place, Jack Hewitt had pulled out to a really good lead. He was a whole straightaway ahead of me and everybody else.

> **JACK HEWITT,** USAC Silver Crown and sprint car champion: "I was driving for Bob Hampshire, and Hamp had a little trick he used on a dry-slick racetrack: he'd back up the [ignition] timing just a little bit. What that does is kill the bottom-end power, so you don't spin the tires and you get a good bite. We'd won quite a few races that way, and I really thought we had Granite City won, too."

Well, lap by lap I gained on Jack, and before long I was on his tail. It just so happened that Hewitt and I were running exactly the same line: up on the cushion in turns one and two, and right down on the inside rail in three and four. That stalled my progress, because his car sat right where I wanted to put mine. Finally, when I was running out of laps, I came off turn two really strong and ducked to his inside on the back straightaway. We were side by side when we reached turn three.

Now, the common mistake for a young driver in that situation is to try too hard; he'll charge into the corner and his car will slide out, and

This is one of my all-time favorite photos, just because I'm sharing the victory lane stage with one of my heroes, Jack Hewitt, at Eldora Speedway. (© John Mahoney)

the wise ol' veteran will dive back under the kid and retake the lead. But that night I pulled a trick I'd learned from a lot of guys, including Hewitt himself: when we got to turn three, I slowed up early and kept Jack alongside me. That left *him* out of the chosen groove, fighting for traction. My guys told me later that by the time we got out of turn four, I was eight or ten car lengths ahead. I never saw him again until after the race.

To beat Jack Hewitt, one of my all-time heroes, and to do it on the kind of dirt track where he really excelled, was a huge personal victory for me. It was a way to gauge how far I had come.

In fact, one of my favorite victory lane photos was taken later that same month, after the 4-Crown Nationals at Eldora. All three USAC divisions compete at the 4-Crown, and I had a huge night: I won both the midget and sprint features, and finished second to Hewitt in the Silver Crown race. We ended up sharing the stage when they took the traditional postrace photos. Jack Hewitt is tough everywhere he goes, but Eldora has always been his signature place; he's the king in the grandstands and the king on the track. To stand beside Jack on that stage, both of us as winners, was an enormous thing for me.

> **JACK HEWITT:** "Tony has talked about watching me when he was a kid, and how he liked the way I raced, and that stuff is neat to hear. I mean, here's Tony Stewart, who has gone out and beat the best in the world in every division he's tried, saying that it was really big to beat Jack Hewitt. He's one of those guys who's making history every day, and just to know that maybe you've been a part of that history has to make you feel good. Anybody who'd say it didn't feel good would be lying."

Between Granite City and Eldora, we squeezed in a pair of pavement races, running fourth in Kansas City and winning on the high banks at the I-70 Speedway in Odessa, Missouri. That put us far enough ahead in the USAC standings that our 4-Crown victory clinched the sprint car championship, even though we still had a race left to run at Winchester. And that was a good thing, because we ended up crashing out of the lead at Winchester when a wheel broke.

After Eldora, I was as happy for Glen Niebel as I was for myself. For all the winning he'd done, Glen had never been a USAC champion, and I was glad to be a part of him becoming one.

> **BERNIE HALLISKY:** "I had known Glen since the late seventies, and that was something I'd heard him talk about a lot: he wanted to win a USAC championship, but he'd never had the right opportunity. Now he had done something he'd waited his whole life to do."

You don't always realize how draining it is to run for a title until the chase is over. Sure, I was still absorbed in the Silver Crown and midget points battles, but as far as the sprinter was concerned I had a mission-accomplished feeling.

It had been an amazing season. We won seven features, tops in the series, and I was proud that our wins were split as evenly as could be: four on the asphalt, three on the dirt. We ended up winning just over a quarter of the races, and in almost half of them—twelve of the twenty-six—we finished in the top three. That, I figured, was the way to win a championship: by running right at the front.

SILVER CROWN

I wish I could say our Silver Crown season went the same way, with us having the car to beat, but it didn't. To be honest, I never expected it to. All along, I figured our least likely shot at success would be in the Silver Crown division.

The biggest thing was, I had a lot more doubts about the V6 as a Silver Crown engine. For one thing, even though the USAC rules gave us a weight break in the Silver Crown series—a V6 car could run lighter than a V8 car—the *total* weight of those cars was much higher than the sprinter, so we were asking a lot of that little engine. Even though the long races mean that handling and tire conservation play a key role, Silver Crown racing really puts a premium on horse-power.

Exactly half of the ten races were on one-mile dirt tracks, where you need lots of straightaway speed, and we also had to go to the paved mile at Phoenix and to the paved Richmond International Raceway in Virginia, which measures three-quarters of a mile around but is awfully fast. At those tracks, I wasn't convinced that any weight advantage would offset the horsepower deficit of the V6.

And it wasn't just the engine; I was also concerned about the Silver Crown car itself. Specifically, the fact that it was a *car*, singular, rather than *cars*, plural. Glen and Bernie had put together a great new piece, but the specialty-car situation in Silver Crown racing had only deepened. If you were running a single car on both surfaces, you couldn't help but feel handicapped.

I knew that if anybody could make our program work, it was Niebel. Still, my Silver Crown goal was to enjoy racing with Glen, and maybe get some satisfaction out of the challenge of running that V6. As it turned out, we did get plenty of satisfaction. We also had a hell of a lot of fun.

The season opened at Phoenix, where we had a pretty good run, coming from twenty-third at the start to finish fourth. But that was canceled out by the second race: we barely squeaked into the field for the Hulman Hundred at the Indiana State Fairgrounds in May, then fell out of the race with an overheating problem.

Then we started to find our stride. We finished fifth at Richmond, sixth at Terre Haute—where I really thought we'd struggle—and then a real good second at Indianapolis Raceway Park.

I was surprised to discover that our run at IRP actually put us on top of the standings; it didn't feel like things were going that well. I guess what was helping us most was that nobody else was having a spectacular season, either. I mean, the guy I took the points lead from was Dave Darland, and he hadn't even entered the first race.

> **DAVE DARLAND,** USAC Silver Crown and sprint car champion: "It was like we all had something happen that cost us some points. Me, it was my first full season in the Silver Crown division, and I hadn't gotten my ride with Galen Fox until late in the winter, so we didn't go to Phoenix. But we won the next race at the Fairgrounds and that put us in the hunt, so we started thinking about the points. Hewitt was right up there, and Tony was, too. From there, it was like we all stayed pretty even."

Niebel was still trying to figure out this new car, and so was I. In hindsight, our biggest obstacle was trying to distinguish the setups that worked so well on Glen's sprint car from the setups the bigger Silver Crown car needed. But there was one thing about Glen: once he got close to a good setup, he'd fine-tune it until it was right on the money. And we definitely seemed to be going in the right direction.

> **BERNIE HALLISKY:** "The Silver Crown car took a different setup, yes, but it also took a different driving style. It was heavier than the sprint car, so it was even more important to keep up the momentum because of the V6. Tony had no problem with running that little motor at Phoenix or IRP, because he knew from his midget experience how to maintain his momentum at those places; he knew how to roll through the corners really fast. But at some of the other tracks, it was tough. Tony had to adjust, and so did we."

The sixth race of the season was at Springfield, on a Sunday that should have been renamed Kenny Irwin Day. Right after he beat me to win that afternoon's USAC midget race, Kenny came from twenty-eighth to win the one-hundred-mile Silver Crown show. I started eighteenth, moved forward a little at a time, and finished tenth. The only bright spot, from a selfish point of view, was that Hewitt and Darland both fell out, so we were looking more and more like a force in the standings. I still didn't see us as a championship threat, but we had the potential to finish in the top three.

On the first weekend in September, we hit a stumbling block. We were back at the Indiana Fairgrounds for the Hoosier Hundred, and we time-trialed far enough down the list that we missed the cut. Then, in the semi-feature, I made a dumb mistake. On Glen's car, we ran three-wheel brakes—every corner but the right front—which is a trick that helps the car turn but obviously doesn't do much for its stopping power. Well, I was chasing Tyce Carlson into turn one, and I just couldn't get slowed down. I slid into Tyce, and we both crashed. I felt terrible about that, because he was a buddy of mine and he missed the race because of a wreck that was strictly my fault. My car got bent, too, but I picked up a ride for the feature in a car that had been qualified by Brian Hayden. I started last because of the driver change, and ended up finishing *next* to last, twenty-ninth, when the engine broke. I was really down after the Hoosier Hundred because, obviously, screwing up one race in a ten-race season is like throwing away 10 percent of your effort.

Darland won that race, and then stretched himself a little points lead by finishing third at DuQuoin, where Hewitt ran fourth and I was sixth.

Frankly, our primary competition for the title, Darland and Hewitt, had been faster than us almost everywhere. Both of them had won races; not only hadn't I won, but I hadn't led a single lap all year. We were hanging tough, but barely.

Race number nine was the Eldora 4-Crown, the night when Hewitt and I shared the stage after he won and I ran second. Darland finished third, which didn't exactly help my cause.

Going into the season finale, a one-hundred-miler at the CalExpo Fairgrounds in Sacramento, it looked like a two-man run for the championship. Darland led Hewitt by eight points; I was so far back that the polite thing to say was that I had a "mathematical chance." It would have been more accurate to call me a long shot, a *very* long shot.

If either Dave or Jack finished in the top seven, I was out of the picture. Even if both of them dropped out, I needed to either win or run second. It seemed like an impossible scenario: not only did we need two great drivers in two great cars to have two bad days, we also needed to match our best finish of the year.

"Mathematical chance," I decided, is another way of saying something ain't gonna happen.

> **DAVE DARLAND:** "Going in, Jack was really the only guy I was worried about."

But the Sacramento race itself was absolutely nuts. At the start, things couldn't have looked worse for me. I lined up twelfth, and fell way back in the opening laps. The car was pushing badly, which is common when you're carrying a full load of fuel, so I just kind of logged laps, hoping the handling would improve as the fuel burned off.

Then, just as my car was beginning to behave a little better, we caught a huge break: only eleven laps into the race, I saw Darland's car coasting down the track, on fire.

> **DAVE DARLAND:** "We had a bolt break in the oil filter adapter base. It wasn't any big deal, really, until a bunch of oil shot out onto the header and the thing went up in flames."

As I rolled past him, I felt bad for Dave; he's a friend of mine, and he'd really had a great season, especially considering that his team, like ours, had run just a single car. Still, it was a psychological lift, because my odds had improved dramatically. I was like, "Wait a minute. Now we've only got to worry about *one* guy. This isn't out of the question."

My car was working better all the time, and before long I climbed up into the top ten. I even passed Hewitt, who was running maybe eighth at the time. But that didn't give me the boost you might imagine it would have; it seemed to me like Hewitt was running a pace which would get him into the top seven, which was all he needed.

A few laps later, the yellow light blinked on. When I rolled through turn three, there was Jack's car, with the front end knocked out of it. He and Billy Boat had tangled, and Hewitt slid into the fence.

The race was exactly one-third gone—thirty-three laps down out of one hundred—and the two favorites for the championship were parked in the pits. I was stunned, thinking, "This just can't be . . ."

But even with all that, the championship still seemed unreachable. I just didn't think we had the speed to run first or second, and if we finished third or worse the title would go to Darland. Then, like magic—Glen Niebel's magic, I guess—my car just got faster and faster, and I could see the guys ahead of me starting to slip and slide. I passed one here and there, and, slowly, things started to work in our favor.

USAC allows radios in the Silver Crown division, and I started to hear an excitement in Glen's voice. Maybe we had a prayer after all.

From what I could see and what I heard from Glen, we had the second-fastest car on the track, next to Donnie Beechler's. And, boy, Donnie *was* fast; he started eighteenth, passed me early, and then passed everybody else to take the lead.

As it turned out, I passed everybody but Beechler. At one point I thought I could run him down, too, but all I did was wear my tires out. We finished second with a right rear tire so bald it probably wouldn't have made two more laps.

All I knew about second place was what had been drilled into my head by all that prerace publicity: if we ran first *or second*, and Darland and Hewitt fell out, we were the champions.

I hollered over the radio, "Did we get it? Did we get the championship?"

The crew said, "We're checking. We'll let you know."

For the entire cool-off lap, there was silence. I asked the question again and again, and I heard nothing. I figured my guys were huddled with the officials, calculating the points. But when I got to our pit, I saw the real reason they hadn't answered me: Glen and the guys had pulled off their headsets and were jumping up and down, celebrating. We had won the Silver Crown title. By two points.

I guess all the hype was true, after all: we really *did* have a mathematical chance.

> **DICK JORDAN:** "Everything fell into place for Tony at Sacramento. I mean, he wasn't supposed to win that championship; he had to finish first or second, and both Darland and Hewitt had to drop out, and the likelihood of all that happening was pretty small. But that's exactly what did happen."

> **JACK HEWITT:** "Sure, Tony winning that Silver Crown championship came at my expense, and Dave Darland's, too, and maybe it seemed like a freak deal. But all of us have won races and won championships because somebody else gave 'em away. Sometimes, it's just your turn."

Even today, it's hard to describe the emotion that second championship brought out in Glen Niebel and me. In our first year together, we had beaten *everybody*. I thought that was pretty cool, and I could tell by his grin that Glen thought so, too.

Glen and I had a wonderful relationship. I had always admired him, the way any young racer admires someone who has done a lot of winning. But in 1995, we developed something close to a father–son bond. When I saw him after that Sacramento race, I got the same sort of feeling I'd had when my dad and I won the karting Grand Nation-

On the way to winning our two championships in 1995, Glen Niebel and I grew incredibly close. He was a huge influence on my career and my life. (© John Mahoney)

als in '83. Glen threw his arm around me, and we just savored our moment.

> **BERNIE HALLISKY:** "What Tony and Glen had was definitely special. To watch them work together at the racetrack was really neat. Glen would stand directly in front of him, put both his hands on Tony's shoulders, look him right in the eyes, and they'd talk. They just had a chemistry."

No, we didn't have the fastest Silver Crown car, but we were competitive in most of the races. And, obviously, we must have been more consistently competitive than anyone else, because that's the only way you become a champion.

By the way, as we celebrated in Sacramento, all my previous nonchalance about chasing three titles in a single season went out the window. I was leading the midget standings, and as far as I was concerned, it was two down, one to go.

MIDGETS

I remember having a burning desire to repeat as USAC midget champion, to back up what we had done in '94. I also remember thinking that we had to be the favorites. After all, the Potter team and I were coming back with the same basic package.

Then, in the course of just a few months, we found out how quickly a championship package can fall apart.

First, Ralph Potter had some health problems over the winter, and his doctors got after him to slow down a little bit. Like most racers would, Ralph ignored that advice. In fact, he decided to step up his racing program a bit by adding a second car for a young guy named Jeff Hunt. Jeff was just sixteen years old, but he brought with him a lot of financial support from some family friends.

The Potters had run two cars before; in '94, I teamed up on occasion with guys like Tony Elliott, Jimmy Kite, Brian Gerster, and Randy Koch. But it's hard to jump from running two cars sporadically to running two on a steady basis. Sometimes an owner will play favorites, and because

Jeff had brought some sponsorship, the racer in me began to worry that the emphasis might shift toward Jeff's car.

I say it bothered me as a racer, because as a human being I completely understood it. Ralph Potter and his family deserved the kind of help Jeff brought; they had always raced out of their own pockets. Plus, I really liked Jeff. He was a great kid, and he was trying to get his career going.

But I felt like we had taken a championship-caliber team and split it in two: we had to divide our people, divide our parts, divide our time. And the more I looked at it, the more I felt like my half of the operation couldn't sustain another serious run at the title. I wasn't happy, and I didn't hide that from Ralph, or from his son Tracy, who had started looking after my side of the team.

> **RALPH POTTER:** "At the time, Tony was too much of a kid. He was a hell of a race driver, and I would never, ever say he wasn't, but he was like a spoiled kid. I'd had some heart problems, and I was too far into my racing career to put up with that stuff. I just didn't want to fool with him, so I turned him over to my son."

> **TRACY POTTER:** "My dad passed Tony off on me, but I still couldn't see us continuing for very long. See, in his own way, Tony could be pretty demanding. When my dad took on the Hunt kid, Tony was almost jealous, thinking maybe he was getting pushed back a bit."

Some of the stuff that happened early in the '95 season backed up my opinion, or so it looked to me. In the first two races we ran a decent fourth at Phoenix and a good second at Winchester, but then we ran fourteenth at IRP, where we should have run in the top five, easily. To say that I was frustrated would be an understatement, and I wasn't shy about expressing it. In fact, after the IRP race, Tracy and I got into it a little bit.

> **TRACY POTTER:** "At Raceway Park we had a bad night. Tony came sliding into the pits with the tires smoking because he was mad,

> and I blew up at him. Looking back, I think he was just going through a stage, a growth period. He just wanted to win so bad. But I'd had enough."

By then, I was sure that the team wasn't going to change its approach, so I began to think about changing mine. That wasn't an easy process, by any means. I've never considered myself a quitter, and bailing out on a team has never come as easily to me as it does to some drivers. The idea of leaving the Potters, just a few months after we'd celebrated a championship, was something I never thought I'd face. Now, after IRP, it was the foremost thing on my mind.

I thought about who might have an open seat, or who might *know* of an open seat, and the guy who kept popping into my mind was Bob East. For one thing, Bob maintained Steve Lewis's team; sure, they were running a car already for Jay Drake, which would have put me in the middle of another two-car situation, but the Lewis team had run two and even three cars at a time without a hiccup. For another thing, Bob also had a thriving chassis business, which meant he was in constant contact with car owners.

> **BOB EAST,** proprietor, Beast Chassis: "Obviously, we deal with a lot of owners and drivers here. When owners want to change their programs and they're looking for a new driver, they'll call and ask if I know who's available. It's the same with drivers; they call and ask if there's any rides opening up. I guess we're pretty much in the loop, so we usually know what's going on."

I jumped into my car—in those days, I was driving a little Mazda RX7—and headed over to Bob's shop just before five o'clock in the afternoon on a Monday. The only reason I mention the time of day is that it ended up being very important. It taught me a lesson in how small a town Indianapolis really is, and how quickly the rumor mill there can spin.

Bob's shop is on a street called Gasoline Alley, which is lined with businesses that relate to racing: fabrication shops, parts suppliers, T-shirt vendors, Indy car teams, sprint car teams, you name it. Well, at five o'clock those places emptied out, and when all those folks drove past Bob's shop and saw my car sitting there—in Indianapolis, everybody knows what everybody else drives—word got around pretty quick that something was going on. My success with Potter made me one of the lead Stealth chassis drivers, so it didn't make much sense that I would be at the Beast shop unless I was thinking about jumping out of Potter's car.

Inside the shop, I hadn't given a single thought to who might be saying what outside; I was just trying to make sure I'd have something to drive. I told Bob I was thinking about making a change, and he mentioned that he might be able to run me in a second car. One of my big concerns was that Jay Drake and I were friends; it was important to me that this wouldn't take away from Jay's program. Bob understood that, and he called Steve Lewis to ask what he thought about adding me to the team.

STEVE LEWIS: "From a driver's standpoint, when you're out there on the track and you see an opportunity, you can't sit and think about it. You don't get a chance to go to some sort of group session and discuss it. You have to make up your mind in a hurry, and either take it or not take it. So the idea of taking advantage of an opportunity is something race drivers become accustomed to, and that's true off the track, too. Well, something had occurred between Tony and the Potters, and the opportunity to talk about him driving our car was there. And Bob East, being a former driver himself, was thinking the same way about Tony: here is a great opportunity walking in off the street."

Steve wanted some time to think about this, so Bob said he'd call me in the morning. Sure enough, first thing the next morning my telephone rang. I was certain it was Bob, but instead it was Tracy Potter. Somebody told him they'd seen my car outside Beast, and he wanted to know what was going on.

We had a conversation that wasn't very pleasant, and it ended with Tracy saying it was time we parted ways.

TRACY POTTER: "Basically, I fired his ass."

It was a traumatic moment for me. I was terrified that if things didn't work out with Lewis, I'd be without a midget ride, and without any midget *income*, which would have killed me at that point.

In the end, everything worked out. An hour or so after I talked with Tracy, Bob called and told me Steve was ready to field a second car.

I ought to add that, eventually, things worked out between me and the Potters, too. No, it wasn't a friendly breakup, but as time went on I think we all wrote it off as one of those things that happens in this sport. I still see those guys from time to time, and I'd like to think we're on good terms. We *should* be, because those folks played a critical part in my career. Hell, I won my first national championship in their car, which will always give them a special place in my heart.

TRACY POTTER: "Things went bitter for a while, but we're friends today. I tell everybody, just joking around, 'Yeah, I fired Stewart. Really hurt his career, didn't I?' But I think the world of him. In fact, I'd run Tony again anytime."

RALPH POTTER: "I don't have anything bad to say about Tony. He was pretty temperamental, but, you know, a lot of these young guys are that way. Maybe they have to be that way to run good."

The silver lining to this whole thing was that I moved from one championship-level team to another. Steve Lewis and Bob East had a huge presence in midget racing; they'd won USAC titles and a ton of races. They had done especially well in the TV events, making the Lewis car—the white number 9—probably the highest-profile car in the series USAC.

Our first race together was in mid-May at IRP, a place where I'd done well in other cars and they'd done well with other drivers. We all had high hopes, but we didn't come out of the box too strong: we broke early in the feature, and finished dead last. Two weeks later, at IRP again, we ran fifth. Fifth isn't necessarily bad, but it wasn't exactly what I had hoped for, and I was sure it wasn't what Bob and Steve hoped for, either.

> **BOB EAST:** "You know, Tony came to us with a reputation for having his tantrums. Well, the first two times he drove for us, we struggled. So, to avoid any problems, to nip things in the bud, I sat him down and said, 'Tony, we don't normally break down, and we don't normally struggle. That's just the way it goes sometimes. But I guarantee you, we're a team that wants to win as bad or worse than you do. Everyone involved with this program gives a hundred percent.' And the look on his face when I said that was like, 'Hey, this is all I've wanted.' After that, he was the model driver."

I love this shot: I'm hanging the tail out in Steve Lewis's midget at Terre Haute. I won my first race with Steve and Bob East that day. (© John Mahoney)

In our third outing, I won my first race in the Lewis car by tracking down and passing Drake at Terre Haute. Jay ended up second, which reinforced my feelings about the depth of that team.

It really was a terrific operation. Bob East built the cars, and Kelly Drake was the chief mechanic. The team's strong points were its preparation at the shop and its readiness at the track. That combination not only makes the cars fast, it can also make the *driver* fast; you're so confident in your equipment that you'll drive your heart out. You know that if you bend the front axle in a heat race, your guys will get it fixed, and fixed *right*. That means everything to a race driver.

Still, for a good part of the season we played catch-up as far as the points were concerned. The bad races I'd had early on had really put me in a hole.

> **STEVE LEWIS:** "When Tony came to us, he was a hundred points off the pace, or some rather large deficit. But he said, 'I can still do this.'"

Just like in '94, I saw Andy Michner and Kenny Irwin as the guys to beat. Michner, in particular, was the guy I focused on; he had run second in the standings the previous year, and Andy had a great mechanic in Tim Schutt.

But the guy who really got our attention as the season unfolded was Danny Drinan.

Drinan had always been super-fast on pavement, so when he won at Phoenix and then at IRP in May that was nothing out of the ordinary. I never really saw him as a title threat, because on dirt he was a hit-or-miss guy and a third of the USAC national races were dirt-track shows. But, as it turned out, Drinan was consistent enough early on to get into the thick of the points battle.

In early July we all went down to a quarter-mile dirt track in Richmond, Kentucky. That night was the start of a little war between me and Drinan that ended up being one of the hot stories of the 1995 USAC season. I've been in a few public scraps in my career, but that might have been the first major one.

Danny is a guy who can beat you on the track or in the shop. He has an incredible amount of talent for designing and fabricating fast cars. On top of that, he's got as much desire as anybody I've ever raced against. The only problem—not necessarily for him, but for me—was that all that desire made him a very aggressive driver, and for a period in '95 it seemed like I kept ending up on the wrong end of that aggression.

At Richmond, I passed him for the lead in turn two and he came right back at me in turn three, but he slid into me and I crashed. I wasn't happy—the way I saw it, I got knocked out of a probable win—but I was willing to chalk it up to hard racing. Then, just a few weeks later, we had another run-in, again when I was leading. This time, at IRP, Drinan tried to pass both me and Michner in the same corner. It was an impossible move, and he rode me right into the fence.

Looking back, I'm sure Danny wasn't running into me on purpose. I think he was just trying hard to win races, and maybe get the right career breaks that go along with winning. I understand as well as anybody how that works. But in the summer of '95, I was incredibly frustrated with him; when you're racing for a championship, you can't afford to fall out of races, and you *really* can't afford to give away wins.

That IRP race was the low point of the year for me, and, as things turned out, for Drinan, too: USAC suspended him for two races for what they called "overaggressive driving," and that was pretty much the end of his title chances.

After that second incident with Drinan, I got on a roll that shot us right to the top of the standings. Over the next eight races we finished first at Kansas City, second at I-70, first at IRP, second at Springfield, second at Kokomo, first in the Hut Hundred at Terre Haute, first in the 4-Crown at Eldora, and first at Louisville. Eight races, eight top-two finishes. In the next race, at Winchester, we must have been slipping, because we fell all the way to third.

Though it was far from being officially clinched, the 1995 USAC midget championship was won and lost right there, in that ten-week stretch between Kansas City in August and Winchester in October.

> **STEVE LEWIS:** "Tony just kept nipping away: second, second, win a race, second, win a race. And it was like, all of a sudden we looked up and we had a big point lead."

Michner, who as late as mid-September seemed like the best bet to win the title, was now playing catch-up, and Irwin had slipped out of the picture. In fact, Brian Gerster, an up-and-coming kid from Indianapolis who had won two races, pushed Kenny back to fourth in the standings.

The longer the season went, the better Bob East and I jelled. He understood more about what I wanted, and I understood more about his cars. We had reached the point where, instead of letting Bob diagnose all our problems, I could actually recommend the changes we needed.

BOB EAST: "In every team you've got three main elements: the car, the mechanic, and the driver. Tony helped us by being able to give us great feedback; he always knew exactly where he had to be faster."

What happened, really, was that Bob and I had developed the same kind of chemistry that I had established with Glen Niebel, and earlier with Larry Howard; we didn't have to *say* a lot to communicate, because each of us pretty much knew what the other was thinking.

The longer Bob East and I raced together, the better we clicked. At one point in 1995, we either won or finished second in eight straight USAC midget races. (© John Mahoney)

Winchester closed out the midwestern portion of the USAC schedule. Then came the usual three-week break before the November races in California: Ventura on a Saturday night, the one-hundred-lap Turkey Night race at Bakersfield, and the finale at Perris. Michner had only a slim chance to beat me, but, remember, the Silver Crown battle had shown me that slim chances could pan out.

I was getting a lot of attention in the media, locally and nationally. USAC really pumped up how unique this whole thing was; Dick Jordan had me visiting TV stations, doing radio programs, and sitting for a bunch of newspaper interviews. I felt like I was running for president instead of racing for a midget championship. It wasn't unpleasant at all—in fact, it was kind of flattering—but the idea of getting all this acclaim for something that hadn't actually happened yet unnerved me a little bit. It just didn't seem right.

JOHN MAHONEY: "There was a point near the end of the season, after he had locked up the second championship, when Dick

> Jordan wanted me to shoot some photos of Stewart. They run a portrait of each division champion on the cover of the USAC media guide, so Dick needed three shots of Tony: one looking straight ahead, one looking up, one looking down. Well, Tony was reluctant to do that. He hadn't won the midget title yet, and he didn't want to count anything as a done deal. He posed, because he's always been cooperative that way with me, but he was very sensitive about the whole thing."

When it finally came time to leave for California, I was ready to get it over with. I knew I had three races to get the points I needed, so my game plan was just to race smart. Yes, I wanted to win those three races if I could, but not at the expense of throwing away a championship. Particularly *this* championship.

At Ventura I finished second to my old rival Billy Boat, and there was no shame in that; Billy absolutely dominated the Western States series that year, winning eighteen of the twenty-seven races. At one point, he'd won eleven in a row.

> **BILLY BOAT:** "Looking back, I'm grateful that Tony had been around so much in '94, because the competition between us made my team so much better. When we won all those races in '95, a lot of that was because the battles we'd had with Tony the year before made us pick up our effort."

Ventura extended our streak of top-three finishes to ten. Michner struggled there, and ended up eleventh. That opened up the point lead considerably. Now, even if Andy won Turkey Night, we only needed a halfway decent finish to clinch the title regardless of what happened in the final race.

It was a good thing we had such a big margin, because we really had an off night at Bakersfield. The car got extremely loose, so I settled into a safe-race mode. The track had developed a tall cushion, and a bunch of cars were getting tipsy as they bounced off it; I wanted no part of being involved in one of their wrecks. I just sort of rode this one out.

I ended up seventh, far enough behind that I had no real idea where

I'd finished. All I knew was that Michner was behind me. After the checkered flag, I saw Boat—who else?—pull into victory lane, and I looked to see if the officials were signaling *me* to stop, too. I figured they'd want the champion right there alongside the race winner, and that would be my sign that we'd clinched it.

I didn't see anybody gesturing at me, so I continued around the track, thinking, Well, I guess we'll have to lock it up at Perris. But when I got to turn two, I saw the whole Lewis team waving and running onto the track, and I knew we had it won.

What I felt most was an enormous wave of satisfaction, like a big sigh. I mean, three national championships! In the pictures from that night, I look more relieved than happy. I guess the weight of what I'd done hadn't sunk in yet.

> **DICK JORDAN:** "I'm not sure Tony realizes even today what he was able to do. To tell you the truth, I'm not sure it's even set in with me. Because, when you look back at the guys who might have been able do this but never even got close, it's remarkable And I don't think it'll ever happen again."

The strange thing was, I didn't do much celebrating after Turkey Night. I was too drained, emotionally, to really gas it up. My family had come to California to see me clinch that third title, and it was nice to share that moment with them. And one of my Bakersfield buddies, Bruce Wilson, threw a party at his house, so I went over there for a while. It turned out to be a really nice night, because a lot of the other drivers came over and hung out with us. But it wasn't exactly a wild time.

Two nights later, the season ended at Perris, and I really wanted to go out in style. Things started out well enough—we set a track record in qualifying—but went downhill from there. We got bent up in a tangle early in the feature, and couldn't finish any better than thirteenth.

I rolled the car to a stop, undid my belts, and climbed out. The 1995 USAC season was over.

I went to bed that night reflecting on a lot of things. Obviously, I was thankful I'd had the cars and personnel to do something like this. But I also thought about luck, or fate, or whatever you want to call it. Whatever it is, it sure was on my side that year.

For instance, if one or two rainstorms had reshuffled the schedules, I'd probably have missed out on at least one of those championships. As it was, the only direct conflict came in July, when USAC scheduled a sprint car race at Wilmot, Wisconsin, opposite a midget show at Indianapolis Raceway Park. I went north to run the sprinter, and that ended up being the wrong decision: Wilmot rained out and IRP didn't. But, hey, I can't complain. There were a total of sixty USAC national events run that season, and I made fifty-nine of them. *That's* luck.

JACK HEWITT: "You know, when you get high mentally and things are rollin' along just right, it's like you can't do anything wrong. That's how it was for Tony that year."

At the USAC awards dinner, Indianapolis Motor Speedway president Tony George presented me with the Triple Crown award. Nobody had ever won it before, and nobody's won it since! (© John Mahoney)

That winter, at the USAC awards dinner, they announced the creation of a new award: the Triple Crown. It came with a custom ring and ten thousand dollars.

That was an unbelievable, unforgettable season. Best of all, it's in the record book forever: Dick King, the USAC president at the time, wrote it up as "Tony Stewart's remarkable, unprecedented Triple Crown." Sure, another driver might duplicate it one day, and win those same three championships—the odds are against it, but, hell, the odds were against *me*, too—but I'll always know that I did it first.

It's like A. J. Foyt winning the Indy 500 four times; Al Unser and Rick Mears matched him, but A.J. got there first, which put him in a league of his own. Even today, when somebody says "four-time Indy winner," I'll bet the name that comes to your mind is Foyt's. They can't take that away from A.J., and they can't take 1995 away from me.

JACK HEWITT: "Let's put it this way: Tony had already baked a heck of a cake with the career he was having. Well, in '95, he put the icing on it."

EIGHT ▓ TRANSITION: BIGGER TRACKS, BIGGER DREAMS

AT EIGHT O'CLOCK ON THE MORNING AFTER THE 1995 USAC MIDGET FINALE, maybe ten hours after the biggest season of my life, I left Los Angeles International Airport on an airliner headed for Sydney, Australia. Midget racing is huge in Australia, so every December the track promoters down there import a few of the hottest American names. My '95 season made me the special guest star.

It was a long flight, something like fourteen hours, but that was just what I needed. I was so damn *tired*. The roller coaster I'd been on for the previous few months had finally taken its toll. I was in one of those moods where all you want to do is stare out the window and think.

I thought about my life, and about the direction of my career. For a couple of years it had seemed clear that racing was taking me someplace. I had no real idea where that might ultimately be, but I tried to be ready for it. I had organized myself to the point where my hobby became a legitimate business—Tony Stewart Racing—run in the beginning by Janie Vogel, a friend who lived in Indianapolis. Janie worked hard to promote me when plenty of people in this sport had never heard of me.

And I had just established a relationship with Cary Agajanian, a Los Angeles lawyer who had racing in his blood: his dad, J. C. Agajanian, was a car owner who won the Indy 500 in 1952 with Troy Ruttman and

One of the biggest days of my life: My first test with Team Menard, January 1996.
(© 1996 IRL by Ron McQueeney)

again in '63 with Parnelli Jones, and the Agajanian family had promoted major races, including the Turkey Night Grand Prix, for decades. Between me running Turkey Night a few times and Cary showing up at other USAC races, I had gotten to know him a little bit, so when I needed representation it seemed like a natural fit.

> **CARY AGAJANIAN,** attorney: "I'm not sure how this got into his mind, but Tony had the foresight to put people around him who could assist him. We had talked several times on the phone about me looking at some of the things that were being presented to him, and at the end of '95 he came to see me in my office."

Looking back on it now, I guess I did a pretty good job of planning ahead. I mean, not many short-track racers have business phones or lawyers looking after their best interests. But at the time, these just seemed like steps I ought to be taking. It pays to be ready, even if you're not sure what you're getting ready for.

Growing up, I had always dreamed about racing in the Indy 500. Then my dad took me to the Speedway for what they call Carburetion Day—the final prerace practice on the Thursday before the 500—when I was nine or ten years old, and that dream grew roots. Once I moved to Indianapolis, I drove past that joint almost every day for a long time. It was nothing for me to go a few miles out of my way just so I could go by that old track.

I used to drive south on Georgetown Road, which runs just behind the main straightaway grandstands, and I was very conscious of how long it took me to get from turn four to turn one. The whole time I'd be thinking about how fast the Indy cars covered that same distance, and what it would be like to be on the other side of that fence, where all the old Indy heroes—Foyt, Parnelli, Mario Andretti, Johnny Rutherford, Al and Bobby Unser, guys who had run midgets and sprint cars just like me—*became* Indy heroes.

The problem was, so much had changed since those guys broke into the sport. Under CART, which sanctioned Indy car racing through the

1980s and the first half of the nineties, the emphasis of the series switched from ovals to road racing, and costs rose out of sight. There were still a few midget and sprint guys who showed up at Indianapolis every May to take a shot at qualifying for the 500, but they faded away as the price of a good ride zoomed to a million dollars, then two million. Unless you had that kind of money, or you could go out and generate that level of sponsorship, you were not going to get to Indianapolis. Period.

Well, I would have been lucky to scrape together an extra two *hundred* dollars, let alone two million. So I sort of switched off this lifelong dream, because that was easier than pretending it might somehow come true.

But if all of that was bad timing for me, I had some good timing, too: I had grown up right in the middle of the NASCAR boom.

I had followed stock car racing as a kid, but no more than I followed, say, Formula One. Even when Winston Cup started showing up every week on television and its popularity soared, it was still just another form of racing to me. Then, a little at a time, I noticed something: it became apparent that if you were a young American oval-track driver who wanted to advance your career, stock car racing gave you that chance.

In the mid-eighties I saw Kenny Schrader, a USAC Silver Crown and sprint car champion, jump to Winston Cup and win races. Then Jeff Gordon joined the Busch Series in the early nineties, and Jeff won, too. In NASCAR, you could see all the right doors opening for short-track drivers. No, not everybody was going to get in, but the doors were open at least a crack.

In CART, not only were those doors locked, but none of us were seen as being worthy of even *knocking* on those doors. I saw guys like me racing their guts out every weekend across this country, and nobody in CART seemed the least bit interested. There were some amazing drivers with grassroots backgrounds who never even got considered for Indy car rides, and yet you had amateur road racers with shaky credentials on the starting grid at the Indianapolis 500 because they were able to bring sponsors.

In NASCAR, things were different. It didn't do a team owner any good to hire a guy based on the size of his wallet because, whether you were talking about Winston Cup or the Busch Series, the fields were too competitive. A dirt-poor driver who was talented enough to make the qualifying cut was a better bargain than a millionaire who couldn't.

I was about three-quarters convinced that my future was in NASCAR when, in September of 1994, a guy named Lorin Ranier took care of the other quarter.

Lorin's dad, the late Harry Ranier, had owned Winston Cup teams in the 1970s and '80s, and they were *good* Winston Cup teams: Cale Yarborough and Buddy Baker won the Daytona 500 in Harry's cars, and he'd also won with Bobby and Davey Allison, Benny Parsons, and Lennie Pond. Harry was an accomplished man, but he'd been out of racing for several years.

I was at the Eldora Speedway, watching time trials for the USAC sprint cars and passing time until it was time to qualify my midget. I wasn't exactly loafing; I wanted to check out the lines the best sprint cars guys were running. Anyway, this fellow walked over and said his name was Lorin Ranier, explained who his dad was, and told me that their cars had won the Daytona 500 three times. That was all pretty neat, and Lorin seemed like a nice guy, but at that moment I was more interested in the Eldora groove than some Daytona race from ten years earlier.

But when Lorin asked me if I might like to drive a stock car, the sprinters didn't seem so important anymore.

> **LORIN RANIER,** team principal, Ranier Racing: "I first noticed Tony when I watched a replay of the '93 Copper Classic at Phoenix, the Silver Crown race. I had actually tuned in to see another driver. I had never even heard of Tony, had no idea who he was. But I watched the first eight or ten laps, and Tony was leading, so I called my dad and said, 'Turn on the TV. I want you to watch this kid.' Anyway, Tony ended up finishing second, and from that point on I paid attention to him, following the schedule in the papers and watching whatever races I could on TV. Then, in '94, I went to Eldora. I introduced myself, and said, 'Are you interested in doing any stock car racing?' He said, 'Hell, yes!'"

That one conversation started a relationship that has lasted ever since. Within a couple of months, Lorin and I had a loose agreement to do a handful of Busch races together in 1996. In the meantime, Lorin came up several times in '95 to watch me run in the various USAC divisions. He and I got to be good friends, and when I met his father, Harry and I hit it off really well, too.

> **LORIN RANIER:** "After I watched Tony run at Eldora, I called my dad and said, 'I just saw the best race car driver I've ever seen.' He said, 'You're joking.' I said, 'Dad, you need to listen to me on this one.' From that day on, he was very excited about Tony."

We took our first stab at the Busch Series in the '95 finale at Homestead, with a car the Raniers leased. We were relatively fast in practice— I think we were fourteenth on the time sheet—but then things went bad. We blocked off the grille with tape, to make the nose aerodynamically slick like you'd want it for time trials, and I made a mock qualifying run. Well, I hadn't learned yet that taping up the nose adds so much downforce on the front end, just because of the increased surface area, that it makes the car loose. The back end stepped out, and before I knew it I had banged the wall. We got the car fixed for time trials, but I missed the race.

Still, I'd had enough of a taste for NASCAR that I thought it was something I'd like to do. Come Daytona in February of '96, I told myself, we'd do better.

Meanwhile, things in Indy car racing had changed a bunch. Tony George, the president of the Indianapolis Motor Speedway, had gotten as fed up with the state of Indy car racing under CART as a lot of us had. He was going ahead with plans to form his own Indy Racing League, an all-oval series which he planned to launch in '96. One of his intentions, he said, was to give American oval-trackers a path toward the Indy 500. That was music to my ears.

While I was in Australia, Cary Agajanian was talking on my behalf to several IRL teams—with Harry Ranier's blessing, because our limited Busch schedule would leave me lots of spare weekends—trying to see

By the end of 1995, it seemed like I was turning all the right heads.
Not only did A. J. Foyt join me at center stage at the USAC banquet,
he also let me test his Indy car. (© John Mahoney)

whether any of them were interested in putting a short-track guy like me into an Indy car.

Already, one team owner had shown an interest: in October of '95, I had flown to Phoenix and done an extended test with A. J. Foyt. I'm still not sure how Foyt chose me, but I'm sure George Snider played a role. George and A.J. are great friends, and they'd been partners in a Silver Crown team for years. Snider had introduced me to A.J. the previous May, and when I was offered this test I could sense George's hand in there someplace.

GEORGE SNIDER: "I'd started watching Tony pretty close, thinking, You know, this kid's gonna be a hell of a racer. You could see the potential in him. Anyway, I told A.J. that Tony was one of the best drivers I'd seen in a long time, but I don't know if I had that much to do with the two of them getting together. I mean, Tony was winning races, and A.J. pays attention to that stuff."

A. J. FOYT, four-time Indianapolis 500 winner: "What first caught my attention was that Tony was a versatile driver, and very few of them come along. I kind of admired him."

To say that I was flattered would be an understatement. A. J. Foyt was one of my heroes, and I was being handed an opportunity to test for him, and *with* him.

I knew he planned on supporting the Indy Racing League, and that he was looking for a driver, so I went to Phoenix believing it was some sort of tryout. At the same time, I looked at it like this: even if that trip didn't do a single thing to advance my career, it still would be worth every minute, just because I'd be able to say I drove Foyt's car.

And it was definitely *Foyt's* car. Sure, Tommy LaMance, A.J.'s nephew and team manager, and Craig Baranouski, his chief mechanic, were the two hands-on guys, but there was no doubt who was in charge. A.J. was constantly tutoring me.

Actually, he was more like a principal than a tutor. A.J. had his rules, and if you broke them he had his own special form of detention: he'd send you to the trailer to think about what you'd done wrong.

He was especially big on having you learn the car at *his* pace. He'd send me out and tell me to run a bunch of laps at around 22.5 seconds; the way that works is, they show you on a pit board how fast you're running, and once you're at the proper pace you concentrate on sustaining that rhythm. It sounds difficult, but it's not. My first lap would be a 23.4, then I'd nudge it down to 22.9, and by the third or fourth lap I'd be at 22.5. The only trouble was, it was easy to sense—even for a rookie like me—that 22.5 was nowhere near the car's limit. Even though I hadn't driven a rear-engined vehicle since my karting days, I was comfortable. So, after a couple of laps at A.J.'s speed limit, my curiosity would get the best of me and I'd run, say, a 22.1. When that happened, Foyt would wave me into the pits.

Then he'd squat down, lean in toward the cockpit, and say, "What are you doing?"

"Just trying to be smooth and run some laps."

"Go sit in the trailer."

So I'd sit in the trailer and look out the window while they got the car ready for its next run. It was like being kept in your homeroom during recess.

TOMMY LAMANCE, team manager, A. J. Foyt Racing: "The thing is, A.J. always puts that restriction on a young driver. I've seen him do it with Tony, Billy Boat, Kenny Brack, several guys. Whenever he sees them getting really comfortable in the car, he'll sit 'em down before they start thinking they're invincible. He's trying to stop them from losing sight of how tricky an Indy car can be, and how fast things can go wrong. I don't think Tony under-

> stood why A.J. was sitting him down; I guess he figured he was in trouble, so he'd kinda walk off and pout a little bit. I'd tell him, 'Tony, it's OK. Everything's fine.' But he'd sit there in the trailer with his head down. It was pretty funny."

Foyt is a tough, hard guy. At the same time, he was the perfect guy for me to learn from, because he came from the same basic background I did. A.J. was a tremendous midget and sprint car driver and, even after all he had accomplished, he still respected a dirt-track racer like me.

A.J. and I spoke the same language. Communication is critical in racing, especially when you're trying to describe a car's behavior, and Foyt and I definitely used the same dictionary. Most Indy car engineers speak in precise technical terms; if you say your car is "pushing" or "loose," they tip their heads and stare, the way confused puppies do, because they don't understand what you're talking about. To them, the correct terms are "understeering" and "oversteering." Well, if you tell A. J. Foyt that the car is pushing, he knows exactly how it's acting.

The whole time A.J. was there, we never really ran flat-out, never really tried for the perfect lap or the ultimate speed. We just worked through a bunch of phases he laid out for us. But on our final day in Phoenix, A.J. left for the airport early, because he had to be someplace that evening. He let us keep running, but he left his guys strict instructions not to let me exceed his speed limit.

Well, I'm not sure if they ever told A.J. this, but Tommy and Craig let out my reins a little bit. I think they could see how frustrated I'd been at 22.5, so they kind of winked and told me to go out and see what I could do.

I ended up running twenty-one seconds flat.

If Foyt had been there, I'd have been sent to the trailer forever. Detention for life.

A.J. is an interesting character. When it's time to get serious, he's as serious as any racer who ever lived; he was a guy who would beat on his car with a hammer, who would chase reporters out of his garage at Indianapolis. But when the pressure is off, that man is the biggest cutup in the world.

Foyt is one of those guys who *needs* somebody to bust on. Usually it's whoever happens to be the new guy on the block, so at this test I got nominated to fill the role as A.J.'s whipping boy.

The funny thing was, when A.J. and I were alone he was like my best buddy. But as soon as he had the crew for an audience, he'd aim both barrels at me. It started at breakfast on our first morning there—a big breakfast is as important to Foyt as Sunday Mass is to the pope—and it only got worse at the track.

For a while, I didn't know what to make of it. I mean, I had gone to Phoenix wearing my best professional-racer face, trying to make a solid impression on Foyt. In return, A.J. was busting my chops nonstop and making me feel about two inches tall.

> **TOMMY LAMANCE:** "I think that when he first came out to Phoenix, Tony looked at A.J. like an icon, a hero. And here's A.J., ripping Tony apart about everything he can think of: the way he dresses, the way he drives. That's the way A.J. gets close to people; he picks on 'em, jokes with 'em. That's how he bonds. But it took Tony a while to realize that."

My wise-guy instinct told me to bust him back, and I thought of some great responses. But I bit my tongue because, after all, we're talking about A. J. Foyt. After an entire day of him laughing his ass off at my expense, I went back to the hotel feeling humiliated. I was walking toward my room with Tommy LaMance, and I said, "If that man busts my ass again tomorrow, I'm gonna bust his. I've got all these comebacks ready, and I'm tired of keeping them to myself."

Tommy said, "Tony, the fastest way for you to leave Phoenix early would be to embarrass A.J. like that. Just keep quiet."

I said, "Okay, I'll try. But it's going to be tough."

> **TOMMY LAMANCE:** "Tony had the big idea that he was going to stand up to A.J., just tell him off. And I said, 'Uh, Tony, I wouldn't do that just yet.' I didn't want him to come off as just a smart punk."

Well, if day one was brutal, day two was worse. All morning, I gritted my teeth and just sort of smiled. Finally, I'd had all I could take.

A.J. had brought along a Winston Cup car which he was testing himself when we weren't busy with the Indy car. He was climbing into that stock car, mouthing off at me over his shoulder. Well, as everybody knows, Foyt has gained a few pounds over the years; he had both his legs in the car, and he was leaning way back, trying to squeeze fifty years of big breakfasts through that window.

I saw my cue.

"Wait a minute," I yelled.

Foyt stopped, looked in my direction, and said, "What's the matter?"

I said, "Let me get some wheel-bearing grease and smear it on that belly of yours. It'll help you slide in easier."

Well, you could have heard a pin drop. It was like the only living creatures in the whole state of Arizona at that moment were me and A. J. Foyt, because every member of his team was too stunned to even breathe.

Finally, maybe five seconds later, A.J. burst out laughing. I mean, he laughed so hard that I thought he might fall backward out of that car. Once he laughed, everybody else laughed, too.

Looking back, I think our relationship changed in that one instant. For the next couple of days, A.J. busted my ass harder than ever, but I busted his right back, and he loved it. The more we jawed back and forth, the closer we got, and it was the start of a friendship I really value.

> **TOMMY LAMANCE:** "You get those two guys together now, and it's a nonstop jab contest. I think Tony gives A.J. a harder time than A.J. gives him."

It's funny, but I've always sensed that this same sort of give-and-take is the basis of Foyt's relationship with George Snider and most of his other friends. I think he enjoys being around guys who don't suck up to him just because of who he is.

In all, I spent five days in Phoenix with Foyt. It was a great experience, but when I left I didn't have the slightest idea where we stood regarding

1996. It was impossible to read whether he thought I'd done a good job. I felt like I'd driven well—smooth, no mistakes—but I got no confirmation of that from A.J. himself.

Over the next couple of weeks I called Foyt's shop a few times, talking to Tommy LaMance every chance I got, but even he didn't have a real handle on what A.J. was going to do.

Then there was some action. In November, those guys needed somebody to drive the car during the filming of a TV commercial at the old Texas World Speedway, and they called me. I took that as a positive sign, because A.J. could have plugged in any number of drivers, but he chose me.

We did a day of filming, had dinner with the team, and that night I went to A.J.'s house. Unfortunately, some kind of bug got into my system, and I was really ill. Here I was, in A. J. Foyt's home, so sick that I couldn't do anything but lie on the couch. The only thing that kept me from being completely disgraced was that A.J. was feeling lousy, too; his knees, which have bothered him for years, were really hurting. I still remember Tommy shaking his head as he looked at the two of us laying around in agony.

> **TOMMY LAMANCE:** "It was a pretty pathetic sight. A.J. was sore, and Tony was sick. They each had a big ol' bowl of ice cream, and they were sprawled out on the couch. I said, 'Look at these two. This guy right here is the greatest racer of all time; this other one wants to be the next great racer. This is embarrassing.'"

Once we recovered, we went down to A.J.'s ranch in southern Texas, where he and I spent some real one-on-one time. I remember riding around on a four-wheeler while he sat on his tractor, clearing acres of brush. I could see in his eyes how much he enjoyed that; he was obviously proud that this was *his* land, and proud that he was shaping it just the way he wanted it. We talked about racing, and also about things that had nothing to do with the sport. I think he was trying to size me up.

Before I left the ranch, A.J. offered me a ride for the '96 IRL season, which actually amounted to just three races: Disney World in January,

Phoenix in March, the Indianapolis 500 in May. Those would fit nicely between my Busch commitments, so this seemed like a dream deal. But there was a hitch: A.J. didn't like the idea of sharing his driver with another owner, in this case Harry Ranier, and he let me know that. That put me in a bind. As much as I looked up to A.J., and as badly as I wanted to go Indy car racing with him, I had made a verbal agreement with Ranier.

In the end, I had to tell A.J. that I wasn't comfortable backing out of my deal with Harry. That was difficult, because the possibility existed that I was closing the door not only on driving for Foyt but on driving Indy cars at all.

It was an agonizing decision, but it was the correct one.

> **PAT SULLIVAN:** "When this rumor started getting around that Tony had turned down a ride with Foyt, I was talking to Larry Martz and I said, 'I just don't understand that.' And Larry said, 'You know, Pat, I don't understand it, either. But let me tell you something: I've watched this kid enough to know that he always lands on his feet. He always seems to make the right decisions.' And that's true. Tony has that savvy about him."

So there I was, racing midgets in Australia and having so much fun that my planned three-week stay turned into five weeks. As the visiting American hero, I got treated like Michael Jordan. I also piled up a bunch of trophies: as I remember it, I ran twelve races and won nine times.

While I was over there, there was plenty happening back home. Cary Agajanian and Harry Ranier worked out the details of my stock car contract. Once that was out of the way, Cary kept hammering away at the IRL team owners he knew, trying to find me a seat. But I wasn't getting my hopes up; I honestly believed that the only Indy car guy who could appreciate what I had done to that point in my career was Foyt, and that avenue was closed.

As it turned out, Cary was a more persuasive guy than I'd given him credit for.

I got home from Australia early in January. My girlfriend Amanda picked me up at the airport at four o'clock in the afternoon and we drove straight to her apartment, where I fell asleep as soon as I got in the door. The jet lag had just wiped me out. Well, at ten o'clock that same evening, Amanda woke me to tell me I had a phone call; it was Cary Agajanian calling. I remember not being sure whether it was morning or night, because I'd been in such a deep sleep.

Cary said, "You need to catch the first available flight to Orlando tomorrow morning."

"What for?"

"For an Indy car test in one of John Menard's cars."

I said, "You're kidding, right?"

"No," Cary said. "They're running Eddie Cheever, and if you get there in time they'll put you in the car."

CARY AGAJANIAN: "I had called John Menard and told him what a great talent Tony was, and how it would be good to have him in the IRL. I'd say he was somewhat taken aback; I'll never forget him saying, 'Well, he's only a midget driver.' That's an exact quote. And I said, 'Yeah, but he's a great one.' Then I told him about Tony's test with A.J., how it had been successful. We went back and forth, and I said, 'I really think you should give this kid a chance.' He said he wasn't sure, and that's how it was left, with John saying, 'I'll think about it.' Then at some point, we were told that Tony would be given the opportunity to test."

I didn't know much about John Menard, other than that he owned a big chain of home-improvement stores and that prior to the formation of the IRL the only race his team entered was the Indy 500. But it had always been an impressive operation; Menard seemed willing to spend whatever it took to go fast. The team had developed its own engine based on the Buick V6, and at Indianapolis it was usually as fast as anything anyone else had.

Menard had been a vocal supporter of the Indy Racing League, and the papers said he planned on running Cheever and Scott Brayton in all the races. Given his resources, Cary and I agreed, it was not out of the question that he might run three cars.

So I started packing for Orlando. I remember Amanda, who had been with me since 1989, being unhappy about that, which I understood. Over the previous couple of months, she had put up with a lot: first the tension of those three USAC titles, then my extended stay in Australia. Now, after being home less than a day, I was off to the airport again. The only explanation I could give was that this was too great an opportunity to pass up. I guess if you get involved in a relationship with a race driver, that's a phrase you're bound to hear more than you want to.

I flew to Orlando, drove out to the track, and introduced myself to Larry Curry, who ran the team. We made some small talk there, and then had dinner together. That evening, I had a little déjà vu experience; I had the same feeling about Curry that I'd had in the spring of '94, when I first met Larry Howard. I mean, the exact same sensation: this is somebody I could enjoy working with. Curry and I just seemed to be on the same wavelength when it came to race cars, and that put me at ease.

> **LARRY CURRY,** former team manager, Team Menard: "I don't know why this is, but there are certain combinations of people that just come together, and they click instantly. With Tony and me, from the first time we started working together it was almost like we could finish each other's sentences."

I went back to the hotel, flopped on the bed, and told myself I might get to be an Indy car racer after all.

I spent most of the next day watching Cheever. In fact, I got a lot more out of watching the guy than I did out of talking to him. I tried to chat with Eddie, but it was clear that he didn't see me as somebody who was on his level. Fair enough; Cheever had spent several years in Europe racing Formula One, and he had driven Indy cars for Foyt and Chip Ganassi. Who the hell was I, some kid off the dirt tracks, to enter into a conversation with Eddie Cheever?

When it came time for me to run some laps in the afternoon, Eddie didn't even stick around. The last thing he said before he headed to the airport was, "This is a good race car. If you crash it, I'll kill you."

The 1996 IRL rules essentially matched the '95 CART specs, so Menard's car, a Lola, was similar to the one I had tested for Foyt. Curry explained to me that he dialed out a lot of the turbocharger boost, cutting down the horsepower, and had made the car stable for me by setting it up to have a slight push. He said, "Go ahead and run it hard. It won't do anything crazy."

Little by little, I found the speed. The Disney World mile had a strange, three-cornered layout, but I figured it out fairly quickly. I don't remember what our times were, but I do know that I ended up very close to what Cheever was running.

Not bad for a lowly dirt-track racer.

Apparently, Larry Curry and John Menard agreed. That night, they decided to stick me in as a third entry for the Indy Racing League opener.

Right from the start of my Indy car career, I had a great rapport with Larry Curry. He was the perfect guy to help ease along a rookie like me. (IMS/IRL © Jim Haines)

I signed that first IRL contract outside the restaurant, on the roof of a rental car.

LARRY CURRY: "I had been there for two solid weeks, testing with Eddie Cheever and Scott Brayton. Well, Tony came in there, and in thirty-six laps, with a car that was set up really conservatively, he ran as quick as either one of those guys had run. When you see that, you think, My God, we've got a pretty good one here."

CARY AGAJANIAN: "We did a deal just for Orlando, and it was all written on a paper napkin in a restaurant bar. Larry and I were there, and John Menard was on the phone. We did a contract for one race, and it was virtually three lines: Team Menard will pay Tony Stewart x percent of the winnings, and Tony Stewart will drive the car, and that was about it."

— — — — —

By the time the Disney Indy 200 rolled around, an interesting thing had happened: the series really caught the attention of grassroots racers. Davey Hamilton had signed with Foyt and had been fast in testing, and my times in the Menard car were right up there. Now it was like every good open-wheel racer believed he had a chance—not a guarantee, by any means, but a *chance*—to get his foot in the door. Sure, the bulk of the initial IRL roster was made up of guys with road-racing backgrounds, but on the weekend of the race there were great midget drivers like Billy Boat and great sprint car drivers like Jac Haudenschild and great supermodified drivers like Joe Gosek wandering around, talking to team owners. It was a nice to see.

At the same time, it sort of put Davey and me under the gun. I think we felt obligated to show that guys who came from places like Winchester and IRP could get the job done at this higher level.

> **DAVEY HAMILTON:** "There was some pressure, that's for sure. I mean, I think Tony and I are the kind of drivers who put a lot of pressure on ourselves to do well anyway, but there was that extra pressure going into Orlando. But, you know, we both ran well right from the start of that weekend. When we got done with the first day of practice, there were smiles on both our faces. At that point, we both were thinking. 'We can do this.'"

At the end of the first session, I was fifth on the time sheet behind Richie Hearn, Buddy Lazier, Roberto Guerrero, and Buzz Calkins. Hearn had won the '95 championship in the Toyota Atlantic series, Lazier had been considered a rising star in CART, Guerrero had scored three top-five finishes in the Indianapolis 500, and Calkins had shown a lot of promise in the Indy Lights series.

In other words, I was in pretty good company.

Team Menard hadn't planned on running three cars until after my test, so we were a little bit understaffed. That left me with sort of a makeshift crew; Cheever and Brayton had their own engineers, and Larry Curry—who was busy enough already, overseeing the preparation of all three cars—served as mine. That was fine with me, because both of the regular engineers were foreigners, and I'm sure anything they

said would have sailed right over my head. I relied heavily on Larry and on Bill Martin, my car's chief mechanic, and everything went smoothly.

The way we had things set up, it was understood that, as the rookie, I'd be free to lean on Scott and Eddie. That would have been interesting because, even though Scotty couldn't have been nicer, Cheever was still acting as if I didn't exist. Thankfully, that never mattered. I was the quickest of the three Menard drivers in practice, and I outqualified both of them.

That's not to say that I was setting the world on fire, because I qualified only eighth. But anytime you're in a multicar team, you always want to be the fastest guy.

> **LARRY CURRY:** "We were having a debrief after one of the practice sessions. I said to Scotty, 'Are you happy with your car?' Scotty said yes. I asked Eddie the same thing, and he said, 'Yeah, my car is good.' So I took out these data printouts and I laid 'em down, and I said, 'All I can tell you two is that this guy'—and I pointed to Tony—'is eleven miles an hour faster than both of you through turn one. Now, are you sure you're happy with your cars?'"

> **CARY AGAJANIAN:** "I never like to say I was flabbergasted, because that makes Tony mad. He'll say, 'What, you didn't have any faith in me?' So I wasn't flabbergasted, but I was so pleased that he had done so well so quickly. That's just unheard of. It was thrilling to me."

On race day, Larry shifted back to his customary role calling the race for Cheever, and he assigned Stu Hackett, who ran the parts department at the Menard shop, to call the shots for me. But as we waited on the starting grid, Larry gave me some last-minute advice. He told me not to worry if a bunch of cars ran off and hid; he thought that with our setup, the car might be a little bit tight until it burned off some fuel. And he warned me to learn as quickly as possible how the car behaved in the turbulent air you encounter in heavy traffic.

> **LARRY CURRY:** "I told him, 'Tony, you need to run behind some people and make sure you understand how the car will react.'

> See, in the cars he grew up in, aerodynamics isn't too big a deal, but in Indy cars it's very important. They react one way when you're on the track by yourself, and another way when you're tucked under somebody's rear wing and you lose the downforce on your front wings. My main concern was how he would handle that. But I also told him, 'Once you're comfortable with how the car feels, hey, you're a race driver. Go race it.'"

At the green I fell into line and tried to run at my own pace, and, sure enough, everything Larry told me came true: the lead guys—Lazier, Arie Luyendyk, Guerrero, and Scott Sharp—did drive away; my car did twitch a few times in the turbulence, which was hairy until I got used to it; and the longer we ran, the better my car handled.

The opposition started coming back to me, and coming back fast. I got past Hamilton for sixth, Calkins for fifth, Sharp for fourth, and Guerrero for third. Then we had a yellow, and just after the restart I went around Arie Luyendyk into second.

That put me on Lazier's tail, but not for long: a few minutes later I dove under him as we hit turn two, and we had the lead. It had taken just twenty-eight laps to get there.

> **LARRY CURRY:** "I was on the radio with Cheever, and, you know, there had been some friction between those two guys. Eddie believed that Tony was getting the best stuff. The fact is, Tony was driving the worst car in the stable. It was our test mule, a car that had been crashed more than any car we had. Well, in the race, Tony was coming around to put Eddie a lap down, so I radioed Cheever, 'The leader is behind you.' I didn't tell him who was coming, just that it was the leader. Cheever said, 'Ten-four.' There were a couple of seconds of silence, and I'm sure he was looking in his mirrors. Then Cheever came back and said, 'What did you say?' I told him again that the leader was behind him, and Cheever said, 'You gotta be shitting me!' Right about that time, zing, Tony disposed of Cheever."

It was cool to be up front in my first Indy car race, but I still had a lot of things to worry about. Pit stops, for one. Until that point in my career,

I had *never* made a real pit stop; I mean, I had limped into the pits with damaged midgets and sprint cars, but I never made an honest-to-God, time-sensitive stop for fuel and tires. We had simulated a couple of stops during practice—I'd roll in, stop, and take off again—but it's always tougher when the pressure is on for real.

Then there were all the onboard controls, which we never had time to study in practice. In a midget, your only in-car tools are your hands, your feet, and your experience: you alter your line to correct a handling problem, or play with the throttle to change the traction you're getting. But this Indy car had levers to stiffen or soften the front and rear antiroll bars, and all sorts of knobs governing every engine system. I had no idea what any of them did.

Early on, I got a radio call telling me to change the fuel mixture, just one of the things they monitor with the car-to-pit telemetry. Well, I had to ask them which knob that was. Then they asked me to cut back on the turbo boost, and we went through the same thing.

I was afraid to mess with the antiroll bars at all, because I was afraid I'd only turn a small problem into a big one. Generally, those Indy cars loosen up as the fuel load burns off, and today I would correct that by stiffening the front bar or softening the rear. At Orlando, I lived with it. In fact, when it got a little bit too loose, I just backpedaled for a while. Calkins passed me for the lead on lap 66, and I just hung on until we could get some more fuel in the thing to balance it out.

It's amazing, really, how little I knew.

> **LARRY CURRY:** "When Tony says he didn't know what was what inside that cockpit, he's not kidding. I had told him, 'The only things you need to know are the gas pedal, the shifter, and the steering wheel. Just get this race under your belt. All that other stuff is for another day, another time.' He just drove the car the way we had set it up, and instead of adjusting the car he adjusted his driving style."

> **CARY AGAJANIAN:** "The thing that fascinates me about that day is this: when those drivers adjust the boost on the turbocharger, they've got a little tube that goes into their helmet, right to their ear, so that they can hear exactly when the pop-off valve opens;

they want to run the engine as close as they can to that point. That was how they all thought: like you could not possibly be competitive unless you got all this important stuff right to the absolute edge. Well, here's Tony, with no idea how to even adjust it!"

I figured that as the day rolled along, the more experienced guys would get their cars better and bring the fight to me and Calkins, but that never happened. By halfway, the only guys on the lead lap were me and Buzz. Lazier broke a suspension, Luyendyk lost a gearbox, Hamilton faded with chassis problems, and we just outran everybody else.

Toward the end, it looked like second was the best I could do—Calkins had pulled away—and I had pretty much accepted that. But then, with about a dozen laps to go, Cheever crashed with Scott Sharp in turn one. I was just coming onto the main straightaway, and my radio man hollered, "Yellow, yellow, yellow!"

I thought, Perfect: we'll be on Buzz's tail for the restart, and I'll get one last shot at him. But by the time I processed that thought, I just about got crashed myself.

I could see a bunch of debris flying around down in turn one. I slowed down and prepared to pick my way through the junk, but I hadn't even downshifted out of sixth gear yet so I was still moving pretty fast. All of a sudden, two safety trucks pulled out of the infield and into my path. Apparently, some official had given them the all-clear sign. I had nowhere to go but up the track, and once I got into all the dust and loose rubber it slid me toward the wall. I glanced off the concrete, which ricocheted me straight toward Cheever's crashed car. I made a big swerve to miss him—steering, braking, downshifting—and ended up driving through a minefield of debris. Somewhere in the middle of all this, one of the safety trucks clipped my front wing.

My guys asked me if I'd hit anything. I radioed back, "I hit *everything.*"

Knowing what I know now—how easy it is to break the suspension pieces on an Indy car, how easily racing tires are punctured—I'd pit in an instant if that happened today. Back then, I just didn't know any better.

It didn't feel like I had a flat tire, and when I zigzagged the car the steering seemed okay, so I didn't see any reason to pit. Besides, I had Calkins right in front of me, which meant I had a chance to win the race.

When the restart came—194 laps down, 6 to go—I put the condition of the car right out of my mind. I took a stab to the outside when we got to turn one, hoping to catch Buzz sleeping, but instead my car pushed badly. It continued to push until the end of the race. It turned out that in the course of bouncing off the wall and getting nicked by the safety truck, my front wing had cracked. Instead of giving me the downforce I needed, it was just flexing.

I chased Calkins to the finish, but he beat me there by 0.866 seconds.

Very rarely am I happy with second place, especially if I feel like I had a car that could have won. Well, that first IRL race was an exception. I was absolutely satisfied with my finish.

I was trying to be objective. We may have finished second, but we were a *fighting* second. On top of all that, I had driven a race that was basically mistake-free. Sure, I might have missed the perfect line here and there, and I'm sure I played traffic wrong once or twice, but I got things right almost all day long. My only close call had been that incident with the safety trucks, and they couldn't pin that one on the rookie.

John Menard told the media later that I had "all the poise of a veteran." And Robin Miller of the *Indianapolis Star*, who had been critical of the lack of experience in the IRL, wrote, "Stewart quickly stamped himself as one of those Parnelli Jones naturals that surface once every thirty years," and said that I had "handled traffic like [I] was running a midget at Kokomo."

I took special pride in that last remark. I really did think I'd done a good job upholding the hopes of all those short-track people who had been watching so closely.

CARY AGAJANIAN: "Tony's finish was so gratifying to me, not because I had recommended him but because guys like him were what the IRL was all about. If a guy like Tony Stewart couldn't succeed, what were those other drivers going to do?"

BILLY BOAT: "At the time, we were pretty intense rivals, so I couldn't imagine myself rooting for Tony. But on that particular day, I really wanted him to win. I knew that if Tony did well, and showed that the type of background he had could prepare you for driving Indy cars, it was going to help not only me but a lot of guys in midgets and sprint cars. So I was a big, big Tony Stewart fan that day."

That may have been the only time I ever felt like I was racing for anybody besides myself and my team. I hadn't let anybody down, and that was a giant relief. I left Orlando knowing I didn't have to prove anything for drivers like us anymore.

We opened our '96 NASCAR season a few weeks later, and it was like going from the penthouse to the outhouse. At Orlando I had been one of the highest-profile guys all weekend. At Daytona, you had to look hard just to know I was there: we qualified thirty-fourth.

Still, I was not unhappy. The Busch Series race at Daytona brings out the best in every team from that division, as well as a dozen or so Winston Cup drivers, so just getting into the field was good for a rookie team like ours. A lot of good cars and good drivers went home after qualifying, but we stuck around.

We had some help from Waddell Wilson, a legendary engine builder who had been a big part of Harry Ranier's glory days, so we weren't *all* rookies. But we were far from the smartest team there, or the best equipped. We had a decent superspeedway car, but nothing as slick as the stuff the top guys had.

And the driver was a little bit behind the eight ball, too. Drafting is everything at Daytona, and I really thought I understood the science behind it. I had done some drafting in my enduro kart days, and the midgets actually draft pretty effectively at places like Phoenix. But anybody who goes to Daytona for the first time thinking he knows a lot about drafting finds out in a hurry that he doesn't know much. I got taken to school on a regular basis in most of the preerace practice sessions.

One of my guys put a little decal on our dashboard poking fun at my rookie status. If you looked quick, it resembled the "No Fear" clothing logo, but it actually read "No Idea." That was a pretty good description of my drafting ability.

On race day we moved up quicker than I thought we might, and I was thinking that the race might go better than expected. Then I felt the engine lose power; a rocker arm had broken, which left us running on seven cylinders. We used the rest of the day as a practice session, the team trying different things with the car and me trying different things behind the wheel. We ended up twenty-first, two laps down.

Man, what a winter. The 1995 season had been over less than three months. The weather around home hadn't come close to warming up. And here I was, just a couple of weeks into February of '96, with an Indy car race and my first Busch Series start behind me, and big things ahead of me.

Cary Agajanian and John Menard had worked out a deal extending our cocktail-napkin contract through the Indy 500. Meanwhile, Harry Ranier and his team put together a Busch program that would take us to a nice mix of superspeedways, short tracks, and intermediate ovals.

The way I looked at it, that kind of schedule would tell me a lot by the end of 1996. More than likely, it would tell me which type of racing—stock cars or Indy cars—was right for me.

Best of all, for at least the next few months I'd be able to do both.

Tony Stewart

NINE WORKING TWO SHIFTS

I NEVER GAVE MUCH THOUGHT TO *HOW* YOU WERE SUPPOSED TO DRIVE INDY cars or stock cars. I just showed up and did the job. Don't get me wrong: I had wondered about, say, the cornering forces of an Indy car, and I was curious about how different a stock car might feel to me. But in 1995, I had run 106 total races. That doesn't leave much time to sit around thinking about your IRL and NASCAR techniques.

Looking back, I don't believe I ever changed my style, my basic approach. I just kept doing what I'd always done: I drove according to what I felt in my hands, and in the seat of my pants.

I paid attention to the feedback I got from the car, whether it was a Pontiac or a Lola. Wherever we went, I tried to creep up on the limits of a car, instead of trying to do that in big chunks. And I did my best to never *over*drive whatever I happened to be in; if all you do is try for the ultimate lap, you'll spend more time trying not to crash than you'll spend learning how to go fast.

But, again, that's the same approach I'd always used.

Sometimes you quickly pick up the cars and the tracks, you and your new team jell instantly, and you look like a hero.

And sometimes it's not quite that easy.

— — — — —

You're never completely at ease at Indy. The magnitude of the 500 brings pressures that are unique to the event. (©1996 IRL by Ron McQueeney)

Everyone connected with the Ranier team was happy with the way things had gone at Daytona. An engine component had let us down, but we hadn't let ourselves down. We left there feeling good about our entire program. Well, it took the Busch Series about one week to bring us back down to earth. At Rockingham, we missed the field by .006—which is six *thousandths*—of a second.

And that's pretty much the way our 1996 Busch Series effort went: we balanced a few flashes of brilliance with an awful lot of disappointments. Take Atlanta, the race after Rockingham. We qualified fourteenth and ran in the top ten, which I thought was awesome, but then the ignition failed and we dropped out.

Anytime you start racing in a new division, it's critical to build up your own reference data. You need to get a feel for that particular type of car—how it changes on a long run, how the tires behave, things like that—and the only way to do that is to log laps. You don't learn much when you miss a race, or when you fall out early.

We finally had one of those solid learning days at Bristol. We qualified seventh and ran in the top ten until the last few laps, when I got tangled up with another guy and spun out. We ended up sixteenth, but still it was a good day. At both Daytona and Atlanta, we'd had moments when we felt like we were getting the hang of this stuff; at Bristol, some other people noticed, too.

LARRY MARTZ: "When Tony ran that first time at Bristol, we went down to watch him. We got to the track early, wished him well, and went up to sit in the stands. This one group of people sat near us, and we struck up a conversation. I found out they were from Virginia, and I told them I was from Indiana. One of them said, 'Hey, you got any tickets for the Winston Cup race tomorrow?' I told him no, that we were going home that same night. He said, 'Why would you come all the way down here just to watch a Busch race?' I told him that the guy in the number fifteen car, Tony Stewart, was a friend of ours. He said, 'Tony Stewart? I never heered of him.' That's just the way he said it: 'never heered of him.' Well, about ten laps into the race, Tony had moved up to fourth. This guy turned to me and said, 'Kid's purty good, ain't he?'"

TRUE SPEED

Unfortunately, we had more occasions when things didn't go so well. We missed qualifying at a couple more places, including Indianapolis Raceway Park. That one really bothered me, because IRP was the closest thing I had to a home track, and I wanted to go there and have a solid run. Instead, we weren't even close to making the field. And in the nine races we did run, we never went home with much to show for our efforts. Like I said, we had flashes of brilliance, but they were overshadowed by bad luck and bad results.

> **LORIN RANIER:** "We just couldn't put a good finish together. Milwaukee was an example. We had a great car, and Tony was in the top five when, basically, his spotter wrecked him. I know, because I was the spotter. What happened was, they had just repaved the track and it came apart, so there was no outside groove. Mike McLaughlin passed Tony, but there was a small gap before the next guy, which was Hermie Sadler. I wanted Tony to get back to the inside real quick, and I told him he was clear when he wasn't. He turned down into Hermie, and they wrecked. It was 100 percent my fault."

I made my mistakes, too. At Talladega I threw away what might have been a top-five finish by getting too racy when I should have been biding my time, learning. My car got away from me, and I spun into the wall. Worst of all, my mistake also wrecked Mark Martin, who hardly ever makes that kind of mistake himself. Mark is a guy who drives hard but who also drives *smart*—the kind of driver I've always tried to be—and I ruined his race. I was angry after I crashed, and I complained to the TV interviewer that the Winston Cup guys in that race wouldn't draft with me. Well, today I can see why: those guys knew I didn't have the draft figured out, so they shied away from me. And when one of them finally did run with me, I screwed up and took him out.

I think anyone who has had success learns to hate failure. That's how it works for me, anyway. I was trying hard to be upbeat about the way our Busch season was going—"It's just the growing pains of a new team," I told the reporters—but that wasn't easy.

— — — — —

Fortunately, I could always count on the IRL car to boost my ego a bit. Every time I climbed into that thing, we were fast. At Phoenix, my second race with the Menard team, we were as good as anybody. Arie Luyendyk won that day, and if you look at the stats he pretty much dominated: he led well over half of the two hundred laps. But we definitely made things interesting. About halfway through the race, we cut down a right front tire; I had to limp around the entire track, and by the time we got in and out of the pits we were four laps down. But the car was so fast that we made up three of those laps, and I was closing fast on Arie to get back on the lead lap when we broke a crank trigger, an ignition part you never even think about until one fails.

They always say that nobody remembers who finished second. Well, that day we didn't finish at all, but everybody knew that we had the best car on the track, and that the guy in the cockpit was coming along pretty well, too.

MARK DISMORE: "Good equipment won't make just anybody look good, but it will make a good driver look good. And Tony was a good driver."

Phoenix was the last IRL race before Indianapolis. That season's 500 was going to be the first one in years without the CART teams, and in the spring of '96 there was all this talk—mostly from the CART side—about how the IRL was full of no-name drivers and second-rate talent. I mostly ignored it, because my job is to beat whoever shows up, not to defend myself against people who *don't* show up.

But it was hard not to take some of it personally. I read stories that said things like, "Sure, this Stewart kid is doing well, but who is he racing against?" Well, nobody was calling Luyendyk, Cheever, Lazier, and Guerrero a bunch of bums when they raced in CART, and I don't think they lost any of their ability just by switching leagues. And how did guys like Richie Hearn and Robbie Buhl, who were supposed to be two of the top prospects in the CART feeder system, go from being promising young racers to being nobodies just by joining the IRL?

Michele Alboreto, who ran fourth at Phoenix, had won five times in Formula One. John Paul Jr. and Johnny O'Connell were two of this country's best sports car racers. Scott Brayton had beaten the CART guys to win the pole at Indianapolis in 1995. Scott Sharp was a Trans-Am champion who had done more than a full season of CART racing, as had Mike Groff, a former Indy Lights champ. Sure, there were some drivers in the IRL who didn't have the greatest credentials, just like there were in CART. But there were also some really solid racers in the league.

I wasn't ashamed to run with those guys. I was proud to run with them, and thankful when I was able to run *ahead* of them. If you had listened to the CART side of things for the previous ten years, that should have been impossible. In fact, I think part of the reason they bashed the IRL was that they just couldn't accept the fact that a short-track guy like me could run up front against a quality field.

CARY AGAJANIAN: "We had been brainwashed into thinking that a guy could not drive an Indy car unless he'd had what was supposed to be all the proper training: the Formula Atlantics, the Indy Lights. You'd hear all these technical reasons about how a guy with only front-engine experience couldn't possibly feel what a rear-engine car was doing. You can see now that all of that was both a defense mechanism and a method of keeping everybody out of their sandbox."

I'm the first to admit that I had a much better first crack at the 500 than most rookies get. John Menard placed such a high emphasis on Indy that he let us do as much testing there as we wanted. In April I actually ran some laps at 235 miles per hour, which was as fast as anyone had ever gone around that place. By the time the Speedway officially opened in May, I was as comfortable as a rookie can be.

Still, you're never completely at ease at Indy. The magnitude of the 500 brings pressures that are unique to that event.

Indianapolis is the only track in the world where you're required to take a rookie test, no matter what else you might have done in this sport. It's pretty simple, really: you pass through three ten-lap phases, with the speed of each phase a bit higher than the last. Then, in the fourth and final phase, a team of observers, generally race officials and a couple of 500 veterans, watches you run ten laps at your own pace. It seemed almost silly that I had to take the test at all, because, trust me, our fast testing laps had been pretty closely observed. But at Indy, rules are rules. A lot of Formula One champions have come over to run the 500, and they had to take rookie tests, too.

I breezed through the first three phases with no trouble, playing things by the book. By the time my fourth phase rolled around, I was getting bored, so I kind of let my hair down a bit.

> **LARRY CURRY:** "The officials said, 'Have him run ten laps at whatever speed he's comfortable.' I told Tony, 'Look, do the ten laps, and we'll get this over with. No showing off.' Well, his second lap was over 235, and I think all ten were between 234 and 236. I turned to the USAC official and said, 'He looks pretty comfortable, doesn't he?'"

I passed with flying colors. Later that day, I ran 237.338 mph, which to that point was the fastest timed lap in the history of the Indianapolis Motor Speedway. Larry asked me over the radio how the car felt. I told him, "Like a Cadillac."

The next day the veterans joined the rookies for the official start of practice, and a bunch of us took turns trading fast laps. Cheever hit 233, and both Brayton and Luyendyk got above 235, but when the day ended I was quickest with a 236.121. Even today, it gives me a chill to think about that: my very first day of open practice at Indianapolis, and there we were, at the top of the time sheet.

Luyendyk edged ahead of us over the next couple of days, and got everybody's attention with a 239.260 on the day before the opening round of time trials.

At Indianapolis, qualifying is spread over two weekends; that's just part of the tradition. The first day is called Pole Day—with uppercase letters, just like Opening Day in baseball—because that's the only day the top spot is available. Winning the pole at Indy carries a ton of pres-

tige, so if you're really fast there's as much tension on Pole Day as there is on race day anywhere else. And we were really fast.

I was a nervous wreck.

LARRY CURRY: "I remember strapping him into the car for the morning practice on Pole Day, and his right leg was bouncing up and down, shaking. I reached in and grabbed his chest, and I said, 'Tony, you calm down. This is just another day on the calendar. Go out and do what you know how to do.' "

Another tradition: unlike most qualifying sessions, where you take two timed laps and the fastest one counts, at Indianapolis you run four laps and the average is your official speed. There's a lot of pressure to get every corner right, because one bad corner means a slow lap, which, obviously, drags your average down.

We were the eighth car to qualify, and probably the first of the serious pole threats. I concentrated on being consistent, and I did all right: my lap speeds, in order, were 233.040, 233.179, 233.076, and 233.106. At Indy, speeds

The Indy 500 has all kinds of traditions. They had my name in lights at the Speedway Motel after I qualified for the front row as a rookie. (IMS/IRL © 1996 Jim Haines)

rise and fall dramatically according to things like wind velocity, wind direction, and changes in the temperature, and the track had clearly slowed down since we all turned those monster laps earlier in the week. My average of 233.100 was the best to that point; I didn't think it would be quick enough for the pole, but it was a safe bet to put us somewhere in the first two rows.

My qualifying run took just over two and a half minutes. In that short span of time, I crossed the line between those drivers who dream of making the Indy 500 and those drivers who have that dream come true. I remember my dad standing there when I rolled to a stop on pit road, and it was a dramatic moment for both of us.

NELSON STEWART: "I've never had a feeling like that in my life. You've got to look at it from this perspective: way back when I was in the third grade, the teacher asked us to list three goals for our lives. I only had two. The first was to win the Indianapolis 500, and the second was to own a farm. Well, I don't own a farm, and obviously I never raced in the 500. But to have Tony there, the pride was just unbelievable."

I made my laps at two-thirty in the afternoon, then sat back and watched everybody take their best shots. Cheever and Guerrero ran 231s, Eliseo Salazar a 232. Then Scotty Brayton went out and ran a 231.535, slower than we'd all expected.

It's funny how your emotions change. I never expected to sit on the pole for my first 500, but the longer I looked up and saw our number, 20, at the top of the scoring pylon, the more I wanted it to stay there.

Then, at five-thirty, just a half-hour before closing time, Arie Luyendyk went out. For a while it didn't look like he had the speed to beat us: his first two laps—a 231.756 and a 233.058—were below my average. But Arie really stepped it up on his last two, both of which were over 234. His four-lap average of 233.390 knocked me back to second.

What happened next was one of those moments which makes Indy so thrilling. Once Luyendyk beat me, John Menard, who really wanted that pole, decided to withdraw Brayton's car and have him requalify in a backup car. It was a gutsy move. After all, Scotty had qualified fifth, and that's an awfully good starting spot to throw away, especially when you're talking about the biggest race in the world. But I had to admire that spirit; if your goal is the pole, well, go for the pole.

There was a ton of pressure on Scotty, but that guy got the job done. He ran four straight laps above 233.5 mph, averaged 233.718, and won one of the most dramatic pole positions you'll ever see.

The ironic thing was, we found out later on that a Menard car would have been on the pole anyway. Luyendyk's car came up light in the post-qualifying inspection, and his time was disallowed. So the guy Scotty was actually knocking out of the top spot was me.

That was tough to take, at first. I mean, to win the pole my first Indy 500 would have been special. But today, I'm glad Scotty won that pole.

See, six days later he took one of our backup cars out on a routine practice run, just trying a few different race setups. But when you're talking about Indianapolis, maybe there's no such thing as routine. Scott's car cut a tire and spun into the wall with incredible force. A head injury killed him.

Scotty was a great teammate, and we were on our way to becoming really good friends. It was a huge loss for so many people: his parents (Scott's father, Lee, was a former Indy car driver himself), his friends all over the country, his buddies at Team Menard, and especially his wife, Becky, and their young daughter, Carly. He was just thirty-seven years old, and he should have had plenty of racing, and plenty of life, ahead of him. The whole thing was just so sad.

But I took comfort from this: Scotty's last-minute run for the pole had him on top of the world. He wanted to be the fastest guy in the place, and, damn it, he was.

Anything I went through that month was obviously minor compared to what the Brayton family had to endure. Still, May of 1996 was a traumatic time for me.

May 1996 should have been an enjoyable time for me. Instead, it was an emotional roller coaster. (IMS/IRL © 1996 Jim Haines)

Before we lost Scotty, he was going to be on the pole with me in the middle of the front row. I took a lot of comfort from knowing I'd have him there. I had planned to ask him how he thought we ought to conduct the start, and how to approach the 500 from a strategic point of view. After his crash, I had the strange feeling that I'd be alone out there, especially in those early laps. On top of that, I inherited the pole position, which is a huge responsibility.

I felt a combination of emotions: confidence one minute, anxiety the next.

LARRY CURRY: "Think about it. Tony comes into that race as this heralded rookie who'd had a great performance at Orlando, who had dominated Phoenix until he broke. Now he loses Scotty, a guy he had a lot of respect for, and who had a lot of respect for him. The harsh reality started to set in, I think. I mean, we're loading up buses to go up to a funeral, and we're dealing with that, and at the same time here's Tony, going into that race as maybe the guy to beat if his car runs all day. It was a roller coaster for him."

A lot had changed on the personal side, too. Amanda and I had split up after the IRL opener at Orlando, and I was dating another Indiana girl, Krista Dwyer. We ended up staying together for several years, and, considering all the stuff I put her through that May, that's almost surprising. It couldn't have been a very smooth road.

Even before Scotty's accident, I was dealing with a huge lifestyle change. Racing at Indianapolis had turned me into something of a celebrity. Before May of '96, I could sit at McDonald's or walk around at the mall, and it was almost guaranteed that nobody would recognize me. If anybody did, it would be a hard-core fan: "Hey, man, don't you race midgets with USAC?" But in that one month, things changed. Everywhere I went, there was somebody wanting to talk, somebody wanting an autograph.

Obviously, I went through an even bigger wave of that later, once I got to Winston Cup, but in 1996 it was all very new, very *strange*. It was one more thing to get used to, one more change in my life.

When I first showed up at the Speedway in the beginning of May, everybody was full of advice about how I ought to handle the place. They talked to me about the speeds, about the proper lines, about the wind and the traffic and a dozen other things I'd face out there. What they all failed to mention was that the really overwhelming stuff happens when you're *out* of the car.

There isn't a race morning anywhere like Indianapolis. On one hand, you feel a sense of calm: after being there for most of the month, you're finally going to do what you went there to do. On the other hand, everything that's going on around you reminds you that you *can't* be calm, because, after all, this is the Indy 500.

Everybody with a media pass stops by your garage to ask for one last interview. That's one of the funny things about Indianapolis: from the moment the track opens, you answer so many questions that you can't imagine there's anything left to say by race day. And yet that's when everybody wants to talk the most, especially if you're one of the fast guys. The TV people want to know how you slept last night; the newspaper guys want to know what you had for breakfast; the radio guy wants to know what kind of butterflies you're feeling.

But it's when you walk out to the grid that the size of the event hits you for real. The Indy 500 is the largest single-day sporting event in the world; they jam four hundred thousand people into the Speedway, and there's a constant hum of noise. Every now and then, you hear some-

body call your name. That happens at every track, but the first time you hear something like, "Go get 'em, Tony," on the starting grid at Indianapolis, *that's* cool.

Then there are the pre-race festivities: the playing of "Taps" in honor of Memorial Day, Jim Nabors singing "Indiana." It's impossible not to be distracted by all of that. As focused as I was, I still felt chills when I heard that opening line: "Back home again . . ."

We had everybody covered in the early stages of the '96 Indy 500, leading the first round of pit stops. In the end, though, a pop-off valve broke and put us out of the race. (IMS/IRL © 1996 Jim Haines)

Larry Curry did a great job of keeping me steady. Just before we fired the engine, he leaned close and said, "Just treat today like another practice session," and that was exactly the right thing to say. It reminded me that we'd been fast all month, and that the important thing was to just stay cool, stay smooth.

Which is what I did. I got a great jump, and led the first lap; in fact, I led right up until my first pit stop on lap 32, which set a new Indy record for most consecutive laps led at the start by a rookie. Once all of the cars cycled through their stops, we were back up front for another thirteen laps. Unfortunately, that was all the glory we got; the engine started losing power—a pop-off valve on the turbocharger was going bad—and finally broke after eighty-one laps. We finished twenty-fourth.

It was a tough way to end the month, but there was a lot to feel good about, too. Leading that race was great for me, and great for grassroots racers and fans. It had been the first time in years that a guy straight off the dirt tracks went to the Speedway with a realistic shot to win, and that had a lot of people excited about Indy car racing again.

JACK HEWITT: "I told Tony, 'You say that I'm your hero, but you've got to realize something: you've opened up the eyes of everybody who can now see what these sprint and midget drivers can do. You've made it possible for me to maybe run the Indianapolis 500.' And I meant that."

On the Monday night after the race, at the formal awards dinner, I was named the Indianapolis 500 Rookie of the Year.

After Indy, I signed a new contract keeping me at Team Menard through the end of '97. And I was happy to do that, because the team's mind-set at the time was just like mine: they wanted to win, and they were dedicated to doing whatever it took to achieve that. Sure, our budget enabled us to do things most of the other teams couldn't, but we also worked their brains out.

For example, we tested like crazy in the two months between Indianapolis and the next IRL race at Loudon, New Hampshire. We devoted ourselves to learning everything we could about our cars, and about the tracks, too.

We went out to Las Vegas in the dead of summer in 1996 to test at the new speedway there. In fact, I was the first guy to turn a lap there in a race car, which was neat. It was ungodly hot, as you might expect, because the track is on the edge of the desert. But the heat didn't stop us; we simply adjusted our schedule. We'd start running at six o'clock in the morning and quit at noon, when the sun grew unbearable. It was torture, but no one complained. The name of the game was to come up with the fastest car, and we all knew that.

LARRY CURRY: "Tony was ideal to test with, because he did what you asked him to do and his feedback was very good. He just had a really good feel for those cars."

All that testing made our cars better, made me better, made our *team* better. The only thing it didn't seem to improve was our reliability. That issue popped up again at New Hampshire, where we suffered one of the toughest losses I've ever dealt with.

For some reason, I didn't qualify well; we started seventh. But once the race started, it was like Orlando all over again: the field just backed up to me. I took the lead on lap 14, and checked out. The only thing that slowed me down was lapping other cars, and that didn't slow me down much.

> **LARRY CURRY:** "Tony was phenomenal, especially in traffic. He'd pull up next to another car, and you could actually see the other guy react, like, 'What are you doing there?' They just didn't expect him to be there. At New Hampshire, he made 'em all look stupid."

The race was two hundred laps long, and by halfway we were so dominant that it was a joke. Larry kept calling me on the radio, saying, "Take it easy, take it easy," and yet every time I backed off my pace, my rhythm would smooth out and we'd go even faster. My fastest lap of the day came on lap 179, and the tires had thirty-odd laps on 'em at that point. There was nobody—I mean nobody—in the same league.

I was up by two full laps, and within five seconds of putting the second-place car down three laps, when we broke another crank trigger on lap 182.

In case I haven't made myself clear, 1996 was getting kind of frustrating.

I don't care what level of racing we're talking about, the name of the game is winning. Every year since I'd started, I had put up better numbers than the season before, and after awhile you start using those numbers to judge your progress. Well, in '96 I couldn't see that progress, and it bothered me a little bit.

Today, it's easy to put it all in perspective; I had plenty of dues to pay in both stock cars and Indy cars. But at the time, I was getting awfully sick of losing.

This is a fickle sport, a fickle business. One day you're the hot young guy, and six months later everybody's looking right past you, at the *next* hot young guy. It's not that you've changed one bit as a driver; if anything, you may have gotten better in that six months. But if you're not putting up the numbers, you're afraid nobody else can see it.

That's the way I was feeling one Monday morning in the summer of '96. I had been off all weekend, running an IRL car or a Silver Crown car or who knows what, and the telephone woke me.

A buddy of mine said, "Hey, that's pretty neat how Darrell Waltrip wants you to drive his car."

I said, "What do you mean?"

"That's what Darrell said on TV the other day."

The guy explained that Waltrip had been the color commentator on a Busch race, and mentioned that of all the young drivers he had seen lately, I was the one he'd hire to drive for him. I saw a replay of that race later on, and sure enough, there was DW, saying all these nice things about me.

That was a bigger boost to me than anybody could have known, surely bigger than Darrell intended, and it couldn't have come at a better point. Every time I looked at my stats that season, I wanted to throw up. We had lousy numbers in the Busch car, lousy numbers in the Indy car; even our good days seemed to end up bad. It was reassuring to know that there were still people out there—and highly respected people, like Darrell Waltrip—who noticed that I was doing a good job.

When you're not winning, you take inspiration where you can get it.

My 1996 season came to a crashing halt in the middle of September, in the IRL finale at Las Vegas. I was running second when the inside of my right rear tire blew out. My car did a 180-degree spin through turn one, and I smacked the concrete wall at about 220 miles per hour. I had never hit anything so hard in my life, and I hope I don't ever hit anything that hard again.

> **PAM BOAS:** "I was way up in the grandstands, and I really didn't get too excited when it happened. To me it didn't look that bad, and Nelson had always conditioned me never to get hyper until you assess the situation. But it seemed to take them forever to get Tony out of the car, and that's when I decided I'd better go to the infield to see what was going on. When I finally got [into the track hospital] to see him, he said, 'It hurts, Mom.'"

This was one of those solid hits, flat on the side of the car, where it feels like the brunt of the impact goes right through you. My entire left side was beaten up: I had a broken collarbone, a fractured pelvis, a fractured hip, and a cracked scapula. I hadn't ever felt that kind of pain in my life.

And yet all I could think was, Man, how long before this *mess* heals up?

> **PAM BOAS:** "It never entered my mind that he might not want to race again. I know Tony too well. It would take something huge to keep him out of a race car, and to him this wasn't anything huge. It was huge to me, but not to him."

I was in the hospital in Las Vegas for just under a week, and then I got flown back to Indianapolis and spent another week at Methodist Hospital, the best place in the world if you're a busted-up race driver. The staff there has studied plenty of racing injuries, so they're very thorough about getting everything patched up the right way. Best of all, those folks know how a driver's mind works; the average guy might milk an injury like a broken pelvis because he's not eager to get back to his nine-to-five job, but a racer wants to get back to work as soon as possible.

Still, there's no such thing as good hospital time; when they released me from Methodist, I was ready to go. The only problem was, my apartment was on the third floor, and I wasn't exactly in top stair-climbing form. I solved that dilemma by moving into my mom's house for a couple months. It was a great place to recover, because not even the best nurse in the world will give you the kind of attention your mom will.

> **PAM BOAS:** "He was anxious, he was impatient, he was hurting. Tony can't stand not being well; he just can't handle that. To keep him busy, we played a lot of games. But finally, he just needed out of there. He needed to be home again."

When I got back to my apartment, I was antsy for several days. I couldn't even drive a street car; I didn't have enough mobility in my shoulders and arms, and I couldn't hold myself up under even the slightest little cornering force.

One day, just to get out for a while, I went with my girlfriend Krista to an indoor go-kart track owned by Stefan Johansson, the ex–Formula One driver. It's on the west side of Indy, and it's always been a magnet for the racing crowd in that area. The karts are fast, and the layout is tricky enough to be a lot of fun. I watched some guys buzz around there, and I started thinking that between the reclined seating position and the fact that those karts don't require a whole lot of steering input, I might be able to drive one.

I said to Krista, "I think I'm going to take a few laps." She told me I was crazy, but I promised I'd take it easy, and that I'd stop if I had any pain. I did four or five laps, just feeling things out. There was *some* pain, but not enough to discourage me. It was a good pain, like exercise pain.

I started my very own rehab program that day at Stefan Johansson's.

A friend of mine named Sean Britz was the general manager of the place, and he was a tremendous help to me. The track didn't open to the public until eleven o'clock in the morning, but Sean's shift began a lot earlier. Every day, he'd come by my apartment at eight, help me down two flights of stairs, and drive me to the track. Then he'd sit me down in a kart, and I'd be on my way.

At first, I could only stand five hard minutes at a time. In a few days, it was ten. After a couple of weeks, I was putting in two and a half hours on those karts, from eight-thirty in the morning until the place opened. It was absolutely the best therapy I could have had, physically and mentally.

> **PAM BOAS:** "I could see it: getting into those go-karts changed his whole world again."

As a side benefit, I also became the fastest gun in town when it came to go-karts. For a long time, I had the track record at Johansson's. I bet I could go there today and, with a little bit of practice, whip anybody in the joint.

The 1996–97 off-season was the beginning of the end for my relationship with Ranier Racing. Harry was anxious to move our team up from the Busch Series to Winston Cup; he kept insisting we were ready, and I kept insisting we weren't. The way I saw it, if you aren't running up front at one level, you have absolutely no business graduating to the next level. As a group, we had not passed that test in the Busch Series.

The easy thing for me to do—and the thing a lot of other young drivers might have done—would have been to go along with Harry. Everybody wants to be a Winston Cup driver, and I did, too. I just didn't believe I had earned the right to be one yet.

LARRY CURRY: "As good as he was, Tony was unsure of whether he was ready to go to Winston Cup."

I'll admit it: my reluctance to step up to Cup was based on fear. To be exact, a fear of looking bad, and what that might do to my career. I had seen it happen to Steve Kinser in 1995. Steve is one of the greatest sprint car drivers of all time; he had won fourteen championships with the World of Outlaws. But when he decided to try Winston Cup racing, everything went wrong. He signed with a struggling team, missed qualifying for a few races, and got labeled as a guy who couldn't drive a stock car. In Steve's case it wasn't the end of the world; he just packed up his helmet bag, went back to sprint cars, and became a champion again. His life went on, and nobody who knows anything about racing thinks any less of Kinser because of that one stumble. But I wasn't Steve Kinser. I was a kid trying to climb the ladder. If I jumped to Winston Cup and had an experience similar to his, my career might suffer permanent damage.

At that point, I was twenty-five years old. I knew I had lots of time ahead of me, so I wasn't in any hurry. I wanted to go Cup racing, sure, but I wanted to do it with the right team. And, with no disrespect to anybody connected with Ranier's operation, that just *wasn't* the right team, at least not yet. To me, the smart play was to spend another year in the Busch Series, getting both the organization and the driver up to speed. But Harry didn't want any part of that. He wanted to run a Winston Cup team, and that was that.

All this put me in a tough spot, professionally and emotionally. The Raniers had worked hard to reestablish themselves in the sport, and I

didn't want to do anything to hurt them. At the same time, I had worked awfully hard, too, building whatever reputation I had. I didn't want their decision to hurt me, either.

LORIN RANIER: "Tony always said that he had spent his whole life trying to get into the right position in racing, and he didn't want to do anything that might set him back. I can't blame him for that. When it comes down to it, business is business, and his business is holding that steering wheel. I understand it now better than I did at the time."

It was a very uneasy winter. Harry stuck to his guns, and I stuck to mine. When the 1997 NASCAR season opened, the Raniers were at Daytona with their Winston Cup car, but they had somebody else driving it.

Luckily for me, there were other stock car options presenting themselves. The most interesting one had kind of a strange beginning. After my Las Vegas crash, the doctors had me on some prescription painkillers while I rested at my mom's house. I don't handle medication too well, so I was feeling kind of slaphappy. One day the phone rang, and my mom came into the room and said, "It's Joe Gibbs."

Now, a couple of my buddies had been calling me on a pretty regular basis, using every fake name they could think of, so I never even considered that it might actually be Joe Gibbs. Obviously, I knew that Joe had a race team, but we didn't exactly travel in the same circles.

I took the phone, and said something like, "Hey, Joe, what's up?"

This voice said, "Hi, Tony. How are you feeling?"

As groggy as I was, I recognized that it wasn't one of my pals after all; it really *was* Joe Gibbs. I was embarrassed about how casually I had greeted him, but Joe didn't seem offended, and we had a nice chat. He asked how my injuries were coming along, and we talked racing a little bit. He wanted to know if I was happy in the situation I was in, and I told him, yeah, I *was* happy; my IRL program was solid, and at that point I was still under the impression that the Raniers and I would be back for another season in the Busch Series, where I felt like we had a great chance to do well. Joe listened to all that, and then he said, "Well, if anything ever changes, please be sure to give me a call. I'd like to talk to you again."

I thought that was pretty cool. I mean, Joe's team had already won a Daytona 500 with Dale Jarrett, and was turning into a real force in the Winston Cup series with Bobby Labonte driving. The fact that he had even the slightest knowledge of me was a nice surprise. But what amazed me most about Joe's call was that very few people knew where I was staying, and only my closest friends had my mom's telephone number. To this day, I don't know exactly how Joe got in touch with me.

Several months later, in March of 1997, I flew to Phoenix for an IRL race. By this point the Raniers were doing their Winston Cup deal, and my NASCAR plans were up in the air. I checked into my motel room, threw my bags on the bed, and the phone rang. It was Joe Gibbs.

That night, Joe laid out the reasons for his interest in me. He planned to expand his Winston Cup operation to include a second team with an up-and-coming driver, but he wanted to do it gradually: by starting that driver in the Busch Series in '97, easing him into a Cup car with a solid testing program, and then attacking the Winston Cup series when the guy was ready. Joe said that in the discussions he'd had with his key people, including Bobby Labonte and his crew chief, Jimmy Makar, I had gotten the nomination.

JIMMY MAKAR: "We didn't just want a second driver. We wanted somebody who could push Bobby, who could challenge Bobby, who could elevate this team to another level. And as we looked at the different people who were available, we kept coming back to Tony."

BOBBY LABONTE: "We tried to figure out the pros and cons of every driver out there, and Tony's name kept coming up to the top of the list. We had all seen what he'd done in the IRL, and what he had done in all the open-wheel divisions on asphalt and dirt. We just kept coming back to his name, even prior to any of us meeting him or speaking to him. Then it was Joe's job to recruit him."

My first thought after I hung up the phone was obvious: I was honored to hear that those people thought so highly of me.

My second thought was, How in the world does Joe Gibbs keep finding me? That question persisted when Joe called me a few more times, catching up with me in the craziest places. I was like, Does this guy have somebody tailing me, or what?

> **JOE GIBBS:** "Tony didn't know this, but before long I had everybody's phone number: his home number, his girlfriend's number, his mom's number, his dad's number. I mean, I had more phone numbers for that guy! When I wanted to talk to him, I'd just start checking them off. That was part of my football background coming in; I had gotten used to chasing down young players, staying after them and not giving up."

The Gibbs organization had a lot to offer: a great staff, plenty of resources, a long-term plan, and, best of all, an understanding that a move like the one they had in mind would require a lot of patience. That was the flip side of what went on with Ranier's team, where there was this big rush to be in Winston Cup no matter what the odds were.

If selling me on his program was Joe's objective, he succeeded. The problem was, I was still legally bound to Ranier. Thankfully, that detail worked itself out without much input from me. After some negotiating, Joe bought my contract from Harry.

It ended up being the right move for me, for sure. Obviously, the Gibbs situation has been great, and Harry's team never really found its footing. By the end of 1997, he was out of Winston Cup racing.

Both of the Raniers, Harry and Lorin, were unhappy with me for a while, which I guess was inevitable. Anytime you develop personal relationships with your business partners, those friendships are bound to suffer if the business arrangement dissolves.

> **LORIN RANIER:** "That was a tough time for Tony and me. Not only were we involved in the same team, but we had become good friends; we'd done everything together. There was a period of

> time, probably from April of '97 when we finalized things with
> Joe right up until about October of '97, when Tony and I didn't
> talk much."

Harry and I patched things up later on, and I'm glad we did, because he passed away in 1999. That saddened me, because no matter what sort of disagreements we had, he provided me with my first opportunity to go NASCAR racing, so I'll always be grateful to him. And Lorin and I, we're good friends again. We hang out quite a bit, and in a lot of ways we're the same two pals we were in 1994 and '95. You know, before business got in the way.

Between our late start with the Gibbs team and the fact that my priority in '97 was the Indy Racing League, I only did five Busch races that year: Indianapolis Raceway Park, Richmond, Charlotte, and the last two events of the season at Rockingham and Homestead. I'm not sure we turned a lot of heads, because it's hard to make a huge impression on any series when you only drop in occasionally. But there were some bright spots: we qualified second at Rockingham, seventh at IRP, eighth at Richmond; at Charlotte, we started thirteenth, ran down the front group, stayed with them all day, and finished third. I could certainly see some potential there.

The best part was, the team kept telling me not to worry about stats; the idea, they said, was to build something for the future, to look at the big picture. I liked that.

> **BOBBY LABONTE:** "We had a goal in mind, so we didn't really pay much attention to the actual results. We paid attention to how we were coming along with this plan."

Just like in 1996, anytime I wanted to feel like a hero in '97, all I had to do was step into my Indy car. Right from the first practice session at the opening race, we were fast. We won the pole at Disney World, and we were on our way to winning the race when, on lap 146 of the scheduled 200, an oil line broke and slicked up my right-rear tire. I did a half-spin out of the final corner, barely nicking the wall. The crazy thing was, just after the yellow flag waved for me, it poured down rain and the race was halted. If the rain had come two minutes earlier, we'd have won. Instead we were scored tenth.

Still, it was a satisfying day for me personally. See, in the '96 IRL season, a lot of people gave all the credit for my speed to our car, specifically the Menard V6. Now, that was a hell of an engine, and I was glad to have it. But nobody ever mentioned that I was usually quicker than my teammates, who had the same stuff. All I ever heard was that I had the best car, the best engine.

Well, all that bullshit went out the window at Orlando in '97. Under the new Indy Racing League rules, there were only two chassis brands allowed, the Dallara and the G Force, and two engines, the Oldsmobile Aurora and the Nissan Infiniti. Our car was a G Force/Aurora. There were a bunch of Aurora-powered G Forces in that race, and we were quicker than any of them. Quicker by a lot.

We had started out that winter with the same blank sheet of paper everybody else had. No one could say I was relying on Cheever's notes or Scott Brayton's notes or *any* notes other than the ones Larry Curry and I came up with. I took a lot of pride in that: if we had an advantage, it was an advantage I had helped us acquire.

> **LARRY CURRY:** "Tony wanted to know everything. He wanted to know about the aerodynamics of the car, wanted to know about this, wanted to know about that. I would explain these things to him, and explain how any changes we made would affect the car. The more I did that, and the more he saw that the effects were what I told him they would be, here came his confidence. That gave him the feeling that he could take that car and drive it anywhere he wanted to put it. And, boy, he did that."

We brought that same advantage to Phoenix, but we managed to lose again. We found ourselves pitting on a different sequence from the other lead-lap cars, and at the end of the day I had to chase down Jim Guthrie, a real underdog who had a big margin. In fairness to Guthrie, I had my shot; there was a restart with ten laps to go, and he beat me fair and square. But we had a great car again, and, even if I wasn't satisfied with the finish, I was satisfied with the way I drove it.

Orlando and Phoenix were similar that way: we didn't win, but it was enjoyable to have a car so good that I could just drive the hell out of it.

Indianapolis was enjoyable in 1997, too. We didn't have the best car there, but we were still very competitive. I qualified second to Arie Luyendyk and led the most laps, but in the second half of the race the speed just wasn't there. Still, I found myself locked in a great five-way battle with Luyendyk, Jeff Ward, Buddy Lazier, and Scott Goodyear that seemed to last forever. At lap 190, just ten to go, the order was Jeff, Scott, me, Arie, and Buddy, and the caution was out. Ward and I both needed fuel, and when we pitted I think we both figured we'd have time to get back to the front. Unfortunately, another quick yellow for debris cost us critical catch-up time. On lap 198, I was fourth behind Luyendyk, Goodyear, and Ward, and I was gassing it hard, probably *too* hard. I brushed the wall out of turn four, and Lazier got by me. At the checkered flag, I was fifth.

I had a big grin on my face when I got out of the car. I told the reporters, "I don't mean to sound happy about finishing fifth, but that was one of the most fun races I've ever had."

The next event, at Texas, was another fun one, right up until the last couple of minutes. We were cruising around, leading again, when the engine blew up and spun me into the fence with the white flag waving.

You might not recall that race, but you probably remember victory lane. A. J. Foyt was celebrating the win with his new driver, my midget buddy Billy Boat, when Luyendyk walked in and protested that the scoring had been wrong, and that *he* had won. I didn't see how that could be, because in the closing stages my guys assured me that Arie was a couple laps down, and I actually let him pass me. Anyway, Foyt gave Arie a backhand slap for interrupting his party, and that made all the sports shows. But it turned out Luyendyk was right: somehow, the electronic scoring system failed to register two of his laps, and Arie had actually beaten Boat.

I'm still not sure where I stood in relation to Arie, but in hindsight

it's probably a good thing my engine broke. If I found out later that I had moved over and given him the lead instead of just handing him back a lap, I'd have slapped somebody, too.

Texas was the ninth race of my IRL career, and I had been a factor in every one. I'd started on the pole four times, I'd led every race but one— in fact, I'd led more total laps than anybody—and I'd been involved in some of the league's most exciting finishes. I had done everything but win.

Which, come to think of it, is like saying I hadn't done a damn thing.

Well, on June 29, 1997, we finally did something in the Indy Racing League. We went to the new Pikes Peak International Raceway outside Colorado Springs, and won ourselves a race.

For a while, it felt like every other Indy car race I'd run: we started outside the front row, led early, and got into a really nice rhythm. Pikes Peak tends to get slippery when it's hot, and it was really hot that day, but my car slipped and slid just a little bit less than everybody else's, and we kept pulling away.

Still, the racing gods couldn't let us have our first win without the usual Team Menard drama. We had to go through two

After a year and a half of frustration, I won my first IRL race at Pikes Peak International Raceway in June of '97. I was more relieved than happy, I think. (IMS/IRL © 1997 Jim Haines)

restarts in the last fifteen laps, the final one with just three to go. Then, as we started that final sprint to the checkers, Stephan Gregoire came out of nowhere and made a real run at the lead, but I held him off.

When I finally got that checkered flag, I felt this strange combination of happiness and relief. When you have as many near misses as we had with that team, you're sure the bad luck has to run out sometime, but in the back of your mind you're thinking, What if it doesn't?

At Colorado Springs, the bad luck ran out.

It was my first Indy car win, and John Menard's, too. We've had our problems in the years since that day, but I'm still proud to have been the first Team Menard driver to get to victory lane.

The next two races were kind of puzzling for us. At the first-ever IRL visit to Charlotte, we qualified on the pole with a lap of 217.164 miles per hour, which had everybody buzzing because the track record for Winston Cup cars was only 185.759. We dominated the first part of the race, but faded to seventh at the finish. Then, at New Hampshire, where we had been so fast the previous summer, I had the single worst race I'd ever had in an Indy car: we qualified fourteenth, fought like hell all day just to edge into the top ten, then blew an engine.

The only upshot was that our good finishes early in the year, coupled with that Pikes Peak win, had put us into the points lead by just a slim margin over Davey Hamilton, who was doing a great job with A. J. Foyt's team.

To me, it was perfect that the fight for the 1997 Indy Racing League title came down to me and Hamilton. The two of us had been the kind of "no-name" guys a lot of folks snickered about in '96 when they bad-mouthed the IRL. Well, maybe we were unknown to those CART fans who were raised on road racing, but Davey and I had raced two and three nights a week for years, in front of thousands of people each time. I guarantee you, more people watched us race in person before we got to the IRL than had watched Michael Andretti or Paul Tracy before they got to CART.

By the autumn of 1997, Davey and I had shown that we could handle any challenge an Indy car gave us. And I ought to throw Billy Boat in there, too, because straight out of midgets he'd run seventh at Indianapolis and second at both Texas and Charlotte in Foyt's other car.

BILLY BOAT: "I think all three of us had established that we had what it took to get the job done in Indy cars. We were for real; we could race, we could be competitive, and we could win. We couldn't come in and buy rides, but we had worked our way into that series."

CHRIS ECONOMAKI, editor emeritus, *National Speed Sport News:* "It was terrific to see those guys doing so well. You know, many years ago, the Indianapolis Motor Speedway had special parking areas for buses which brought in fans from short tracks all over the country. I mean, when Mario Andretti first arrived, there were busloads of fans coming in from Pennsylvania! I think Tony George understood that when he created the IRL."

Davey Hamilton and I always had a lot of respect for each other, going all the way back to 1993, when we shared the front row in the Copper Classic. I think each of us had developed a real appreciation for the other guy's talent, and the hardest part about wanting to win the championship so badly was that it would mean beating another guy who deserved that same title.

DAVEY HAMILTON: "Tony and I developed a great relationship that year. We were each there to do a job and beat each other, but off the track we didn't dwell on racing or act like there was a big rivalry. We'd just laugh and joke the way friends do. Before that last race, we did a lot of promotional stuff for the Indy Racing League; I flew to Indianapolis and we did some things there, and when we got to Vegas we posed together for photos with the championship trophy. I think we were both enjoying that moment, two short-track guys racing each other for that title."

Going into Las Vegas, I led the standings by just ten points. Larry Curry and I figured out all the scenarios: if Davey won the race, I needed to finish eighth or better; if he ended up second or worse, a ninth-place run would win the title for us. I'm sure A.J. and Davey were doing the same sort of equations.

As it turned out, we all could have put away our calculators, because neither one of us got anywhere close to victory lane. My car pushed all night long, and I brushed the wall twice; Davey's car was loose, and he *almost* hit the wall twice. It was kind of ironic: here we were, each of us battling for the right to call himself a champion, and we were riding around in the middle of the pack, hanging on for dear life.

> **DAVEY HAMILTON:** "It was like neither one of us wanted to win the title. I was right behind Tony when he hit the wall out of turn two, and I was sitting there saying, 'Buddy, I'm not wishing you any bad luck, but I need all the help I can get right now.' Because, man, I was running terrible, too."

I'm sure there were people who thought we were just riding around, being careful, collecting points, but I guarantee you I never had a scarier ride in an Indy car. And I watched Davey have enough close calls to know that he felt the same way.

I finished eleventh, an embarrassing four laps down. Davey's junk car was better than my junk car, but he only managed to get to seventh, not far enough ahead to overcome our margin in the points.

Larry Curry told me on the radio that I was the Indy Racing League champion. I couldn't wait to get back to pit road, so I could celebrate with him and the rest of the team. But even more than that, I wanted to climb out of that evil race car.

It had been a heck of a season, and a heck of a

In the final race of the 1997 season, we clinched the Indy Racing League championship at Las Vegas. (IMS/IRL © 1997 Jim Haines)

title fight. I had said before the race that no matter who won, it wasn't going to impact my friendship with Davey. It didn't that night, and it still hasn't.

> **DAVEY HAMILTON:** "I still have special memories of that weekend. You know, I really wanted to win that thing, but if I had to lose, there was nobody I'd rather lose to than Tony. He's a friend, so I was happy for him."

That championship closed out an amazing four-year stretch for me. Between 1994 and '97, I had won four USAC championships, competed in my first Indianapolis 500, driven my first race at Daytona, and won an Indy Racing League title. It had been one incredible ride.

Everything had changed.

Well, almost everything.

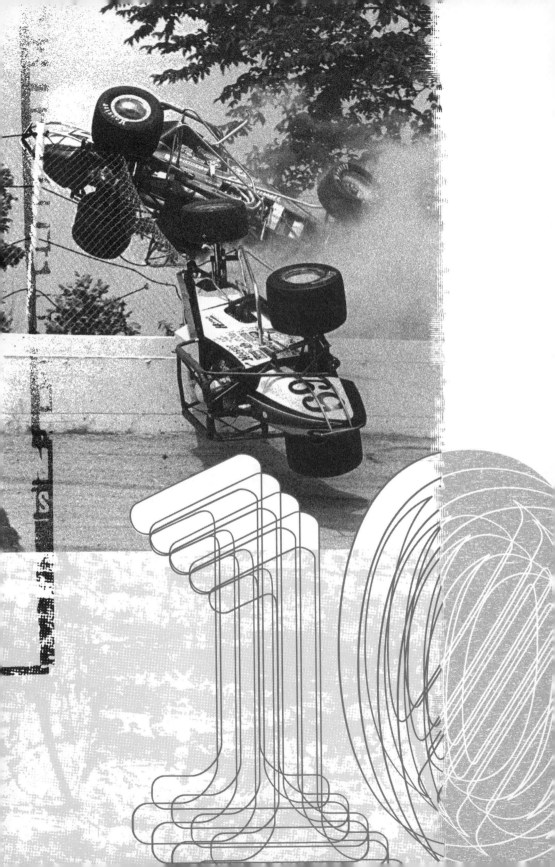

TEN NEW BLOOD FROM AN OLD SCHOOL

ONE THING THAT DIDN'T CHANGE WAS THAT, EVEN AS MY INDY CAR AND stock car schedules got busier, I kept showing up at the short tracks whenever I could. Most of the time I brought my helmet bag with me.

That meant I got this question a lot: "What are *you* doing here?"

Actually, that's not quite right. It was more like, "What are you doing *here*?"

In other words, why was I fooling around on the bullrings now that I had made it *out* of the bullrings?

My answer was always the same: I'm a race driver. I drive race cars. Stock cars and Indy cars aren't the only race cars on earth. And, unless I'm mistaken, there's a race here tonight.

I've never been able to figure out why people found that so difficult to understand. I mean, racing was never just a *job* for me; it was the thing I loved to do most. Was I supposed to love it less just because I had moved up the ladder?

What did they want me to do in my spare time, play tennis?

And, don't forget, I had a *lot* of spare time, particularly in 1996. That year, I ran only five IRL events and nine Busch Series races. Fourteen races in a season didn't add up to enough seat time for me to stay happy; I'd have felt like I was wasting my time just hanging around the rest of the year.

Something I did cut out of my schedule: racing sprint cars at places like Salem, where in 1992 I had flipped Steve Chrisman's car right out of the track. (© John Mahoney)

A lot of midget fans thought it was pretty cool that I kept running the short tracks after I'd made it to Indy and Daytona. For me, it just felt natural. (© John Mahoney)

So I didn't hang around. I raced. In 1996 and '97, I drove TQs, midgets, Silver Crown cars, sprint cars, dirt late models, and pavement modifieds. Every weekend, I was sitting in *something*.

I had a lot of people tell me that I was wasting my time, because none of that stuff was going to make me a better Indy car driver or a better NASCAR driver. They might have been half right about that, because there's not a lot of information that translates from, say, a dirt midget to a Busch Series car. But what *does* translate is the intensity you only get from racing often, and that was important to me.

I always felt that the extra stuff I've done has helped keep me sharp. In the 1960s and '70s, guys like Foyt, Parnelli Jones, and Bobby Allison operated under that same theory, running just about every race they could, and those guys didn't get to be champions by being stupid. You race your best when you're *ready* to race, and I was always ready.

PARNELLI JONES: "The thing about Tony is that because of all the racing he's done, he's been able to stay so fine-tuned. I remember when I was doing the same thing. We'd go to a track and I'd be quick right away, and it was just because I was always geared up to race. I believe racing is like anything else: if you do it on a day-to-day basis, you're bound to be better than the guy who isn't."

BOBBY ALLISON: "For me, it was important to keep running those short-track races because it was a way to continue to hone my personal skills. I felt like that was really, really valuable. The way I looked at it, to push a car to its limit as often as possible—and to constantly have to recognize that limit—kept me on top of my game. It absolutely helps you stay keen, right on that edge. And, let's face it, you have to be right on that edge if you're going to be at your best."

I'll give you an example: when I went to Orlando in January of '96 for my IRL test with Team Menard, I didn't feel the least bit rusty because I'd been racing midgets all winter in Australia. I didn't have to shake off all the cobwebs that build up when you're inactive. Some of the other drivers testing that week hadn't been behind the wheel since the previous autumn. They might have kept themselves physically fit during the layoff, but they hadn't been doing the kind of workouts I had.

Did that make me more ready than they were? I can't say that for certain, but I sure outran a bunch of them.

BOBBY ALLISON: "If a baseball pitcher decided, 'Well, I'm going to sit around for a couple months, and then I'm going to go out and pitch this real important game against our number-one rival,' he would be so rusty that the ball would never find home plate. He didn't lose his talent, he just didn't practice it enough. It's like, nobody ever forgets how to ride a bicycle, but you're definitely going to ride better if you do it frequently."

And another thing: the idea of me doing all this outside racing wasn't anything new. I had *always* run every race I could, right from the time I found car owners willing to hire me.

Throughout my open-wheel career I was primarily a USAC racer, but I also ran a ton of non-USAC races. Every January I'd line up a ride for the Chili Bowl, the big indoor midget race in Tulsa. Every August I'd head out to Kansas for the Midget Nationals at the Belleville High

Banks. And on any open Sunday you could find me up at Sun Prairie, Wisconsin, one of the neatest midget tracks in the country.

I'll tell you a story that shows how eager I was to race. In 1995, I had a lot on my plate, running midgets, sprints, and Silver Crown cars. There was a national midget race set for the first Saturday in May at Indianapolis Raceway Park, and I was going to run it for Ralph Potter. My old landlord Larry Martz was going to enter his new car in that same event, with a local kid named Matt Lux driving. Well, I stopped to visit the Martzes on Thursday, and somebody mentioned that there was a USAC regional event on Friday at the Indianapolis Speedrome.

I said, "Hey, Larry, why don't I run that race in your car?"

He was absolutely against the idea, because he had put a lot of effort into getting ready for Raceway Park. What happened next, though, was a classic case of a driver twisting a car owner's arm to go racing.

Literally.

> **LARRY MARTZ:** "I had been working on the car for quite a while, preparing it for IRP, and now here's Tony, saying, 'Come on, why don't we run the Speedrome tomorrow?' We kidded back and forth, but I was absolutely not going to budge. So Tony comes up with this idea: 'Let's arm wrestle.' If he wins we go to the Speedrome, and if I win we don't. We're going to go two out of three. Now, Tony's left-handed and I'm right-handed. We go left-handed first, and he beats me. Then we go right-handed, and I beat him. We decide to flip a coin to see which way to go the third time; heads we go left-handed, tails we go right. Well, the coin goes up in the air, comes down on the floor, rolls out of the kitchen and makes a right turn, where nobody can see it. My son Tate goes after it, finds the coin, and comes running back into the room: 'It's heads, it's heads!' So we arm-wrestle left-handed, and Tony beats me, and I tell him, 'Okay, a deal is a deal. We're going to the Speedrome tomorrow night.'"

What makes that such a good story is that we absolutely spanked 'em at the Speedrome. After working so hard to get that midget just right for IRP, Larry threw his best bullring setup at it, and that thing was perfect. We won the feature by half a lap.

> **LARRY MARTZ:** "The funniest thing is, we were sitting at the kitchen table a year later, retelling that story, and Tate said, 'You know something, Dad? I lied. It was really tails!' He was like Tony: he wanted to go race at the Speedrome."

It just made sense to me to run that race. I didn't have anything else to do that Friday night, and Larry had a great car.

The same type of thing happened later that year, on the night Glen Niebel and I clinched the Silver Crown championship at Sacramento. The preliminary event was a USAC Western States midget race, and Steve Lewis and Bob East said they'd bring a car out there if I wanted to run it. So instead of sitting around all night, worrying about the Silver Crown points, I ran that midget show. And won it.

> **PARNELLI JONES:** "When you're a good young race driver, like Tony is, you just want to do everything."

For a long time, the only major-league driver who still made a habit of moonlighting on the short tracks was Kenny Schrader. I had even raced against Kenny a few times myself in the early nineties, in indoor midget races. He was a guy who had won at the Winston Cup level, and I thought it was cool that he still enjoyed going back and racing the kinds of cars he had grown up in.

> **KEN SCHRADER,** USAC champion and NASCAR Winston Cup veteran: "Let's say you like to play golf with your buddies on weekends, and all of a sudden, boom, you're on the PGA Tour. Well, wouldn't you still like to play golf with your buddies sometimes?"

As cool as I thought it was for Schrader to do that, I could imagine how it must have been back in the days when this stuff was common. When I was a kid, I saw Bobby Allison race a late-model car against the local hotdogs in Indiana; Bobby did that sort of thing all the time. And years before that, all the top Indy car drivers—Parnelli and Foyt, like I mentioned, but also Bobby and Al Unser, Jim Hurtubise, Roger McCluskey, and a bunch more—filled up their schedules by running sprints and midgets.

I guess that by doing that sort of thing myself, I brought back a few memories for people who were old enough to have seen those guys. There were a number of times when fans came up and said, very emotionally, "You know, I remember when A.J. used to do things like this after he won the 500."

Or, "I remember when Parnelli used to come back and run midgets."

Now, I'm not comparing myself to those guys; they're legends. My point is, a lot of people clearly liked the idea that they could watch somebody race an Indy car one week, and then see that same guy running sideways in a midget the next week. The fact that this sometimes made them mention me in the same breath with those heroes was an enormous source of pride for me.

That wasn't something I ever talked about, and it certainly wasn't the reason I kept jumping into short-track cars. But there were a few late nights when I'd drive home from the track, thinking about the way those old-timers spoke and how sincere they were, and I'd say to myself, "What I'm doing here *means* something."

CHRIS ECONOMAKI: "I was so pleased to see Tony doing that sort of thing. It showed that he hadn't shut out his past."

It was in this period that one of the T-shirt vendors in Indianapolis printed up a shirt with my name on it, along with pictures of an Indy car and a midget, and these words: "NEW BLOOD FROM AN OLD SCHOOL."

I liked that.

As popular as all this bouncing around was with a lot of the fans, it didn't always go over so well with my employers. The only one of my bosses who never seemed to have a problem with it was Harry Ranier, who got a kick out of the fact that I still wanted to do that stuff.

Both John Menard and Joe Gibbs would suggest, sometimes gently

and sometimes not so gently, that I ought to back off a bit on my outside activity. Obviously, one thing that concerned them was that I could get banged up on a Wednesday night someplace and have to miss a NASCAR or IRL race that weekend. But neither of them ever came right out and asked me to quit, which in hindsight was probably a good thing, because I'm sure I would have fought that.

After awhile, both John and Joe adopted the public position that they were willing to be patient until I got over this "phase" I was going through. Joe told one writer that he thought I was going "through a period of withdrawal," and John said, "We're going to let Tony get some of this stuff out of his system."

The mistake they made is that racing wasn't just something that was in my system. Racing *was* my system.

KEN SCHRADER: "The people who tell you that you ought to stop, they don't understand what makes you do that stuff in the first place. I mean, if they have an office job, I'm sure there's something they like to do for relaxation. Why don't they quit doing that? Racing is what I grew up doing, and it's the same with Tony; he grew up running every race he could find, every opportunity he got. Then he got the opportunity to run that IRL car and some stock cars, but that didn't mean he suddenly didn't want to do that other stuff anymore."

I was lucky to have Larry Curry on my side whenever the question of my schedule came up with Menard. Larry looked at it from the standpoint of a team manager who wanted his driver to be happy; anytime I wanted to go off and run a midget or a Silver Crown car when we weren't busy with the IRL team, Larry was very supportive.

In time, I think John Menard started to see it the same way. I knew I was starting to win the battle when he told one reporter, "I understand it more than I did before. What makes Tony so good is that he races all the time. All he thinks about is racing."

And, honestly, over time I also began to look a little harder at things from Menard's perspective. He used to tell me all the time, as Joe did later on, that I had a lot of people depending on me; it wasn't just him or Harry Ranier or Joe Gibbs, John always said, but also our sponsors and all the guys who worked on our cars.

I have to give John Menard credit for that. He was probably the first car owner who got me to look seriously at weighing risk versus reward.

I did start making a few changes to my short-track program, and that risk/reward thing was at the bottom of most of them.

I stopped running sprints and midgets at Winchester and Salem, just because history has kind of shown that mixing those cars and those tracks can be pretty chancy. I'd had one of the most dramatic wrecks in my career at Salem back in '92, when I was driving Steve Chrisman's sprinter. A couple of guys tangled ahead of me during a heat race, and my car rode over another's car's tire. That launched me over the wall, through a steel mesh fence, and down an embankment into a wooded area which separates the track from the little airport next door. I wasn't even slightly injured; in fact, I hopped into another car and ran the feature. But when I saw the photos of that incident later on, I knew I'd gotten away with one that day.

Since 1996, I've run a lot of Silver Crown races for George Snider, and a lot of midget races in Larry Martz's 32. (© John Mahoney)

PAM BOAS: "I think the only time I ever really got totally upset when Tony crashed was when he went completely out of the track at Salem. I mean, he was tumbling into trees, and I had no clue what was happening because I couldn't see him anymore. Then, when I finally saw him come climbing back up the bank, I just wanted to go down there and beat the tar out of him for scaring me to death!"

I also cut way back on the kind of ride-jumping I had once done pretty regularly, and settled in with certain teams for whatever open-wheel racing I did. Your odds of getting into trouble increase if you're constantly hopping into unfamiliar equipment, and I had done a lot of that in the early nineties. Since 1996, the bulk of my midget activity has been with either Steve Lewis or Larry Martz, and the only Silver Crown racing I've done has been with George Snider. I knew those people really well, and I trusted them to give me safe, reliable cars. I also appreciated the fact that they were always willing to get a car ready for me anytime I felt like racing, sometimes on short notice.

I trust George and Larry to give me stuff that's fast and safe.
(© John Mahoney)

STEVE LEWIS: "To this day, we've got a car sitting there that we consider to be Tony's car. He can just call us, come to the track, and hop in that car. The interesting thing is that even though this obviously creates more work, our chief mechanic, Kelly Drake, has never looked at it that way; he sees it as an opportunity to have a driver of Tony's talent in a car that he's prepared. So it's not, 'Oh, God, I've got a lot to do.' Instead, it's, 'Boy, we've got Tony coming.' People will work for Tony, because they know he's going to put forth the effort to win."

LARRY MARTZ: "Having Tony Stewart drive for you is the ultimate fun, because you just know that everybody's going to be watching your car. You know it's the center of attention."

––––––

Coming back to drive for Steve Lewis put me in the strange position of being a teammate, at least occasionally, to a guy I had always seen as the enemy. When it became clear in the winter of 1995–96 that I couldn't commit to another midget season, I recommended to Steve and Bob East that they ought to hire Kenny Irwin. I was pretty qualified to make that judgment, because I had kept a close eye on Kenny over the years. He had always been fast, always been aggressive, and I couldn't really see any weaknesses in his game. He was the kind of guy Steve and Bob needed.

So they hired Irwin, and he drove their cars to the 1996 USAC midget championship. I dropped in and ran a few races in the second car—ten in all—when I wasn't off running a Busch or Indy car race. Kenny and I definitely kept our bosses on their toes. We finished first and second on the big track in Richmond in June, with Kenny winning, and then I turned the tables when I beat him at Kansas City in August. But if those one-two finishes were exciting for Steve and Bob, they were

If you think this battle looks good, you should have seen it later on. That's me (in the foreground) racing Kenny Irwin in the 1996 Hut Hundred. We ended up crashing as we fought for the lead. (© John Mahoney)

nothing compared to what we had in store for them in the Hut Hundred at Terre Haute.

I was really pumped up to find that the Hut Hundred happened to land on a quiet weekend for me. I still had great memories of winning that race in '93; at the same time, I had a feeling—and so far I've been right— that I might never get to run another Hut Hundred, just because of scheduling conflicts. So when we went to Terre Haute for the '96 race, I *really* wanted to win that thing.

> **BOB EAST:** "Before that race, Tony and Kenny were in the trailer, and my son Bobby was standing between them. Tony said to Bobby, 'Hey, does Kenny know what it pays for second?' That was his way of saying he was there to win."

I qualified on the pole and led the feature for quite awhile. Then I started to feel pressure from behind, and it was coming from Irwin. I kind of expected that, because I had chosen a right rear tire much harder than Kenny's, trading speed for durability. Anyway, we proceeded to have ourselves a hot little battle for the lead.

Now, nine times out of ten, Kenny and I were really solid team players. But on September 4, 1996, it was clear that the only thing either one of us had on his mind was to beat his teammate and win that Hut Hundred.

The fast groove at Terre Haute that night was up high, against the cushion, and I had that lane covered. So, heading into turn one, Kenny tried the classic slide job; carrying a ton of speed, he steered his car across the bottom, hoping to clear my front end before he slid back out to the cushion at the center of the corner. It worked; he didn't clear me by much, but he did clear me. The trouble was, I had the tail of my car hung way out, and my eyes were riveted on the cushion. In other words, I was basically looking out over my right front tire when, out of nowhere from my left, here came Kenny. He was still busy catching his car, while I was already mashing the gas. I hit him before I knew it, and the wreck knocked both our cars out of the race.

I thought the whole thing was Kenny's fault; he was so much faster than me, I figured, that he could've waited another lap or two and passed me cleanly. But Kenny always insisted that I caused the crash, because he'd cleared me and gotten run over. Maybe the truth was somewhere in the middle, and we were just two aggressive young guys trying too hard to win an important race.

From that day on, Kenny Irwin and I raced each other more fiercely than we raced anyone else. Our last really good midget battle came the following February at Phoenix, in the Copper Classic. I won, and Kenny ended up second. One-two again.

Part of the challenge of jumping back into a midget, particularly as we got into the '97 season, was that there was a real changing of the guard happening. Guys like Irwin, Andy Michner, Mike Bliss, and Stevie Reeves had either moved on from USAC or were in the process of moving on. There was a pretty stout group of us who stepped away within a few seasons, and that created plenty of opportunities for the next batch of hungry, talented guys.

Racing has always been like that, and always will be: when there are shoes to be filled, even big shoes, somebody will come along to fill 'em.

In the midgets, guys like Jay Drake and Jason Leffler stepped in and picked right up where the rest of us had left off. I had raced with all those guys in the past, but now they were in different situations, *better* situations. Maybe they were in better cars, or maybe they had just become better drivers. All I knew was that in that short span of time, they had really come into their own. Whenever I climbed into a midget, they made me scrap for every spot.

It was interesting to match wits with those guys, particularly at some of the dirt races we ran. There's probably no better way to size up an opponent, to really see what he's got, than to race him head-to-head on a good dirt track.

A. J. FOYT: "The thing about dirt is, you can control the car with your throttle foot, as long as you've got an educated foot. It's something you have to learn: how to slide the car into the corner, and feather the throttle, and control that thing while you keep it driving forward. Most drivers today only know one thing: on the throttle, or off the throttle."

KEN SCHRADER: "On dirt, there's so much more that the driver can do with the car. It's not that the driver doesn't do anything on pavement, but he has more of an input on dirt."

Of the ten events I ran in that year, eight were on dirt tracks, and I spent a lot of time checking out all the newer guys, the same way I'm sure Stan Fox and Page Jones checked me out when they were the top guns. These guys were good, *real* good—Leffler won the next three USAC midget championships, Drake won lots of features, and some of the other kids were winning, too—but I held my own.

I won two USAC features at Beaver Dam, Wisconsin, and another at the 16th Street Speedway, a little bullring that ran for a couple of seasons inside an old minor league baseball stadium in Indianapolis. I'll tell you, 16th Street was an interesting track; it was shaped like a square, but you drove it as one big circle, just clipping the inside of every corner. The speeds were relatively slow, which made guys aggressive as hell, and yet you needed a lot of finesse and throttle control to get around there quickly. On the opposite end of the spectrum, I also had a great run in the 4-Crown Nationals at Eldora, a big, wide-open track, where I ran a strong second behind Drake and in front of Leffler.

It was really satisfying to climb out after that Eldora race, my last midget outing of 1997, and know that I could still run dirt with the best of 'em.

LARRY CURRY: "Tony is one of these guys who has to keep proving his ability to himself. I went to Terre Haute with him one night in 1996 for a midget race. He hadn't run dirt for a while, but that night he won the feature. He got out of the car and said to me, 'I can still do this. I've still got it.'"

RALPH POTTER: "Years ago, when I first started running midgets, I went to Terre Haute, and Foyt was there. He probably hadn't been in a midget on dirt for ten years, but he went out and set fast time. Fast time! There are drivers and there are great drivers, and to the great drivers it's automatic. And Tony has that."

– – – – –

Of course, we had our moments of glory on pavement, too. In May of '97, I qualified for the Indy 500 and then fought the traffic to hurry over to IRP for a USAC midget race. We got there late, missed practice,

In May 1997, I qualified for the Indy 500 on a Saturday afternoon and then won a USAC midget event at Raceway Park that night. Now that's old school! (© John Mahoney)

and only managed to qualify ninth. Still, I had high hopes; I was driving the Steve Lewis car, and that thing was a rocket. Coming from ninth would be tough, but I thought we might be able to do it.

As it turned out, we did it from a lot further back than that. Somebody up front slipped on the first lap of the feature, and a bunch of us were caught in a pileup. I got pushed back to the pits, where Bob East and his guys swarmed all over the thing and got it patched up just in time for the restart.

When you see your team put out that much effort, it makes you want to do something special as a reward. And, boy, we sure did that night.

> **BOB EAST:** "The fuel tank was smashed in, so we had to raise the back of the car a bit, and I made a couple of [suspension] changes to compensate for that. I told Tony what we'd done, and that everything looked okay. He looked up at me and said, 'Well, it's showtime.' Then he went out and restarted dead last, and it was lap thirteen when he took the lead. He passed every car and won the race."

One thing I noticed was that by the end of 1997, nobody seemed surprised anymore when I showed up at a short track. Nobody bothered to ask, "What are you doing here?"

They knew I was there to race. Same as always.

CARY AGAJANIAN: "I'm a sentimentalist, and Tony Stewart is truly one of the few drivers that I can say belonged in another era. He belonged in the 1950s and '60s, racing with Roger McCluskey and Don Branson and Parnelli Jones and Jim Hurtubise and A. J. Foyt. Those guys raced all the time, just because they loved it. As soon as the Indy 500 was over, they'd be driving to St. Louis or someplace for the next midget race they could find. They'd drive for peanuts. What I love about Tony more than anything—I'm almost getting choked up talking about this—is that he reminds me of that era, an era when I admired real racers. That's what he is, and I mean this with all my heart: he is a real racer."

ELEVEN ⫶ TUG OF WAR: INDY CARS VS. STOCK CARS

MY ARRANGEMENT WITH JOE GIBBS CALLED FOR FIVE BUSCH STARTS IN 1997 and a busier schedule—which ended up being twenty-two races—in '98. We signed that deal in April of '97. The very next month, I extended my IRL contract with Menard through the end of '98.

Like I've said, quite a few people, particularly the old-line fans, seemed to like the fact that I wanted to race everything. But there were lots of others who didn't agree. When I started doing well in both Indy cars and stock cars, all I heard from some folks was that I needed to make up my mind, *right now*, which path I wanted my career to take. Over and over, I'd hear, "You can't drive a stock car one week and an Indy car the next week. That sort of thing just isn't done."

And I'd think, Sure it is. *I'm* doing it.

I knew in the back of my mind that sooner or later, there would come a day when something would push me toward one form of racing or the other. Maybe it would be a case of the two schedules having too many conflicts, or maybe I would simply discover that I wasn't happy enough in one series or the other. But at that point in my life I was doing my best to put that day off as long as I could.

I was like a school kid facing a final exam: he knows it's coming, and he knows it's important, but he's still a kid, so he's going to just have fun right up until it's time to start cramming.

In my heart and head, there was a pretty good tug of war going on. What kind of racing was I heading toward? Did I want to stay in Indy cars or move on? (©1997 IMS by Michael Haley)

The way I looked at, I'd have been crazy to just walk away from the IRL, because Team Menard was on top of that world; I'd have been just as dumb to turn my back on NASCAR, because the Gibbs program was obviously headed in the right direction. As long as nobody stopped me from doing both, that's exactly what I was going to do.

It seemed so simple to me, and I couldn't understand what all the fuss was about. I looked at it like, Why is it such an unwritten rule that an Indy car driver, assuming he's a *good* Indy car driver, can't be a stock car driver, too? That didn't make any sense. The fact that I was fast in a midget had never stopped me from being fast in a Silver Crown car. Winning sprint car races on dirt didn't stop me from winning in a pavement modified.

All of a sudden, just because I had reached a certain level of racing, whatever skills I had were no longer transferable?

It used to be that versatility was seen as a *good* thing. In the 1970s, stock car guys like Cale Yarborough and the Allisons, Bobby and Donnie, raced in the Indianapolis 500, and did a great job. It worked the other way around, too: Indy car guys used to jump into stock cars all the time. Hell, Foyt and Mario Andretti each won the Daytona 500. It seemed to me that the history of American motorsports had proven that a good race driver was a good race driver, no matter where he took his helmet.

But for some reason, by the 1990s that kind of thinking was considered outdated. All I heard was, "Well, that might have worked in Cale's day, or in Foyt's day, but in this modern era you can't do that."

That's the term they used: "this modern era." And they insisted that to win in this modern era, a driver had to be a "specialist," concentrating on one particular form of racing. Well, to hell with that. I didn't get into this game to be a *specialist*.

In my USAC days I beat a lot of so-called dirt-track specialists, and a lot of so-called pavement specialists. Beating the best Indy car racers *and* the best stock car racers might have been a taller order, but it didn't seem impossible. I mean, we're not talking about rocket science, or developing a cure for cancer. We're talking about driving automobiles.

Stock car people look at an Indy car, and to them it's so fast and so *different* that they forget it's just a race car. Indy car people do the same thing: they look at a stock car and see a big, heavy thing that's a challenge to turn and a challenge to stop, and they lose sight of the fact that it's also just a race car. Every race car has four wheels, a throttle pedal, a brake pedal, and a steering wheel; if you drive them too hard, every one of them either pushes, gets loose, or does a four-wheel drift. None of that has changed since the early 1900s, never mind the 1970s.

So maybe the reason nobody in this modern era had succeeded at both stock cars and Indy cars was that nobody had bothered to try. Because I'll stick with what I said a minute ago: a good race driver is a good race driver.

> **A. J. FOYT:** "In my lifetime there's probably been only two or three guys I've known who could drive just about anything they sat down in, and Tony Stewart is one of 'em."

The real trick to jumping from series to series is learning how to shift your focus quickly, and I'm sure there are drivers who can't do that. But I never had any trouble hopping between the Indy car and the stock car, whether we were testing or racing. When I drove for Team Menard, those guys got my full attention; if I was with Joe Gibbs Racing, same thing. I never sat around thinking about one car while I was on the job with the other.

Well, I should say *almost* never, because there were exceptions.

The guys on each team were always curious about how things were going with the other side. The Menard guys would ask me how my last Busch race had gone, so we'd talk about stock cars for a few minutes; when I went to a NASCAR race, there might be a short discussion with the Gibbs guys about the most recent IRL event. But once we got past the small talk, all my thoughts were on whatever series I was competing in.

Maybe my best answer to all of this stuff came in October of 1997. I had the best Busch Series finish of my life to that point, a third at Charlotte; exactly one week later, I clinched the IRL championship at Las Vegas. I guess my focus must have been pretty good at both places.

It's kind of funny, but for a guy who has a reputation for sometimes being hard to get along with, during that 1997–98 stretch I used my people skills as much as my driving skills. I was somehow able to keep lots of different groups happy, against pretty tall odds.

Both my IRL and Busch teams seemed to understand that my commitment would sometimes be to the other camp. In other words, John Menard might not have always appreciated it when I was off running, say, a midget race, but he did cut me plenty of slack if I had to be someplace with my stock car team. Joe Gibbs was the same way about the IRL program, because he knew it was my top priority through the end of '98.

I'm sure there were times when one party or the other must have resented that a little bit. It can't be easy to want to sit down for a talk with your driver, only to realize that you can't because he's off racing for somebody else. But I always dealt in an up-front way with both John and Joe, always made my intentions clear, which kept any discomfort to a minimum. For the most part, both those guys seemed pleased with me.

And so did our sponsors, although that sometimes required some diplomacy. In the course of '97 and '98, I drove cars sponsored by two major oil companies (Shell in the Busch Series, Quaker State in the Indy Racing League), three tire companies (Goodyear in NASCAR, Firestone in the IRL, Hoosier in USAC), and two hardware chains (Menards in the IRL, TrueValue in the Silver Crown division).

I kept thinking, How in the world do I get away with this?

The nice thing was that, generally, my sponsors were understanding. I think they respected the fact that, with all the racing I was doing, it would have been almost impossible *not* to have a conflict or two. They didn't exactly give it their blessing, but they didn't hold it against me, either.

Besides, I didn't have any real say in what went on sponsor-wise, anyway. Joe Gibbs made his own deals, John Menard made his own deals, and my USAC owners made their own deals. That was fine with me, because whenever a conflict popped up I could shrug, put on my most innocent face and say, "Hey, I'm only the driver."

I was like Sergeant Schultz on the old *Hogan's Heroes* TV program: "I know *nothing*."

— — — — —

What finally convinced me that I'd better start deciding what I wanted to do with my life was plain old logistics. You can only juggle rides for so long until it backfires on you, and you're forced to choose between a major race over *here*, and a major race over *there*. At the Indy Racing League and Busch Series levels, every event is major, but some are certainly more important than others. I'd been pretty lucky that while I was committed to the IRL, not many of those races conflicted directly with the biggest Busch dates.

Still, I had to do quite a bit of hustling. I rented enough airplanes to realize that it'd be cheaper and more efficient in the long haul to have one of my own, so toward the end of the '97 season we bought a used Twin Commander, a fast turboprop. I had to admit, that was a significant step up from driving to midget races and hoping I'd earn enough gas money to get home. But even though the plane eased the scheduling hassles, it didn't eliminate them altogether; there were quite a few late-night flights from, say, IRL tests to NASCAR qualifying sessions.

As 1997 wore on and all these questions about my future got louder, I tried to laugh them off by joking, "You know, if only I could get NASCAR and the Indy Racing League to schedule their races without any conflicts, this would be no problem." But deep down, I knew I was only kidding myself. It was time to start making some decisions.

In my heart and in my head, there was a pretty good tug of war going on.

At Team Menard, we had a team that clicked together and won together. The only guy I couldn't seem to get along with was the owner. (© John Mahoney)

Joe Gibbs was really anxious to get his second Winston Cup team up and running by 1999, and that was obviously the crux of the whole issue. With the way the Cup series has taken off in the last ten years, I'm sure lots of people would see the choice to go NASCAR as a no-brainer. But if you grew up when I did, and where I did, that wasn't so simple.

From the time I got that yard kart when I was a kid, I had been wrapped up in open-wheel racing. My reputation was made in midgets and sprints and Silver Crown cars; later on, in 1997 and '98, I was much better known for what I had done in Indy cars than for anything I did in stock cars. More than anything, I was an open-wheel racer. That was a part, a *big* part, of who I was.

I also felt a strong sense of attachment to the Indy Racing League. Let's face it, my career might never have reached the point where a guy like Joe Gibbs was interested in me—or at least it wouldn't have reached that point as quickly—if Tony George hadn't developed the IRL. One of the things Tony wanted to do was to reopen the road between America's short tracks and the Indianapolis 500, and I'm living proof that he did that. Tony George was directly responsible for me running that race. Under the old CART system, the only way in was to buy a seat, and for me that was out of the question. You can add up all the relatives and friends I had, and together we didn't have enough money to get a CART owner to shake my hand, much less give me a ride. Without the IRL, I wasn't going to get my shot, period. That meant something to me.

And it meant something to other folks, too. When you went to Indy in the late 1990s, you ran into all these retired drivers and retired mechanics, guys with backgrounds similar to mine, who were genuinely thrilled to see racers like me and Billy Boat and Davey Hamilton there. It was an emotional thing for them, that connection between our day and their day. You'd see tears in their eyes, and these are some pretty *hard* men. They'd say, "I'm so proud to have you kids in this race." It was impossible *not* to be touched by that.

My heart may have been leaning toward sticking with the Indy Racing League, mostly because of that one event, the 500.

But my head was telling me to take a long, hard look at NASCAR. It was obvious that in the eyes of most people, the premier form of American racing was Winston Cup. Everywhere you looked, you saw Dale Earnhardt bumper stickers, Jeff Gordon T-shirts, Mark Martin jackets.

To a lot of folks, Winston Cup *was* auto racing; if you weren't there, you were nobody.

I didn't buy into that line of thinking, because I had raced in enough places to know that there are great drivers in every series. Still, I'm a competitive person; if you tell me that the best drivers are over *here*, that's where I want to go, and those are the guys I want to beat. I want to race at whatever is perceived to be the top level of the sport, and NASCAR obviously had everybody else covered in that department.

What really got my interest up was the fact that there were friends of mine with deep connections to Indy car racing who pointed out that, in terms of my long-term prospects, NASCAR might be the way to go.

> **LARRY CURRY:** "I remember talking to Tony, and telling him, 'This is difficult for me to tell you, because I'd like to run with you in Indy cars for the rest of my career. But that's me being selfish. You need to do whatever is best for you, and if that means going to NASCAR, that's what you have to do.'"

Even Cary Agajanian, who had worked with USAC and the Indianapolis Motor Speedway and had a hand in shaping the IRL's rules and philosophies, urged me to strongly consider a full-time career in stock cars. Sure, as an attorney Cary is used to putting aside his emotions and looking strictly at the facts, but, given his love of Indy car racing, I saw that as a pretty strong endorsement for NASCAR.

> **CARY AGAJANIAN:** "My personal history at Indianapolis dates back to 1959, and my family's history goes back to '47. That's fifty years of heritage, so many of my most wonderful memories come from Indianapolis. I worked on the pit crew in '63, when Parnelli Jones won in my dad's car, and I still wear the special ring that Parnelli gave each member of the team. So sometimes [in regards to Tony] I thought, What would my dad say about this? Everything I've learned came from him, and his love of open-wheel racing was as deep or deeper than mine. But I will add this: my dad was also a businessman, and he would have recognized the commercial success of NASCAR."

I guess maybe every major career decision comes down to two things: money and happiness.

Money was a factor in my case; there was no getting around the fact that Winston Cup drivers earn more than any other racers in America. But it was by no means the biggest factor. I mean, I like the things money can buy as much as the next guy does, but I can honestly say that I've never driven a single lap, much less chosen a specific series, *just* for the money. If you race for the money, you're doing it for the wrong reason. Do it for the glory, meaning the victories and the trophies, and the dollars will come. All the money floating around in NASCAR had caught everybody else's attention, but it wasn't something I dwelled on.

Besides, it's not like I was starving running Indy cars. I wasn't getting rich, but I was certainly living more comfortably than I ever had.

CARY AGAJANIAN: "John Menard was—and I'll say this nicely—frugal. But he paid Tony pretty fairly. I think he recognized Tony's talent, and we were able to get what I thought was a good, fair salary, probably upwards of what anybody else in the IRL was making."

So once you get past the money, you've got to look at your own happiness. The logical thing was to examine which type of racing I enjoyed best. That's something I'd been asked about in a hundred interviews, and my answer was always the same: "My favorite race car is the one I'm sitting in that day." And I meant it; I love the challenges all these different cars present.

Okay, so if I liked both Indy cars and stock cars, which was I *better* at? Well, that was a tough call, too. I'd obviously had much better results in the IRL, but, relatively speaking, I'd had better *equipment* there. I could definitely see progress in our Busch Series effort with Gibbs; finishing third at Charlotte was proof, because that race was loaded with Winston Cup guys as well as the usual Busch teams.

The one thing that kept popping up as I weighed one series versus the other was my personal relationships on each side. I thought the

world of my IRL team—meaning Larry Curry and the guys at the shop—but my relationship with John Menard wasn't so cozy. He seemed to enjoy nitpicking about this and that, to the point where I felt like he was really busting my chops. He'd make big issues out of little things, just to show me who was boss, I guess. For instance, at one point I missed a scheduled appearance at one of his stores because of a miscommunication between someone in Menard's office and someone in my office; they simply got their dates mixed up. That shouldn't have happened, but it did. When I heard about it, I was really upset, because I've always done my best to meet my commitments to my sponsors and teams. Anyway, to make it up to John, I offered to reschedule that appearance, plus

This is me in winning form at Pike's Peak International Raceway, 1997. (© 1997 IRL by Jim Haines)

throw in another one at one of his other stores. To me, that was fair, especially because it hadn't been my mistake; it might have been a clerical error on his end, and it might have been a clerical error on my end, but it sure wasn't something *I* did. Well, Menard wouldn't even consider that. He pointed to a clause in my contract which allowed him to dock me a percentage of my salary if I missed an appearance, and, sure enough, he held back the money.

It was hard for me to believe that the owner of a successful, winning race team would choose to interrupt his team's harmony by bickering with the driver that way, but that was John Menard. He just *had* to show me who was in charge.

The longer things went on like that, the more it took away from the enjoyment I got out of the job.

As a team, we'd had our on-track disappointments. Generally speaking, I can live with that stuff, because it's just part of racing. But piling these ridiculous conflicts with the team owner *on top* of those disappointments began to wear on me. It soured me on Indy cars a little bit.

At the same time, there was nothing sour about the stock car side of things. I got along great with Joe Gibbs, got along great with Bobby Labonte and Jimmy Makar, got along great with my crew chief, Bryant Frazier. Every time I climbed into that Busch car, it seemed like I was driving smoother, learning more, going quicker.

In other words, getting happier.

Every day, stock cars were looking better and better.

Probably the biggest obstacle I faced was mental. I couldn't escape the idea that switching from the Indy Racing League to NASCAR was a matter of leaving the *known* for the *unknown*. I said a moment ago that I was going quicker all the time in the Busch car; well, in the Indy car I was already quick, already a champion.

It's a hell of a gamble to leave a situation like that, especially to jump over to NASCAR, where things are so competitive that a good driver can get lost in the shuffle in a heartbeat. I didn't doubt that I could drive stock cars, and I didn't doubt that Joe Gibbs was building a strong team. But, again, the only way to prove all that was to walk away from what already *was* a championship team.

> **KEN SCHRADER:** "It had to be a big struggle for Tony, because he had good opportunities in both places. He was right there, at the top of his game in the IRL cars."

But the more I thought about it, the more I realized that every positive step I ever took in my career meant leaving behind a winning situation. In order to run TQs, I had to step away from go-karts; in order to run USAC, I had to step away from TQs; in order to run Indy cars, I had to step away from USAC. That's just the natural order of sports, I think.

It's kind of a cliché, but I really believe that in these tough spots you have to listen to your own best instincts. In the end, mine pointed me toward stock car racing.

Most of that was directly attributable to Joe Gibbs. The more time I spent around that man, the more impressed I was with him. He's the kind of guy you want on your side, whether you're entering an autobile race or a football game. Our relationship got stronger by the day.

> **JOE GIBBS:** "I worked on him hard. I mean, I really did a sell job on Tony. He still had that thing inside that pulled at him, that love of open-wheel racing. But I think that when he really took a look at NASCAR, he saw that it had so much going for it."

It wasn't an easy move, but it was the correct move for me. I knew it then, and I know it now. Add it all up on your own: on the NASCAR side I saw the stronger series, and the better team/driver dynamic. I saw the right situation for me.

What absolutely clinched the deal was that Cary and I were able to negotiate a clause in my Joe Gibbs Racing contract that allowed me to run in the Indianapolis 500 each May, if I chose to. I knew that my stock car commitments would make that tough, if not impossible, but I definitely wanted to keep that option open. The idea of being locked out of that race was more than I wanted to think about.

The Indy car racers I talked to were pretty supportive of my decision. That had been a concern of mine, because when all this first came to light I was still the defending IRL champion. I didn't want my leaving to be seen as a slap in the face to the series. But I didn't get that feeling from anybody in the IRL paddock. Most people said, "Hey, we hate to see you leave, but we wish you the best."

MARK DISMORE: "The way I felt about that whole deal was, if you were to turn the whole racing universe around—if Indy cars were the premier series, to the point where every convenience store and souvenir shop had Indy car stuff on the walls, and NASCAR was the fledgling series—you'd have had guys jumping the other way. Tony's not stupid; he saw that he could go someplace where he could make a heck of a living and better his quality of life."

BILLY BOAT: "We've all been faced with decisions like that in life. At that point, Tony could go somewhere else and make a better living, and be in a competitive situation, too, so that was the choice he made. Obviously, it turned out to be a good choice for him. But I was definitely sorry to see him go."

One thing I felt good about was that, as I looked around, I could see much more of a grassroots presence in the Indy Racing League than there had been when I had started. Billy Boat wasn't just an IRL racer, he had become an IRL star; and as the '98 season shaped up, short-track guys like Brian Tyler, Andy Michner, Jimmy Kite, Tyce Carlson, J. J. Yeley, Jason Leffler, and Dave Steele were developing ties to IRL teams. That same year, my old sprint car hero Jack Hewitt realized his lifelong dream of racing at Indy.

I'm not sure how big a role my success played in any of that, but a lot of people, including some of those drivers, gave me credit for helping that process along.

DAVEY HAMILTON: "What Tony did with the IRL helped open the door for a lot of other short-track guys to get opportunities in that series. There's no question about that."

If that's true, it's something I'm very proud of. It makes me feel like I've contributed to the cause, so to speak. I got where I got because of whatever talent I had shown on the bullrings, and if I turned some of the right heads toward other young bullring drivers, that's a good thing.

Don't get me wrong, I didn't do it for them. I did it for *me*. But, hey, if it helped, I'm glad. Because any good short-track racer who wants a crack at the Indianapolis 500 ought to get it.

There was one last thing that weighed heavily in my mind about all this. It didn't make sense to live in Indiana if I raced in NASCAR, which kind of revolves around North Carolina, so I knew I'd have to relocate. The only problem was, I really didn't want to leave home.

That sounds crazy, I know, because for me the word "home" had meant so many different places. Once my mom sold the house I'd grown up in, I never stayed in one place long enough to put any roots down. Still, if you gave me one of those word-association tests and said "home," I'd have pictured that old house in Columbus.

I still had a lot of friends in my hometown, so throughout my short-track days I spent plenty of time there. Whenever I got the chance, I'd take a detour past that house. It always had a strange, calming effect on me; no matter how bad a day I was having, or what else was going on in my life, I could put my problems on hold just by seeing that place.

One evening back around 1993—it was winter, and there was a heavy blanket of snow—I cruised past the house and noticed a light burning in my dad's old garage. On a whim, I decided to stop in. Because of the snow it was impossible to distinguish the driveway from the grass, but I drove right around that house without skipping a beat. I knew *exactly* where the edges of that driveway were, because I had been up and down it a thousand times on tricycles, go-karts, you name it. You don't forget things like that.

I knocked on the door of the garage and walked in. There was a fellow on his back, lying under a Jeep. I started to introduce myself—"Uh, I used to live here"—and he said, "I know who you are." We talked for a while, and the guy was really nice. He worked at the Cummins Diesel plant right there in Columbus, and he followed racing a little bit.

Over the next couple of years, I stopped in every time I saw those garage lights on. At some point in 1994 or '95, the fellow mentioned that his goal was to buy some property out in the country and build a new home there. I said, "Do me one favor: before you sell this place, let me know. I might be interested in buying it."

Well, in '96 he called. He was interested in selling the house if I still wanted it. It took me about a second to say yes.

Once I moved in, I made a lot of changes to the place. It had always been a fairly small house, so I expanded it quite a bit and put in all kinds of bachelor amenities: a hot tub, a big-screen TV, video games, stuff like that. And I found a couple of roommates: Barry Medaris, a local guy I'd known since we raced go-karts together as kids, and Jason Leffler, who was driving midgets for a team out of Columbus.

Jason was from California, and I'd known him from the days when I drove Western States midgets. I guess I saw in him the person I had been a few years earlier: knocking around far from home, trying to climb the racing ladder. When I was young and struggling, so many people had opened their houses to me; I felt like I could repay that, in a way, by giving Jason a place to hang out.

> **JASON LEFFLER,** USAC champion and NASCAR driver: "Tony knew I needed a place to live, and he just said, 'Hey, I've got an extra room. Why don't you just move in?' It really helped me out."

I was running the entire IRL series and a bunch of Busch races, and Jason had a pretty hectic midget schedule, but whenever we were home we'd kind of compare notes. I'd give him a little debrief on how my weekend went, and he'd get me up to speed on all the USAC action.

And then we'd unwind a little bit, the way only racers can. I had a couple of four-wheelers and off-road motorcycles in the garage, and Jason and I took recreational riding to a whole new level.

> **JASON LEFFLER:** "Before long, we had the backyard all dug up. Tony had a little garden back there, and one night we tore that up, knocked all the little wooden barriers down. It was wild, because the house was in a residential neighborhood, pretty quiet, and we'd ride until midnight or later, but the neighbors never complained. They all knew Tony, I guess."

After all my bouncing around, I had finally found a home. *My* home. And I found it just in time to leave it behind.

I had already bought a small condo on Lake Norman, outside Char-lotte, and I'd been bunking there whenever my schedule had me in that part of the country. The place was pretty bare for a while, but little by lit-tle I found myself moving things in.

There was no way I was going to sell the house in Columbus—I still have it, and I just might have it forever—but as 1997 and '98 rolled along, I found myself spending less and less time there. That bothered me more than I'd ever imagined it would. I'd lock the front door behind me, realize I might not be back there for months, and feel really depressed about that.

In 2000, I did a television commercial for the folks from the Home Depot, spotlighting some houses they were helping build for Habitat for Humanity. My main line was, "There's something about a home that preserves memories." That sentence wasn't scripted; those words were all mine, and they came from the heart. I had that house in Columbus on my mind when I said it.

But waving good-bye to that home and those memories, at least for a while, was something I needed to do. When you have a tug of war, even winning can be painful.

TWELVE   1998: LIVING FOR THE MOMENT

I'M A COMPETITIVE PERSON, AND I'M AN OPTIMIST, TOO. YOU ADD THOSE two qualities together and you end up with a driver who attacks every year flat out. I always start a season edgy, anxious, ready to get out there and race.

But, looking back, I really threw myself into 1998.

I had plenty to accomplish, at least in my mind. On the stock car side of things, it wasn't necessarily a make-or-break year, but I knew I had to get things right. On the Indy car side, '98 was going to be my last fling, at least for the foreseeable future, at a lot of tracks and events. And as far as short-track racing went, I wasn't sure *what* the future held; I was pretty sure I'd still be able to sneak off to do a midget race here or a dirt late-model race there for the rest of my career, but I knew all of that would be tied into how I performed in the stock car.

So what 1998 was, really, was a year of beginnings and endings. The beginning of what looked to be a long NASCAR career, the end of a great—rocky, but great—Indy car stint, and my last real blast of complete short-track freedom. I wanted to make the most of it.

I had a pretty good reason for feeling as anxious as I did. For my whole career, I had operated according to my own schedule: if I did well in one

In the 1998 IRL opener at Orlando, we spanked 'em bad. Won the pole, won the race, took the trophy, and went home. (© 1998 IRL by Jim Haines)

class, I'd move up to the next one. But in 1998, I was following somebody else's time line; all the key people at Joe Gibbs Racing—Joe himself, of course, plus Bobby Labonte and Jimmy Makar—had their minds made up that I'd be their second Winston Cup driver in 1999. Because of that, I *had* to be good in that Busch car by the end of '98.

I was going to do everything in my power to meet that schedule, and to prove to those guys that they'd made the right choice. So the big job in 1998 was simple: to get competitive. Right now.

In the early days of that season, it seemed as if we were solidly on track. In the Busch Series opener at Daytona, I was third with ten laps to go when we had a left rear tire go down on a restart; I bobbled, Mark Martin got into my back bumper, and instead of challenging for the win I was bouncing off the wall.

At Rockingham the next week we won the pole, and then I came about as close as a racer can come to winning without actually taking the checkered flag. On the last corner of the last lap, Matt Kenseth got into my left rear quarter panel, nudged me up the track, and drove past me while I was wrestling to stay out of the fence. He led the last quarter-mile of the race, and I ended up second.

I've never been a big fan of those bump-and-run finishes. Where I come from, the open-wheel cars, your instinct is to *avoid* leaning on another car if you can help it, while in stock cars that rough stuff is pretty much tolerated, especially on the final lap. Needless to say, I wasn't happy with the way Rockingham ended. Still, it was the second race in a row where we'd been competitive, and I think everybody on our team felt pumped up as we headed into the heart of the season.

Unfortunately, it ended up being another up-and-down year. I hadn't seen that coming, not after we'd had those two "ups" right out of the box.

I was still having trouble getting the feel of a stock car. On the biggest speedways, I had things pretty well figured out; at those tracks, as long as the equipment is right, speed is mostly a result of being smooth and running consistent lines, and I had that figured out. The places that troubled me were the stop-and-go joints like Nashville, Bristol, and Myrtle Beach, where you had to slow the car down a bunch, get it turned, and then get it back up to speed.

On those types of tracks in a midget or a sprint car, I felt like I could throw a car around with the best of them. But I was learning the hard way that you cannot throw around a full-sized stock car. That's not to say that the driver is less important in NASCAR than anywhere else, because in the same equipment a good driver will almost always beat a mediocre driver. But you just can't hustle a Busch car the way you can hustle an open-wheel car.

It's all a matter of weight. A midget weighs 900 pounds, a sprinter weighs 1,400 pounds. Hell, even an IRL car, with all its horsepower, weighs around 1,650 pounds. You could double the weight of my Indy car and it would just about match the 3,300-pound Busch car I drove in 1998. All that weight means you're dealing with an entirely different animal, and it's not an animal that's easily controlled.

Here's the best analogy I have: get yourself a tennis ball and a four-teen-pound bowling ball, and have somebody roll them at you from across the room. You can change the direction of the tennis ball with a flick of your wrist, but changing the path of the bowling ball isn't so simple. It can be done, but it requires a whole different technique.

I had grown up driving tennis-ball race cars, and now I found myself in a really competitive bowling league called the Busch Series. And, well, let's just say that there were weekends in 1998 when I rolled a few gutter balls.

BOBBY LABONTE: "Tony tore up some race cars, which definitely wasn't what he wanted to do. It was probably the worst year he'd ever had, as far as results."

The only cure for all of this was seat time, and I got better as the months passed. That was no different from jumping from a kart to a TQ, or from a sprint car to an Indy car; even if you do well right away, you're going to get smoother as you pile up laps. Your comfort level increases, and that builds confidence, and before you know it you're as proficient in one division as you were in the other.

It just goes to show you: you really can teach an old dog new tricks.

— — — — —

In retrospect, I was kind of tough on myself in that '98 Busch season. By almost any other newcomer's standards, it would have been a pretty impressive year.

I matched my runner-up finish at Rockingham with a strong second at New Hampshire, and had two more nice finishes at Atlanta (third) and the Gateway track outside St. Louis (fifth). I had a great third at Dover, where I battled side by side for about twenty-five laps with Mike McLaughlin, one of the more established guys in the series. And there were other good days: we qualified in the top ten eight times in twenty-two tries, including two poles at Rockingham.

So, realistically, it wasn't that bad a year. I was simply putting too much pressure on myself, certainly more than the team ever did.

> **JOE GIBBS:** "What I saw was that everywhere we went, every kind of track, he handled it without any problem at all. At Loudon, which is a slick, flat track, he finished a real good second; at Daytona he was running third when he had that flat tire. That's what I looked at. I said, 'Man, there's nothing this sucker can't drive.'"

Whatever the numbers said, I can see now that I came an awful long way as a stock car racer in '98. Just getting used to the different tracks was a major step, because it obviously cut down on the learning I'd have to do as a Winston Cup rookie in '99. I had raced well enough in the Busch car at places like Rockingham, Charlotte, Dover, Texas, and Loudon to believe I'd be okay there in Cup cars, too.

No, I wasn't quite where I wanted to be yet, because where I wanted to be was in victory lane. But I guess I wasn't as far out of touch as I'd been afraid I was.

Meanwhile, I hadn't exactly backed off on the Indy car side. With the Team Menard car wearing the number 1 signifying our '97 championship, we won the season opener at Disney World after starting from the pole. It made for a really cool box score.

Car number: 1. Start position: 1. Finish: 1.

When we backed up that run with a strong runner-up finish in the next race at Phoenix, I started thinking I might be in a position to grab another title in my final full-time season with the IRL. But things sort of slid downhill from there.

Indianapolis in May typified the way my Indy car season went. We had the kind of month that lulls you into a false sense of promise—fast every day in practice, a stout fourth in qualifying despite the car being too loose—only to break your heart when you least expect it. In the 500, I followed the early leaders for a handful of laps, and then I made a move toward the front. On lap 17, I passed my teammate Robbie Buhl for third, and immediately passed Billy Boat for second. On lap 19, I turned the fastest lap of the race. Two laps later, as we came down the frontstretch, I passed Greg Ray for the lead.

The car felt great. *I* felt great. Everything was perfect in my little world.

For about, oh, forty-one or forty-two seconds. My engine blew up on the very next lap, in the exact spot where I had taken the lead.

They towed me back to the pits, where I gave a television interview which included a little bit of, uh, colorful language; I'll tell you more about that later. Then I headed back to the garage, as brokenhearted as I had ever been at a racetrack. What bothered me most was that I had no idea when I might get back to Indy for another 500. My NASCAR contract left that door open, but there was no way to be sure.

I had been in three 500s and had a car fast enough to win each time, and again I was walking away empty-handed, for God only knew how long.

> **JEFF "GOOCH" PATTERSON,** motor coach driver, Tony Stewart Racing: "Tony was miserable that day. He wasn't mad as much as he was, um, down. I guess he was more sad than anything."

Things didn't get a whole lot better from there. We had one great day at New Hampshire, where we scored a dominant win, but that was our last real high point in '98. Oh, we finished a decent third at Pikes Peak and fifth at Atlanta, but those results didn't come close to reflecting how hard we worked, or how fast we were.

If you look back at the Indy Racing League stats, you'd think we had a fairly good year: two victories, four poles, third in the standings behind Kenny Brack and Davey Hamilton. But we sure weren't *feeling* very good. Even today, when I look at some of the other numbers from that season I get sick.

In 1998 we set IRL records for most laps led, most races led, most consecutive races led, most times leading the first lap, most consecutive times leading the first lap, and—worst of all—most laps led by a driver who didn't win the race. For all of that obvious speed, we had only two victories in eleven starts. We were supposed to be the team to beat, and that's what we became: a beaten team. Engine-related problems knocked us out of three races; a radiator split at Texas; at Dover, the bumpy track rattled the car so badly that the dashboard actually fell into my lap.

It was a long, frustrating year.

I need to emphasize this: our problems weren't all the team's fault, by any means. Dover shook a lot of cars to pieces, so that wasn't a preparation issue. As for the other failures, well, Indy cars have always been more fickle than stock cars; they rev higher, they use more exotic materials, there are more sophisticated electronics involved. Things are going to break from time to time as you push the development envelope, and the Menard guys pushed that envelope as hard as any outfit in the league. That's the only way to find speed, but, unfortunately, it can bite you sometimes, too. It just so happened that I got bit a lot during my time in the IRL.

Too many times, I was changing into my street clothes before the race ended.

JEFF "GOOCH" PATTERSON: "He'd get back to the bus and just be so pissed off. Sometimes it would last for a couple of days, that mood."

I don't want to sound overly negative about my Indy car experience, because my time with the IRL certainly moved my career to another level. On top of that, after three years together, a lot of the guys on our team had become friends of mine. But between the car problems that always seemed to happen at the worst times, my own troubles with

John Menard, and the idea that I was on my way to a solid future with Joe Gibbs Racing and NASCAR, I was ready to call it a day.

Let's just say that when I climbed out of that Indy car after the '98 season finale, I wasn't exactly overwhelmed with sadness.

One thing that did have me feeling a little sad was the uncertainty over my short-track future. It was clear that once the Winston Cup program was up and running, the reins on me were going to get tighter. The team would tighten 'em a bit, our sponsors would tighten 'em a bit, and, obviously, Joe Gibbs would tighten 'em a bit. Even in '98, when my Cup activity was limited to testing, Joe worked pretty hard to convince me that there were things far more important than a Saturday-night midget race.

> **JOE GIBBS:** "We tried to get Tony to realize that the Winston Cup schedule was going to be much more strenuous than he thought. You're either racing, or testing, or traveling, or doing a sponsorship deal."

To be honest, I thought I might even want to tighten those reins a bit myself. If Winston Cup was the last step on my career ladder, I was going to do all I could to see that I was successful there. If testing or even a personal appearance could contribute to our team's success, well, that really *was* more important than having fun at some bullring.

So, at the time, 1998

What a day: As soon as I'd won the Copper Classic midget feature and celebrated with Steve Lewis . . . (© John Mahoney)

looked like my last real chance to satisfy my short-track addiction, and I made it count. I didn't do a *lot* of that stuff, but I found a way to run the races that were really important to me. In a way, the year had kind of a bachelor-party feel; I was like a guy going out to play with his buddies one final time before he tied the knot.

A week after winning the IRL opener at Orlando, I went out to

... I jumped into George Snider's Silver Crown car and won that race, too. (© John Mahoney)

Phoenix for the Copper World Classic and had an amazing time: I won the midget race with Steve Lewis, won the Silver Crown race with George Snider, and was on my way to winning the first race I'd ever driven in a supermodified when a tire went flat.

The Copper Classic was televised, and a lot of NASCAR people told me later that they'd watched it. It was the first time they'd ever seen me run the kinds of cars I'd cut my teeth on, and they talked as if they were pretty impressed. I think it gave them a window on my past; they understood that I had raced my way to wherever I'd gotten.

The same sort of thing happened that May, when Indianapolis Raceway Park held a USAC Silver Crown race after pole qualifying at the Speedway. As the night wore on, you could tell by looking at the shirts in the pits that a lot of Indy car team members had drifted over to IRP. It was another great race for me and Snider, and we won going away.

In July, I got to show off in front of the big-timers again when, as part of its IRL weekend, the Charlotte Motor Speedway hosted a USAC midget race on its small infield oval. Bob East brought an extra car for me, and I led every lap.

In all, I ran eight USAC national events in 1998—five in the midget and three in the Silver Crown car—and won exactly half of them.

RUSTY KUNZ: "A guy like Tony, once he takes a few laps and knocks the rust off, he's back in the saddle. He makes it look easy."

Toward the end of 1998, the promoters at the 16th Street Speedway in Indianapolis held a special "Tony Stewart Night" in conjunction with a USAC midget event. I had tried to support that track whenever my IRL and NASCAR schedules allowed; there were times when they advertised that I was coming, and times when I just showed up unannounced and raced, and either way I always had fun. I won

Big laughs: A bunch of my old pals roasted me pretty good on "Tony Stewart Night" at the 16th Street Speedway in Indianapolis. The emcee was my friend Pat Sullivan, who has announced a ton of my open-wheel races. (© John Mahoney)

twice there in Larry Martz's car, and also had a handful of seconds and thirds. It was really a neat little place.

On my night, they had a ceremony patterned after the old *This Is Your Life* television program, with me standing on a stage as they brought out a collection of people I had been associated with over the years. For me, it was a great evening.

It could have been better, though. See, I was determined not to just make a speech and stand around signing autographs, so I asked Larry if I could drive his midget. That was fine with him, and we worked our tails off all night to get the car fast.

> **PAT SULLIVAN:** "I was walking through the pits at 16th Street, and Stewart was leaning down, grooving a tire. Just to bust him, I said, 'Geez, you come back here and they even make you groove the tires.' He said, 'Whaddaya mean, make me? I love this shit!'"

Unfortunately, we had some kind of trouble in qualifying—I don't recall exactly what went wrong—so we started the feature dead last. It was a forty-lap run, and I had twenty-odd cars to pass, but I gave it hell. In fact, I had already put away more than a dozen of them when the engine quit before we'd even reached the halfway point.

The guys who finished up front might disagree, but, I promise you, I would have won that race. That would have been cool, just to look at the headlines later on: TONY STEWART WINS ON TONY STEWART NIGHT . . .

Whenever he felt like it was time to nudge me toward slowing up on my short-track activity, Larry Curry used to fall back on one particular line: "You know, Tony," he would say, "I went to high school once, and I had a lot of fun there."

Pause. "But I graduated."

I'd nod like I understood, but my habits wouldn't change. Hey, every class has to have a slow learner, right?

But as '98 rolled along, I began to appreciate Larry's point. It was time to rethink things. And I came to feel the way everybody feels as a graduation approaches: happy one minute because life is moving onward and upward, and sad the next minute.

I'd show up for a midget or Silver Crown race at a track I liked, and I'd be grinning all night, thrilled that I got to run there again. Later, on the way home, I'd think, God, was that the last time I'm going to see that place? Was that the last time I'll ever *drive* there?

I flew out to Kansas to run the Belleville Midget Nationals in August specifically for that reason: I had no idea whether I'd ever get there again.

Belleville is a three-night show, with the first four rows for Saturday night's finale locked in through preliminary events on Thursday and Friday. I couldn't get there until Saturday afternoon, because I'd been tied up with the Busch race at Indianapolis Raceway Park. Obviously, that put us in a hole, because even though I did well in the last-chance race, I'd have to come from behind in the forty-lap feature. But I had a strong ride in a Steve Lewis car, so it was an interesting challenge.

We didn't win it; in fact, we couldn't do any better than fourth. Still, I had a hell of an exciting race. I spent the last dozen laps trading slide jobs with Ricky Shelton, a fast kid from California who was driving a car wrenched by my old pals Keith and Rusty Kunz. Things got pretty nasty; it wasn't the smartest driving either one of us ever did, because Belleville is a fast, dangerous place. But it was as though each of us was determined to out-brave the other guy. I got in the last good slider, and beat him for the spot.

> **KEITH KUNZ,** veteran midget mechanic: "I was standing there watching those two, and I was like, 'What are you guys doing?' But Tony is a real racer, and he was going for it. That's just what the guy is made of."

My instinct tells me that whenever another driver puts up a fight, like Shelton did that night, I *have* to fight back. I happen to think that's one of my best qualities. And yet it was also the best argument in Larry Curry's favor, and in Joe Gibbs's favor, and in favor of everybody who thought I ought to scale back on all this barnstorming. Scraps like the one I got into at Belleville had the potential to jeopardize a career I'd spent my whole life trying to build. One wrong move by either one of us—and, believe me, I was being every bit as hardheaded as Ricky was—could have screwed up everything I had going my way for '99 and beyond.

And for what? Fourth place in a midget race?

It really made me think.

At around the same time, I had several old friends, people I never thought would want me to get out of open-wheel cars, tell me, "Stop doing this stuff. What's the point?" These people were devout midget and sprint fans who loved seeing me drive those cars, but they cared enough about me that they didn't want me taking unnecessary risks.

> **CROCKY WRIGHT:** "This may sound ironic coming from me, but I wish Tony would focus entirely on the Cup races and forget about open-wheel racing."

To hear them talk that way, it startled me. It made me realize, probably for the first time, that it really didn't make sense to do *all* of the things I was doing. What was important was what I could accomplish down the road, not what I could do tonight on some dirt track.

I still do plenty of short-track racing, and I'm sure I always will. I just don't do it with the same urgency I once felt. I don't *have* to run every midget race I can fit into my schedule; I run the ones I want to run. And I'm cool with that.

As the whole Winston Cup rookie thing started getting closer and closer, I wasn't exactly the most confident guy on the planet. I hadn't yet won a race in a stock car, and I was having a hard time gauging how prepared I was for this step. Plenty of people told me, "Look, you've been successful in everything you've climbed into. This will be no different." I appreciated their votes of confidence, but, you know, most of them had never raced Winston Cup cars.

In the end, one guy who *had* raced Winston Cup cars did the most to put me at ease. Bobby Labonte had watched me closely, and he told me all the time that I'd be fine. In fact, he suggested that because the Cup cars were so much more powerful than the Busch cars I'd driven, I'd probably adapt better to them since most of my previous racing had come in high-horsepower machines. Hearing that sort of thing from Bobby—who is not the kind of guy who just gives the answers he thinks you want to hear—was exactly what I needed.

> **BOBBY LABONTE:** "If I helped him with anything, I think it was his confidence. Maybe Tony thought he wasn't cut out for this, I don't know. But I knew that with the equipment

> and the people we had, we could build a good, solid place for him. And I felt sure that with his ability, we could make it work. I had no doubt about that."

We did a fair amount of testing with the Cup car late in '98, and, little by little, I began to believe what Bobby had said. I *was* more comfortable with the way it responded than I had been with the Busch car; the extra power meant a driver could play with the throttle more, and even allowed me to use a few throttle-control tricks that had worked for me in sprint cars and midgets.

> **JIMMY MAKAR:** "Once Tony got into a Winston Cup car and found that he had some horsepower under his right foot, his true driving talent came out."

I still wasn't sure how I'd stack up against the competition, but I did know this: somewhere in the middle of all that testing, the *mystery* went out of driving stock cars. I went from being apprehensive to being eager.

You already know how things have gone from there, but that's really where our Winston Cup success started: in '98, with a driver who wasn't sure he was up to the job and another driver convincing him that he was.

Today, I have fond memories of 1998. It's funny, but that has become kind of a lost year when people talk about my career. They mention the three USAC titles in '95, the big Indy car debut in '96, the IRL championship in '97, the Winston Cup rookie award in '99, the six races we won in 2000 . . .

But they skip right over 1998. I guess that makes sense, because that season was like a bridge from one part of my life to the next. But, man, it was an interesting time for me. Most of the big decisions facing me in '96 and '97 had been made. I knew where I was going, and I could look back at where I had been. All I had to do in '98, for better or worse, was live for the moment. And I did that.

SINCE I SETTLED INTO WINSTON CUP, NOTHING ELSE HAS EVER BEEN MUCH OF a distraction. Sure, people still love to talk about the short-track racing I do, but that's all back-burner stuff. Driving that Cup car is my job, and it's pretty hard to steer my attention away from it.

Except, of course, in the springtime, when I still find my mind wandering off toward Indianapolis and the 500.

I can't help it. When you grow up spending your after-school hours camped in front of the television set every May, watching the live reports from practice at the Speedway, you never get that race out of your system.

It's impossible to put into words how much the Indy 500 means to me. It is still the one victory I'd most like to have. Whatever is considered the biggest Winston Cup race—probably the Daytona 500—would rank second. A really good second, sure, but still second.

People ask me to explain why I've gone through the trouble of trying to fit the Indy 500 in with our Winston Cup schedule—which I've done twice now, in 1999 and 2001—and I always get the feeling that I come up short, because a lot of them still don't seem to get it. But, I mean, how do you explain a lifelong dream?

Luckily for me, Joe Gibbs is a competitive enough guy that he *does*

I came awfully close to not doing my first Indy/Charlotte run in '99: I had to jump the slight hurdles of a restraining order and a court date ... but as you can see, I made it! I'm still waiting for that Indy victory, though. (© 1999 IMS by Ron McQueeney)

understand. And even though my competing in the 500 presents us with a heck of a dilemma, because it runs on the same date as NASCAR's Coca-Cola 600 at Charlotte, Joe has been incredibly supportive of my desire to win that race.

I'm not sure how much he actually *likes* me doing Indianapolis, but I do know this: he fully appreciates why I do it.

> **JOE GIBBS:** "This is something we addressed the very first time we sat down and talked about a contract. Tony said, 'Hey, I want to go Winston Cup racing, but I'd also love to race Indy.' I look at it like, he's got a dream, and he's got the talent to make it happen."

I'm not the first guy to try doing both races on the same day—John Andretti did it in '94, and Robby Gordon's attempt in '97 got messed up by rain—but I'm proud to be the first guy to *finish* both, and I've done that two times. I may have gotten more attention out of those two days than anything else I've done so far in racing.

The first time we did the Indy/Charlotte thing in '99, somebody started calling it "Double Duty." In 2001, it became "Double Duty II," with a big involvement from the Home Depot and Target department stores and a charity connection with the Victory Junction Gang Camp for kids with chronic illnesses, founded by Kyle and Pattie Petty as a tribute to their late son Adam. With so many people and companies involved, there's a lot of publicity generated, and plenty of press conferences; we've done 'em at Indy and we've done 'em at Charlotte, trying to keep everybody happy. You sit there and answer questions about scheduling, about the logistics of getting to both places, and about the business arrangements between the involved parties.

But for me, none of that stuff is what really matters. Running the Indianapolis 500 is not a *business* decision for me. It's a decision I make with my heart, not with my brain.

I guess I just want to be there too much to stay away.

There are a lot of obstacles in doing that Double Duty thing, but they're not the ones everybody thinks of first. For instance, I always get asked about the travel, but that isn't my department. We've always had other people look after that stuff. They make sure I'm at the right track at the right time, and I just climb in the car and drive it.

Honestly, the biggest thing you've got to overcome if you want to do both Indy and Charlotte is all the hype. Everybody knows how big Indy is, but the Coke 600 is a major deal in its own right. Charlotte is where most of the NASCAR teams are located, so there's a ton of home-race pride on the line for everybody in every shop, right down to the floor sweepers. It's easy to get caught up in all the hoopla of both events.

You'd better be good at keeping your mind on the job you're there to do.

> **LARRY CURRY:** "The first time Tony did both races [in '99], I was a little bit apprehensive about that. He had run Richmond in the Cup car the night before practice started at Indy, and of course he'd been getting ready for Charlotte. Naturally, I'm hoping he's ready for all this. Then he shows up at the Speedway, and on his eighth practice lap he's at 222 miles per hour. Think about that. He had not been in an IRL car since the previous October, and immediately he was, like, fifth-quick on the time sheet. I said to myself, 'Well, that didn't take long.'"

When things go badly, like they're bound to at one point or another, the whole Double Duty thing can be a pain in the neck. But when it's going right—like when you're fast in drastically different cars at drastically different tracks on the very same day—it's a very fulfilling thing.

It's almost comical to think about now, but I came awfully close to not doing my first Indy/Charlotte run in 1999. I had put together an IRL team with Larry Curry and Andy Card, an Indiana businessman we both knew, and The Home Depot agreed to sponsor us in the 500, which was perfect for me. Then John Menard, who seemed intent on making my life miserable whether I was racing for him or not, threw a monkey wrench into the whole thing.

I had just won a Winston Cup pole at Martinsville in April when I learned that Menard had been granted a temporary restraining order barring me from racing at Indy for anybody but him. He was also asking for a judgment of five hundred thousand dollars against me for breach of contract. He claimed that Team Menard's reputation and ability to attract sponsors had been "damaged" by my decision not to drive a Menard car at Indy. I'm not sure how that was possible; Menard's cars still had a reputation for being super-fast, and his own stores had always been the team's primary sponsor. Still, it was impossible not to be worried. I didn't have a half-million bucks lying around, and I damn sure didn't want to sit out the Indy 500.

Menard's lawyer suggested that the best way to settle the whole thing would be for me to drive his car, but that wasn't going to happen. My contract with Joe Gibbs tied me to The Home Depot, and driving for a team sponsored by a competitor of theirs was out of the question. I knew that, and John Menard knew it, too. Or at least he should have, since he'd agreed to it in the last contract we did together.

CARY AGAJANIAN: "The agreement Tony signed for '97 and '98—which was finalized in a hotel room in Indianapolis over a period of hours between myself and Tony and John Menard—contained this addendum: 'Driver agrees to give first option to Team for Driver's services in the 1999 Indy 500 at terms to be agreed upon by parties, and if the option does not conflict with Driver's existing contract for 1999.' It's a very simple thing: 'if the option does not conflict with Driver's existing contract for 1999.' I put that in there specifically because there was so much we didn't know about the Gibbs situation, including who the sponsor was going to be. And Menard said, 'Okay.' Well, a few months later Gibbs signed Home Depot. As we got close to the end of '98, Menard was saying, 'Is Tony going to drive for me in the 500?' We said, 'No. Home Depot won't let him.' But Menard kept saying, 'Well, I'm exercising the option.' He would not take no for an answer, and, finally, he filed [suit] and said that Tony had breached his agreement."

Menard's suit was filed in Wisconsin, his home state, so we had to hire some attorneys from up there to go to bat for us. Cary Agajanian kept me up to date on what all the lawyers were doing, and went up there himself for the preliminary hearings. As it turned out, that was a good thing for us. For *me*.

> **CARY AGAJANIAN:** "Typically at a hearing over an injunction, the judge reads affidavits and statements; most of the time, it takes half an hour. The judge looks at everything, and if he sees that something that might cause irreparable harm is going to occur, he will stop somebody from doing something until there can be a full-blown trial. That's a temporary restraining order. In this case, the bad thing that was going to happen [to Menard] was Tony Stewart driving for somebody else. We had great lawyers, but I flew to Eau Claire because this was so important to Tony. I mean, if we lost, he wouldn't have been able to run the 500. So I was sitting there in court, and here comes Menard with his lawyers, and John takes the stand! This was unusual; it's one out of a thousand that they take any live testimony in a hearing like this. [Menard] testified that the word 'conflict' [in the contract] only meant a conflict in times or dates. I leaned over to our attorneys and said, 'You know, that's my handwriting on that contract; I drew it up myself. You'd better put me on the stand.' So I got on the stand, and I said that by 'conflict' we meant any kind of conflict with the [Winston Cup] contract.' I had a copy of Tony's contract with Joe Gibbs, which said that Tony couldn't drive for any conflicting sponsor. I said, 'Your Honor, Mr. Stewart would be in breach of his contract with Joe Gibbs if he were to drive for John Menard.' The judge looked at everything, and said, 'I find that there is a conflict, clearly, between Menards and Home Depot. Therefore, I am going to deny this injunction.'"

And just like that, I was allowed to race in the Indy 500.

There were quotes in some of the papers saying that Menard felt "crushed" by the decision. I can't say that bothered me a whole lot.

It's got to be a pretty big leap of faith to watch your driver leave town, knowing that in a few hours he's going to strap into something that is completely out of your hands. But I have to say, from the very start my Winston Cup team has stood behind me through all the headaches that come along with this Double Duty thing. I mean, they've been terrific.

JOE GIBBS: "Obviously, you don't like to see anybody who means so much to you driving other cars. That always makes me nervous, and I'm not just talking about Indy cars; Bobby [Labonte] has gotten hurt in a Busch car. But it's a calculated risk."

GREG ZIPADELLI: "I worried about it at first. But I think that now we just look at it like, 'Hey, he's going to do it, so let's hope he runs good up there.' Because, you know, if Tony runs good at Indy, we can feel like we've played a little part in it."

It takes a pretty big leap of faith to let your driver go off and do something like the Indy 500, but Zippy has been great about it. (© 2001 Mike Adaskaveg)

It didn't take me very long to put their faith to the test. On May 20, 1999—my twenty-eighth birthday—I smacked the wall at Indianapolis. It was the first time I had ever crashed at the Speedway. I guess you'd call it a minor wreck by Indy standards, since the car was repairable, but it was major to me because it was my fault.

I had been experimenting with different lines through turn three, which can be dicey because the wind tends to swirl there. We had been catching a strong tailwind, which makes the car push because the front wings are tricked into acting like they're not going through the air as fast as they are. Say you're running 220 miles per hour, but you've got a twenty-mile-per-hour tailwind; the penetration speed of the wings is only two hundred, so that's the level of downforce they generate. Not enough front downforce means the car pushes, and you've got to ease out of the throttle. It's that simple.

Anyway, on this particular lap the car felt stable. The wind had died down for a instant, and that gave me a false sense of security. I kept my foot in it. Well, midway through the corner the wind picked up again and the push returned, and there was no way to keep it out of the wall.

> **JOE GIBBS:** "Somebody called me at my house and said that Tony had crashed. I asked, 'How bad?' They told me it didn't look bad at all, and they had seen him on an interview after the crash. So by the time I heard about it, it was good news; we knew he was all right."

I was pretty upset, because I should never have been caught off guard that way. This wasn't some huge, sudden gust blowing in; it was the same wind that had been there all day, just catching my car in a slightly different spot. I should have been ready for it.

Coincidentally, we had a press conference scheduled later that afternoon. The Speedway's PR staff, most of whom I knew from my time in the IRL, presented me with a surprise birthday cake. They asked me to blow out the candles and make a wish, and I did: "I wish I didn't crash the car."

Two days later, on Pole Day, it was cool and damp—in fact, there were raindrops in the air—when it came my turn to qualify for the 500. But I had to get to Charlotte for The Winston all-star event that same night, so we didn't have the luxury of waiting for better weather. It didn't feel like a super-fast run, and it wasn't: we ended up qualifying twenty-fourth. Still, that wasn't bad considering the conditions.

> **LARRY CURRY:** "In normal circumstances, we don't even make that run; instead, that car comes out of line, we wait for it to warm up and dry out, and we [qualify] in the front two or three rows. But we had no choice."

Then we buzzed down to Charlotte, where things went incredibly well. First we won the Winston Open, which allowed me to start twenty-first in the Winston finale. Just being included in that race was a huge bonus for our rookie team, and then we almost won the thing; I finished second to Terry Labonte, who outsmarted us by taking four tires to our two before the final ten-lap sprint.

I had a week to go before our big Double Duty Sunday, but it wasn't exactly time off. On Monday we taped a TV interview; on Wednesday night we qualified for the Coke 600; Thursday was Carburetion Day practice at Indy; and on Saturday we had our final practices at Charlotte.

I went to bed on the eve of the 1999 Indianapolis 500 feeling remarkably relaxed.

Looking back, maybe I was *too* relaxed. If I'd been more worried about the long day ahead, I might have eaten a healthy breakfast on Sunday morning. Instead I settled for a couple of mini-bagels, which, as I found out, didn't build me a great nutritional base.

On the starting grid, I was amazingly calm. That might have had something to do with our position; when you're up front there's a big temptation to lead, but from eight rows back you go into a patience mode.

Still, I was confident, like I always am.

When the green flag waved, we moved forward pretty quickly. We were in the top fifteen after something like thirty laps, which had me feeling pretty good. Then we caught what looked like a lucky break: a caution waved at just the right time for me, and I jumped to fifth during that round of pit stops. But as soon as the green flag waved again, the guys ahead of me—Arie Luyendyk, Greg Ray, Sam Schmidt, and Kenny Brack—drove off into the sunset. I knew right then that a win was absolutely out of the question.

Our biggest problem was that the car wasn't balanced. At a high-speed place like Indy, where you're on a knife edge all the time, a driver can live with a slight push or a slight loose condition, but too much of either one and he's a candidate to hit the wall. Ours was maybe the worst scenario of all: at mid-corner, the car would snap from push to loose, just like that. At 210 miles per hour, in traffic, that's no fun.

We didn't give up, though. On pit stops, Larry tinkered with wing angles and tire pressures. Inside the car, I was moving the chassis-

adjustment levers like they were gear shifters. At times we improved the car enough that our lap speeds matched the leaders, but that never lasted.

We were running ninth, four laps behind winner Kenny Brack, when the checkered flag came down. I was objective about the whole thing; we fought hard all day, and we basically finished where we deserved to.

Physically, I felt pretty good. I had a blister on my right hand and another on my left knee from the steering shaft, and I also had some muscle soreness, all of which is typical after an Indy 500.

We helicoptered over to Indianapolis International, jumped onto a Home Depot corporate jet, and got to the Concord airport near Charlotte in just under an hour. On the way, I ate part of a nutritional bar and drank some PowerAde, and slept maybe twenty minutes. Then we climbed aboard a chopper we borrowed from Rusty Wallace for the ride into the racetrack; I'll never forget the people pointing up and waving as we made our entrance. When I stepped out onto the infield grass and heard that crowd cheering, I felt like a new man.

And that new man was almost—*almost*—good enough to win at Charlotte. I'm pretty sure his car was good enough, and I know his team was good enough. But the driver came up a little bit short.

We had qualified twenty-seventh for the 600, but I had to start last as a penalty for missing the mandatory drivers meeting. But when they threw the green flag, man, we were ready. We broke into the top ten after sixty laps, and that was with no cars dropping out; every spot we moved up was a legitimate pass. A hundred laps later, I was in the top five, and the car was perfect.

Unfortunately, I wasn't. I radioed Greg that I was starting to feeling nauseous and hot; the hot part was as bad as the nauseous part, because, remember, once I start to overheat my claustrophobia usually kicks in. I needed something to settle my stomach, and something to cool me down, too.

> **GREG ZIPADELLI:** "Tony complained that he wasn't feeling good. We got him some ice on his chest, we gave him a [nutrition] bar and some PowerAde, and that helped him a little bit."

Everybody figured that getting some food into me would help, but as soon as I took a couple bites out of that bar I realized it was melting onto my glove. All I could do was fling it out the window.

The Coke 600 is 400 laps long, and I was still 250 from the end. There were very few caution periods that night, and on those long stretches of green-flag racing the exhaust got the seat and the floorboards good and hot. I remember sitting there, roasting.

Still, we had a great race for a while. At one point our car seemed to be the class of the field: between laps 251 and 267, I passed Mark Martin for third, Jeff Burton for second, and my teammate, Bobby Labonte, for the lead. But it wasn't long after that—lap 310, 320, or so—that I started feeling sicker.

First came more nausea, then some slight dizziness—which isn't as uncommon during a race as it may sound—and then my neck muscles gave out. I rarely lean on the headrests in my cars, but that night I spent the last sixty laps laid up against the one to my right.

Bobby and Jeff got back around me, but I still thought we'd end up third because I had a nice cushion over Mark. Then, with twenty-five laps to go, under green, we made our final pit stops; I got four tires, but Mark took only two. His shorter stop put him on my tail, and from there that guy just wore me out. Mark messed with my mind just by being there, and drained the last of my energy. On lap 387, thirteen from the end, he got me.

Burton won, Bobby was second, Mark was third, and we ran fourth. I had run 600 miles at Charlotte after going 490 at Indy.

The rest of that night is a blur. I remember stopping in the garage area, and the medics hustling me over to the infield medical center to get some IV fluids into me. And I remember a couple of neat things happening in between.

One was Dale Earnhardt making his way through the crowd, and then teasing me—"Aw, are you all right?"—once he saw how tired I was. But I knew Earnhardt wouldn't have stopped by if he hadn't respected my effort, so I could live with the razzing.

The other was Kenny Schrader thumping my car on the right-side window and giving me a big thumbs-up even before I'd gotten out of the car.

KEN SCHRADER: "I just wanted to let him know I was proud of him. I really appreciated what Tony had done. We're talking about the longest stock car race of the year and the biggest race of the year, period, in one day. That kid is just a hell of a good racer."

I didn't try to pull the double again the next year, mostly because we'd finished up the '99 Winston Cup season so strongly that I thought we might make a run for the 2000 championship. I just didn't want to complicate things by getting tangled up in another Indianapolis try.

I was feeling pretty much the same way about 2001, at least until an old friend of mine named Andy Graves called in mid-April. I had been saying I wasn't going to run Indy because I hadn't gotten any interesting offers, and Andy called my bluff. He works for Chip Ganassi's Winston Cup team, but in 2000, when Chip decided to buy some IRL cars and enter the Indy 500, Andy oversaw that project. Well, Chip and Andy ended up going to victory lane at the Speedway with Juan Montoya driving.

Andy and I shared similar backgrounds. He'd grown up around the short tracks, working on supermodifieds, midgets, and sprint cars. He knew how much the 500 meant to me, and he also knew that Ganassi was looking for a couple of drivers; Chip had planned to run Indy with his two CART rookies, Bruno Junqueira and Nicolas Minassian, but those guys were short on oval-track experience and I guess Chip wasn't comfortable throwing them into the deep end of the pool.

Andy said, "Hey, do you think you'd like to go back to the Speedway?"

"Hell, yeah."

Andy got on the phone with Chip, and I got on the phone with everybody I knew, trying to figure out if this was something doable. I had to have The Home Depot involved, and Ganassi's primary sponsor was Target, and even though those stores aren't direct competitors it seemed like there might be a conflict. Thankfully, everybody involved agreed that this might be a good deal for all of us. Target agreed to share some signage space with Home Depot, not just on my car but also on the other Ganassi car, which Jimmy Vasser had signed to drive.

CHIP GANASSI, owner, Chip Ganassi Racing: "The Target people understood that to have a little Home Depot sticker on the car didn't hurt them; this was still the Target car, which has become kind of an icon in this sport. Plus, you know, I think everybody realized that if you put Tony Stewart in your car, you've got a chance to win. Anyway, in the end, you had two very large companies making an accommodation for a guy who deserved it."

We officially announced our arrangement on the day the Speedway opened for practice, and we threw in an extra twist: for every lap I completed at both Indy and Charlotte, The Home Depot, Target, Joe Gibbs, and I were each going to donate one hundred dollars toward the building of the Victory Junction Gang Camp. If I managed to complete all six hundred laps, that would add up to $240,000. That gave me an extra incentive heading into the month of May.

As if I ever needed one.

As soon as word got around about Double Duty II, a lot was made about how that deal had whipped me in '99. Out of nowhere, the papers were full of letters and columns about how dangerous this was, and how I was going to be a hazard, particularly to my Winston Cup rivals at Charlotte, if I tried to run both races again.

Well, I need to say a few things in my defense. First, I have always put the interests of my fellow racers at least on a par with my own. Look at '96, when I passed up what would have been my Cup debut while I was healing up from my Indy car injuries. There was a chance I might get tired, and I didn't want to risk ruining anybody else's race. A lot of guys would have climbed in that car, hurt or not, but I resisted.

Also, my condition at Charlotte in '99 wasn't exactly as bad as it looked. I was dehydrated, and the medics wanted to get me out of the mob around our car. The best way to do that was to plop me onto a gurney, pack me into the ambulance, and go. While they were doing that, they loaded me up with ice and got me breathing cool, clean oxygen, but it's not like I was on the verge of dying if I didn't have that stuff right away.

Look at it this way: I was fighting Mark Martin for third place. You know how many "healthy" guys would love to be in that position, running that well against that guy? Hell, I couldn't have been *too* sick.

I think what happened was, I had just come to the end of this incredible month, and as soon as the 600 was over every last drop of adrenaline just seeped right out of me. My work was done, and so was I.

And that wasn't unusual. Over the years, I've developed a knack for being able to perform at a high level, mentally and physically, for just as long as a race requires. I'm up to the fight until the checkered flag falls, but not much longer. It's like I somehow budget my energy to fit the length of the race.

> **BOB BURRIS**, chief pilot, Tony Stewart Racing: "It doesn't matter what he does, Tony is exhausted when he's done. It might be a thirty-lap midget race, or a five-hundred-mile stock car race. I think it's because he puts 100 percent into everything he does. I mean, if you go against him on a go-kart track, he'll put 100 percent into that go-kart race."

I used to have the track record at Sun Prairie, Wisconsin, for a twenty-five-lap midget feature; it was pretty quick, a little bit over six and a half minutes. That might not sound like much time, but, I promise you, that was six and a half minutes of pure punishment. If you're a serious racer, you put out everything you have. *Everything*.

Anyway, in May of 2001 we wanted to be absolutely sure that this time there were no doubts about my fitness. We got Al Shuford, who oversees the training and fitness programs for all the employees at Joe Gibbs Racing, to baby-sit me throughout the month, looking after my diet and also putting me on an exercise program.

I've always been a pizza-and-burgers guy, which I'm sure goes back to my days driving midgets and sprint cars. When you follow the kind of schedule I did then, you eat whenever it's convenient, even if that's a taco stand at 1:00 A.M. That's a habit that followed me right through my IRL days and into Winston Cup. I mean, my idea of fine dining meant supersizing my Value Meal at McDonald's.

Al, who worked as a trainer with the Carolinas Panthers NFL team and both the Texas Rangers and Kansas City Royals baseball teams, had been leaning on me for a while, trying to show me how better nutrition could improve my health. It seemed to all of us that Double Duty II would be a good time to prove that. Right from the start, Al was my shadow. If I ate in my motor home, I ate stuff Al bought. If I ate in a restaurant, Al usually ordered for me.

By mid-May, I was probably in the best shape of my life.

One thing I noticed when we started practicing at Indy was that the fans gave me a really warm welcome every time we rolled the car onto

Being back at Indianapolis in 2001 was like coming home. The fans were great all month long and really made me feel welcome. (© 2001 IMS by Jim Haines)

pit road. They'd always been good to me there, but I hadn't really been sure how I'd be received this time. For one thing, I'd been away from the IRL for a couple of years, doing my NASCAR thing. Plus, Ganassi Racing was a CART team, and there was still a lot of bad blood on both sides of the CART/IRL.

But I got some incredible ovations from the Speedway crowd. It was a special homecoming, for sure. Over the years, I'd heard those kinds of cheers for guys like Foyt and the Andrettis and the Unsers, and I used to wonder how it felt to be on the receiving end of all that noise. Now I knew: it felt *good.*

Between my commitments in Charlotte that month and the fact that Chip's guys had to be in Japan to run a CART event in mid-May, practice time was tight, so we focused mainly on race-day setups. That put us a little behind on Pole Day, but nobody in the team was disappointed when I timed seventh and Vasser ended up twelfth.

CHIP GANASSI: "We didn't think it was worth making a big, big effort for the pole. To us, the real prize is the one they give out on Memorial Day weekend, not in the middle of the month."

In fact, Chip proved just how confident he was the day after Jimmy and I made the race, when he rolled out our backup cars, stuck his two CART drivers into the seats for practice, and got both Junqueira and Minassian qualified for the 500. Then I borrowed my spare car back from Junqueira and crammed in all the practice I could, because my mechanics were leaving for Japan the following day. I sat in that car for four straight hours, either making laps or hanging tight while the team made adjustments.

Then I headed back to North Carolina to race in The Winston—we finished a decent third behind Jeff Gordon and Dale Jarrett—and relax a little bit. Things didn't get busy again until the Thursday before Memorial Day weekend, when we had Carburetion Day practice at Indy in the early afternoon and Charlotte time trials at night. But we got through all that; I timed twelfth for the Coke 600, even though we knew I'd miss the drivers meeting again and have to start last. We lay around on Friday, did our final Charlotte practice runs on Saturday, and then headed back to Indiana, where I got a good night's sleep in my motor home at the Speedway.

Race day at Indianapolis felt a bit unusual in 2001. Unlike the years I had run there with Menard, there were no season points to worry about, no "big picture" to look at. And unlike in '99, when I co-owned the team, all I really had to do was show up and drive. I was there for one thing, and one thing only: to win the Indy 500.

We didn't get that done, but it wasn't from lack of effort.

Right from the start of the day, I was on my game, or at least my *new* game. I had a solid breakfast—a waffle, a bowl of fruit, two glasses of orange juice—and did some brief hospitality visits with sponsors before wandering over to the Ganassi garage.

Our only real concern was the weather. Rain is common in Indiana in the springtime, and every year it disrupts at least *something* at Indy, whether it's practice or qualifying or the race itself. The forecast for race day included some showers; nothing that was likely to wash out the race, but with our tight schedule even a small delay would be a major thing.

Indy is the bigger race, but Charlotte is the number one priority, because of my commitment to Joe Gibbs. Missing the green flag of the Coke 600 is out of the question, since in the NASCAR standings all the points go to the starting driver. With that in mind, what we do on these Double Duty weekends is look at the Charlotte start time, then work backward—how long will the plane ride take, how long are the helicopter flights, and so on—to establish a time at which I absolutely *have* to be out of the Indianapolis Motor Speedway. In other words, even if I'm leading the Indy 500 with fifty laps to go, if that deadline comes I'm out of the car and gone, period, no question about it.

Ganassi and I had decided that in the event of a serious rain delay in the morning, I wouldn't even start the 500 if I didn't have a clear chance of finishing it. It just wouldn't be fair to Chip for me to run two-thirds of the event and then say, "See you later, I've got to go to my regular job." The best thing to do in that situation, we figured, would be to let another driver run the race, and we had Richie Hearn lined up for that.

As it turned out, the 500 started on time, but we almost needed Richie anyway.

I laid back early on, feeling out the car, seeing how it behaved in different situations. In practice, we had developed three aerodynamic setups—basically, three levels of downforce—which we could utilize as circumstances dictated. If things got hot and slippery, we had a high-downforce package to give us grip; if we got in a shootout at the end of the race and needed maximum straightaway speed, we had a low-downforce setup ready; and, of course, we had a compromise setup. Well, right from the start my car had too little downforce, and it was really sensitive to the turbulence thrown off the other cars. We added downforce on our first couple of pit stops, and by the midway point I thought we were in pretty good shape.

I was fifth by lap 120 or so, then I got past Robby Gordon for fourth. But we still had three pretty tough guys ahead: Roger Penske's two drivers, Gil de Ferran and Helio Castroneves, were running one-two, and Michael Andretti was third. The Penske cars were really quick, and I thought Michael and I were pretty even on speed, so it seemed like fourth might be the best I could do for a while. Then we caught a fortunate break. Actually, it was a series of breaks.

We got a yellow flag, which brought all the top cars into the pits. My guys got me out ahead of Andretti, and as I was leading Michael toward the end of pit road, the two Penske cars, which were pitted right at the pit exit, finished their stops. Each of them was trying to beat the other, and Castroneves forced de Ferran out into the main pit lane rather than the middle merging lane. I had to slam on my brakes to avoid de Ferran, and when I did, Andretti slid into the back of my car, damaging his nose wing. The officials penalized both Penske drivers a spot for jumping straight out into the exit lane, and that put me out front. Castroneves and de Ferran restarted second and third, while Andretti, our other main competitor at that point, had to pit again for a new nose.

It was a strange way to go from fourth to first.

As soon as we got going again, I knew the Penske cars still had the edge on us. They couldn't just drive up and pass me, because I had the best line and the cleanest air, but I could sense that if they got out front they'd just ease away.

Eventually Castroneves got the lead, but he didn't take it from us; we gave it to him. It started to spit rain, which caused a caution. Ganassi saw on the radar that this was only a passing shower and that the race would probably restart; he also saw that there was a second storm off to the west, and that we might get more rain before long. So, on lap 149, Chip called me out of the lead and into the pits. His plan was to load me up with enough fuel to last until that next shower came, *if* it came; if the rain held off, all we'd need later was a quick splash, while everybody else would have to take on a full fuel load. If those stops happened under green-flag conditions, we might end up with a big lead.

It was a pretty brave move. Think about it: if the track doesn't ever get dried out and the race is declared official, Ganassi has just thrown away the Indianapolis 500 with a trick call. But you don't accomplish the kinds of things Chip has—between 1996 and 1999, his teams won four straight CART championships with Vasser, Alex Zanardi, and Montoya—without being a pretty fair gambler.

CHIP GANASSI: "Hey, we were going for the win. We weren't there just to try for a top-ten finish. We knew that all we'd need later on was a three-second stop, fuel only, and we'd pop out with the lead. It was a gamble, sure, but we were there to win."

We ran a few more laps under yellow, but then the rain got hard enough to bring out a red flag. Even though it seemed certain that the skies would clear, this was bad news for us, because the drying-out period was going to take awhile.

In another way, though, the break actually came in handy. My right leg and foot had started aching early in the race, and by the red flag they were just about numb. There was some talk later that maybe my new diet had caused cramping, but that wasn't it. We had simply packed so much setup work into our practice time that I never gave enough thought to finding the ideal seating position, so my leg fell asleep. I hopped out of the car and headed to the first-aid station, where the staff gave the leg an aggressive massage.

That set off a little bit of a circus among the media people tracking my day. When they saw me get out of the car, they figured I was turning the wheel over to Hearn and heading for Charlotte, so I had a pretty good group of reporters and photographers chasing me. They waited outside the first-aid room, and when I came out it was like I gave them a giant head-fake: they all started to go one way, toward the helicopter pad, but I went the other, toward pit lane.

When I jogged back to my car, the crowd was screaming.

The race restarted twenty minutes later, in bright sunshine, on lap

158. Our pit stop had dropped me to fifth. That was okay, because we still had our fuel strategy going for us. But then, with thirty-five laps to go, Robbie Buhl spun while running second; that gave everybody a chance to pit under yellow, which wiped out our splash-and-go scenario.

At this point, our only chance of winning was to find every ounce of raw speed we had. I told myself, "We've got a low-downforce setup especially for this situation." I radioed the crew and suggested we go for broke. They supported me 100 percent, making the changes I asked for.

Sometimes, that kind of call can win a race. This wasn't one of those times. Right from the restart the car skated around, getting really skittish in turbulence. I had no choice but to backpedal into a comfort zone. When my teammate Bruno Junqueira came up and challenged me for fifth, I didn't even put up a fight.

I finished sixth, behind Castroneves, de Ferran, Andretti, Jimmy Vasser, and Junquiera.

We might have run in the top three if I'd only left the car alone. Still, I'd rather gamble on a win and run sixth than just *settle* for third. If the same scenario presented itself tomorrow, I'd roll the dice the same way.

CHIP GANASSI: "I can't blame Tony for that call. He was going for the win, and that's something we had to try. I don't think we had the absolute best car there that day; what we had was a car that could have won if everything had fallen our way, and it didn't."

Until we did the Indy 500 together, I didn't know much about Chip beyond his record, but I really enjoyed working with him. He's a committed, supportive owner who will do whatever it takes to help his team win, and that's exactly the kind of boss I like.

I thanked the guys on my crew, said some quick good-byes, and then headed for the helipad and the rest of my day. In other words, my one-race deal with the Ganassi team ended the same way it came together: in a hurry.

We had ourselves a stylish trip to Charlotte: Tony George had his helicopter jump us over to the airport, where the Home Depot folks had set us up with a Citation X, the fastest business jet in the world. It took only forty-seven minutes to do the 435 air miles—eight or ten minutes quicker than we'd done the same ride in '99—but that was enough time for me to eat half a turkey sandwich and a bowl of fruit. We also had a couple of doctors on board, and they got two liters of fluid into me through an IV hookup.

Even with the rain break at Indy, we made it to Concord with time to spare. I changed uniforms at the airport, and even took a few minutes to just sit and relax. Then we jumped onto another chopper for the hop over to Charlotte in plenty of time for the prerace introductions. My Winston Cup team seemed happy to see me, and I was definitely glad to see them, and to get that race started.

The fact that we were starting last didn't faze me a bit: I thought our car could win the Coca-Cola 600, and I was sure that this time, I could win it, too.

Of course, before long I might have been the *only* one who was thinking that way. I drove down into turn one to start the second lap, and spun the car out.

I knew right away what people would be thinking: that the spin was due to fatigue, or me having trouble adapting to the stock car. Well, I'll tell you what really happened. You drive race cars from memory; what I mean is, your best reference is always what you felt the last time you ran that car on that track. It just so happened that at the start of the 600, the conditions were extremely different from what they were at the end of our last practice. The surface was greasier, and when I got to turn one for the very first time at speed, the car got away from me. Period. It had nothing to do with Indy, nothing at all, and that's a fact.

The 600 is the most challenging race on the NASCAR schedule from a mechanical point of view. It starts in sunshine and ends under the lights, and Charlotte is probably the most temperature-sensitive track in the series. The surface changes drastically, so your car's handling does, too. Generally, the cars tighten up as the temperature cools, so to compensate you tend to start with a loose setup. Well, we had overcompensated, and our Pontiac was incredibly loose in the early laps.

But just like they had done so many times for me, Greg Zipadelli and

his guys kept working away; I'd describe how the car behaved as the track cooled, and they'd make small adjustments during pit stops. And, little by little, things got better.

> **RONNY CROOKS:** "Tony has an amazing feel for grip. He can feel things—changes to the car, changes to the track—that go undetected by a lot of other drivers. That kind of thing is so helpful."

By the time the race was two-thirds over, they had it just about perfect. And right at the end, it *was* perfect.

We had hung around the top ten for a while, but in the closing laps we just took off. I passed Dale Jarrett for fifth with thirty laps to go; eight laps later, we blew off Jimmy Spencer for fourth. Mark Martin was running third, and he had a little bit of distance on us, but I ran him down with thirteen laps to go.

The only thing that wasn't working in my favor was time. The two guys up front, Jeff Burton and Kevin Harvick, were too far ahead for me to do anything about them. But we ended up third, and in the process I became the first guy to run the full distances at Indy and Charlotte on the same day. Of course, the previous record—1,090 miles—was mine, too, but I felt proud of doing the full eleven hundred.

And I was still on my feet.

Just like in '99, a swarm of folks met us when the race was over. Mark Martin came over to congratulate me, which I really appreciated, and Al Shuford, who had taken such good care of me all month, was right there. I asked the reporters if any of them knew of a dirt track running that night, because I was ready for another race.

Of course, I couldn't resist throwing a jab at all the letter writers and columnists who had speculated that I'd be such a hazard. In a TV interview, I said, "For those people that had any doubts, and thought I was putting everybody in danger, you're a bunch of idiots, because I was the fastest car on the racetrack at the end."

I wasn't just running my mouth: according to the NASCAR timing, my last-lap speed was faster than any other driver's last-lap speed. Not bad for a guy everybody expected to be on life support.

— — — — —

The further we've gotten from that second version of Double Duty, the more I've come to appreciate it.

Going the distance in both races meant that the Victory Junction Gang Camp got the maximum donation we'd pledged, and Kyle Petty told me that the awareness we created pushed the contributions even higher, well over a quarter-million dollars. When you can help a great cause *and* do something you love, it's impossible not to feel good.

Returning to Indianapolis also gave me a chance to get back on the track with guys I'd known since my short-track days, like Billy Boat, Davey Hamilton, and Donnie Beechler, and guys I'd had some great IRL battles with, like Arie Luyendyk, Buddy Lazier, and my old karting mentor Mark Dismore. It was also a nice treat to run against Jimmy Vasser, who I had met but never competed against, and especially Al Unser Jr. and Michael Andretti. When I was just getting started in racing, I always identified with Little Al and Michael because they were the hot young drivers beating the veterans. Unfortunately, the CART/IRL split meant I never got a chance to race with those guys in my Indy car years, but I always maintained a ton of respect for both of them.

If I'd had my way, the 2001 race would have come down to a dog-fight between the three of us, but that didn't happen. Little Al got crashed out early, and even though Michael and I swapped positions a couple of times it was usually because we were on different pit strategies; we never had what you might call a duel.

Sometime down the road, I would love to go up against Michael and Al at a place like Phoenix, where there's more pure driving involved than there is at Indianapolis. I'd really enjoy measuring myself against those two guys at a place like that.

I'm pretty proud of the career I've had to this point, but I'm not going to consider my résumé complete until it's got an Indianapolis 500 victory on it.

At the same time, that race is getting harder and harder to win. For one thing, the level of the competition in the Indy Racing League has gotten considerably higher in the time I've been gone, so dropping in once a year and thinking you can win the 500 is a very tall order. Sure, Ganassi and Penske did it as car owners, but they came with multiple entries; from a driver's standpoint, only one car gets to pull into victory lane.

And trying to do that while you're running a full Winston Cup schedule only makes it tougher. The racing is difficult enough, but when you factor in the logistics, the sponsor and media obligations, and even the weather, it's an enormous task.

Still, my dream of winning the Indy 500 is no less intense today than it ever was. It's still *the* race. It's still *the* goal. And as long as I feel this passionately about it, I guess I might as well keep after it.

That race hasn't seen the last of me.

FOURTEEN ▓ I WASN'T RAISED TO BE A LOSER

IN MY DAY-TO-DAY LIFE, I'M PRETTY LAID BACK. I GET OUT OF BED WHEN I want to, I eat when I want to, and unless I've got to meet some kind of obligation to my team or my sponsors, I basically *do* what I want to. I take life as it comes, and I don't let a lot of things get to me.

Like I said: most of the time. When it's time to go racing, all that laid-back stuff goes right out the window.

> **JACK ARUTE,** veteran race broadcaster: "I think anybody who has a real passion for something is going to be emotional about it. And when it comes to racing, Tony is one of the most emotional people I've ever been around."

> **JOE GIBBS:** "The thing about Tony is, he wears everything on his sleeve."

I can't help it; when it comes to my racing, I'm intense.

Everybody likes to win, and I'm no different. But I guess I'd have to add this: I'm not a good loser. In fact, I'm a bad loser, plain and simple, and I'm not ashamed of that.

I think it all goes back to this: I wasn't *raised* to be a loser. I don't

Me and my game face. (© Mike Adaskaveg)

mean to be boastful, but I've been able to do things that a lot of drivers haven't done, and I believe my desire is part of the reason for that. Yes, I'm sure that natural talent—whatever ability I've been blessed with—enters into the equation somewhere, but I've seen a lot of talented racers who just didn't want to win as badly as I did.

NELSON STEWART: "Some other drivers, yes, they like to compete; yes, they like to win. But when they don't win, their attitude is, 'Well, so what? Tomorrow's another day, and we'll try it again.' It's like they have a certain level of desire, and Tony has another level, a higher level."

I've read in different places that I put on a "game face" on race day. That's not something I do on purpose, but it's been pointed out to me enough that I suppose it's really there. I don't recognize the moment when I switch it on, so I guess it must be second nature. Then again, after twenty years of doing something, you shouldn't have to think about how to get ready. When it's time to go to work, you just go to work.

If I put on a game face as a race approaches, it's because I know what I'm there for. I always have.

LARRY MARTZ: "Every time I've gone to a race with him, the moment we got in the car to drive to the track was the moment he changed. Until then, he'd cut up, jack around; but now he had put on his game face, and he wasn't kidding around anymore."

NELSON STEWART: "When Tony and I were driving to Oskaloosa for the [karting] Grand Nationals in '83, a neat thing happened. I started telling him how tough the competition was going to be, that we'd be going up against teams with better equipment than we had. I just wanted him to be prepared for whatever happened. He sat there and listened, and he didn't say anything for probably twenty minutes. When he did finally speak, he looked me square in the eye and said, 'Dad, I'm gonna win this race.' He was only twelve years old, but you could see that determination in him. And, of course, he did win."

From day one, I've wanted to be the best guy out there, and that meant being about as serious about the sport as I could be. Even when I got into Indy cars and NASCAR, where it's easy to get distracted by the fame and the money and the headlines, my basic approach did not change.

The way I looked at it, you stay with whatever works. I stuck with the attitude that got me there, for better or for worse.

Looking back over the past few years, there were times when it might have been "for worse." My attitude has caused me a few problems along the way. But, you know, when you're a bad loser, every now and then you're going to have bad days.

> **PAM BOAS:** "For the most part, I think he's handled himself really well. But there have been times when he's been pushed to his limit, and he's not handled it in the best way."

I've been in hot water occasionally with the media, and with various officials. Sometimes it feels like I've gotten as much notoriety by misbehaving as I have by winning races and championships. I haven't ever looked for trouble, but it sure has seemed to find me. Of course, I wasn't always hard to find; sometimes all you had to do was listen for the shouting.

NASCAR hauls around a big red trailer that serves as its mobile office at Winston Cup events. It's where the officials do their private business, and it's also where you're summoned anytime you step out of line and they feel the need to give you a heart-to-heart talk. They don't exactly have a regular seat reserved for me, but let's just say I've been in there enough that I could probably dodge all the furniture in the dark.

My first high-profile visit to the red trailer came at Martinsville in October of '99. I'm sure you saw the video clip of how it all started; it opened with me standing beside my wrecked car in turn one, waiting for Kenny Irwin's car to come along. He and I had collided three times in the first 147 laps of a 500-lap race. The last time, he sent me into the wall, hard.

I had a little scuffle with Kenny Irwin at Martinsville on October 3, 1999, and it cost me five grand for conduct "detrimental to stock car racing." All I knew was, Kenny running into me had been detrimental to my car! (© Chad Fletcher/Winston Cup Scene)

Standing there, I had no idea what I wanted to say or do to Kenny. All I wanted was to look him in the eye and let him know how mad I was. But while I was waiting for his car to roll around the track under the caution, I took off the fireproof heel pads I wear over my driving shoes. I was holding them when he rolled up, and, out of pure instinct, I just threw 'em at his windshield.

> **NELSON STEWART:** "Tony's always had a temper. He threw his helmet one night in the go-kart days, and I told him that if I ever saw him do that again, that would be the last time he raced. I can't say for sure that he's never done it again, but he never did it again while I was around."

Kenny stopped for a second, but not because he wanted to chat. He had no choice, because the driver in front of him, Dale Earnhardt, had stopped; Earnhardt told me later that he knew I wanted to confront Irwin, so, being his mischievous self, he was just trying to help me with that. Anyway, as Irwin sat there, we let each other know how mad we were, him through the usual hand gestures and me by trying to get at him through his right-side window.

The whole thing was a case of emotions piling up.

The first contact between us, only twenty-nine laps into the race, was all my fault. It was just carelessness, really. We were running at mid-pack when I tagged his bumper in the third turn. I wasn't trying to rattle him, or nudge him out of the way; I just got into him accidentally, and spun him out. Kenny lost a lap, which pretty much ruined his day.

Now, remember, Kenny Irwin and I had a history. Our midget wreck at Terre Haute in '96 had kind of cemented our rivalry. But none of that had anything to do with the start of our problems at Martinsville. There was nothing more to that first bump than this: I messed up and drove into him. Period.

This kind of thing happens all the time at tight places like Martinsville. Most times, the guilty party apologizes, either through hand signals or through messages relayed by radio. I told my team that I hadn't meant to spin Kenny, and asked them to pass that along to his crew, which they did.

I didn't expect Kenny to simply forgive and forget. But I did hope that, mad or not, he'd understand that the bump had been unintentional, and let things be.

Well, it didn't go that way. The next time I came up to pass him, Kenny ran me around a little bit. That was frustrating, because I was on the lead lap and he wasn't, but I figured, Hey, if this is his way of paying me back, at least now we're even.

But, obviously, Kenny didn't think we were even just yet. Later on, during a period of the race when his car was faster than mine, I gave him room to pass me cleanly, but he knocked my car sideways. Well, that did it; the way I saw it, now I owed *him* one. So we went down into turn three, and I spun him around again.

Looking back, keeping score like that was the wrong thing for Kenny and me to be doing, especially so early in a five-hundred-lap race. I mean, if he had only given me the benefit of the doubt about our first contact, things would have ended right there. By the same token, I certainly could have cut him some slack about running into me later.

Instead I got mad enough to spin him again, and he got mad enough to punt my car into the wall.

Hindsight, of course, is twenty-twenty. I wasn't seeing quite that clearly as I threw my little tantrum.

They told me later that the crowd was going crazy, cheering this show I was putting on, but I was too mad to notice. In that moment, I wasn't seeing anything beyond what had happened with Kenny and me. I never stopped to think about what NASCAR might say. But as I walked back toward pit road, an official stopped me and gave me the word: "They want to see you at the trailer."

My sophomore season hadn't even officially started yet when I got my second summons to the NASCAR office.

On the Wednesday leading into the 2000 Daytona 500—the day before the Twin 125 qualifying races—I was leading a line of four or five cars in the final practice of the day. You see a lot of tight packs in that Wednesday practice, because it's the last time you can play around in traffic, figuring out what works and what doesn't from a drafting stand-point, before everything starts counting for real.

My group was bearing down on Robby Gordon, who was running by himself on the backstretch. I went to pass him on the bottom, but he started easing to his left; he may have been trying to put himself in position to lead our train. But we had too much momentum going for me to just throttle back, so I kept coming, and he kept easing left.

I moved over as much as I could, but as we edged closer to the infield grass we touched, my right-front fender to his left-rear quarter panel. Robby went for a wild spin through the infield, and I could tell from the *thump* that my car had a bent nose.

I drove back to the garage and was checking out the damage with my guys. I'll admit, I was mad as hell. I mean, this is the day before we've got to run a qualifying race at a track where aerodynamics is everything, and we've got a fender caved in. I happened to glance up, and here came Robby Gordon, walking toward our garage.

Now, where I come from, when you walked into somebody's pit after a tangle it meant one thing: you were looking for trouble. Maybe you

wanted to swing at somebody, or maybe you only wanted to argue, but you were definitely looking for trouble.

I met Robby at the door. No sense keeping a visitor waiting, right?

SCOTT DIEHL: "All I know is that we were all talking, and Robby came walking by. Tony caught him out of the corner of his eye, and he started toward the back of the car. They just got jabbering back and forth, and, well . . . "

I don't remember exactly what was said, but essentially Robby wanted to know why *I* had crashed *him*. The more he talked, the madder I got. Finally I shoved him a little bit and said, "Get out of here." Well, he came back at me like he wanted to fight, and I moved toward him. At that point my crew got involved, and for a minute it seemed like we had a brawl on our hands; the whole thing happened in front of a TV crew, and even when you see the tape today you'd swear there's a rumble about to break out. But the officials were right there, and Robby walked away, and the whole thing ended as quickly as it had flared up.

NASCAR had us both in for a sit-down meeting the next morning, but by then Robby and I had straightened things out. He stopped by my motor home Wednesday evening, which I thought was a pretty cool move, and we calmly discussed how one little practice spin had gotten so far out of hand. Neither one of us had meant to wreck the other one, that's for sure. And looking back, I'm sure that when Robby showed up at our garage, he wasn't trying to stir things up. He's an up-front guy who speaks his mind, and he just wanted to talk things over right away. Maybe I misread that a little bit.

So NASCAR gave us both the lecture we deserved, and that was that. Or so I thought. That confrontation, like the one from Martinsville, still plays from time to time on TV. The funny thing is, they use that video every time they talk about my temper. There I was, standing around with *my* team, looking at *my* car, in *my* garage, when another driver initiated an argument. But all that film clip shows is me pushing Robby.

You know, whether trouble finds you or you find trouble, the bottom line is this: you're in trouble.

— — — — —

I guess the most infamous incidents of my Winston Cup career—so far, anyway—were two scraps I had with Jeff Gordon, in 2000 at Watkins Glen and in 2001 at Bristol. I'm not sure *why* those moments got so much attention, but I'm sure it's partly because Jeff and I are two young guys who both run up front, and people want to build that into some kind of a rivalry.

Well, I don't know if we'll ever be rivals in the classic sense of the word, but I do know this: I've always thought the world of Jeff's ability. He comes from a background very similar to mine, and I know how good he is. When I get up on any Sunday and think about the guys I have to beat that day, Gordon's name is always right there.

At Watkins Glen, we had just completed the first lap of the race, and as we all went down into turn one I had a golden opportunity to dive under Rusty Wallace. But I resisted that urge, partly because of some things I had picked up from a lot of the Cup veterans, Gordon included. See, Jeff has always been a guy who advocates patience; there have been times when I've made an aggressive move to pass him on a restart, only to have him wave me off, as if to say, "Hey, man, not yet. Let the tires come up to temperature. Take it easy." In races as long as the ones we run, that's a smart way to think.

Anyway, I stayed in line instead of putting a big kamikaze pass on Rusty, and here came Jeff, putting a kamikaze move of his own on me. He was carrying too much speed to make it work without sliding into me, and he pushed me off the track as we exited the turn. Nobody saw that, because we were back in sixth or seventh and the cameras were focused on the leader. But once he shoved me into the dirt, I made up my mind that I wasn't going to give up that spot without a struggle. Patience, hell.

So off we went, side by side through the fast uphill esses, with me on the left and Jeff on the right. Everybody says you can't run through there two abreast, and, as Jeff and I found out, everybody's right.

At the top of the hill, where the road bends to the left, I clipped the inside curb—my fault—which got my car loose. The back of my car nudged Jeff's car and got him out of shape, too; then, as I counter-steered to the right to correct my slide, the *front* of my car slammed into Jeff's. By now, our momentum had carried us to the outside of the track,

and Jeff ran out of room. He bounced off the guardrail, and I bounced off him again.

Both our cars were bent up, his worse than mine. I ended up finishing sixth; Jeff lost a lap pitting for repairs, made it up later, but finished only twenty-third.

It just so happened that his transporter was right beside mine, and when we pulled our cars to a stop we jawed a bit before climbing out. That's when the real fun started: I suggested to Jeff, in language I won't use here, that he should have practiced some of the patience he was always preaching; he threatened to slam my car "right into the wall" the next chance he got. I told him in very clear terms that he'd be making a big mistake if he did that.

Naturally, the TV guys got it all on camera, and there I was, one more time, flipping out on all the racing programs.

> **PAM BOAS:** "I get angry at Tony at first, for letting his emotions control his mouth. It's embarrassing, because people come up and say, 'Well, he lost it again.' But then I'll look at his side, and I'll think, Well, I understand his frustration. I understand his passion."

Two days later, Jeff and I got it all smoothed out. NASCAR had several Winston Cup teams at Daytona, testing some new aerodynamic rules. The participants had been selected well before Watkins Glen, and Jeff and I were on the list. I was sitting in a room with the other drivers and a handful of officials, going over what would be involved in the test, when Jeff came in. He walked right over and sat down next to me.

He grinned and said, "Hey, you still mad at me?"

I grinned and said, "No."

And the two of us went about our business.

The same thing happened after our Bristol get-together in 2001: some bent sheet metal, a lot of noise, a face-to-face meeting, and then Jeff and I getting back to work.

The two of us had been fighting for fourth over the last twenty or so laps of the race. I had the spot, but Jeff's car was better than mine at that point, so he was working me over pretty hard. I held him off for several laps, protecting my line, but it wasn't easy. Coming off turn two on the last lap, my car slipped a bit. Jeff got a strong run on me, and I knew automatically that he'd try to use his momentum to make an inside pass as we hit turn three. My spotter could see that, too, and told me that Jeff was "looking low."

In a moment like that, you rely on instinct. If you think the other guy is far enough alongside you that he now owns the line, you give way; if your gut tells you that you still have position on him, you take your line and expect *him* to give way.

At Bristol, I took my line, and I got spun out.

Now, Jeff's version is different. In his television interview, he said, "I got underneath Tony, and he just turned down on me. I don't want to take a guy out on the last lap, but, hey, I got the position."

Well, I watched the tape later, and I'd say that he had gotten maybe eighteen inches of his car alongside mine by the time I turned into the corner. Is that position? Who knows? All I can say is that in the past, whenever the roles were reversed and I was the guy trying to pass, Gordon had always taken his line and expected *me* to lift.

Anyway, Jeff finished fourth. By the time I got my car gathered up, a long string of cars had driven past me. I ended up a miserable twenty-fifth.

I was pretty hot. Like I said earlier, I hate bump-and-run finishes. If you flat-out steal a guy's spot on the last lap, you ought to be held accountable. It shouldn't be a freebie. I decided right then that this *wasn't* going to be a freebie for Jeff Gordon. I might not get fourth spot back, but he was going to know—*everybody* was going to know—what I thought about the whole thing.

I tried to catch him on the cool-down lap, but he was already on pit road by the time I tracked him down. Then I nudged my front bumper against his back bumper, gassed it, and spun him out. I didn't wreck him—I barely put a wrinkle on his car—but I let him know that I could have wrecked him. Then I left him sitting there, parked sideways on pit road.

I think I got my point across.

> **BOBBY ALLISON:** "I've been on both sides of deals like the one Tony and Jeff had, and I understand how your temper can get away from you. I had an incident with Curtis Turner in 1966 that was somewhat similar. We were at Bowman Gray Stadium, a tight, flat quarter-mile track in Winston-Salem, North Carolina. Early on, he spun me out. I got going again, but I lost lots and lots of positions. Eventually I raced my way back up to Curtis, who by now was leading. I attempted to pass him, and he wrecked me pretty good. Well, that was all I was going to take. The caution flag came out, and he was riding around behind the pace car, and I just drove right across the infield and T-boned him in the side. From that point, we had ourselves a destruction derby: he backed into me, and I drove into him. It was really something."

Naturally, NASCAR summoned Jeff and me to the trailer immediately. They wanted to make sure that any tensions between us ended right there, and they did. As far as I was concerned, I had registered my disappointment with him, and it was over.

The NASCAR folks also wanted me to know that they didn't think too highly of drivers running into each other on pit road. I understand that, because it opens up the potential for a crewman or an official to get injured. Not that this was a factor in our case; I heard all the talk about how I spun Gordon "on a crowded pit road," but, believe me, I'd never have laid a bumper on him if there had been anybody standing even close to his car. I'm not saying I was thinking rationally, but I wasn't thinking recklessly, either. I mean, when I bumped into Jeff we were going maybe fifteen miles per hour. It's not like I came in full throttle and body-slammed him.

One last thought about that Bristol deal: when they asked Jeff on TV if I had caught him off guard by turning his car around, he laughed and said, "That didn't surprise me one bit." Well, it shouldn't. Jeff Gordon and I are two hungry, aggressive racers, and in the course of a season we'll run probably ten thousand laps together. It's inevitable that we'll have a run-in or two along the way.

Again, I have immense respect for Jeff, and for his driving talent. But that doesn't mean I'm not ever going to get mad at him again, or that he won't get mad at me.

Meanwhile, we'll just go right on racing.

Jeff Gordon is a guy I have a lot of respect for. But we're both young, and we both drive hard . . . I guess it's inevitable that we'll have a run-in (or two) along the way. (© Phil Cavali/Winston Cup Scene)

I think the reason Jeff and I were able to put that stuff behind us so quickly is that none of it was new to us. What happened at Bristol and Watkins Glen is the same sort of thing you'll see weekly at any short track in this country: two guys will disagree about something, and one of them might get spun out, and then they'll holler a while. Maybe they'll even throw punches. By the next week the whole thing is forgotten, because there's something new to holler about.

Old-line racers and old-line fans don't get too excited about this stuff.

For some reason, a lot of today's fans are different. Many of them discovered racing through television, and they haven't received the kind of education, if that's the right word, that you have after a few seasons at the bullrings. They don't seem to understand that in this sport, cars are going to bump now and then without it always being intentional, without it always being *somebody's fault*. They sit at home glued to the TV, staring at the replays, and they feel like they need to be judge, jury, and executioner after every little incident.

Well, television is a great thing, but it isn't God. And I'll tell you something else: the term "pictures don't lie" does not always apply when it comes to analyzing racing replays, especially if you don't know what to look for.

My Watkins Glen collision with Gordon is the perfect example. I'm sure that to a novice fan, it looked like I just drove him into the wall. You could see my hands, plain as day, steering toward Jeff's car. But you have to understand that when your car is sliding around like mine was, you're sawing at the wheel, just trying to regain control. The back end of my car had stepped out to the right; well, anybody who has driven a car on snow or ice knows that you *always* steer into a slide, which in my case was toward Jeff's car.

People watch footage like that, and they make these snap judgments: *Stewart wrecked him on purpose.* If they'd only take a moment to think, really stop and analyze the issue, they'd ask themselves, "Why would a guy with a very competitive car just drive into another guy? Why would he risk taking himself out altogether just to skin up somebody's door?" At Watkins Glen, all of that bumping around cost me any shot of winning the race. Why would anybody throw that away on purpose?

They wouldn't. But that doesn't stop some guy from screaming at his TV, from writing critical letters to the editor of every racing paper he subscribes to, or from sending nasty e-mails to the website of the driver he thinks is guilty.

If I saw it once, I saw it a hundred times: "Stewart drove right into him! We saw his hands!"

When I was a kid, I noticed a driver wearing white gloves at a local track, and I was amazed at how clearly I could see his hands. I thought it was so cool; if you paid attention, you could actually understand how hard the guy was working at that steering wheel. I decided right then that I was going to wear white driving gloves someday, and for years I did. I made that choice specifically because I thought it might add some enjoyment and insight for the fans. Well, I wear black gloves today. You figure out why.

By the way, misbehaving ain't cheap. NASCAR fined me five thousand dollars for the fit I threw at Martinsville in '99, and another ten grand for looping Gordon's car after the Bristol race. Both penalties were for what the rule book calls "actions deemed by NASCAR officials as detrimental to stock car racing."

That's kind of funny. I mean, I'm not saying that what I did on those two occasions was right, but I wonder if the promoters of the events *after* those races found my actions detrimental. Everybody wants to frown and act concerned that a little scuffle might hurt the sport's image, but they sure don't mind using that same scuffle to sell tickets the following week.

It's funny to me that some people in NASCAR were surprised to find out that I showed a little bit of temper now and then. It's not like I kept that side of my personality hidden until I got myself a Winston Cup ride.

In 1998, when my engine blew one lap after I took the lead in the Indianapolis 500, I gave what is probably still my best-known interview. As soon as I climbed out of the car on pit road, here came Jack Arute from ABC-TV. He asked me how I felt, and I told him.

Boy, did I ever tell him.

"This," I said, meaning the 500, "is the only thing I've ever wanted to do in my life. This has been my number one goal."

Pause.

"And every year, I get shit on doing it."

It was not the most graceful moment in the history of sports broadcasting. But, again, you have to understand this: it wasn't about that one race, that one result. It was another case of emotions piling up. I'd had three tough losses at Indy, so what you heard was three years of pent-up frustration coming out all at once, unfiltered.

A lot of people took me apart for having the nerve to use profanity on national television. Well, maybe my choice of words wasn't perfect, but I can tell you this: it was perfectly honest. That loss took a huge toll on me, and I think my interview reflected that. I was mad, and I didn't care who knew it.

What I hadn't stopped to consider was that these days, a race driver apparently isn't supposed to show anger. He isn't supposed to display his feelings. He's expected to talk about how gosh-darn great his car and his tires and his engine were, and then he's expected to grin and say he'll get 'em next time.

LARRY MARTZ: "Today, with the media as big as it is and the sponsorship deals like they are, you're expected to smile and say all the right things. But when it comes to racing, Tony is just so truthful. He's not one of those guys who can stand there and put on a performance if he's not happy."

PAT SULLIVAN: "I guess what bothers me when people get on Tony after he's had a bad day is this: all of a sudden, race drivers cannot have warts. They cannot have faults. Well, we used to love race drivers because of who they were, because they were so colorful."

Because Indianapolis is such a big event, it tends to bring out the extremes in your emotions. When you lose the 500, it's like your dream is shattered for another year. Deep down, you know it might be shattered forever.

Less than an hour before the start of that race in '98, Jack Arute interviewed me for ABC's prerace show. He asked me to explain how I felt about Indy. I said, "I'd give up every win and every championship I've ever earned in my life to win this race just one time. I'd give up everything I've done in the twenty-seven years I've been alive."

Now, by that point I had put together a pretty good career. But I meant what I said: I would have traded it all to stand in victory lane at the Speedway.

Even if none of this makes up for my language after falling out of that race, I hope maybe it explains it a little bit. At that moment, the 1998 Indianapolis 500 was the most important thing in my life. *In my life.* One minute I was leading, and the very next minute I was finishing dead last. You can't hide that kind of pain. At least *I* can't.

So when Jack put his microphone in front of me after I'd dropped out, what you heard was that pain. In my mind, Indianapolis really *had* shit on me again. How was I supposed to act? What was I supposed to say?

JACK ARUTE: "I looked in Tony's eyes when he got out of that car. I know what Indianapolis means to him, and I think we both

> knew that this might be his last really good chance to concentrate on the 500; he had already committed to the Joe Gibbs NASCAR thing for 1999. So I asked him an honest question— 'How do you feel?'—and he answered it honestly. It's not for me to say whether that moment was great television, but I can tell you this: that moment was true Tony Stewart."

People always tell me to be careful not to say the wrong thing, but you can get in just as much trouble for saying nothing at all.

After that TV interview at Indy, I holed up in the Team Menard garage, shutting out the world. For the next couple of hours, a huge pile of cameras and microphones built up outside the door. I guess everybody in the press room had heard my comments, and now they wanted some hot quotes of their own. But as far as I was concerned, I had done all the talking I was going to do.

I knew that every guy out there wanted to ask me the same thing Jack had just asked: "How do you feel?"

Well, hadn't I answered that already, on television? And hadn't I sort of answered it again by closing myself off in the garage? Damn, how did they think I felt?

The way I looked at it, they didn't need another sound bite to know what was on my mind. The trouble is, racing has gotten so big and so well covered, and the drivers are usually so accessible, that our accessibility is now taken for granted. When one of us decides *not* to talk, the reporters take it as a snub. And sometimes they retaliate, which is what happened after the 500. For the next few weeks, a bunch of different reporters called me a spoiled brat and worse, all because I wouldn't poke my head out of the garage and talk into their microphones and tape recorders.

> **A. J. FOYT:** "When you lose, you're not in the mood to hear their bullshit. You already know what happened, and why you got beat. I mean, the media has been good to me through the years, and they're still good to me, but they need to realize that if you're the type of driver who hangs everything out, you

don't want to be bothered after something drastic happens. The way I look at it, they ought to have a lot of respect for a guy like Tony, who gives 100 percent every time he goes out there."

Personally, I thought I was a damn good story at Indy in '98. I didn't hide the fact that I wanted to win that race, and I didn't hide the fact that it destroyed me to lose it. Instead, most of the media decided that the real story was that I wouldn't talk with them, like that part of my job was somehow more important than what I did on the track.

That happened again in July of '99 at New Hampshire, when we gave away what should have been our first Winston Cup victory by running out of gas with three laps to go. It was another one of those days when I didn't want to hear even one person ask how I felt, so as soon as I climbed from the car I headed for my motor home. Rather than facing the choice of talking to the reporters or just ignoring them like I had at Indy, I planned on being long gone before they made it from the press room to the garage area.

I knew it was going to cause me some grief, leaving the way I did. But it would have caused me more grief if I stood there and told people how I felt. I was not happy about what had happened, and I needed to deal with that.

KRISTA DWYER, longtime girlfriend: "We went back to the motor home, and Tony locked himself in the bedroom and unwound as much as he could. He said later that he had a screaming fit, but I didn't hear anything, so I think maybe that was all in his mind."

The flight home to North Carolina took three hours, and I didn't say a word the whole way.

As time goes by, I try to look for the positives in a situation. That evening I laid in bed thinking, Okay, we should have won, and we didn't. But we were in a position, as a rookie driver with a rookie team, to run up front all day long in a Winston Cup race. That's something to be proud of." That helped put things in perspective, and by the time I fell asleep I was starting to put the whole weekend behind me.

Unfortunately, the rest of the world wouldn't let me forget it. By Monday it was clear that the press wasn't about to forgive me for ducking them. One more time, what I did *after* a race became a bigger story than what we had done *during* that race.

This time, thankfully, the pounding didn't carry on quite as long. Maybe that was because, without intending to, I did a bit of damage control. On the Tuesday after the New Hampshire race, I happened to be the scheduled guest in a NASCAR media teleconference. I took the opportunity to say that I regretted any inconvenience I had caused by leaving the track so quickly, and that seemed to calm the uproar. Within a day or two, it seemed like every newspaper in the country had mentioned what they called my "apology."

Well, I was glad that things had cooled down, but I didn't feel—and I *still* don't feel—that I had anything to apologize for. I mean, when I'm at any track, whether it's Indianapolis or some fairgrounds joint, I'm there to do my job, which is to drive a race car. The media is there to do its job, which is to report on what goes on. And nothing I do keeps them from that.

The way I look at it, if I stand there and answer every question they ask me, sure, it makes their job easier. But it's not like me keeping my mouth shut is going to keep them from meeting a deadline.

I should point out that despite these experiences at New Hampshire and Indy and a few other places, I think have a pretty good relationship with the media. I've always had friends in the press, guys and girls who covered whatever form of racing I was in at the time. In most cases, we just happened to connect as *people*, and we'd have probably been friendly if I still worked at McDonald's and they came in twice a week for a lunch.

For the most part, I try to treat all media people with the same respect they show me. In other words, as long as they give me the room I need to focus on my racing, I do my best to be as open and as candid as I can be with them. Most of the time, I think we're pretty fair to each other.

JOHN MAHONEY: "Tony's like so many great drivers: when he's doing his job, don't mess with him. I've always tried to be sensitive to that. If he was working on his car, or if I could sense it was a bad time, I left him alone. And I think he respected that, because when he wasn't busy, or if he knew I needed something important, he always made time for me."

JACK ARUTE: "The great thing about Tony Stewart is that, to my knowledge, he never lied to anybody in an interview. Now, don't get me wrong; that doesn't mean he's an easy interview. Tony will make you work, and you'd better ask the right questions. But if you do, he'll answer you, and he'll answer you honestly."

One day at Indianapolis, I tried to explain to a group of reporters, in terms I thought they could relate to, why I sometimes behaved the way I did. I said, "You guys want to be the best you can be each time you write an article or do a report, and I'm no different as a driver. I'm not a guy who'll be out there running around, saying, 'Hey, I'm in the top five, and I'm settling for that.' I always want to be the best I can be, and I feel like that's helped me get to where I am."

I guess what I wanted from the media that day—and what I still want—is

I'll admit this: I'm not always the easiest guy to interview. But I do think I'm one of the most honest, and that's not going to change. This photo was taken after my scuffle with Kenny Irwin . . . I wasn't in the best mood. (© Phil Cavali/Winston Cup Scene)

for them to understand that if I'm tough to get along with sometimes, it's nothing personal. I want them to see that what got me to Indianapolis and Charlotte and Daytona in the first place, my desire, is the same thing that makes me a pain in the butt when I fail.

> **MARK DISMORE:** "Tony's a sore loser, and I don't think that's a bad thing when it comes to racing. When you get beat, how you handle it in the public eye is one thing; but the bottom line is, when you've lost and you're sitting in a room all by yourself, you'd better be pissed off about it. And that goes right to the heart and soul of Tony: he wants to be the winner."

I absolutely believe that I'm hungrier than the next guy is. And I think part of the reason I've been criticized by reporters and by fans is that most people don't understand that kind of hunger. Unless they've been that passionate about something in their lives, they can't possibly understand it. So they try to put you into some kind of context that makes sense to them. They compare you to other drivers, other athletes. In my case, if I'm less gracious in defeat than, say, Dale Jarrett, they'll be sure to point that out.

The funny thing about all this is, the Winston Cup media is always complaining that today's drivers all seem to come from the same mold, that they all give the same answers, and that it's rare for a driver's personality to stand out anymore. And yet, as soon as you let your personality show, you get hammered for doing it.

When I first came to Winston Cup, there were stories calling me "refreshing," and a lot of the regular reporters told me, "Don't ever change, man. Keep being yourself." But before long, some of those same writers were lining up to throw me under the bus for speaking my mind, or for acting the way I'd acted right from the day I started racing.

This same sort of thing has happened to drivers who came before me, and it'll happen to other drivers down the line. So what happens? Those drivers start toeing the line, and giving the same standard cookie-cutter interviews the media claims to hate, just to keep out of hot water.

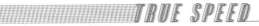

Me? I hate to think I'd let that happen. But it sure would make my life easier sometimes.

> **JACK ARUTE:** "I think there are people who would like to make Tony something he isn't. They'd rather put the mold around him and say, 'Okay, Tony, you will conform to this.' Well, those people ought to just leave him alone, because he is probably the truest, most honest racer I've ever known, along with Foyt."

More and more lately, it seems like people have been comparing me to A. J. Foyt. That's flattering, but it's not something I'm completely comfortable with. After all, Foyt is a living legend in this sport, and sometimes I feel like I'm still trying to find my place in it. But I've heard from some of Foyt's friends that we do have a lot in common, and I've spent enough time with A.J. to believe that maybe we really are cut from the same cloth.

> **TOMMY LAMANCE:** "They're very similar people, A.J. and Tony. They're driven, and they're not going to let anybody stand in their way. They're very hardheaded, they're very selfish—selfish in the sense that they'll do what it takes to be better—and they just want to win."

Just like me, Foyt came up on the dirt tracks. Just like me, Foyt had his scrapes with the press. And just like me, Foyt always wanted to win so badly that losing seemed to kill him. Hell, the night he smacked Arie Luyendyk in victory lane for disputing that Texas win in '97, A.J. was sixty-two years old. *Sixty-two!* That's a long time to carry around that kind of fire.

I guess ol' Super Tex has a pretty mean game face, too.

> **A. J. FOYT:** "My PR skills wouldn't have carried me very far, just like Tony's PR skills wouldn't take him very far. But you know something? People love winners, so he'll be all right."

All I know is, Foyt did a lot of impressive things in his career, and I think I'm doing okay, too. And whatever we've done, we've done our own way. But I've never consciously tried to be like A.J., and I'm not sure that you could do that, anyway. Guys like Foyt—and maybe like me, I guess—are just born to be the way they are. You're either that intense, or you're not. It's not something you can develop in someone, not something you can teach. It's hard enough just to get people to understand it.

Being intense, passionate, emotional—pick your own word—isn't the best way to win popularity awards, and I'm sure my behavior has cost me a fan or two. I hear the boos during the prerace driver introductions, and they bother me. Nobody wants to be disliked, and I'm no different.

But you know something? For every fan who has let me know that he or she didn't like my conduct in a certain situation, I've had another one tell me, "Hey, I'm glad to see you stick up for what you think is right."

> **PAM BOAS:** "I once got an e-mail from Arie Luyendyk; actually, Arie was trying to get to Tony, but the only e-mail address he had was ours at the office. And he said, basically, 'Tony, just relax and be cool. You will get through this.' It was so great of Arie to point out that, look, these things happen, and then they pass. I think that helped me as much as it helped Tony."

The way I see it, you're never going to please everybody anyway, so why try? If you just be yourself, and you're true to your own pattern, I think people eventually come to understand *why* you are the way you are, and why you do the things you do. They come to realize that there's a difference between somebody who's a loudmouth or a crybaby and somebody who simply has a lot of passion about what they do. Look at Foyt: it took awhile, but today A.J. is celebrated as much for his fighting spirit as for his racing record.

I hope it doesn't take people quite that long to accept me, but I do know this: whether they accept me or not, this is who I am. And this is who I'm always going to be.

A. J. FOYT: "If he changed, he wouldn't be Tony Stewart. A lot of people used to say I had mellowed with age, but then I got in that trouble with Luyendyk and they said, 'Well, maybe not.' You know something? I think you stay the way you are as long as you live."

FIFTEEN ☰ EXTREME HIGHS, EXTREME LOWS:
RACING AS A HEAD GAME

YOU HEAR A LOT OF TALK ABOUT HOW DRIVING RACE CARS IS AS MUCH MENTAL as it is physical, and I think that's right. This sport can play a lot of head games with you.

Some of them are kind of comical. A lot drivers get into the traditional racing superstitions—some hate the color green, others go crazy if somebody's eating peanuts near their car—but I never got too wrapped up in any of that. Maybe I've just been too busy; I mean, when you run ninety or a hundred races in a year, like I did in my open-wheel days, you don't have a great deal of time to go through all these private rituals.

There are, however, a couple of car numbers I steer clear of. Years ago it occurred to me that I had driven a few different cars numbered 81, and I had flipped in every one of them. And I'm not too crazy about any car with 13 on the side, just because it seems like you're tempting fate to run a number everybody else thinks is unlucky.

In 1995, when I drove for Glen Niebel, he wanted to run the number 20 on his Silver Crown car, but it had already been assigned to another team. Glen didn't have a preference for any of the numbers that were available, so he just picked 76. We ran it that way once, but when we got home I leaned on Glen to change the number; I told him I didn't like 76,

Racing cars plays a lot of head games with a guy. The trick is to keep your mind in the game.
(© Mike Adaskaveg)

Mr. Magoo at the wheel. (© 2001 Mike Adaskaveg)

because if you add those two digits together you got thirteen. Glen was kind of amused by that, but he was the kind of owner who thought it was important to keep the driver happy. By the time we got to the next race, our car was number 25.

But not all the head games in this sport are that silly. There's a lot of very serious thought that goes into this stuff. Driving race cars takes more brains than some people might think. Just look around, and you'll find that most of the guys who win regularly are bright, intelligent people; they might not have had great formal educations, but they're all quick thinkers, fast on their feet, with a lot of street smarts. Or, I guess, track smarts.

LARRY HOWARD: "Tony's always thinking about the best way to win. What I mean is, a lot of drivers get caught up in battling the guy next to them. That's all they care about.

With Tony, that particular battle with that particular guy is just part of the overall picture: 'How can I win this race?'"

RONNY CROOKS: "That kid doesn't just rely on his talent. He uses his head, too."

Maybe the best way to say it is like this: you take one driver with a ton of raw ability, and another driver with the exact same skills but more brains—more awareness—and I'll put my money on the second guy every time.

It's a commonsense thing.

Every race car has limits to what it can do: it can only brake so hard, it can only corner so hard, it can only accelerate so hard without breaking loose. Every now and then you can sneak over those limits and get away with it, but if you try it too often you're going to bust your butt. A lot of drivers are very good at finding those limits, but only a few have the track sense to run right to those limits all day long without stepping over them. That's why certain guys seem to end up on the wrong end of a tow truck so often.

When I first jumped into an Indy car, everybody warned me that nothing I had learned on the dirt tracks would apply in this new environment. I heard the same type of thing when I started running stock cars. But I think that, in both cases, I had enough common sense to know that I was driving something completely different, and that I had a new set of limits to explore. The good drivers, I think, understand that stuff right away. Nobody needs to explain it to them.

But that didn't mean that I was starting completely from scratch each time. Your talent goes with you; it's just that it needs to be tempered a little by that commonsense approach.

Talent can make you fast, but only brains can make you a champion. That's what I mean about this being a mental game.

No matter where a guy races, he won't be successful if he doesn't learn the peculiarities of that division. Look at the Winston Cup series: people always talk about how the restrictor-plate races are like rolling the dice, because they're so unpredictable. Well, sure, there's usually an underdog in the mix at some point in a plate race. But for years Dale Earnhardt dominated those events, and now you always see guys like Jeff Gordon, Dale Jarrett, Bobby Labonte, Mark Martin, and even Dale Earnhardt Jr. at the front when it counts. That's not just because their cars have great engines or the slickest bodies; it's because those guys were smart enough to see that restrictor-plate racing is a completely different game than the one we play on all those other Sundays, and they made it a point to learn its peculiarities.

I've always tried to take that same approach, no matter what division I was in. If you can't figure out the game, you're not going to stand a chance.

> **LARRY CURRY:** "When Tony ran his first IRL race at Orlando in '96, I warned him about the way the car would develop a push if he ran too closely behind another car. Well, Tony told me, 'Hey, I figured out that if I just flank a guy instead of running right behind him, I can keep one of my front wings out in the clean air and the car doesn't push as bad.' That's how he was; he very quickly figured out a lot of things that other drivers never learn."

> **RONNY CROOKS:** "Tony is like a data-acquisition system. He can tell you what the car did at any point in the corner, and then how it acted when he picked up the throttle. We were testing someplace, and he was explaining to me how the car felt on a very specific part of the track. Then he said, 'Let's look at the [computer] data.' So I did that, and he was exactly right about what the car was doing, right down to within a foot of that particular spot. He feels that stuff in his hands and his feet, and then he files it away."

I think that's part of the reason why I've never really found anything—a particular type of race car, a particular type of track—that I couldn't eventually get comfortable with. It was just a matter of figuring out what the job required.

The smartest drivers of all, I think, are the ones who realize that wherever they go, there's usually somebody a little bit smarter. What I mean is, there's always another racer with more experience, more know-how about that certain track or series. Most times, if he sees that you're a serious racer who uses his head, that guy will be willing to help you out, which will shorten up your learning curve tremendously.

I think our sport is unique that way. There's a serious contradiction there, helping a rival; I mean, Michael Jordan didn't teach his greatest moves to Reggie Miller or Allen Iverson. But it happens all the time in racing. Coming up, I got a lot of help from some of the top midget and sprint drivers in the country, guys like Mel Kenyon and Jack Hewitt. Later on, I had A. J. Foyt and Scott Brayton and others showing me the ropes in Indy cars. In NASCAR, Bobby Labonte was obviously my biggest help, because as teammates it's only natural that you end up talking about techniques at different tracks. But Dale Earnhardt and I weren't teammates, and he gave me some great advice, too. Mark Martin and Jeff Burton were two more guys who spent a lot of time with me.

Anytime you have an opportunity to get good, solid information from winners—drivers who have been there, done that, and have the trophies to prove it—that's a privilege you'd be stupid to pass up. They are handing you knowledge that can't be picked up from a book or a schoolroom; it's knowledge you couldn't buy for any price if those guys thought you didn't deserve it, but if they respect you they'll give it to you free of charge. They won't tell you all they know, but they'll get you headed in the right direction.

It's like Al Unser Jr. says about Al Unser Sr.: "My dad taught me everything I know, but he didn't teach me everything *he* knows." Whatever percentage of his wisdom Big Al passed down, it was obviously a great starting point for Little Al.

In a way, the ultimate sign that a driver is finding his way is that he'll notice the advice coming a little less freely. There were times toward the end of my rookie Winston Cup season when I'd ask a question of one of the veterans, and he'd say, "Hey, you're going faster than I am. Why do you want advice from *me*?"

I took that as a heck of a compliment.

– – – – –

One thing I've found is that some tricks apply no matter what series you're in, and every good driver knows them. For instance, there's a wise old saying about how a race can't be won on the first lap. Well, that's true, but a driver can damn sure *help* himself win on the first lap. For one thing, that's when the cars are bunched the tightest, so if you pass one, you'll likely pass the guy beside him, too. For another thing, all that wise old advice makes the younger drivers so careful that they're sitting ducks.

> **LARRY MARTZ:** "Tony has always been one of the most aggressive drivers at the start of a race. I remember him telling me a long time ago, 'Those are the easiest positions you'll get. If they give 'em to you, take 'em.'"

And the way you approach slower traffic, lapped cars, is pretty constant no matter where you race. A good driver does a lot of planning ahead; when he sees a cluster of slow cars ahead, he'll start figuring out ways not to let them slow *him* down.

Sometimes you'll see the leader of a race go charging right up on a lapped car only to find himself boxed in, unable to pass, as they enter a tight corner. That's a great way to lose a big lead in a hurry, because while his forward progress is slowed, the guy in second place is closing fast. The key is to avoid letting slower cars dictate *your* momentum; if you catch them coming *out* of a turn rather than entering one, you can drive right past them on the straightaway. That's an old trick, but if you have a good sense of timing you can make it happen. You back off here and there while you're catching them, which goes against the instinct of a young charger. But it's better to lose a tiny fraction of a second on *one* lap than to get bottled up in a pack of slow cars for two or three laps.

Of course, when things are going right, *really* right, it seems like even the lapped cars can't slow you down. There have been races when I got on such a roll that I just passed people when I caught 'em. It seemed to take no effort at all.

A big part of that was having cars that behaved the way I wanted them to. But another big part was confidence; was able to convert my confidence into a rhythm, and when you find that rhythm, it's like you get into a zone.

> **RALPH POTTER:** "I used to call him Mr. Magoo, after the old cartoon character, and he could never figure out why. Well, see, Mr. Magoo would come out of his house, looking all quiet and peaceful with that little brown derby. But then he'd get into his car, and slide behind the wheel, and his eyes would change and he'd grow horns out of his head. That was Tony; he'd get in that race car some nights, and he was a different person."

There have been times in some of my very best races when I muscled the car around more than I should have, getting really aggressive when I didn't need to. But I was having so much fun that I *had* to keep on pushing it, pushing myself. I was in that zone.

While we're on that subject, there's a definite line between being aggressive and being *over*aggressive, and I've always tried to stay on the right side. I've raced in as many divisions as anybody, and I don't think I've been considered a dirty driver in any of them. I've never been the kind of racer who takes out his frustrations with his car.

That's not to say that my career has been incident-free. I've had days when I've drawn a line in the sand and said, "Enough." And sometimes when you do that, somebody ends up in the wall.

At New Hampshire in '96, I was running away with the IRL race when I came up to lap Buddy Lazier for the second time. Buddy was running a strange line; he'd enter the corners really high, then slice left across the groove and exit the corner on the bottom. With every lap I kept sticking the nose of my car deeper into the gap he left on the inside, only to have him chop down on me. I was standing on the brakes just to keep from hitting him, and I told my guys on the radio, "If he keeps this up, I'm gonna be in there so far that I won't be able to back out, and he's going to get spun out."

That's the line in the sand I'm talking about. I was hoping Buddy wouldn't keep chopping me, but if he did, whatever happened was on him.

Sure enough, eventually I got under him in turn three, and when he came down I was *there*. The right-front corner of my car hit his left-rear corner, and he spun hard into the fence. I wasn't happy about that, because Buddy had broken his back in a crash several months earlier, and I didn't want to see him get reinjured. But I knew inside that I hadn't crashed him; he crashed himself.

As it turned out, he hopped out okay. To this day, we've never had another problem on the racetrack.

In 1998, I had a similar disagreement with Dale Earnhardt Jr. in a Busch race in Colorado Springs. Junior was charging through the pack on new tires, and I was running fourth or fifth, trying to hold my own on old rubber, but it was so late in the race that I wasn't about to just roll over and give him the spot. That's when things started to get a little bit heated; it was a deal where we *both* drew our lines in the sand, and then finally each of us decided to just jump right over the other guy's line.

DALE EARNHARDT JR.: "I caught Tony, and he raced the hell out of me. I could get all the way alongside him, with me on the bottom, but when we'd get into the corner I'd get loose. Every time I got loose, I'd slide up into the side of his car. I'm sure it appeared to him like I was just banging into him, trying to bounce him around, but I was just so loose. I guess he was getting sick of me running into him, and I was getting sick of not being able to pass him. So I started running into the back of him on the backstretch; that was my way of saying, 'Dude, come on, I'm so much faster, let me go.' I mean, I could see the leaders, and I knew I could catch 'em, and I was getting frustrated. Anyway, I finally got past him, and a caution came out. Now, Tony's behind me. Well, on the restart he got into the back of me, and that put me up into the marbles. I slapped the wall, tore up the right side of my car. After the race, they called us into the NASCAR trailer. Well, Tony was cool about it. He said, 'You and I are all right.' I was cool, too. Hell, I could see Tony's

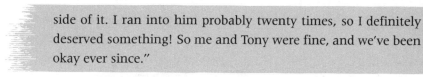

side of it. I ran into him probably twenty times, so I definitely deserved something! So me and Tony were fine, and we've been okay ever since."

I'm sure that to a lot of people watching that race, Junior and I were both over the edge. But if he had been a dirty driver, he could have easily just knocked me out of the way and stolen my position. And if *I* had been a dirty driver, I was certainly in a position to do more than bounce him off the wall on that restart.

It might not have looked this way at the time, but I think Junior and I both used our heads when it counted most. Neither one of us ever really lost control.

The way I look at it, racing has enough inherent risks; you don't need to go looking for more. I'm very aware of the dangers this job can present. I've had all the reminders I ever want to have.

Maybe it's because I've raced in so many different disciplines that I know more drivers than most of my peers do, but it sure seems like I've seen an awful lot of my friends get hurt and killed.

In September of 1994, I was watching Page Jones lead a USAC sprint car race at Eldora. I was supposed to be in the same race, but I was nursing a broken hand from a crash the previous weekend. Anyway, Page was running that scary old joint wide open, skimming along the wall, really hanging it out there. At one point there was a red flag for somebody else's wreck, and during the break I told him, "Man, stay away from that fence, or it'll bite you."

Sure enough, the next red flag was for Page. He clipped the wall and flipped, and as his car bounced down the banking, another car slid in and nailed Page's car right in the cockpit. He suffered serious head injuries.

Most times when I'm racing, I'm too busy to be scared. That day at Eldora, Page's wreck frightened the hell out of me.

I had just gotten to know him really well that spring in California, when I started driving Larry Brown's midgets. Our mechanic, Larry Howard, was like a stepfather to Page and his brother P.J., so Page would stop by our shop quite a bit. He came out to Indiana that summer to run the USAC national series, and we had some fun times.

Nobody ever talked more trash than Page and I did to each other. He'd say he was going to blow me off in the feature, and I'd tell him he'd be lucky just to finish on the same straightaway as me. If a stranger happened to overhear us, he'd have thought we were bitter enemies. We were only kidding, of course, and yet there was a serious side to all of that ribbing. I wanted to beat him, and he wanted to beat me.

> **BOB EAST:** "When Page was driving for us in '94, Tony won a race at Bloomington after he'd passed Page on the outside. Well, Page pulled into the pits and said, 'That's the last time that guy gives me a driving lesson!'"

The funny thing was, at the end of the night Page and I would usually end up shooting pool together. That was our second form of income: hustling the other racers in billiards. We also golfed quite a bit, Page and me and Mike Bliss. Actually, the three of us redefined the rules of the game: instead of being about who could put the ball into the hole in the fewest strokes, it was a contest of who could get to his ball quickest. We took back a few golf carts that looked like they'd been wrecked at Talladega.

For a while I was afraid that I had lost a really good friend, and that Parnelli and P. J. Jones had lost a son and a brother. Even when it was clear that Page would survive, for a time it seemed like we had lost him anyway; he was unconscious for a long time, and even later he couldn't speak for weeks. For me, if Page Jones wasn't busting my chops, he couldn't really *be* Page Jones.

Fortunately, Page has made a terrific recovery in the years since that crash. In April of 2001 he got married, and every now and then I'll see him at a race someplace. I love running into him, because I've got so many great memories of that period when we hung out every day. Seeing him helps me get over that one bad Eldora memory, which affected me for a long, long time.

> **NELSON STEWART:** "When Page got hurt, that shook Tony up quite a bit. It was almost as if he was afraid to get too close to another driver for a while, for fear that something might happen."

I wasn't naive about the dangers of racing, by any means. Just that spring, Robbie Stanley, a three-time USAC champion and the guy I passed to win my first career sprint car feature in '92, had died in a crash at Winchester. But Page was probably the first truly close friend of mine who had ever been hurt that badly.

I'm sad to say he wasn't the last.

Looking back, we were all a little young for that sort of drama. At the time of Page's wreck, I was twenty-three years old. Then again, maybe you're never really ready for this sort of thing.

On July 7, 2000, I was buckling into my Winston Cup car, getting ready to make my first practice laps for that weekend's race at New Hampshire, when I heard everything go quiet. The red flag had come out, which isn't uncommon; usually it's somebody dropping oil, or debris on the track, something like that. One of my guys leaned down and said, "Hang on. Kenny Irwin hit the wall in turn three, and it's going to be a minute."

As I sat there, that minute turned into several minutes. I kept asking if Kenny was all right, and nobody knew anything. That's usually not a good sign. If a guy hops out okay after a wreck, you hear about that right away. Even if a guy breaks a leg,

Sometimes Kenny Irwin and I were friendly, and sometimes we couldn't be, because each of us stood in the other's way. But I tell you this: I respected the hell out of Kenny, and I sure miss him.
(© Phil Cavali/Winston Cup Scene)

same thing; nobody *wants* to tell you about an injury, but they figure you'd rather know the facts than sit there wondering. When there's nothing but silence, you get nervous.

The track reopened for practice after a long delay, and I got back to work. It wasn't until later, after the session had ended, that my guys gave me the bad news: Kenny was dead. It was a stuck throttle that got him, they told me.

Even though that earlier silence had been a warning for me, this hit me like a thud. *Kenny Irwin*?

Our relationship went back to the start of our USAC careers in 1991. Kenny was a bit older than me, but we broke in together as midget rookies at the Indianapolis Speedrome. We were the top two candidates for the Rookie of the Year award, but toward the end of the season I won two features, which clinched it for me.

Anytime you compete with a guy for a specific honor, you're bound to look at him as more than just another driver. Kenny and I didn't know each other personally, and we hadn't communicated any further than maybe nodding at each other, but, right there, the rivalry was on.

Before long we had branched out into national midgets, sprints, and Silver Crown cars, working our way up the USAC ladder. He beat me some, and I beat him some, and, like I've mentioned, he was the guy I feared most during my championship runs in '94 and '95. It was like that Speedrome rivalry never went away, and Kenny Irwin became my benchmark.

Sometimes it seemed like my career had jumped ahead of his, like when I graduated to Indy cars in '96; other times, like when he signed on with Robert Yates to run Winston Cup cars in '98 and then won that year's rookie award, it felt like he'd slipped ahead of me. Either way, it made perfect sense to me that by 1999 we had both found homes in the Cup series.

In the back of my mind I figured, Okay, I guess this is going to go on forever, me and Irwin, battling it out. Even when I started winning Cup races while Kenny struggled, I knew—I mean, I just *knew*—that this was just a temporary lull in the action.

There wasn't a practice or qualifying session that went by without

me looking for Irwin's name on the time sheets. If I was ahead of him, great; if I wasn't, I had to get going, damn it. Sure, there was a long list of other guys I should have been worried about, but I always wanted to know one thing first when I saw those sheets: *Where's Irwin?*

And now he was gone.

I didn't know what to do. I had some friends with me at New Hampshire, and that day we talked about everything except the only thing on all our minds, which was Kenny. I asked Bob Burris to fly to Charlotte to pick up Krista, who had stayed home that weekend, and when she arrived we did the same thing: we talked about other things. All I could think about was Kenny, but I just didn't know how to face what had happened.

> **PAM BOAS:** "That's the way Tony has always dealt with things that hurt him. He has to sort those things out in his own mind first, and when he's ready to talk about it, he will. It's a defense mechanism, I think, something to prevent himself from being hurt any more."

Two days after Kenny's death, I won the race. I said this in my post-race interviews, and it might have sounded corny, but I meant it: from the time I climbed in the car that day until the time I climbed out, I had Kenny Irwin in my thoughts. There were times when I felt it so strongly that it was like having a co-driver with me; it was eerie, but it was also comforting.

On the trip home, I protected that trophy like it was the last one I'd ever win. In a way, it was the last one Kenny Irwin won, because I gave it to his mom and dad after Kenny's services in Indianapolis that week.

Going to Kenny's funeral was one of the hardest things I've ever done. I knew I would go, there was no question about that. Still, I wondered how it might be received. Kenny's family—particularly his dad, Kenny Sr., but the rest of the family, too—always had the same fiercely competitive spirit Kenny had. They were his biggest supporters. I'm sure there were times when they didn't think too much of me, because of the run-ins we'd had, and I was worried about that.

Well, his mom, Reva, put me at ease. We embraced at the service, and she said, "I was afraid you weren't going to be here." It made me realize, again, just how much a part of each other's lives we had been. I had known the Irwin family for years without really knowing them at all.

I think about Kenny a lot, and when I look back I can see that ours wasn't a bad relationship. There were periods when we hung out, and periods when we didn't, or *couldn't*. See, Kenny looked at me as a guy who stood between him and his goals, which was the same way I looked at him. It was just easier to not get too close, so we both took the easy way out.

At times we disagreed over certain situations, and at times I didn't want to see him, much less talk to him. But there was never, ever a moment when I hated the guy. There was too much respect there for that. I understood what that kid could do with a race car. I couldn't *help* but respect him.

I've said this before, and I'll always believe it: Kenny Irwin helped me get to where I am today. Some guys keep you sharp, but Kenny made me sharper. It was the only chance I had to keep up with him.

I think—I hope—that he thought that way about me, too.

Boy, I miss that guy.

And everybody, of course, misses Dale Earnhardt.

I thought I knew how big Earnhardt was in our sport. As it turned out, I had no idea. I think a lot of people in racing felt that way: shocked by what a huge news story his death became. For a week after he was killed at Daytona, he was on the front page of every newspaper in the country, even the big-city ones that never cover racing. And they talked about him for days on the network newscasts, which hardly ever mention sports except for the Super Bowl, the World Series, or the Olympics.

We knew Earnhardt was an icon in the garage area and in the grandstands, but I'm not sure any of us understood what he meant to people across the country, and even around the world.

I was only around Dale on a regular basis for my first two years of Winston Cup racing, plus a handful of times when Dale Jr. and I ran the Busch Series. I really enjoyed that guy, and I felt like I was just getting to know him.

If you watched Earnhardt on TV, like I did for years, studying his races and listening to his interviews, you probably came away with the same perception I did: that he was just a stubborn, determined hardcase. Well, he was that, yes, but there was a lot more to Dale Earnhardt.

On one hand, he was like royalty; to be accepted by Earnhardt was something every young driver wanted, and that part of him was as intimidating as having him on your bumper. To be honest, I worried about that, because of some scrapes I'd had with Junior in Busch cars. But Dale understood that those incidents had been just hard racing between two hungry kids; he never made me feel anything but welcome once I got to Winston Cup, and to be welcomed by that man was a blessing. It was like you had been officially greeted, and now you were part of The Show.

Then there was this other side of Dale, a much less intimidating side, that I wish everybody had gotten the chance to see. There were times when it was just the two of us together, leaning against a fender or a toolbox, and Earnhardt would open up, talking a little about racing and a lot about life. In those moments, he was nothing like the hardcase he was supposed to be. He was just a really cool guy—to me, an older, wiser guy—who had a lot to offer.

Beating Dale Earnhardt to win the Budweiser Shootout just a week before he died is one of the highlights of my career. Getting to *know* Dale Earnhardt, and to feel the start of a bond with him, is one of the highlights of my life.

Everybody always mentions my accident when they talk about the crash that killed Earnhardt. I was supposed to be the guy in big trouble that day at Daytona, because my car flipped and tumbled a dozen times and Dale's wreck looked much more routine. All I know is that it took me some time that day to comprehend that he was gone. When he hit the wall, I was already at the hospital, getting my shoulder X-rayed and my head treated for a concussion. They told me he was hurt bad, maybe dead, but I was in a drugged-up state of disbelief. Then there were people crying in the hospital hallways, and when we got back to the track the place was stone quiet with grief. There was even some talk about a memorial service being planned for later in the VIP motor home area. This was *real*.

My own wreck started when Robby Gordon bumped Ward Burton, who bumped me, and then all hell broke loose. All I remember is feeling a thump on my right rear, and nosing into the backstretch wall before I took a short nap. Then, out of a thick fog in my head, I saw Bobby Labonte at my window with some rescue workers, and I knew I was going to be all right.

I mention the origin of my wreck only because of something that happened that evening, at the memorial service for Dale. Robby Gordon spotted me in the crowd, and walked over to check on me. Of course, we had a history even before that day, and I guess there were a few people there who got a little nervous, wondering where this situation might go. But when Robby asked if I was all right, I didn't care about the wreck. I didn't care about my headache. I didn't care about my aching shoulder. All I cared about was that Robby and I were standing there, basically healthy, and that Robby's mom, who was right beside him as we talked, wasn't in the same situation Teresa Earnhardt was in. Robby hugged me, and I hugged him back.

We were two race drivers who happened to tear up a couple of stock cars. On this day, that was no big deal.

Since we're on the topic, this is what I feel about the chance of me getting injured, or worse, in a race car: I don't worry about it.

Yes, I know this stuff can hurt you. There aren't many things as painful as a broken pelvis, and I've been down that road. And, obviously, I'm well aware that you can lose your life doing what I do. But I believe this: I've got a better chance of dying of cancer than of getting killed in a race car. I've got a better chance of killing myself on some interstate highway than on some speedway.

Sure, I have a risky job, but lots of folks do: firemen run into burning buildings, truck drivers crash, factory workers face all kinds of industrial hazards. There's danger in a hundred occupations. The difference is, I'll bet I love my job more than most people in those occupations love theirs.

I've worked jobs I didn't like, to pay rent and to buy groceries and to

make enough money to keep racing. Happily, that period of my life lasted just a few years. Well, there are millions of people who spend literally their entire adult lives doing work they can't stand.

I am doing the only thing I've ever really wanted to do, the only thing that completely fulfills me. I'm a very lucky person.

So if I don't make it out of the next race I run, don't cry for me. That's an order.

Sure, there are still a few things I look forward to experiencing, things that don't have anything to do with racing. But I've already gotten much more out of this life than I ever expected. I've been all over the country, won my share of races, and met an awful lot of neat people. And maybe I'm just a simple enough person that that's all I need.

If it all ended tomorrow and I was looking at a replay of my life, there wouldn't be many regrets.

If racing is such a mental thing, then a smart racer ought to be pretty good at analyzing what makes him tick, right?

Wrong. I'm not too big on looking that closely in the mirror.

So when a reporter asks, as one seems to every now and then, why I've been able to be so successful, I usually give them the least analytical answer I know.

"Gosh, I dunno," I tell them. "You'd have to ask somebody else."

> **LARRY MARTZ:** "With Tony, there are several things that make up the package. First of all, he was born with a tremendous amount of talent, and his will to win is so much higher than the average person's. Then, his ability to get the best out of what he has is amazing. Tony Stewart has driven a lot of great cars, but he did not always have the best equipment on the track; he sometimes won with average equipment. So he is able to get the most out of himself, and the most out of the car. Then there's his depth perception, his reflexes, his throttle control; I really think that Tony is the master of throttle control. And, you know, he's got a tremendous amount of nerve. Courage. Balls."

STEVE CHRISMAN: "He's just a natural. His combination of seat-of-the-pants feel, eyesight, hand reaction, and smoothness on the throttle is the best I've ever seen."

ROLLIE HELMLING: "Tony always manages to play the hand he's dealt, and that's what makes a champion. In other words, if the car is perfect, most good drivers can drive it to the front and keep it there, but if the car is just a little bit off, your true winners will make up the difference. There were times when maybe I didn't do my job in preparing the car, or I made a decision that didn't turn out to be correct. Well, Tony never griped, never complained; you could see him just decide, Okay, I'm going to take what I've got, and do the best I can with it. He sees it as his job to make up the difference. No excuses, no alibis. Just, 'Here's the mission. Get the job done.'"

PARNELLI JONES: "It all boils down to two things: car control and desire. You can teach somebody the basics of how to drive, and you can even teach him a little bit about car control as long as they've got the natural ability, but you cannot teach him that will to win. The best drivers, guys like Tony, they don't ever want to lose."

BOB EAST: "When he goes to the track, he's sure he's going to win. And once the race starts and the car's not exactly right, he'll adjust his style to suit it. He still believes he's going to win, but now he's just got to figure out another way to do it. That's how it always is with Tony: it's not, 'God, I hope I can win this race,' it's more like, 'Okay, how am I going to win this race?'"

A. J. FOYT: "It's hard to say what makes Tony so good. I'd guess I'd have to turn it around, and look at myself; I was always able to adapt to just about any type of car, same as Tony, and I can't say why. I guess maybe you're just gifted with that sort of ability. I don't think it's something you can learn. I mean, a lot of people have tried hard to do these things, but they've failed. So I think Tony has been gifted, from the day he was born."

CHRIS ECONOMAKI: "The guy has an extraordinary amount of talent."

SIXTEEN · IT'S MY LIFE

I'VE ALWAYS BEEN FLATTERED BY THE IDEA THAT THERE WERE PEOPLE WHO followed my racing. When I first started running well in the midgets, it was a neat feeling to be at my hometown Dairy Queen and have somebody say, "Hey, aren't you Tony Stewart?"

Now I'm past thirty, and it's still a neat feeling. I've always said that the day I dread most is the day people *don't* recognize me. I'm proud that people know who I am, proud that they care about what I do.

But I've got to admit this: Everything I thought I knew about fame didn't really amount to much. There's a point at which fame takes on a life of its own, when it becomes so big that it has an effect on your daily life. And never again do you feel that same innocent thrill you felt the first time somebody asked you if you really were who they thought you were.

Now, I've gotten into trouble in the past when I've talked about this aspect of being a race driver. Anytime you discuss the relationship between drivers and fans—or, for that matter, between *any* celebrity and the general public—you're in kind of a touchy area. But most of my problems have resulted from things being taken out of context, or at least misunderstood. I think I owe it to myself and to the fans, whether they're my fans or not, to clear up some of this stuff.

When I look back on everything that has happened to me since my rookie Winston Cup season, I'm absolutely stunned. I guess I underestimated the sheer size of that form of racing, and how closely people followed its drivers. Just by taking that one step into another form of racing, everything about my life somehow became *bigger*.

Sometimes the ride has been a whole lot of fun.

And sometimes it hasn't.

I want to say right up front that I'm not *complaining* about any of this. I like my life. I'm having the kind of career that once would have been just a crazy dream. And, let's face it, there are definitely benefits to being successful at this level.

But for every plus, there's a minus. Some of them are actually pretty minor; you always hear the old cliché about getting interrupted while you eat dinner in restaurants, and, sure, it happens. But that's just a tiny headache compared with the overall loss of your day-to-day privacy. That's the single biggest adjustment I've had to make: getting used to the idea that even when I'd like to be anonymous, I can't.

People ask what it's like to be a Winston Cup driver. Well, it's great, as long as that's *all* you want to be. But if you want to be a living, functioning human being at the same time, it has its drawbacks.

I'll be the first to admit that I haven't always handled all this in the most graceful way. But, in my defense, when you grow up the way I did, you don't spend a lot of time preparing for how you'll react to being famous. All I know is, when you realize one day that people treat you differently, talk to you differently, and push and pull you differently just because you've won some Winston Cup races, it is a huge culture shock.

CARY AGAJANIAN: "At the Brickyard 400 a couple of years ago, a crowd of people rushed up to Tony and Krista, and they knocked her down. Well, you tell me, how does somebody learn to be ready for something like that?"

TUTTI MARTZ: "When you think about it, it has all happened so fast for him. It's all been, just, boom-boom-boom! It's not that Tony's in a bad position; he's done very well, and he's doing what he likes to do. But there's just so much pressure."

TARA ARMSTRONG: "I look at it like, Tony is an ordinary person in extraordinary circumstances. And as much as he wanted to be in those extraordinary circumstances, he still wants to be that ordinary guy."

Ten seconds. That's what everybody wants, as in, "Gee, if you just have ten seconds, I'd really appreciate it if you could sign this . . . "

Right about then, there's this strange thing that goes on in your mind. On the one hand, you want to accommodate somebody if you can, because you know that by fulfilling that request you might make their night. On the other hand, you have to consider the effect it could have on *your* night. Suddenly you're caught in a bind; what started out as a pleasant encounter has the potential to ruin an evening.

From their standpoint, it looks so simple: ten seconds hardly seems like too much to ask. But they don't stop to think that once they get their ten seconds and move on, there are now a dozen more people, or a hundred, who each feel entitled to their ten seconds, too. They don't consider that you might be in a private discussion with friends, or a girlfriend, or family members you rarely get to see. They don't realize that to give them their ten seconds, you're *taking* ten seconds from whoever you're with.

In the best-case scenario, you exchange a word and sign a quick autograph, and everybody gets on with their night. Then there's the scenario where one autograph leads to several more, and you just grin and bear it. But the worst scenario is the one where you *don't* give somebody those ten seconds, either because it's not practical or because you're just not in the mood, and they get so mad that they lose their tempers.

It happens more than you'd ever believe, and I can't understand why. People go out for a nice evening with friends, and then they wind up going home angry because somebody—a ballplayer, an actor, a race driver—wouldn't sign his name on a napkin. They have somehow convinced themselves that just because they happened to choose the same restaurant or the same movie theater this celebrity did, that guy *owed* them something, something they could show their kids or their buddies at work.

Well, I'm sorry, but I don't feel like I owe anybody an autograph. I don't feel like I owe anybody anything more than my best effort in the race they bought tickets to. On that score, I've never cheated anybody out of a penny.

Now, that's not to say I don't sign autographs. We have a bunch of appearances every season where I'll do that for hours. And in the course of a normal weekend, I might sign a hundred more just walking through the garage or down pit road. But I don't feel like I'm *obligated* to do that.

Obviously, not everybody shares this belief.

On the evening after I won the Bud Shootout in February of 2001, I was feeling great. I did the postrace interviews, showered and changed at my motor home, and then headed out with some friends to catch a sprint car race at Volusia County Speedway, a dirt track about forty miles up the road.

We were hungry, but we didn't have much time to kill, so we ducked into a Hooters across the street from the Daytona track. We grabbed a corner table and I sat facing the wall, just trying to blend in. We didn't ask the waitresses to turn people away; we didn't ask to have our table roped off. All we did was mind our own business.

A few people stopped for autographs, and I told them as politely as I could that this wasn't the right place for that; if I signed for them, I explained, I'd end up signing for everybody. That's the way these things go: if folks see you sign one autograph, they figure you're in a signing mood. And it's not that I *wasn't* in a signing mood, it's that I really wanted to get to Volusia County. All we wanted was to put away a quick sandwich and get out of there.

Nobody squawked, nobody cussed me out. The general reaction was like, "Cool, we'll let you eat. Oh yeah, congratulations on today's race."

Well, one guy was wearing a Tony Stewart hat that he wanted me to sign. When we turned him away—again, politely—he seemed to take it as well as the other folks did. But after we paid the check and headed out, there he was, standing on the patio, pointing down. And on the ground was that hat, torn in half and charred around the edges. He had actually set fire to the thing, and he wanted me to see that.

I was so shocked, I wasn't sure what to do. Finally I picked up the hat, handed it back to him, and went on my way.

It's strange how hard things like that hit you. I had a great time at the sprint car race, saw a bunch of friends, had a few laughs. And yet what kept popping into my mind as I drove back to Daytona Beach, and even after I'd climbed into bed, was that guy burning his hat.

What bothered me the most was that until that evening, that man obviously liked me at least a *little* bit. I mean, he had bought the hat, and he had come looking for an autograph. But now, just because I hadn't taken a pen and scrawled my name on that hat, the guy hated me. I tossed and turned, trying to balance that out in my head, but I couldn't do it.

> **DICK JORDAN:** "I think it's a difficult thing for Tony. He's such a people person, and trying to blend that with being a star, so to speak, is not easy."

There has been a lot of talk over the past few years about how Winston Cup drivers keep themselves secluded on race weekends. During the day, they're holed up in their transporters; when the practice and qualifying sessions end, they're hidden in their motor homes. Fans complain all the time about how inaccessible some drivers are.

Well, maybe it's because some of those drivers have had experiences like the one I had that night. Who in their right mind would volunteer to go through that again?

Here's the craziest part: if I had been like the drivers those fans complain about—if I had just cut myself off from the public—that guy with the hat would probably have been a fan of mine forever. But because I elected to chill out like a normal person and unwind with my friends, I was a bad guy, because he didn't get that autograph.

The one he figured I owed him.

I wish every fan who ever complained about an athlete or movie star being rude to them could trade places with that person for a week. Not an afternoon, and not a day, but a solid week. I say that because there are friends of mine who see this public side of my life for a few hours, and think it's fun. Wherever we go, people seem glad to see us, and there's always something *happening*.

But once they're with me for a few days, they change their tune.

They begin to see the way it all adds up. And after a week or so, they're as tired of it as I get sometimes.

> **BARRY MEDARIS,** longtime friend: "I kinda sit back and take it all in. First you'll notice people staring and pointing. Then maybe a waitress asks for an autograph. Then she'll show it to everybody she works with, so all the other waitresses and the managers want one, too. Now everybody else notices that there's a group around this one table, so they want to see what's happening. Pretty soon, it's like all the attention is on us. I've kinda grown used to it, but it does get a little frustrating. Hanging out gets harder all the time."

It's tough, because I've always liked having company around. Whether I'm at home in North Carolina or maybe back in Indiana, there are days when all I want to do is get out with my buddies and see what's going on in their lives. By the same token, they're interested in catching up with the nonracing side of my life; guys like Barry Medaris or Mark Hill, who I've known since my karting days in Columbus, they already know where I finished last Sunday. They're wondering what else I've been up to.

> **MARK HILL,** longtime friend: "Most of the time when he comes home, we don't even talk racing. He deals with racing every day, like I deal with my work every day. When we go out, we talk about other things."

In other words, we enjoy just bumming around, like friends do. But the odds of us actually getting to do that, spending time by ourselves, are pretty steep. If we go to a place where there's any kind of a crowd, every five minutes we're interrupted so I can sign somebody's T-shirt or meet somebody's girlfriend. An old friend of mine might be in the middle of an important personal story, and we'll hear, "Uh, excuse me, Tony?"

Well, I'm not sure if that's fair to me, but it's definitely not fair to my friends. They're not out with me because they think it's cool to have a beer or shoot pool with a NASCAR driver. They're out with me because it's a chance to see a guy from their group who isn't around much anymore.

We've figured out that we can avoid a lot of this commotion by going out at odd times, and to places we think will be pretty empty. But, you know, when you have to put so much scheming into a simple night out, it's no longer a simple night out. It becomes more like a scheduled event, and it lacks the spontaneity that makes being out with your friends so much fun in the first place.

People talk all the time about the price of being famous. Well, I look at it like this: if fame means that you're unable to spend quality time with your friends, it's only human to wonder if that price is getting too steep. And I have wondered that a lot lately.

I guess what it all comes down to is, there's a time and a place for everything. The best time and place to get an autograph, like I mentioned earlier, is at a personal appearance; just about every Cup driver makes several per season, so the opportunity is there.

The worst time and place—even worse than the middle of dinner—is on any race weekend in the garage area or on pit road.

Sure, I've signed thousands of autographs there, and most drivers have done the same thing. But what some people don't stop to consider is that when a driver is at the track, he's at work. In my case, it's work that I love, but it's still work. My job

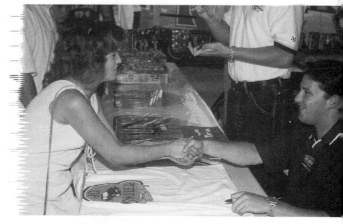

Every year, like most drivers, I sign thousands of autographs at scheduled appearances. But for a lot of folks, obviously, that isn't enough. (© Phil Cavali/Winston Cup Scene)

doesn't begin when I climb into that car, or end when I climb out. If I'm chatting with my crew, or bending down to look at a tire, or even just walking from the transporter to our garage stall, I'm *working*. I'm thinking about that race car. It's all part of the job.

Yet every weekend in the garage area, people approach me—and every other driver—looking for autographs. My position is this: maybe they'll get one, and maybe they won't. And if things aren't going well, they haven't got a chance.

That has always been my philosophy, and I don't think it's hurt my performance any. It *has* hurt me in the public opinion polls, though. See, people who are successful in getting autographs in the garage area walk away happy; people who aren't successful boo you on Sunday and write letters to the editor on Monday. I've lost count of the letters I've read about how rude I was when someone asked me for an autograph at Such-and-Such Speedway.

They don't mention that I might have been discussing gear ratios with my crew, or getting psyched up for qualifying. All they mention is what a bum I was.

Now, I don't enjoy reading that I'm such a horrible person. But you know something? I still believe, and I will *always* believe, that when I'm inside that racetrack fence, I'm in my work area. I'm on the clock. And if folks can't understand that, it's their problem, not mine.

PAM BOAS: "I've said to people who have e-mailed me about this, 'Look, if you were trying to get something from Tony in the garage area, please understand that you were stepping inside his office. How would you feel if you were in the middle of something crucial, and somebody came flying into your office and wanted you to change your focus and just sign something that had nothing to do with what you were working on?'"

DICK JORDAN: "It's hard to put yourself in those shoes, to understand what a person in Tony's position goes through. You see the way the fans react, and there are a lot of, uh, merciless people out there. Some drivers can deal with that, and some can't. I think Tony's kind of in the middle; he can deal with a certain amount of it, but only to a point. The bottom line is, he's just so dedicated to what he's doing that all this other stuff becomes a problem for him, and he'll let people know that because he's not one to hold back. And that's what turns people off sometimes."

A couple of seasons ago, in a press conference and then in an interview that same week, I talked about dealing with the demands of Winston Cup racing, and about how some fans didn't give drivers a moment's peace. It had been a growing issue among people in the garage area, including lots of drivers I had talked with. Anyway, I was very clear about how much I resented the way those kinds of fans intruded on my life.

The stories came out in May of 2000, and I was shocked at the ruckus they caused. I didn't figure I was going to make any new friends, but I was stunned at the number of enemies I generated. I don't think I've ever had one single topic cause me so much grief.

Most of that was due to either me misinterpreting the questions, or the reporters misinterpreting my replies. In my mind, we were talking about a certain type of fan, the pushy, overbearing type. Some of the stories, on the other hand, made it seem as if I was referring to race fans in general. Naturally, my negative quotes about "the fans" got plenty of attention, and they were reprinted in so many places that by the time most people saw them, the original tone of the interviews had disappeared. Instead, there were all these point-blank statements saying, "Tony Stewart is tired of signing autographs and dealing with fans," and that I had "ripped fans" for their behavior.

Not *certain* fans.

Just fans.

It was hard for me to believe that things had gotten so far out of hand.

CARY AGAJANIAN: "We're in a different era now, with the media and the focus on these drivers. I mean, these guys are like rock stars. Everything they do, every word they say, every step they take is examined."

Unfortunately for me, the next Winston Cup race happened to be in Charlotte, which is the hub of all NASCAR hype, good and bad. We tried to set things straight by holding a press conference so I could clarify some of this stuff; it helped a little bit, but not much. By then, everybody had read those stories and formed their opinions. In the driver introductions, I got booed pretty badly.

Now, I had been booed before, and generally you accept that as the price you pay for winning. After all, if you're beating John Doe's favorite driver, there's a chance John Doe is going to boo you. But I had never been blasted like I was at Charlotte. The memory of that still bothers me.

> **PAM BOAS:** "People don't know how much it hurts Tony to be booed. That is really a painful thing for him."

Honestly, I'm still angry about how all that was handled. I'm angry because I'm not the person those stories made me out to be. All I did was address an issue that a lot of people inside the sport had been discussing for a while. Maybe my mistake was assuming that it was okay to talk about these things in public, to say on the record what a lot of us had been saying off the record.

> **PAT SULLIVAN:** "That business Tony went through with the fans, it's all kind of funny today because you'll pick up the papers now and see other drivers and writers talking about that same thing. Yet they let Stewart hang out to dry when he said it, even though he was telling the absolute truth."

Nobody likes to get booed. Personally, it kills me.
(© Phil Cavali/Winston Cup Scene)

By the way, the percentage of fans who cause all these problems is actually pretty small. The overwhelming majority are polite folks who recognize that there's a time for autographs, a time for conversation, a time to just let us do our jobs. Those kinds of people are great to get to know. You walk away after talking with them for a while, and you feel good about yourself and good about this sport.

The flip side is that this small percentage of bad fans still amounts to a large number of people. And those are the ones who leave you feeling, uh, not so good.

At Daytona in 2001, I was driving back to the garage area after a practice run, passing a large group of fans in the paddock, when this lady caught my eye. She was crouched down beside a little boy, maybe four or five years old; I'm guessing it was her son. Anyway, she was giving me the thumbs-down sign with both hands. The boy, of course, was doing the exact same thing, because a child learns from what he sees. I felt disgusted. Here's this little kid, out for what should have been a fun afternoon at the track, and the biggest lesson he's getting is that he's supposed to hate the guy in that orange number 20 car, a guy neither he nor his mother has ever met.

Now, am I wrong to have ill feelings toward that type of fan?

That same week, I raced my late-model car in a couple of events at Volusia County. One night I was strapped into the car, waiting to go out for practice, when a woman reached into the cockpit and asked me to sign her son's Game Boy. I tried to be nice; I explained that it wouldn't be fair to sign something for her if I wasn't going to do it for anybody else, and that because a large autograph session wasn't practical, I couldn't sign her game.

Well, she threw a tantrum I'm sure her son would have been proud of. She started hollering that without my fans, I wouldn't be anybody special. I should have told her that I hadn't gone to the track that night *asking* to be anybody special, I went just to race.

I'll ask you again: how am I supposed to feel about that sort of fan?

With some of these people, it's not about racing. It's about what you can *give* them. It's like dealing with a preschool child: if he doesn't get what he wants, he'll pout and stomp his feet, and too many adults I've encountered are just like that.

Those are the kinds of fans I was referring to in all those stories that got me in trouble. And those are the only kinds of fans I've ever had a problem with.

Here's something that didn't make all the papers. In November of 2001, I spent my Thanksgiving racing midgets in Irwindale, California, at the

Turkey Night Grand Prix, just because the tradition and the history of that event were so important to me. As it turned out, I was able to win the thing after years of trying, and that victory meant more to me than most people will ever know.

Anyway, when that race ended, it seemed like everybody in the grandstands came down and stood in line by my car. Some of them just wanted to offer congratulations, and some of them wanted an autograph on a T-shirt, a souvenir program, whatever. I hung around until everybody got what they wanted, and some people came back three or four times to get different items signed. They were polite, not at all demanding, and they seemed to enjoy the night as much as I did.

But, like I said, you probably didn't read about that.

Everybody wants to write about the fan who felt like he or she got snubbed in the garage area at some superspeedway, but not many columnists mention the thousands of people we've mingled with at tracks around this country.

See, Irwindale was no exception. For most of my life, that sort of thing has been standard procedure.

PAM BOAS: "When he was racing in USAC, and even before that in the TQs, Tony was usually the last guy to leave the track. He would stay until the last person was gone, just because he loved talking to these people. I've actually heard them say on the pit loudspeaker, 'Tony, we're shutting the lights out . . .'"

BOB EAST: "Stewart gets a lot of criticism in the press for the way he is with the fans, but I've seen myself how he takes care of people. I've seen him sit in the pits until one o'clock in the morning, signing autographs. In fact, the way he treats fans is better than any driver I've ever seen."

Sure, I have my bad days and nights. Everybody does. But whenever it's reasonable, I try to do the right thing.

Why wouldn't I? I love those people, the genuine diehard race fans.

You always hear athletes say that the fans are what it's all about, and I used to wonder if they were being sincere about that. Then, in my early IRL days, I spent about two weeks straight testing at Indianapolis without a soul in the grandstands. As much as I love that place, and as special as it feels even when it's empty, the Speedway got pretty lonely after the first few days. Thankfully, some workers showed up to install some new seats, and those guys were the most welcome sight you could imagine.

I mean, driving race cars is only the second-greatest thing in the world. The greatest thing is having people *watch* you drive race cars.

They say you've really become somebody when you make it into a supermarket tabloid. If that's true, it's a whole lot easier being a nobody. Trust me, I speak from experience. In December of 1999, one of those rags thought it was worth pointing out to the world that Krista Dwyer and I had gone our separate ways.

They got that one basic fact right, but not much else.

Krista and I had been together since the beginning of '96, when I was still juggling midget and sprint car rides and hoping that my new Indy car deal would last. Our life together was hectic from the start, and it got busier as I had some success in the IRL and began mixing in more stock car races. But we were able to cope fairly well with most of those changes, because things increased at kind of a steady, progressive pace. Basically, Krista and I adapted to whatever came along.

We got engaged after the 1998 season, and had I led a more normal life we would have been married in May of 2000. But, as I've been telling you, everything normal in my life faded out as '99 rolled along.

Engagements can bring on a lot of tension, everybody knows that. There's so much to think about, so much to plan, so much to discuss. It was a trying period for both of us, just like it would be for anybody. The difference with us was that because of the increased demands that went along with jumping to Winston Cup, I couldn't find enough time in my schedule to keep *myself* happy, let alone another person. We never had time to work on things. And when you don't maintain a relationship, you're bound to run into problems, which is just what happened to me and Krista.

Like I said, lots of folks go through this sort of thing. Most of the time, they get everything solved by devoting the time necessary to see it through. If the guy has to skip a bowling night, that's what he does; if the woman has to miss a night out with the girls, that's what she does. With Krista and I, that spare time just wasn't there. By the summer of '99, the only time we had together—quiet time, just the two of us—was on Friday and Saturday evenings in the motor home at the track. That put us in an uncomfortable spot; naturally, she'd want to use this time to talk out whatever problems we had, while I'd be wracking my brain over how things looked for the race on Sunday.

I'm not saying my way was the right way. I'm saying that there was no way to clear all thoughts of racing from my head temporarily, and deal with something as big and complicated as a relationship. Even when I tried, I just couldn't do it.

That just led to more tension, and it sure wasn't Krista's fault. I mean, all she did was try to use what little time we had to make things better. But we starting butting heads, and one thing led to another, and before long it was like the relationship had become a burden on both of us. By the autumn of that year, when neither one of us could handle that burden anymore, we broke off the engagement.

Anybody who has been through this knows how tough it is. Not only are you torn up inside, you're also embarrassed; it's probably the most personal failure you can go through. We had the added embarrassment of breaking up in the public eye, because everybody who followed Winston Cup racing had seen us together on television or in photographs, and had heard her described as my fiancée. To have everybody find out that things had changed was humiliating for us.

I was doing the best I could to put that behind me, and I thought I was doing all right. Then I was in New York for the Winston Cup banquet, and I got a phone call from Krista. Somebody had shown her that tabloid story, and she was pretty upset. I could understand; I mean, that girl never asked to be a public person, never looked for the spotlight. If a newspaper—the legitimate kind or the sleazy supermarket kind—wanted to pick on me, well, I'm the one who chose a public profession. All Krista did was choose me, or at least go along with me when I chose her.

I actually hunted down a copy of that paper while I was in Manhattan, just to see it for myself. The story had quotes from "a source" and "an insider," which tells you that either the stuff was made up or it

came from people who were ashamed that they would even talk to a publication like that in the first place.

Krista and I have gotten over our differences—in fact, we've dated on and off for a while—but I don't think I'll ever get over the idea that we somehow ended up in a situation like that. The whole thing was a lesson in just how low some people will go. I mean, these so-called journalists will take something from a person's private life, something they will know will cause pain, and exploit that for their own gain. If it happens to ruin your life for a while, they don't care.

The way they see it, you had it coming. You were somebody famous.

You hear folks say all the time, "Boy, so-and-so became a star, and he changed." Well, I'm sure that happens to certain individuals, but in most cases I think the opposite is true: it's not the "star" who changes, it's the people around him. Like I said earlier: everybody looks at you differently, treats you differently, and talks to you differently, so all this forces *you* to act differently.

When I was just a dirt-track racer, nobody ever accused me of letting people down, probably because nobody expected anything out of me. It's not quite the same these days.

TARA ARMSTRONG: "After Tony ran the Silver Crown race at Indianapolis Raceway Park the day after the [2000] Brickyard 400, he sat in the trailer for a while, and then he left. He had hurt his arm somehow, and he was exhausted. Well, there was a write-up in the paper about how he wouldn't sign autographs, like he was too big for that. Now, he'd already been through a tough week; he was at IRP on Wednesday night when they were supposed to run the Silver Crown race before it rained out, then he had the Brickyard on Thursday, Friday, and Saturday, and he had his fan club's picnic on Sunday afternoon. He actually stayed an extra night to run the Silver Crown race, but they made him out to be a bad guy anyway. I almost wrote a letter to the editor, saying, 'You know, he didn't even have to be there! Why can't a guy like Tony be allowed to come back to the places where he cut his teeth and just be normal? Why can't we just treat him like we've always treated him?'"

There have been a few people—people I wasn't especially close to, but who I knew from the old days—who have told mutual friends of ours that I've changed. I hear that stuff, and it makes me crazy, because it's not true. My *life* may have changed, and I've had to adapt to everything that has come with those changes. But I haven't changed at all where it counts: inside.

I believe that, and it's important to me that the people I grew up with believe that, too.

> **JOHN MAHONEY:** "I don't think Tony has changed. At least he hasn't with me. I probably back off from shooting [photos of] him a little more than I used to, just because he's always surrounded, always being bugged. So many people want a piece of him. But he hasn't changed that I can see."

> **PAT SULLIVAN:** "I was announcing a race at Terre Haute in May of '96, the year Tony was going to start on the pole for his first Indianapolis 500. He came to Terre Haute, and they brought him to the booth to be interviewed. Later on, I said, 'Hey, would you autograph my program before you get so damn famous that you won't talk to me anymore?' Well, he went ballistic: 'Sullivan, that pisses me off. You know that won't happen.' I was only kidding, but I think it offended him that I would even suggest that."

I'm only human. I've lost touch with people in the last few years, but not because I've changed, and not because I think I'm somehow above them, and not from any lack of caring. Mostly, it's a consequence of everyday life, mine and theirs; we all get busier, and we all have things that get in the way of staying in contact with people who mean a lot to us. Life goes on, and you can't stop it.

Plus, I've lived in a bunch of different places in the last ten years, and in all that moving around you misplace phone numbers and addresses. Before long, it's been a year or two since you talked to somebody you used to see three nights a week at the track.

But that doesn't mean I don't think about that person and smile every now and then. It doesn't mean we're not still part of each other's lives, just because we're racing in different places now.

— — — — —

The hardest thing for me has been trying to divide my life between the racing side and the personal side. Where do I draw that line? How much of my time is mine, and mine alone? How much of it belongs to the job, to the sport, to the fans? I'm doing all I can to find the right balance. Maybe I never will, but for now I'm going to keep trying.

In the meantime, I'm sure I'll make some mistakes. I'll upset a few more people. I'll say no to the wrong person at the wrong time, and that will create another incident, and the whole world will be booing and writing letters all over again.

But you know something? People are just going to have to deal with that. They're not going to get what they want from me every time. I try to be a good guy, but sometimes I come up short. All I would ask of anybody is that they cut me the same slack they'd look for themselves on their own bad days.

In the end, everybody has got to live his own life, and that includes me.

Because my life is just that: *my* life. Not *their* life.

My life.

And I'm doing the best I can with it.

SEVENTEEN | BLOWING OFF STEAM

NO MATTER WHAT YOUR JOB IS, YOU'RE GOING TO HAVE A CERTAIN LEVEL OF stress. That's just the way of the world. I mean, if you drive race cars in America, the best gig at the moment is a Winston Cup ride. Well, I have one of the premier rides in that series, and I get stressed out anyway.

But even if the stress is higher these days, the cure isn't any different from what it was at any other level of racing. You've got to blow off steam. You've got to find fun where you can. It's the only way to stay sane.

EDDIE JARVIS, personal assistant: "Before I came to work for Tony, I worked for Steve Park for three years, driving his coach and taking care of some other things. After I left I still had one of his credit cards, so when I saw Steve I tried to give it back. He told me to hang on to it for a while, in case I was in a situation where I needed some cash or something. I mentioned that to Tony, and he thought that was nice of Steve. Anyway, we went to Daytona for a test, and Tony and I ended up going out to dinner with a bunch of guys from Michael Waltrip's team, Dale Earnhardt Jr.'s team, and Steve's team, although Steve himself wasn't there. When the bill came, Tony asked me for Steve's credit

As long as I need to blow off a little steam now and then, you'll find me hanging my hat at a short-track race. (© John Mahoney)

> card. I told him I didn't feel right about that, but I gave it to
> him. The check came to something like three hundred dollars,
> and Tony left the waitress a hundred-dollar tip, very generous.
> Then he signed the bill, 'Tony Stewart.' He told everybody at the
> table, 'When you guys see Park tomorrow, make sure you tell
> him thanks. That's it, just thanks.' And that's what happened;
> Steve had six or eight guys thank him, and he kept saying,
> 'Thanks for what?' "

You always hear that laughter is the best medicine. Well, it definitely works that way for me.

Normally, though, my stress-relief methods are a lot more low-key. The busier I get, the more I enjoy those times when I can just do nothing, or at least nothing out of the ordinary. And when I can string a few of those days together, that's a great way to relax.

If I'm back in Indiana, maybe I'll get over to Rushville to see Larry and Tutti Martz and their kids. And I'll always stop and visit with my next-door neighbors in Columbus, Merideth and Joan Mabe, who have known me since I was a kid and who are the unofficial stepparents of Bud, my little shih tzu dog.

> **TUTTI MARTZ:** "When he comes here, he's just Tony. He goes
> down to the basement with the kids, and they play their
> Ping-Pong and pool, and you would never think he's anything
> but the old Tony who just came home from the TQ midget
> track."

> **PAM BOAS:** "Tony will go over to see the Mabes and just lie on the
> floor, playing with his dog. Those people don't care about the
> racing; they care about Tony."

When I spend time with people like that, it takes me completely away from whatever craziness is going on in my life. Sure, we'll spend a few minutes talking about racing, but once that's out of the way we'll talk about other things, everyday stuff.

It's probably like the guy who goes for a walk every evening at six o'clock. It's not just a walk to him, it's a chance to clear his mind. Getting back home and just kind of reinserting myself into that life helps me clear *my* mind.

> **BARRY MEDARIS:** "Here's something that says a lot about Tony. When I was living with him in Columbus and he was just starting to be gone all the time—like in 1997, '98—he'd call and say, 'Don't mow the grass, whatever you do. Save that for me. Go ahead and trim everything up, but I'll mow the grass when I get home.' That was one of those simple things in life that he wanted to keep doing. He had mowed the grass at that house when he was a kid, and he wanted to keep doing it. Nowadays he doesn't have time even to do that anymore, and I'll bet he misses it."

I have the same sort of agenda—or lack of an agenda—if I'm up in Indianapolis. Maybe I'll drop in to see Bob East and nose around his shop for a while, or I'll stop at George Snider's place. I just show up unannounced, same as when I was a local. I was never the type to call ahead and plan an appointment, so I don't see any need to do it now. I'll just pull into the driveway, walk in, and see what's going on.

Anytime I get a chance to kick back with old friends and do the things we used to do, I jump at it. And it's still the same old funny cross-section of people it was when I was twenty-three or twenty-four.

I've played pool with Dick Jordan and Crocky Wright in little dives where you didn't dare go near anything with sharp edges for fear that you'd need a tetanus shot.

> **CROCKY WRIGHT:** "When Tony plays pool, he never mentions anything about auto racing; he's totally focused on the game. When Tony and I have been partners, we usually won. Actually, it was mostly the two opponents against Tony, although once in a while I played pretty good. I was quite a pool player in my youth."

And I've played in poker games all over Indiana—some of them at my own house—where you might see John Mahoney, who has probably

Here's a great way to unwind from the pressures of my regular job: turn me loose with a bunch of my old short-track buddies. This was a poker game at Joe DeFabis's house, December 1998. (© John Mahoney)

photographed more of my races than anybody, dealing cards to Bob Jenkins, who you know from his broadcast work on ESPN but who I know as a guy who loves midgets and sprint cars. And if you kept looking around the table, you'd see race officials, mechanics, announcers, maybe a driver or two. If we stopped and thought about it, we'd probably agree that it was a pretty impressive collection of racing people. The thing is, we *don't* stop to think about it. We just play, because that's what we've always done.

These people knew me when I was a nobody, when we were all just animals in the same traveling circus, and I think that's how we still see one another.

For me, it's like pushing the reset button on my life.

DICK JORDAN: "You get Tony back to his roots, so to speak, and he's not the superstar racer anymore; he's exactly the kid he was when we all met him."

PAM BOAS: "You know why he's so comfortable with those people? Because there are no pedestals."

TUTTI MARTZ: "As much as he likes what he's doing now, I think Tony enjoys it when something takes him back to those less complicated times."

-- -- -- -- --

In July of 1999, the pressure of my first Cup season was just starting to spin out of control. The Brickyard 400 was coming up, and I was dealing with a lot of rookie-comes-home media stuff. Racing at Indianapolis as a Winston Cup driver had gone from being something I really looked forward to to something I almost dreaded, just because of all the extra demands on my time.

Then I had another one of those reset-button experiences.

The weekend before the 400, the folks at Salem Speedway had me come in for an autograph session prior to a Saturday-night race. That went really well, and we saw a lot of old friends and fans there. But once the races got rolling, I skipped over to the airport next to the Salem track, and Bob Burris flew me to Columbus.

Now, the drive between Salem and Columbus is only about sixty miles, so flying seemed a bit ridiculous. But, see, I knew Tate Martz was racing a go-kart at Columbus, and I was afraid that if I drove I might not make it in time to see him run.

It was important for me to be there because . . . well, just because.

There had been so many times in my career, whether I happened be living with the Martzes or not, when that whole family showed up to watch me race. Then, when my feature ended, they would hang out until I was ready to leave so we could get a bite to eat together at some burger joint. They were always going out of their way to do nice things for me, and this was a chance for me to do something in return.

> **TUTTI MARTZ:** "We've always told Tony that he doesn't owe us anything. We did what we did because we liked him. It's just that simple. But it's great when we can spend time together."

Like all the Martz kids, Tate is a little brother to me, and I think he was happy to see me there. He ran well that night, and it was fun for me to see how he was progressing as a racer. But I wasn't about to tell him that. I didn't want Tater to get a big head.

> **LARRY MARTZ:** "Tony wasn't going to pat Tate on the back, that's for sure. Even today, they act the same way they did when they

raced bicycles and minibikes in our backyard, so Tony wasn't going to cut him any slack. Tate had passed something like five or six karts on the first lap, and Tony never even mentioned that. Instead, he gave him a rough time about something Tate hadn't done."

Later, they came over to my house for a while, and we talked late into the night, just like old times. It took away every last bit of stress I had been feeling that week.

It was a strange evening: you start out playing the big hero race driver and signing autographs, and you end up laying low, having fun and just enjoying the company.

From a commonsense point of view, it wasn't the smartest night of my life. Planes aren't cheap to operate, and firing one up just to save an hour of driving time is almost stupid. But the way I looked at it, how do you put a price on happiness?

I had a similar logistical problem in the autumn of '99, when I realized that Greg Zipadelli, my crew chief, and Barry Medaris, one of my oldest friends, were getting married on the same Saturday. Zippy's ceremony was going to be in North Carolina, and Barry's was back in Columbus. On top of that, I was in both wedding parties.

Greg and I had only known each other for a year or so, but we had become really close; to have him and his fiancée Nan include me in their big day was an honor, so skipping that wedding was not an option. And I had known Barry since I was ten years old; we'd raced karts together growing up, and later on we had been roommates. In fact, Barry was living with me in Columbus when he and his fiancée Tanya started dating. There was no way I was going to miss Barry walking down the aisle.

Fortunately, there was a gap between the Zipadelli wedding in the afternoon and the Medaris wedding at night. I stayed with Greg and Nan and their wedding party long enough to take the photos, and then I blasted to the airport. I did a quick tuxedo change in the plane, made a fast flight to Columbus, and everything was going smoothly. Then, just down the road from Barry's church, a policeman pulled me over—I guess he'd never seen a minivan go so fast—and we had a nice little chat. That delayed me just long enough to miss the "I do" part of the festivities. I walked in just in time to see Barry and Tanya hug their parents after they'd been pronounced man and wife.

Counting the Indy 500 and the Coke 600 in May, this was the second Indiana/North Carolina doubleheader I did in 1999.

Two years later, when my sister, Natalie, got married up in Lafayette, it figured that the date would fall on the Saturday evening of the October race at Charlotte. That meant another quick flight, and it also meant missing the final Winston Cup practice. But, the way I look at it, you make whatever sacrifices you have to make for the people you care about.

So many people have supported me over the years—lending me gas money, giving me room and board, offering me advice, and of course, hiring me to drive their race cars—and most of the time that support came just when I needed it most. It would be wrong to say that trying to do nice things for my friends today is my way of paying them back, because, honestly, nothing I can do would even begin to make us even. But, like I said, you do whatever you can for those you care about.

IRISH SAUNDERS: "He's the kind of friend that you're proud to have. I'll tell you a little story. Tony sponsors my son Eric, who races motocross. A while back, I called him and said, 'Hey, next time you're up this way, we need to do a photo shoot with you for Eric's autograph cards.' Well, not only does he come up, but he ends up spending the day with the kid; Tony's on a four-wheeler, and Eric's on his motorcycle, and they're tearing around together."

LARRY CURRY: "Tony is very much misunderstood. People don't know the Tony Stewart who, when my son Dane died [in a traffic accident], sent an airplane to pick me up without me ever asking him to. They don't know the Tony Stewart who offered his plane to Kenny Irwin's family when Kenny died. That's not some guy who's trying to say, 'Hey, look at me, I've got an airplane I can send all these different places when I want to.'

That's a guy who cares about people, and who doesn't care if anybody ever knows about these things he does. You could not ask for a better friend in the world than that guy."

BOB BURRIS: "That kid, he'll do anything for a friend. Anything."

There's one thing I do that seems like a nice-guy deal, but it actually gives as much pleasure to me as it does to my friends. For the last several years, I've dabbled in owning race cars, and it has progressed to the point where we've got a good little inventory going. The last time I counted, I owned a half-dozen sprint cars that Danny Lasoski drives on the World of Outlaws circuit, two dirt late-models I run when I get the chance, a couple of TQs that my dad and my buddy Mark Hill race in Indiana, and a Legends car that my dad plays around with when he has time. Oh, and I'm also a partner in a couple of USAC Silver Crown cars that Bob East takes care of.

The question everybody asks about all those race cars is, Why? Well, being a car owner allows me to contribute something to short-track racing, and in some cases to the places and events that shaped my career, whether it's the Hoosier Hundred or the TQ races at the Rush County Fair.

For the most part, the TQ and Legends department of the Stewart empire is just a fun thing. My dad still loves to race, and helping him compete is my small way of thanking him for everything he's done for me, as if that's possible. Mark's ride in our other car came about because he was playing around with an old TQ that didn't have a prayer of being competitive, and I guess I just felt sorry for him.

MARK HILL: "Tony was looking at my car one night, and he said, 'This thing is a shitbox. You ought to get rid of it.' I told him I knew it wasn't a great car, but I wanted to race. Well, a buddy of ours named Jason Setser was getting ready to move from TQs to full-sized midgets, and he had a nice TQ for sale. The next thing I knew, Tony bought that car and put me in as the driver. Since then we've gotten a newer car, and his dad and I are teammates.

There are probably fifty guys dying to get in that TQ, just because it's Tony's. But Tony tells me, 'Hey, that's your deal. If you want you race it, go. If you don't, let it sit there.' That's just the way he is."

We take the rest of the inventory a lot more seriously. Steve Barnett, an Indiana driver who has done a lot of winning around the Midwest, looks after my late-models, and several times a year we go racing as teammates. It's a great arrangement for me because all I've got to do is show up at the track, and it works out well for Barnett because if he has a problem with his own car, he's free to use mine. Best of all, we've both won races.

My deal with Bob East has pretty much the same feel. A few years back he was looking for a partner to run a Silver Crown team, and it just seemed natural that we should get together; I'd had a ton of success driving midgets for

Owning race cars has been a satisfying thing for me. At Phoenix in 2000, I won the midget race driving for Steve Lewis and Bob East, and then Jason Leffler won the Silver Crown race driving for Bob East and me. (© Jim Haines)

him and Steve Lewis. We've had a bunch of talented young drivers in the Silver Crown car, including J. J. Yeley and Kasey Kahne, and it's nice for me to feel like maybe I've been able to help those kids the way Bob, Steve, and so many other car owners have helped me.

But my most ambitious effort in the ownership business, by far, has been the World of Outlaws team. I had known Danny Lasoski for several years; although we never really ran the same circuits, we'd occasionally compete at oddball races like the Chili Bowl. I had tremendous respect for him as a driver, and I liked him as a person.

The biggest thing was, I could really identify with Danny and the life he was leading. He's a professional short-track racer, and I know how tough that is. It's a hard road, scrambling from track to track, living off your percentage of the prize money, and knowing that if you hit a dry spell you might be out of a job tomorrow. So when the thought crossed my mind that forming a full-time sprint car team might be an intriguing possibility, Danny was the guy I wanted to do it with.

I knew we'd be a good mix. He'd contribute all the driving talent an owner could ask for, and I'd contribute the ingredients Danny needed to build a team that could win for him immediately, and maybe for another driver under his guidance in the years to come.

DANNY LASOSKI, veteran sprint car driver: "When Tony and I first talked about him getting involved with the World of Outlaws, I wasn't thinking about us having our own team, I was thinking about getting him involved with the team I was driving for. Well, Tony brought to my attention that from a driver's point of view, if the car owner I'm working for at any given time happens to quit, all I'm left with is my helmet bag and my seat. He said, 'Why don't we think about building something that can be yours, something for you and your family?' I thought that was an amazing gesture; he was more worried about my future than I was. And the way we've got it set up is, the day I decide I don't want to drive anymore, this team is still mine. He's given me both job security and something to fall back on when I'm done racing."

We hired Jimmy Carr—a good sprint car driver himself, and a guy who is like a brother to Danny—as our chief mechanic. The 2001 season was our first full swing with the Outlaws, and we were incredibly successful. Danny not only won the Knoxville Nationals, the most prestigious sprint car race in the country, but he edged Mark Kinser to clinch the World of Outlaws championship. It was about as sweet a debut season as an owner could hope for.

Obviously, I'm anything but a hands-on boss. But I've been lucky enough to make it to a handful of races and whenever I'm around, Danny and Jimmy put me to work. And I mean *work*: I don't want to get in the way of the guys and their regular job, so I end up doing grunt duty, and I love it.

> **DANNY LASOSKI:** "He'll mount tires, groove tires, change gears, anything we need him to do. When he's around, it's an absolute blast, because he's not there as Tony Stewart the Winston Cup racer or even Tony Stewart the car owner; he's there as Tony Stewart the buddy, the guy who just wants to see that we do well."

Sure, all these cars are a lot to keep track of. There are times when I'm lying in my motor home in the infield of some Winston Cup track, and I can't even remember where they're all racing. And if I think about it long enough, I'll go into full owner mode, worrying about how much money these teams burn up. Then, late at night, the cell phone will ring, and it will be one of the guys calling in with their results. And if it's a happy call, it's all worth it.

A happy call doesn't have to be about a win. Maybe Danny came from the back of the pack and ran third, or maybe my dad just had the time of his life in a TQ race. If I can hear that joy in their voices, that's all the return I need.

Speaking of return on investment, of all the race teams and all the business ventures I've been involved in, guess what has been the most reliable, dollars in versus dollars out?

Dogs.

That's right: racing dogs, greyhounds. I've got a small stable of them in Florida.

It's a strange story. One of the photographers on the Winston Cup circuit was into greyhounds, and, just being curious, I asked her a few questions. She told me about the owner's role, and how the winnings were split, and that you could get into it for as little as five hundred for a single dog. I looked into it some more, and ended up buying eight puppies out of the same litter.

When I went looking for someone to oversee the dog program, I was introduced to a gentleman named Walt Gribben, who has been around greyhounds for years. He didn't know a thing about auto racing and had no clue who I was, which I liked because that meant he dealt with me like he'd deal with any other owner. One of my concerns was what happened to the dogs once their racing days were over, because I've got a soft spot for animals, and Walt steered me toward an adoption program; in fact, I've got a bunch of NASCAR team members interested in giving homes to my dogs when they're retired.

Anyway, Walt and I got together, and it's been a great relationship. I watch how he takes care of these dogs, and I can tell that he loves his sport as much as I love mine. Early on, he took me behind the scenes at a track in West Palm Beach, and when I saw how our dogs reacted when they heard Walt's voice—tails wagging, jumping around—I knew I was with the right guy. Since then, I've even turned Walt into a stock car fan; he's come to see us race at Daytona and Homestead.

I only get to see the dogs run occasionally, but it's a neat feeling to sit in the clubhouse and bet a few dollars on your own puppies. I've even been fortunate enough to see them win. I was proud of that, even though I know the success of those dogs has a lot more to do with Walt than it does with me.

Just to prove that last point, I'll share a little story. Once upon a time, I actually owned a 25 percent interest in a racehorse. This was in '95, when I was still running USAC. My pal Lorin Ranier and his father, Harry, knew a lot of Kentucky thoroughbred people, and Lorin explained to me that the right horse could be a good investment. I guess I just didn't pick the right horse.

I saw him run only once, when the trainers brought him to the Hoosier Park track in Indiana. When he came tearing out of the gate and led the first two-thirds of the race, I was on top of the world. Then, just at the point when you expect the loudspeaker to say, "And down the stretch they come," he started slowing. By the time they galloped across the line, he faded to fourth. As it turned out, he had injured a leg in the course of that race, and he never competed again.

In horse racing, only the top three positions—win, place, show—mean anything. My horse was out of the money. And pretty soon, my money was out of the horses.

Win or lose, the horses and dogs seemed to make sense to me at the time. I guess I'm just attracted to anything that moves. I went through a phase just before I moved to North Carolina when I was dangerously addicted to riding four-wheelers. It wasn't the addiction that was dangerous, it was the way we rode. We'd ride in the woods, in the fields, anyplace. At one point, a bunch of us even helped a buddy of ours carve a little oval out of some property he owned.

> **MARK HILL:** "We worked on that track for hours, which is a typical Tony deal; once he gets something in his head, he'll go non-stop until he gets it the way he wants it. He actually bought a five-hundred-gallon water tank so he could keep the dirt greasy and slick, because that way he'd have everybody covered. Tony and I locked wheels once, and I turned him over. That's always been a big joke with us. We had some great times. Lots of scars."

> **BARRY MEDARIS:** "One day we were riding in some woods we didn't know, with Mark in front, me second, and Tony behind us. At the last second, Mark noticed a hole about four feet deep right in our path, with a little mound of dirt just in front of it. He was able to get on the gas, and he jumped right across it. I didn't see it in time, so I went straight down into the hole. Tony grabbed a tree and bailed off his four-wheeler, or he'd have been down there with me. I'm laying in that hole, trying to gather my thoughts, and I can hear those guys chuckling. I look up, and there's Tony: 'Dude, are you dead?'"

I don't get on the four-wheelers as often as I used to, but I'm still a sucker for anything else that lets me beat and bang around with my friends. Go-karts have proven to be a great form of therapy. You put together a handful of friends and a few karts, and you never know what might happen.

> **JEFF "GOOCH" PATTERSON:** "We were in Florida for a late-model race, but it got rained out early and somebody decided we ought to find a go-kart track. We started thumbing through the Yellow Pages. Tony called this one place, and the guy says, 'Yeah, we're open. Come on over.' So we all pile into the motor home, and off we go. We followed the guy's directions and ended up way out in the boondocks. The track was right in the front yard of the guy's house, but it was really neat: a banked asphalt oval, nice karts, real good lighting, a flag stand. We were racing in the rain, having a blast. All of a sudden I came out of turn two, and this white hog appeared out of nowhere on the backstretch. Not a regular pig, but a huge hog that had to weigh six hundred pounds. It was the neighbor's hog, and it had gotten out of its pen. We kept racing for a while, steering around the hog, but finally they threw a yellow flag because it would have been ugly if somebody hit that thing."

Generally speaking, I'm more laid back when it comes to driving passenger vehicles. Sure, I got my share of speeding tickets when I was young and dumb, but I'd like to think I'm a bit more responsible these days.

Still, like any red-blooded American motorist, I have my moments.

A couple of winters ago I was in Fort Wayne, Indiana, for an indoor race, and when we got out of the arena we found that it had snowed pretty heavily. The streets were in decent shape, but the hotel parking lot had a layer of snow on it. Well, I'm like any other guy with a driver's license: you give me a snowy lot, and I want to play.

I had a BMW at the time, and a few of my hometown friends were riding with me. I slid the car around, showing off my broadsliding skills, and at one point I just barely clipped a curb which had a bunch of snow packed up against it. That gave the rear tires some bite and launched the car forward; it was like riding the cushion on a nice dirt track. So I made a few more passes at it, getting a little braver each time, doing everything I could to impress my buddies.

Well, on one of my laps I miscalculated, and hit that curb harder than I had planned on. A *lot* harder. The impact blew the tire off the bead, and actually broke the wheel.

> **MARK HILL:** "That wheel just shattered; it sounded like plate-glass breaking. At first I thought he'd kicked up a stone and knocked the front window out of the motel, but I guess the magnesium or aluminum, whatever it was, was so cold that it just busted to pieces."

I don't remember what it cost me to replace that wheel, but it wasn't cheap. But the worst part was listening to all the razzing I got as I limped that car across the parking lot.

It's a funny thing, but if you sit around swapping stories with racers, sooner or later somebody brings up rental cars. Everybody's got a story about doing something silly with one, or to one.

The old joke about Bobby Unser was that the folks from Hertz were so impressed with the way he treated their cars, they provided Bobby with a lifetime VIP membership. *To Avis.*

Then there's the story about A. J. Foyt pretending that his rental car's passenger door was broken so he could trick a couple of tire engineers into riding in the back. Then A.J. got that car running wide open on the freeway and jumped into the backseat with them. When all the swerving stopped, the two tire guys were sitting up front, and Foyt was alone in the back.

I've never done anything *that* crazy, but I have been on the scene for some stupid rental car tricks.

Back in 1997 I was in Daytona during Speedweeks, hanging out with my old Hoosier Tire buddy, Irish Saunders. The rental agency gave Irish a nice midsize car with the emergency brake in the center console, which was a serious lapse in judgment on their part. One day Irish was driving like a typical tourist, looking around, not paying attention to anything. Just to get his mind back on the job, I reached over with my left hand and gave that brake handle a big yank. That did a nice job of locking up the rear wheels, and Irish was all elbows for several seconds until he got that car going straight again. He was mad at me for a minute or two, but once his heart rate returned to normal he saw the humor in the whole thing.

From that moment on, our Florida vacation turned into a week of squealing rubber. We went from amusing each other to abusing every pedestrian we saw.

We'd pass a lady walking her dog on the sidewalk, and lock up those rear brakes: *Eeeeeeeeeeeeeeeeeee* . . .

We'd drive by a guy loading something into his trunk: *Eeeeeeee-eeeeeeeeee* . . .

We'd pull up next to a car parked at a stoplight: *Eeeeeeeeeeeeeee-eeee* . . .

It sounds childish, I know, but we had a blast watching people freak out when they'd hear that squeal. One young guy, maybe eighteen or nineteen, was taking a romantic stroll with his girlfriend when we arrived on the scene, tires screaming. The poor kid jumped back so suddenly that he knocked his girl right into the bushes. I think we laughed for five solid minutes.

> **IRISH SAUNDERS:** "By the time we turned that car in, I swear it had square tires. It vibrated the fillings right out of your damn teeth."

Rental cars are a great release. You want to know why? It's pretty simple: because you don't own 'em. All you need to do is fork over that extra seven bucks a day for the insurance, and then spend a few minutes every morning practicing your best aw-shucks look so you don't arouse any suspicion when you turn in the keys. And always remember, if things go wrong, the answer to every question is, "Heck, I don't know *what* happened."

But keep this in mind: people like Irish and me, and Unser and Foyt, we're trained professionals. Don't you dare try this at home.

– – – – –

Of course, nothing I've ever found helps me blow off steam like a good short-track race. When I'm in the middle of a really hot thirty-lapper, driving my heart out just for pride, the pressures of my regular job are a million miles away.

I know I keep saying that these short-track races are a lot of fun, and they are, win or lose. It's just that they're *more* fun if you walk out with the trophy.

Every summer since I've been in Winston Cup, I've gone back home to run a dirt late-model event at Terre Haute. They promote the show as "NASCAR Night," and they've brought in Kenny Schrader, Dave Blaney, and me to compete against the guys who run that division every week. That's a tall order, beating drivers who are more familiar with the equipment, and when you can pull it off it's something to be proud of. I was

When I show up to run some dirt race, I feel like I work as hard as the next guy does. To me, there's no such thing as a little race. (© Mike Adaskaveg)

fortunate enough to win one of those Terre Haute events, and it was a huge thrill for me. Later that night, Schrader and I flew to that weekend's Cup race, and I think I smiled through the entire trip.

> **JUDY DOMINICK,** former publicist: "It was a kick to see Tony win at Terre Haute, just because of how happy it made him. I think people might expect a driver in his situation—you know, the hot young Winston Cup guy—to look at that race as a trivial little thing. But to Tony, it wasn't."

What other people might consider little things aren't necessarily little to me. If I'm at some half-mile dirt track, I don't feel like a Winston Cup driver that night; I'm a dirt-track driver, and I go through the same things every dirt-track driver does. I sign in at the pit gate just like everybody else, and I work hard to get my car fast just like everybody else. And my goal is to hold that checkered flag at the end of the feature, just like everybody else.

Sure, when you put one race into perspective, and stack it up against the prestige and the money of the Winston Cup series, it might not seem like much. But a race is a race. If five other guys show up, I want to beat those five guys; if it's fifty other guys, same thing. And if I can't beat 'em all, I'll get as many as I can.

> **CHRIS ECONOMAKI:** "I've seen a lot of big-name drivers pull out of local races early because they knew they couldn't win. Well, that's not in Tony Stewart's makeup. Tony is the kind of guy who might finish ninth, and he'll go back there again and try to win."

I've had so many fans walk up during our visits to these short tracks and say, "Hey, thanks for supporting our series," or "Thanks for being a part of this."

I always want to tell them, "No, thank you. It's *my* pleasure." Because it really is.

And then there are the races that, over the years, have become sort of like obsessions to me. Normally, they're events where I've struggled for success, like the Chili Bowl, which until January of 2002, I had never won. Every winter, I'd compare my Winston Cup test schedule with the Chili Bowl dates, and I'd run down a mental list of midget owners who might be interested in hauling to Tulsa. I thought if I could win that thing just once, it probably wouldn't nag at me so much. But, you know, now that I've done it, I'm sure I'll go back anyway.

The Turkey Night Grand Prix bothered me that way for several years. In my days as a midget regular, the best I finished that race was seventh. From 1996 to '98, my own schedule kept me from competing, but when Bob East and Steve Lewis told me in 1999 that they had an extra car ready, I jumped at it.

The race had moved to Irwindale Speedway, a track I had never seen before, and I hadn't run a midget in over a year, which had me a little bit worried. But when we got out there and I set fast time, I felt like the king of the hill.

> **BOB EAST:** "Tony looked at me and said, 'So, do you think I should lap the field?' I said, 'Well, have fun trying.'"

That night I had one of the most fun races I've ever been involved in. Jason Leffler and I were teammates, and we battled for the entire one hundred laps, me leading one lap and him the next. Underneath my helmet I think I was grinning all night, whether I was passing or getting passed.

Until the *last* pass, that is.

I was leading with two laps to go when I felt my engine losing power; we found out later that the oil pump belt broke. Leffler passed me as we took the white flag. He won the Turkey Night Grand Prix, and I finished second.

To be so close to winning—especially in that race—and then to have it slip away because of some fluky thing like a broken belt, that really chewed at me.

> **TRACY POTTER:** "We were sitting in a Denny's restaurant after that race, and Tony walked in. He came over and sat down for a while, just bullshitting, and then he said, 'Man, I really wanted that [bleeping] trophy.'"

I waited 365 days for revenge, but in November of 2000 I went back there and got that trophy.

When I climbed out of the car, I had tears in my eyes. ESPN was there to cover the race, and Gary Lee, a broadcaster I'd known for years, asked why I was so emotional. I told him, "It's cool to win six Winston Cup races," which we had done that season, "but it's damn cool to win Turkey Night."

> **PAT SULLIVAN:** "Watching that broadcast, I was thinking to myself, Tony is reminding every other young gun out there that he's still the best in the business. To him, that means a lot."

By the way, one of the things I get asked most frequently is when is this going to end, when will I stop sneaking away to run these short-track races. I suppose casual Winston Cup fans don't understand it any more than the USAC people did when I kept going back in 1996 and '97.

Here's another shot of me and my friends decompressing, at Roman's in Phoenix. (© 1998 by John Mahoney)

Well, right now the idea of *not* doing the occasional bullring race just seems impossible to me.

I guess the only real answer is, as long as I feel the need to blow off a little steam now and then, you'll see me at one short track or another. It's either that, or I'd be back to tearing up four-wheelers and rental cars. Hey, a guy has to cut loose somehow.

And, you know, there's more to this short-track stuff than just racing. What you have to consider is that if I gave this up, a whole group of people would basically disappear from my life. There are friends I see only at Silver Crown races, others I see only at late-model races, others only at midget races. They can't make it to Talladega or Watkins Glen, and I'm not likely to make it to their neighborhood unless it's for a race.

We'd be talking about reshaping my entire life, and I'm not ready to do that.

DICK JORDAN: "Tony just enjoys everything he's done in racing, and I don't think he wants to leave any of it behind. So every time he shows up and somebody says something like, 'You know, this might be Stewart's last midget race,' don't believe it. Because you can go to that same race two years from now, and Tony might be there winning it."

JUDY DOMINICK: "You know what it is? To Tony, racing is not a career. It's his soul. Racing is his soul. It's who he is."

EIGHTEEN   LOOKING FORWARD, LOOKING BACK

IN THE SUMMER OF 2001, I WAS AT A SHORT TRACK IN LAKELAND, FLORIDA, testing with my Winston Cup team, when I got a message to call Dick Jordan at the USAC office. It turned out I had been selected for induction into the National Midget Auto Racing Hall of Fame—the youngest guy ever to get voted in—and Dick figured I'd want to know right away. He was right. To me, that was a huge honor.

See, midget fans, particularly the old-timers, are a pretty hard-core group. They wouldn't dare stay home to watch a stock car race or an Indy car race on TV if they can get out and catch a midget race instead. That's especially true of the guys on the Hall of Fame board; to them, there's no higher form of racing.

And that's what makes their hall so prestigious, in my mind: you don't get in without earning your stripes in a midget, regardless of what you've done elsewhere. Guys like A. J. Foyt, Parnelli Jones, and Rodger Ward are in there, but not because they won the Indianapolis 500; they were inducted for what they did in midgets, and they aren't considered any better than midget champs like Rich Vogler or Sleepy Tripp.

In my case, the fact that I had won some NASCAR races and an IRL title didn't mean a thing. What mattered was that I was a two-time

I won this bronze "Duffy" trophy in the Grand Nationals in 1983, when I was twelve. I still have a ways to go. … (Courtesy of Pam Boas)

USAC champion, and that I'd won all the right races: Turkey Night, the Hut Hundred, the Copper Classic.

They held the induction on a Sunday at the Angell Park Speedway in Wisconsin, and I wouldn't have missed it for the world. I had won the Winston Cup race at Bristol the previous night, so I was in a great mood anyway, but the Hall of Fame deal topped off the weekend perfectly. My mom and her husband flew up with me, and we brought along Cary Agajanian, whose family has such a deep history in midgets, and Bob Higman, one of the all-time legendary car owners in that division.

And my old pal Crocky Wright, who saw me win in TQ midgets before anybody ever heard of me, showed up with a nice surprise: he presented me with a helmet he had worn himself as a midget racer fifty years earlier. It was as nice a gift as I've ever received.

Almost since I started racing, I've told Crocky Wright that I wanted his old helmet. This is me, trying it on in 1992. It meant a lot that he gave it to me almost ten years later, when I got inducted into the National Midget Auto Racing Hall of Fame. (© John Mahoney)

It was a wonderful night, but at the same time, it gave me kind of a strange feeling. I mean, youngest-ever inductee or not, getting voted into *any* hall of fame is a sure sign that you aren't a kid anymore. When I think of a hall-of-famer, I see a guy who has a little bit of age on him. Heck, one of the guys inducted with me was Gordon Betz, a West Coast official who worked his first race in 1932. *Nineteen thirty-two!*

So on the one hand I felt like a youngster, especially when I spent some time with Mr. Betz, who is in his eighties. On the other hand, the whole ceremony was a confirmation that, hey, I had been around awhile, maybe longer than I had realized.

I was thirty years old, and already I had lived one hell of a racing life.

Anytime I start taking for granted how far I've come, all I've got to do is walk outside my office in Indianapolis. Hanging in the hallway is a framed check dated April 20, 1990, in the amount of $149.36, from my days as a floor sweeper at Irvin's Interstate Brick & Block. I look at that check, and I remember how even later on, when I started having some success with USAC, I had to scrape for every dime. I used to study the purses listed on the entry blanks, calculating to the dollar what my percentage would be if I ran first, fifth, or wherever. Being broke can really help a young driver's math skills.

Obviously, things have changed considerably. I say this not to brag, but because it amazes me: I'm more comfortable financially than I ever dreamed I'd be. I've got homes in Indiana and North Carolina; I own about as nice a motor coach as you can buy; and at the end of my second Winston Cup season, we upgraded from our turboprop plane to a Citation Bravo jet.

I'd have laughed in your face if you told me back in '93, when I rode out to my first Turkey Night race in the backseat of a club-cab pickup, that seven years later I'd cruise out there in my own jet. But there we were, in November of 2000, doing just that.

I used to be late for every commercial flight I booked. I never listened to that stuff about checking in an hour before the scheduled departure; for me, ten minutes was plenty. Not surprisingly, I missed a few flights. Well, I'm still showing up at the airport long after I'm supposed to be there, but our plane never rolls until I'm in my seat.

In the past few years, I've done endorsement deals with Coca-Cola, Nike, Chef Boyardee, Sea-Doo, Old Spice, Pontiac, Worldcom, and a few more companies. I'm proud of all that, and it's not because of the money. It's sort of like what I said about the plane: just the other day I was a dirt-track kid, and now I'm contracted to the same shoe company as Michael Jordan and Tiger Woods. Now I'm pitching products in TV commercials. I'm supposed to be in a convenience store *buying* canned ravioli, not on television *selling* it.

TARA ARMSTRONG: "The first time I realized Tony had actually made it, I was in a store. I saw his face on the front of *TV Guide*, and I thought, Well, that's cool. Then I walked outside that same store, and there was a Coke machine with his picture on it. And I thought, This is not supposed to happen for people you know."

PAM BOAS: "Never in my lifetime could I have imagined that one of my children would be in this position. I was always used to looking in from the outside at somebody else's life, particularly other race drivers: the Unsers, Foyt, and some of the guys in NASCAR. But you never dream that your life will be that way, too. It's overwhelming."

The one thing I hope is that every single person who helped me along the way understands that they're still part of what I do. When I win a Winston Cup race, that's a victory not just for me and Joe Gibbs Racing and our sponsors, but for everybody who, in some way or another, was involved in moving my career forward. They deserve to enjoy those moments.

What's really fun is that every time we've won a Cup race, the number of people who have called to offer congratulations has been incredible. Generally, the postrace interviews keep you pretty busy for a couple of hours, but once I get to my cell phone and check the voice mail there's always an interesting collection of messages. Then I'll get home, and the answering machine will be full. I'll hear from former car owners, former mechanics, and former rivals, all of them old friends.

It's a warm feeling to know that those folks still care about what I'm doing.

LARRY HOWARD: "You think I'm not proud of Tony? Geez, am I proud of that kid. I love him to death. He always referred to himself as my other son, and I just enjoyed the heck out of him. I loved him, and I still do."

RUSTY KUNZ: "Whenever you see a guy who drove your car do that well for himself, you like to think, Hey, maybe I played a part in that."

When we won at Bristol in August of 2001, it was a nice little reminder that while my life had changed drastically, the basics of my life had not. Brad and Tara Armstrong were there as guests of mine, and I was happy they got to celebrate with us. For me, it was like completing a personal circle: ten years earlier, when I'd been hauling broken-down cars for Brad's towing service and sleeping on his couch, he and Tara had been so supportive; it was nice, on this one night, to show them that their friendship and faith in me hadn't all gone for nothing.

> **BRAD ARMSTRONG:** "I'll tell you a story. Back when Tony used to work for me, he would use my cell phone. For a long time after he left, I'd still get calls for him, because that was the number he'd given people. This one guy called for Tony, and after I explained the situation he said, 'Boy, it might be neat, years from now, to say you knew the next A. J. Foyt back when he was just getting started.' I mean, this is in 1991! I just laughed. I told my wife, 'Can you believe that misguided, misdirected guy?' Well, turns out he was a pretty smart fellow."

Yet as far as I've come, in my mind I still have a long way to go. There's plenty of unfinished business, particularly at the NASCAR level.

I've got to win a Winston Cup title. It's not that I feel like I need it to make my career complete, but it would sure go a long way toward rounding out the stock car side of my résumé.

In NASCAR, the championship is the biggest single prize, so much bigger than any one race. It's not that way everywhere; a victory in the Indianapolis 500 is so huge that it makes the IRL title seem secondary, and in sprint car racing it's probably as big an accomplishment to win the Knoxville Nationals as it is to win the World of Outlaws championship. But in NASCAR, every team shoots for that big trophy called the Winston Cup.

It might be the most difficult achievement in all of motorsports, because of the size of the schedule and the depth of the competition. To win that championship, you need great cars for every track, solid pit stops from February to November, and every bit of luck you can get. And you'd better have the right guy behind the wheel.

We haven't put that whole package together yet, because we haven't nailed down the luck part. But we've had terrific cars and terrific stops right from the time I showed up in this series, and the luck is going to come sooner or later. I know that.

I also know this: the driver is up to the job.

Over the past few years, I've heard that I'm too high strung to win a Winston Cup title, but that's just one more case of experts who don't know what they're talking about. I've won races and championships at every discipline I've attempted, and I can switch from trophy-racer to points-racer as quickly as the next guy can. The only real trick is in knowing the system, and then working it to your own advantage.

Before I won any of my titles—in go-karts, USAC, or the IRL—I had to understand what it took to get to the top of the standings. Almost every division in racing has a different points structure; some have bonuses for qualifying, for leading laps, for finishing well in heat races, for all kinds of things. If you're serious about chasing a championship anywhere, you'd better be prepared to exploit all those loopholes. You can't beat the system until you know *the* system.

To me, this is the good side of Winston Cup racing: cutting up with guys like Dale Earnhardt Jr. off the track, and racing hard with guys like him on it. If only it was all this much fun . . . (© Mike Adaskaveg)

I feel like I'm really starting to understand the methods that can lead us to a NASCAR title. In my first three Cup seasons, we were at least in contention to win the thing each time; we might not have been battling for the crown until the last race every November, but it wasn't like we had been written out of the picture early, either.

TRACY POTTER: "That NASCAR deal, Tony will conquer it. There's no doubt. I mean, he's conquered everything else."

Other than being able to walk into my den and see the Winston Cup sitting there, I'd enjoy being able to look at a couple of Daytona 500 trophies, and maybe one or two from the Southern 500 at Darlington, just because that's considered such a driver's race.

And, while I'm getting greedy, I would love to have one of those killer seasons that only happen from time to time at the Winston Cup level. I'm talking about a year when you leave no doubt that you were the baddest team in town, whether you win the championship or not. Dale Earnhardt had one in 1987, when he won eleven races, and Rusty Wallace had one in '93, when he won ten. People talk about how the competition has tightened up too much to do that today, but, you know, Jeff Gordon won ten races in 1996, ten more in '97, and *thirteen* in '98. If those numbers were attainable for Jeff and his team, they're attainable, period.

I've gone through stretches in my career, particularly in midgets, where I felt like I was absolutely *the* guy to beat. I want to have that feeling in Winston Cup, too.

And I think I can do that. Because we've already won a bunch, and in my mind I still have a way to go before I'm the Winston Cup driver I'm capable of being.

JIMMY MAKAR: "Stop and think about what he's done. The boy is still new to Cup racing, really, and what he has accomplished already is tremendous. But I don't think he's come close to reaching his potential yet."

DALE EARNHARDT JR.: "Tony is in a great situation right now, and he's going to get so much better. He's going to be one kick-ass racer; at some point, he's going to have a period, three or four years in a row, where he'll be one of the most dominant guys."

What I wonder sometimes is whether I'll stick around long enough to get all these things done. Because, I'll admit, there are days when this stuff really wears me out.

The amount of politics in this business would shock the average fan. Never mind that, it would shock even the most *hard-core* fan. If you love racing the way I do, just love the pure sport of it, that can get pretty disheartening. When I get caught up in the really petty stuff, I sometimes find myself wondering what the hell I'm even doing here.

When I was fined at Daytona in July of 2001 for losing my temper outside the NASCAR trailer, that weighed on me for months. Some of my friends in the Cup garage couldn't understand why I was so frustrated; well, I had raced with a dozen sanctioning bodies, and this was the first time I ever got a bill for speaking my mind.

In the spring of 2000, after a bad qualifying run at Martinsville, I complained in a TV interview about the tires Goodyear had brought that weekend. Actually, I didn't complain about the tire itself; I was upset because this particular tire was different from the previous year's Martinsville tire, which meant all our old notes from that track were now scrap paper. We didn't get the new tire figured out as quickly as some other teams did—our fault—and that bothered me. I never bad-mouthed the quality of the new tire, and never even mentioned the company by name, but that one little ten-second speech got my team in hot water with Goodyear.

It's like every time a Winston Cup driver starts to talk, he's expected to have a little censor in his head, making sure the speech is okay. If that censor happens to fall asleep at the wrong time, there's hell to pay.

Joe Gibbs has always told people that he likes the fire he sees in me. Lately, just keeping that fire stoked has been a challenge, for all the wrong reasons. (© Phil Cavali/Winston Cup Scene)

All the drivers know this, and that's why some of them don't dare get anywhere close to a controversial subject. One of the biggest names in this sport said to me, "Hey, I'm making more money here than I'd ever make doing anything else. Why screw that up by opening my mouth?"

That's how the game is played. Don't rock the boat, ever.

Well, that's not the way I think racing ought to be. That's not the way I think *life* ought to be. Like I said at the beginning of this book, my parents instilled in me the value of truthfulness, and I'm not about to sell that out just to save whatever dollars NASCAR wants to fine me, or some sponsor wants to penalize me.

But, I'll tell you, I get awfully sick of fighting this battle.

Joe Gibbs has always said that he appreciates the fire he sees in me. Well, I've told people close to me, Joe included, that lately it has flickered more than I ever imagined it would. Trust me, it's not the actual racing that has beaten that fire down. If anything, the level of competition every week is what keeps that flame going; if you enjoy a challenge, Winston Cup racing will give you one. But there are days when all the stuff that goes along with racing at this level is like fire-retardant foam raining down on my head.

When they wave that green flag, I guarantee you I'm going to drive with as much heart as anybody in the field, and more than most. But I don't find myself looking forward to going to the track as much as I used to.

And so, the question is, what am I supposed to do about all this?

Do I just smile my way through the weekends for the next fifteen years simply because I'm making a great living, and because there's supposed to be nothing better on this earth than being a Winston Cup star?

Or do I ultimately decide that enough is enough, and tell myself, Screw the money, racing is supposed to be about you and me strapping in and seeing who's best?

I'm going to have to find that answer. Soon.

When I ran my first go-kart race, I had no concept of rent, no concept of mortgage payments. I didn't know what it meant to pay for groceries. I didn't understand that everything had a price tag, and that the nicest stuff cost the most. And I sure wasn't aware that if he was good enough and caught all the right breaks, a race driver could get rich. All I knew was that I loved to compete.

Even as I moved into midgets and sprint cars and I started pulling in a few dollars, it was still more about the competition than the money. I got paid to race, but I didn't race because I got paid.

> **BOB EAST:** "When Tony ran for us in '95, every time he won a race he went and bought something. You know, toys. He'd stop here and say, 'East, look at what I bought.' With him, no matter how much money he makes, it's still just a big allowance to him."

My attitude about all that has never changed. Yes, you need enough money to survive, and if you're a professional racer you'd better learn how to drive smart and calculate your percentages, the way I did. But at the moment I climb into that car, I'm not thinking about the payoff. I'm thinking, Give me the trophy.

That's what I really want: the trophy, the win. The money is just a way to confirm that you did the best job, whether it's two hundred thousand dollars at Charlotte or two thousand dollars at Terre Haute. The only reason you want the biggest check is because it means you won.

People who don't have a competitive streak in them might not believe that, but I mean every word of it.

> **LARRY CURRY:** "Is Tony making a lot of money these days? Sure he is. But let me tell you something: if he found himself in a situation where on one hand he could drive a race car and not get paid a dollar—just be guaranteed a place to live and enough food to eat—and on the other hand he could take a job in corporate America and be a millionaire as long as he stayed out of a race car, it would be no contest. Tony's going to drive that race car."

The biggest problem with money is that people let it dictate their lives. Sure, that has to go on sometimes when you're flat broke, and I've been there. But once you get to the point where you're comfortable, money shouldn't run the show for you.

Yet it happens in racing, just like it happens everywhere else. There are lots of examples of drivers who made terrible career moves—left a good ride for a bad one, or maybe stuck around too long past their primes—because they got tempted by money. In fact, it's hard to remember the last big star who retired on top, at the peak of his prime earning years; it would probably be Rick Mears, who figured that winning the Indy 500 four times was enough, and said *adios* when he was only forty-one. Rick told everybody that his heart wasn't in it anymore, at least not to a level that he found acceptable, and he walked away.

Too many guys can't do that, and the money an established driver can earn by running just one more season—and then just one more after that—makes his decision easy to rationalize. Yet every time you see one of these guys, he never looks happy, because he's either struggling at the back or fighting just to qualify.

Well, the way I see it, if you're wealthy but you're losing, you're losing. If you're wealthy but you're miserable, you're miserable. And what's the point of that?

If you asked me to name the five happiest moments of my life, I'd have to think about the races I've won, or the times I laughed with my friends when we played pool, or crashed our go-karts, or rode down the highway in a pickup truck. I've never equated happiness with dollar signs, and I never will.

And that's comforting, because if I decide one day that the only way to lead a more pleasant life is to do something that involves a smaller paycheck, I know that I could do that.

NELSON STEWART: "From day one, when he first started racing, the last thing I've always told Tony before he went on the track was, 'Have fun.' I still do that today, because I think it's the most important thing."

There are times when I daydream about finishing out my career like Mel Kenyon, who's in his late sixties and still races midgets just because he loves it. Mel doesn't win like he did in his thirties, but he'll grab himself a feature every now and then, and I think that's what keeps him going. Or I'll see myself running midgets every weekend, and then hooking up with a good IRL team in May to go after the Indianapolis 500. I used to watch Stan Fox and Rich Vogler do that, and it never seemed like such a bad deal.

In those daydreams, I'm always smiling. Nobody's on my case about something I said in an interview, and I'm not being summoned to a meeting to discuss my conduct, and there's not some drunk screaming that I owe him an autograph because he just bought one of my T-shirts.

There's just a bunch of us standing on the gas, racing just for racing's sake.

Until the summer of 2000, I had never raced against my father. His driving days basically ended before mine started, and by the time he started messing around with TQ midgets a few years ago, I was obviously off doing other things. So when we looked at a UMRA schedule and noticed that the club was in Columbus on a night when I'd be in the area for a Winston Cup test at Indianapolis, we both jumped at the chance.

Just for racing's sake.

We qualified through separate heat races, but when we rolled off together for the A-main, that was a special moment.

Not that we raced head-to-head, exactly. I was battling for the lead, and my dad was having his problems, running in the back. Then I got tangled up with another car, spun out, and had to restart at the tail. I could see my dad ahead, and I thought, This ought to be fun. I was smiling as I ran him down, and as I sailed past him on the outside I gave him a discreet little wave, kind of a *see ya* gesture.

But, wouldn't you know it, my dad had the last laugh. I got caught in another wreck, and UMRA has a rule that if you spin twice, you're done. I sat parked in the infield while my dad finished the race. If I remember correctly, in the official box score he was twelfth and I was thirteenth.

The next day at the Winston Cup test, he was telling everybody how he'd blown me off at Columbus.

We still have our discussions about that race. I'll remind him that I was quicker, and how I rubbed it in by waving at him; he'll always point to that box score. And you know something? Someday I'll be old and gray, and I might not have any memory of how fast I was at the fairgrounds, but that box score will always be there. I guess ol' Nelson wins that fight.

That night at Columbus was just pure enjoyment, nothing complicated.

I miss that sort of easygoing fun, and I'd give just about anything to feel that way more often.

You know what I want out of racing? I want to be competitive, no matter what I'm sitting in. If it's a Winston Cup car, I want it to be fast. If it's an Indy car, I want it to be fast. If it's a midget, a dirt late-model, a Silver Crown car, same deal.

I want to win. I don't ever want to be just another guy out there.

It sounds simple, but it takes a lot of hard work.

What I want out of *life* probably sounds simple, too. I'd like to have a family of my own when my career settles down a bit. That's also going to take some hard work. As you might have noticed, long-lasting relationships have not been my strong suit. Maybe someday.

You know what else would be nice? I'd like to make a few less people angry, and a few more people happy.

> **JEFF "GOOCH" PATTERSON:** "The sad thing is, all most people know about Tony is the side of him that they see on TV, when he's mad or cussing or throwing something. Well, yes, that's one side of Tony Stewart. But there are other sides to that guy, just like there are different sides to everybody. I wish more people could have seen him when we went down to New Smyrna [Florida] for the opening of Mark Martin's quarter-midget track. Tony spent so much time playing with the little kids—hell, he's just a kid himself anyway—and he had a smile on his face all night."

The making-people-happy part is something I'm trying to work on. It's going to take some practice, I think.

As far as making them angry sometimes, I can't see where that's going to get any better, at least on any large-scale basis. Almost all the trouble I get in seems directly related to the passion I put into this sport, and I'm definitely not going to start caring less anytime soon.

So I'll continue to lose my cool from time to time. We'll have our occasional explosions. There might be another fine or two to pay. Hey, at least things around me aren't dull for very long.

Joe Gibbs has compared me to Gary Clark, a wide receiver he coached when he was with the Washington Redskins; I guess Clark was hard to handle sometimes, and got a little bit mouthy when he thought he'd been treated badly. That sounds a lot like all those comparisons to Foyt I mentioned earlier.

Honestly, all I want to be is who I am.

I don't expect everybody to root for me. If they don't like me, there are forty-two other guys in every Winston Cup race, thirty-two other guys in every Indy 500, twenty-odd other guys in every short-track race I run. If you cheer for one of them, I won't mind. Just as long as you give me credit for putting everything I have into every lap of every race I run.

A. J. FOYT: "Tony doesn't need to do anything different. If he just keeps on doing what he's doing right now, sooner or later everybody's going to have to respect him. Because he's a winner."

What I want out of racing isn't all that complicated. I want to be fast and I want to win. (© Mike Adaskaveg)

It sure is funny, the way things change.

A dozen years ago, while my school buddies back in Columbus were off at various universities, I was flipping hamburgers at McDonald's. If you just happened to wander by and saw me in the drive-through window, I'm sure I didn't come across as a kid who had a lot to look forward to.

Well, today, some of those friends who were lucky enough to go to college call me from time to time. They're looking for pit passes.

Awhile back, I was actually presented with a key to the city of Columbus. Nobody could have predicted that. I've also received an honorary key to Indianapolis, where I was essentially a bum scrambling not to get evicted, and another to the city of Rushville, which is hysterical, because when I lived there Tutti Martz was always hauling me to traffic court for assorted speeding violations. I was not a model citizen.

In Rushville, they actually named a street after me. You can go there and see it for yourself: Tony Stewart Drive.

LARRY MARTZ: "That street leads right into the racetrack, and the closest office building to it is the police station. If they'd only put a pool hall in there, they'd have Tony's whole life history."

One night not long ago, I pulled over to the side of the highway just as I was entering Rushville. I grabbed an ink marker out of the glove compartment, looked around to be sure the coast was clear, and then ran up to one of those "Home of Racing Champion Tony Stewart" billboards. On the corner of the sign, I scrawled my signature, plus the date and the time. Then, several miles down the road, on the sign at the opposite end of town, I did the same thing, only I wrote down a time that was just a minute or two later than I'd written on the first sign.

I'm not sure whether anyone ever discovered my handiwork. But I laughed for days, imagining some guy noticing those two autographs, comparing my arrival and departure times, and muttering, "Man, he sure passed through in a hurry."

When you think about it, that's not such a bad thing to say about a race driver.

AFTERWORD by BONES BOURCIER

ANOTHER GOAL MET: TONY STEWART CAN NOW WALK INTO HIS DEN AND
see the Winston Cup championship trophy sitting on his shelf. What he
said earlier in this book was right on the money: the driver was up to
the job.

And it couldn't have happened in a more fitting way. Sure, Stewart
would have obviously chosen to clinch the crown by winning the 2002
season finale at the Homestead-Miami Speedway, but that would have
been too neat, too perfect. No, it was only right that he lock up the thing
with what he termed "an ugly day," an eighteenth-place finish after a
race full of highs and lows and emotions pulled in different directions.
November 17, 2002, was more than just the date when Stewart sewed
up his first Winston Cup title; it was a terrific 400-mile metaphor for his
entire NASCAR tenure, and especially for this particular season, one he
called "the most difficult of my career."

And it was an afternoon when, after four years of being pushed and
pressed into molds he stubbornly refused to fit, Stewart was set free to
just be himself. Even on the television broadcast of the postrace championship celebration, you could hear the infectious little-boy giggle that
still comes out of Stewart when he is absolutely free of tension, free of
inhibition. It was a charming scene. There he was, in what was clearly
the most public moment of his life—a life marked by occasional outbursts against having to *be* such a public figure—and Stewart was so
alone in his joy that it didn't seem to mean a damn to him who was
watching.

And so, as he wrapped his arms around his friend and crew chief,
Greg Zipadelli, and as tears welled in Zipadelli's eyes, out came the real
Tony Stewart. Out came that giggle.

Stewart said later, "To see Zippy cry . . ."

(© Worth Canoy/VPS Motorimages)

Then he paused, and onto his tired face there came a sheepish grin that said all there was to say about his 2002 season.

"I knew I could make him cry. I just wanted to do it the right way. I've made him cry before."

Yes, he probably had. Seldom—okay, never—had a Winston Cup championship team ridden the kind of emotional roller coaster upon which Stewart drove his Joe Gibbs Racing mates in 2002. On their best days, they joined him in the victory lane after stunning performances at Atlanta, Richmond, and Watkins Glen. On their worst, many of them were ready to strangle their driver.

"I practically destroyed this team by midseason, single-handedly," Stewart admitted when it was over.

The crazy thing was, almost none of the destruction had anything to do—directly, anyway—with what happened on the track. Oh, there were days when Stewart made it plain that he was less than pleased with his car; he called it a "piece of shit" in one famously bleeped TV interview late in the season. And, yes, there were days when his candor on that subject rankled his mechanics. But neither Stewart nor his team has ever let hard feelings over how the car ran or where it finished linger.

No, what nearly blew apart the Home Depot Pontiac organization was the tension triggered by Stewart's volatility outside the cockpit. If his previous seasons were punctuated by Sunday afternoon run-ins on the speedway—with Kenny Irwin, with Jeff Gordon, with Robby Gordon—2002 was marked by a bizarre string of events and/or nonevents involving Stewart and a handful of folks working and/or lurking on the periphery of the sport.

After the Brickyard 400 at Indianapolis in August, Stewart was directed to park his car in a designated inspection area rather than in its usual spot behind the team transporter. Already frustrated by a late-race slide to twelfth place, he was running through the garage area toward the sanctuary of that transporter when he encountered freelance photographer Gary Mook, snapping away as was his right to do. What happened next is up to which witness you believe: Stewart either punched or shoved

Mook once or twice or several times. In the next eight days, Stewart was docked $10,000 by NASCAR, was hit with an unheard-of $50,000 fine by his own sponsor, announced plans to enter anger management training, and, oh, yes, won the following weekend's Winston Cup event at Watkins Glen. Mook later said that the whole thing had been blown out of proportion. Hell, how do you blow *that* kind of a week out of proportion?

On September 5, Stewart was triumphant at Richmond in a one-off start in NASCAR's third-tier Craftsman Truck Series. The very next day, word swept through the Winston Cup garage that Tennessee authorities were investigating claims that Stewart had shoved a female fan after a Bristol race a few weeks earlier. Stewart vehemently denied the allegation, and a grand jury ultimately found no cause to indict him. The whole thing triggered an intense debate over crowded conditions in the garage area, with NASCAR promising tighter future controls on credentials.

On September 14, New Hampshire's *Concord Monitor* published a story in which an emergency medical technician named Phil Jewett claimed to have been punched by Stewart during a July event at the New Hampshire International Speedway. Jewett had worked that race as part of the rescue crew and had tried to help Stewart climb from his car after a wreck. "As soon as he saw me in the corner of his eye he swung at me and hit me in the left arm," Jewett said. "He hit me pretty hard. He didn't break my arm or anything, but if he had hit me in the ribs instead of my arm it would have hurt a heck of a lot worse." Jewett came forward, he said, because he hadn't gotten an apology from either Stewart or NASCAR. Subsequently, a replay of television footage showed Stewart merely swatting aside Jewett's hand, making light contact at best. A NASCAR spokesman declared the case "a closed issue."

If all these allegations didn't send Stewart into a foul mood, the frenzy of follow-up reporting did. His behavior became such an issue that one respected Internet site, CNNSI.com, actually published a "Tony Stewart

Timeline" chronicling his misdeeds. Scanning its entries, you didn't know if you were checking the sports pages or the police blotter: "Sept. 6, 2002: Reports surface that Stewart is under investigation by Tennessee authorities for allegedly shoving a fan. . . . Sept. 15, 2002: NASCAR officials say they found no conclusive evidence to support an emergency medical technician's claim that Stewart punched him after the New England 300 in July. . . . Sept. 24, 2002: A Tennessee grand jury declines to indict Stewart. . . . Sept. 26, 2002: In his first extensive interview since his Brickyard 400 incident, Stewart says he is trying to protect himself from any more allegations by keeping to himself more in the garage area. . . . Oct. 6, 2002: Stewart takes over the Winston Cup points lead after finishing second to Dale Earnhardt Jr. in the EA Sports 500 at Talladega."

And so Tony Stewart, already edgy at best, stepped over the edge a few times. In postchampionship remarks that amounted to an emotion-filled confessional, he acknowledged that his team's season had not exactly been a day at the beach.

"There were times when guys were wanting to leave this year, and it was because they just didn't want to work for me," Stewart said. "And I don't blame 'em. We did lose a couple guys, and . . . those guys who left, I've never once blamed 'em. They had a reason to leave."

How intense did it all get, really? Check out Stewart's account of some team meetings in crew chief Zipadelli's office: "I've had heart-to-hearts where I've sat and cried in the room. I've said, 'Hey, I'm sorry for what I'm doing to you guys. But I'm not doing it because I want to hurt you; I'm doing it because I'm frustrated. And if you'll bear with me, we'll make it right.' Hopefully, with this championship I've made some of it right."

And what of the man who cried with him in that Winston Cup celebration at Homestead? What of Greg Zipadelli?

"Zippy was the glue that held everybody together," Stewart declared. "Zippy was the friend that got me back on track, and got my mind set right. He wasn't just a crew chief; he had to be a crew chief, a baby-sitter-slash-best friend, and a huge leader. Zippy kept everybody motivated and focused."

Zipadelli claimed it was a matter of making his driver understand that during the season's most trying days "there was a group of people who were really, truly dedicated to him. And sometimes we *all* have those days. If we go back over these four years, together we've been through some tough times. But we've been able to *learn* from the tough times."

And so maybe Greg Zipadelli has become the latest Larry Howard, the latest Glen Niebel, the latest Bob East, the latest Larry Curry, just a younger version of the same figure who has been there through all of Stewart's successes: the wise teacher, the shoulder to lean on, the stabilizing influence. Zipadelli, a straightforward sort of fellow, doesn't much go for such deep analysis. He chooses instead to say that if he and his driver and the men behind them proved anything in 2002, it was that "If you stick together, there's nothing you can't accomplish or overcome."

And, to be honest, there was a lot more to overcome than just the driver's psychological baggage. Stewart's season began not with a bang, but a clunk; his engine let him down three laps into the Daytona 500. The failure was especially stinging, for two big reasons: first, the Gibbs team's Daytona program was stronger than ever, having propelled Stewart to his second straight Bud Shootout victory a week earlier; second, among the team's goals for 2002 had been to change its troublesome pattern of falling behind in the points over the first half of the season.

So what had loomed as a day full of grand possibilities—many insiders had labeled the orange number 20 the Daytona 500 favorite—ended instead with Stewart last in the race, last in the Winston Cup standings, and changing into civilian clothes in the team transporter about, oh, three hours earlier than he had hoped. That was where Joe Gibbs, fearing the worst, found his fiery driver.

"I was expecting him to *really* be upset," Gibbs recalled. "But he turned around, kind of calm, and he said, 'We're gonna still win this thing.'"

Meaning, of course, the championship. And Stewart apparently believed it, putting together top-five finishes in the next three races—including that Atlanta win—and hauling himself into fifth in the standings. A violent crash at Darlington bruised Stewart and sapped the team for a race or two, but he was soon back in form—fifth at Texas, third at

Martinsville, first at Richmond—and back on the move in the points. Never again was Stewart out of the Winston Cup top ten.

His strength seemed to come in spurts: the Watkins Glen victory backed up by a second-place run at Michigan; consecutive top-fives at New Hampshire and Dover in September, and at Talladega and Charlotte in October. It was his runner-up finish at Talladega, race number 30 of 36, that gave Stewart the point lead he never surrendered.

There were others who had looked to have strong hands over the NASCAR autumn. But Sterling Marlin cracked a vertebra at Kansas, Jeff Gordon couldn't seem to be fast and consistent at the same time, rookie Ryan Newman blew hot and cold, and another Cup first-year man, Jimmie Johnson, stumbled at exactly the wrong time after equaling Stewart's phenomenal 1999 mark of three rookie wins. Stewart, meanwhile, was rock steady: second, third, eleventh, fourth, fourteenth . . .

The old saw in the NASCAR garage holds that if a team can run in the top fifteen on a bad day, it is of championship caliber. Tony Stewart's team was running like that as 2002 ground toward a conclusion.

All of which had Stewart saying things like, "To start the season off like we did this year—forty-third in points after Daytona—and to be able to rebound from that, and then to go through all the things we went through this year and still keep our focus. . . .

"I still have a hard time believing that we've been able to accomplish what we have this year."

By the time the series got to Phoenix for its penultimate round in November, it was clear that the champion would be either Stewart or Mark Martin, whose Roush Racing Ford team had been a model of consistency. The one blight on Martin's season came in race 34, at Rockingham, when he finished second but was docked 25 Winston Cup points after NASCAR inspectors found his car carrying a front spring that was marginally out of spec. That controversial penalty threatened to throw a dark cloud over the championship chase, at least until an unlikely source came along to lighten things up. It was Stewart who elevated the last few weeks of this topsy-turvy season by continually singing the praises of a man he had looked up to since 1996 and '97. Back then, Martin was already a Winston Cup superstar and Stewart was struggling to gain a foothold in the Busch Series.

"Religiously on Friday mornings, before practice, I would run down and ask Mark a lot of questions," Stewart remembered, "because I had no clue what I was doing. And with all of his commitments, Mark was always willing to take the time to talk. He didn't know me from Adam, didn't know what I'd driven in the past. But he never cared. He always took time out of his schedule to answer any questions I had.

"There's a lot of guys you hope you never get into a points battle with, because it could get hairy at the end. But I've got a lot of respect for this man. He's one of my heroes in the Winston Cup series."

However muddied things might have seemed, what with Martin's complicated situation and the residue of his own dustups still hanging overhead, there was an air of confidence around Tony Stewart as the season entered its final laps. Not the brash cockiness that has always been there, but a quieter brand, a let's-get-to-it determination. It was as if Stewart understood that, for better or worse, 2002 had been the ride of his life, and there was nothing to do now but finish it out.

Certainly from a career standpoint he had never been more established. Blowups be damned, he was, at thirty-one years of age, a NASCAR veteran held in high regard by his peers, if not always by the outside world. His team was a threat to win everywhere: big tracks, small tracks, road course, *everywhere*. Maybe that was the thing that made Stewart happiest: he had become a complete Winston Cup racer, just as he had been a complete go-kart racer, a complete midget racer, a complete Indy car racer.

And his personal life seemed more, well, settled. From April on, he was most often in the company of a California beauty named Jaime Schaffer, young and centered and seemingly capable of surfing the rolling wave that is life with Tony Stewart.

Even when Stewart sparred with the press on the season's final two weekends—hey, he may have been quieter, but he wasn't castrated—his tone was not so much combative as self-assured. For four years, he had seethed off and on as the racing media urged—no, demanded—that he change his ways. This was Stewart declaring: My way works, at least for me. He was at the top of the pile, the Winston Cup points leader. Who could argue with him?

At Phoenix, the initial word from the Gibbs camp was that Stewart would not be available for interviews over the weekend. This seemed like an interesting-enough angle—"Points Leader Mum, Lets Driving Do the Talking"—but to a pampered NASCAR press corps so accustomed to being provided with access and quotes, both real and PR-generated, this was heresy. An uproar was quelled only when Stewart relented to a media-center session after Friday's qualifying round. But even then, he would not bend. Again: My way works.

Someone asked if, given the title fight, he planned any changes in strategy for the Sunday race. He answered, "I haven't changed anything up to now. Why would I change now?"

Then came a question about whether or not he was approaching his day-to-day routine differently. Stewart: "No. What part of 'We haven't changed anything' is hard for all you guys to understand?"

Asked if he was at least enjoying the championship fight, Stewart answered, "Pass."

His performance did not draw rave reviews. Various Saturday morning reports labeled him sarcastic, exasperated, caustic. What that meant, of course, was that he did not provide the answers the press had come looking for. The truth was that by the time Phoenix rolled around, Tony Stewart—however uncomfortable he might have been with all of the hoopla—was finally comfortable just being himself. If that meant occasionally being a bit of a thorn in the side of some newsman, so what?

He finished eighth at Phoenix and brought with him to the Homestead finale an 89-point lead and the same this-is-me outlook.

In the days leading up to the season's last race, *USA Today* carried a major feature in which Richard Petty, a seven-time Winston Cup champion and the most fan-friendly driver in the history of NASCAR, if not of all motorsports, seemed to suggest that Stewart's attitude needed to change.

"People become role models, not because they want to," the paper quoted Petty as saying. "That's an obligation that they get by doing the job they want to do. . . . That job doesn't just constitute driving a race car. If the people before him had treated the people as he treats them today, then there wouldn't be no Tony Stewart running Winston Cup, because there wouldn't be no Winston Cup."

Stewart's stated response to that philosophy was basically the same as it had been for his entire career: he was a race driver, not a politician, and now he was running for a NASCAR title, not some government office. That is a weighty enough thing to say in the politically polished world today's stock car racers live in, but it became a huge issue now because it involved this smart aleck standing up to King Richard-by-God-Petty.

In a Saturday press conference, this interchange occurred between Stewart and Ed Hinton of the *Orlando Sentinel*:

HINTON: "Tony, you said earlier this week that you were running for a point championship, not a political office. And yet, even since then there's been some reaction [suggesting that] after you get it, it does become some sort of a political office. . . ."

STEWART: "Tell me how that happens."

HINTON: "Pardon?"

STEWART: "Tell me how it happens. Because I don't know. I don't know anything about it."

HINTON: "Well, that's what the people who've been champion before say: that it becomes an ambassadorial role. And so, what I'm asking is, should you win this thing, do you look with some dread on the idea that you might be—not just because it's an ambassadorial role, but because of all that's gone on with you this season—that you might be under a greater microscope than other champions have been in the past? Does that bother you, or do you sort of look forward to the chance to handle that?"

STEWART: "I'm not really even concerned about it. I haven't made a thought about it. Maybe we'll see if we can hire Richard Petty to do it for me."

There was laughter around the room, a great bit of laughter, and then Stewart wrapped the whole thing up by suggesting that maybe it ought to be okay that he and Petty were simply different sorts of people.

"He is a great ambassador for our sport," Stewart said. "I'm not an ambassador for *anything*. I'm a simple kid from a small town in Indiana. All I've done for the last twenty-three years is drive race cars."

It was an interesting moment in an interesting season. Stewart did not put down Richard Petty. He did not insult Ed Hinton. He merely challenged the premise of the question. That is his way, and, after all, his way works.

Toward the end of the press conference, a reporter raised a hand and asked Stewart what was on his schedule for that evening.

Stewart smiled. "That'd be the last thing I'd tell *you* guys."

His last night as a championship contender went smoothly: Stewart and Schaffer passed a few hours playing video games in a Miami arcade, then had a quiet dinner at the home of some old friends.

His last race as a championship contender was a little rockier. Stewart loves Homestead because it is a track where "the driver has to do a lot of work. Nobody has a perfect car there." But he didn't plan on working as hard as he did; his car handled badly from the start, suffering from a loose condition, and Stewart fell a lap down 192 laps into the 267-lap race. In an ironic twist, at one point he slipped as far back as twenty-second, exactly where he needed to finish to clinch the title no matter how Martin fared. The two-way link between Stewart and Zipadelli crackled all day with ideas about how to fix the car. But neither man ever sounded overly anxious.

"We never gave up," Stewart said later. "We never got frustrated with each other on the radio. We did this the [same] way we got here, and that's as a team. We never gave up on each other."

It turned out that Stewart had been right way back in February when he addressed Joe Gibbs through a silent fury after dropping out of the Daytona 500. His team really did have what it took to win this thing.

When a late-race restart lined him up at the head on the lapped-car row, directly beside leader Dale Jarrett, Stewart took full advantage. He drove away from Jarrett, putting himself back on the lead lap, and pulled himself up to eighteenth at the finish. Martin ended up fourth, a gallant effort but futile.

The 2002 Winston Cup championship was Stewart's, by thirty-eight points. That margin, he admitted, was a relief, because it rendered Martin's Rockingham penalty moot.

As he drove slowly down the pit road after the race, toward one giant celebration and one tearful crew chief, Stewart was saluted and high-fived by the members of almost every rival team, including Martin's. Long after the championship trophies had been handed out and all the group photos had been taken, it was that display—that show of respect from his competitors—that seemed to touch Stewart the most.

"I don't care what [size] check Winston writes," he said quietly. "The feeling of satisfaction from seeing those guys out there is more than money can buy. It's like those commercials that say, 'Priceless.' You couldn't put a price tag on it."

Not surprisingly, given Stewart's scraps with the press, the days surrounding his title-clinching run were filled with speculation about how he would handle the added burden—real or imagined—of being the Winston Cup champion. Columnists drew a hundred contrasts between bad-boy Stewart and that nice ex-champ Jeff Gordon, and had a ball joshing about what Stewart might do during his trip to New York City for the NASCAR awards dinner and its related media outings. Would Regis Philbin provoke him into taking a swing? Would Stewart storm off the Letterman set if ol' Dave happened to ask the wrong question? Some of it was funny, but most of it was forced, and all of it was too predictable: *He's busted our chops for four years. Now it's our turn.*

But while some folks wrung their hands in terror—mock or sincere—over this notion of Stewart-as-champion, his fellow drivers seemed completely comfortable with the head upon which stock car racing's ultimate crown now rested.

"A lot of time has been spent this year talking about Tony's negatives," Jeff Burton said at Homestead. "There's been a tremendous amount of conversation about Tony being able to uphold his responsibility as a champion. I think Tony will step it up. I think Tony has respect for this sport.

"I don't know if Tony, a month from now, is gonna be happy he won the championship or not. I think Tony would just as soon take the trophy tonight, go have a party, and that would be it. But that's not the way it's going to work for him. I think Tony's going to step it up, and I think he'll do a great job representing our sport."

Kyle Petty, taking a decidedly different tack than his dad, Richard, suggested to *USA Today* that Stewart could be NASCAR's ultimate "people's champion," given his penchant for running short-track cars at out-of-the-way venues in his spare time. "How cool could it be to have the Winston Cup champion run a dirt race in Iowa somewhere?" said Kyle. "Jeff Gordon [and] guys like that take the sport to the boardroom. I think Tony Stewart can take the sport to the boardroom if he feels like it, but chances are he's going to feel like taking it to Des Moines."

For his part, Gordon claimed not to understand what all the fuss was about, declaring that the Winston Cup title was given annually to the driver who scored the most points—as he himself had four times—and that what Stewart had done on the track in 2002 was enough. Gordon told *USA Today,* "This whole 'I've got to represent the sport and I've got to say all the right things and look pretty and smile,' that's not what makes you a great champion."

If Gordon's view was the right one, then Stewart had another strong backer in 2002 Winston Cup Rookie of the Year Ryan Newman, who praised Stewart's ability "to drive so many different kinds of race cars as well as he has" and said he considered his fellow Hoosier "one of the greatest drivers that's ever lived."

But maybe the best endorsement of Stewart came from the man he had beaten for the crown. Minutes after the season finale, Mark Martin strolled into the conference room just off the Miami-Homestead media center to talk about what it had been like to finish second—for the third time—in the Winston Cup standings. Always an interesting interview because he rarely falls back on the tired clichés preferred by so many of today's big-time racers, Martin spoke eloquently about his career, about his race team, and about coming so close, again, to his sport's biggest title.

Then from the floor came the following question: "Mark, you've been watching and competing in this sport for such a long time. Would you say that Tony Stewart is the most unusual champion that's been crowned in some time?"

Martin paused a moment before answering. When he spoke, his words came slowly, and, as always, thoughtfully: "I admire Tony Stewart. I am a, uh . . . *commercialized* racer. You have to be commercialized in this business, and I've done my very best to do that, and to represent, you know, the sport the best way that I can. But, down deep, I'm like Tony: I'd rather be on the road right now, headed toward the dirt track, or at the quarter-midget track and watching the kids race. That's where I'd really like to be going right now, instead of sitting here talking to you guys.

"I admire Tony Stewart. He's a racer's racer, and he's really, really good. He didn't just step in and get this stuff given to him. He's won everywhere he's ever been. Yeah, he's intense and, yeah, it's gonna be interesting to watch . . . you know, because [being champion] is a tremendous load. I've thought about the load, because this could have swung my way too, and I know it would have been a tremendous load on me as well. Whoever does win the Winston Cup championship carries a big load, and it will be interesting to watch. But I *admire* Tony. I race with him hard, and he races with me hard, fair and clean, and he has respect. I was there first, a long time ago, when he was just a kid, and he respects that. And, you know, it's nice when these young guys come along that are so incredibly talented and also have the respect that you would like to have. So, you know, I'm a Tony Stewart fan."

Then Martin, who has a tendency to lean very hard on words he wants emphasized—I once wrote that he spoke in italics—added one last tip of his hat to Stewart: "He is an *incredible* race car driver."

And from Jim Hunter, NASCAR's vice president of communications, came still more support. Hunter is generally viewed as the sanctioning body's chief liaison to the sport's regular beat writers—so many of whom have taken issue with Stewart's behavior—and thus might have been excused for feeling a tad uneasy about NASCAR's new titleholder. But Hunter, an old newspaperman himself, was looking on the bright side: In Stewart, NASCAR had on its hands an emerging mainstream sports star who, through good times and bad, was never, ever dull. That meant headlines. That meant column inches. That meant more and more publicity for Winston Cup racing, and surely everyone in positions of authority at NASCAR understood that.

Said Hunter to all who would listen, "Tony will be a great champion."

———

It was logical to ask Stewart exactly where among his many accomplishments—the Indy Racing League championship, the USAC Triple Crown, all those race wins—he placed the 2002 Winston Cup title.

"I guess if I had to retype my résumé tomorrow, I'd put it number one," he said. "None of them were easy. They all had their own unique sets of circumstances and obstacles and challenges. But to say the Winston Cup championship isn't my greatest accomplishment, I mean, I'd look pretty stupid.

"The caliber of teams and car owners and crew chiefs and drivers here makes you really respect this championship. That doesn't take away anything from the other ones. But this one—with all the pressures that go along with it—feels quite a bit different."

He talked at Homestead about how he was still finding his way in NASCAR, still adjusting to the high-profile nature of the job. "It's like I've always said: you don't get an instructional video, and they don't give you a freshman pamphlet saying, 'This is what your life is going to be like [as a Winston Cup driver], this is how you do things, this is what's going to happen to you.' None of that is explained to you. It's trial and error. Lord knows, I've had enough trials and errors."

He paused. "More errors than trials."

But, he told reporters, he was nowhere near fed up with the pressures of Winston Cup racing enough to chuck it all and, championship check in hand, head back to the short tracks for good, as some pundits had predicted.

"I still don't agree with everything NASCAR does," Stewart said. "But the things they do, they do for a reason. And you know what? I'm a race car driver, and I don't *have* to understand everything they do. I don't *have* to agree with anything they do. I just have to abide by their rules.

"If there comes a day when I feel like I truly don't enjoy this enough anymore, then I'll quit. I *will* get up and walk away from it. But as much stuff as happened to us this year, I can't imagine any year coming up being any worse than this year has been for us. I'm hoping, I'm *praying*, that I've got the worst of it behind me.

"I've got no plans of leaving."

— — — — —

Except, of course, for a few temporary side trips back to his roots. While Stewart did a bit less short-track moonlighting in 2002 than in past years—partly at the urging of Gibbs and Zipadelli as the NASCAR points situation tightened—he still showed up, helmet in hand, at selected midget, sprint car, Silver Crown, modified, and late model races. When he jetted away from preseason Daytona testing long enough to compete in, and win, the Chili Bowl indoor midget classic in Tulsa, he was only living up to the creed he continues to race by: you can take the boy out of the bullring, but you can't take the bullring out of the boy.

In fact, just ten days after clinching his Winston Cup championship, Stewart headed west for a Thanksgiving weekend reminiscent of his busiest ride-hopping days in the mid-1990s: USAC national midgets and Western States sprints at California's Irwindale Speedway—the fabled Turkey Night event he holds so dear—and a similar program two nights later on a three-eighths-mile paved track in Las Vegas. Stewart, making the most of his holiday fun, had rides in both divisions.

Things started well enough when Stewart ran away with the 40-lap Irwindale sprint car feature. Then, while he was battling for third place early in the 100-lap Turkey Night Grand Prix midget show, Stewart crashed hard after being hit from behind by another driver whose throttle had stuck wide open. The impact left Stewart dazed; back in the pits, he admitted to a headache, a sore ankle, and various other pains. He sounded unsure about whether he might compete at Las Vegas.

But if you ought to know one thing about Tony Stewart by now, it is this: if he *can* race, he *will* race. He was still hobbling come the Saturday-night doubleheader in Vegas, but his driving didn't suffer much. He was the fastest qualifier in the 48-car sprint field, the second fastest of the 36 midget racers on hand, and he won both features.

The next night, Sunday, he was due to fly to Washington for a Monday morning White House audience with the President of the United States, just one of the perks for his Winston Cup championship. But the look in Stewart's eyes at Las Vegas showed nothing but pure joy at being able to show that he still had what it took to be a short-track, open-wheel badass.

Something he'd said at Irwindale two nights earlier rang in the ear. After winning that sprint car feature, Stewart had addressed the huge crowd, saluting the fans for their support of grassroots racing.

"Everybody's always telling me not to change," he said. "Well, I won't change if you won't."

He shows every sign of holding up his end of that bargain.

This sort of thing just doesn't happen anymore. No racer in the world closes out a season in which he achieves his discipline's ultimate accolade by competing in a relatively minor event, and then—and *this* is the trick—takes that relatively minor event so damned seriously that he goes out and wins the thing.

No racer except Stewart, that is.

Dale Earnhardt capped off his seven Winston Cup championship seasons with hunting trips and Bahamian getaways on his yacht. Rick Mears thrived on two things: winning the Indianapolis 500, which he did four times, and then spending his winters as far away as he could from the adulation afforded an Indy winner. The late Ayrton Senna blunted the stress of his three Formula One championship seasons by fleeing Europe for the beaches of his native Brazil as soon as the last race was over.

To find anything comparable to the way Tony Stewart rounded out his defining season in 2002, you have to go clear back to 1961. That was when a rising bullhead from Houston named A. J. Foyt won his first Indianapolis 500—the triumph that truly put him on the map, Foyt will tell you—and then closed out the year with his second consecutive Turkey Night midget win.

Which makes sense. After all, try as both Stewart and Foyt might to keep the comparisons between them from getting out of control—A.J. has joked with his young friend that he's sick of talking about him—there is simply no way to look hard at the young hothead from Indiana without also seeing the old hothead from Texas. Stewart brought up the subject himself almost as soon as he sat down in the Homestead interview room after locking up his championship.

"I think the coolest part about this whole thing," he said, "is that I finally did something Foyt didn't do."

He told the assembled media the story about how he had run his first Indy car test laps with Foyt's team back in the fall of 1995, and if you knew Stewart well you could almost see the memories flooding back: the way Foyt had made him his whipping boy, had ridden him mercilessly about everything from his clothes to his driving ability, had humiliated him daily in front of the entire team. Stewart told the reporters that whenever he had tried to point out that he couldn't have been *that* bad—he had just wrapped up the USAC Silver Crown championship, he had already won the club's sprint car title, he was leading the midget points—Foyt would answer by looking the kid straight in the eye and snorting, "Just check the record books, big boy."

At this point, now able to boast a title that Foyt had never come close to, Stewart gave the video cameras a big, showy nod.

"You're damn right, A.J.," he said, addressing his absent hero. "Check the record books."

There were chuckles all around the room, and Stewart said, "He may have won Daytona, and he may have won Indy, but he hasn't won an Indy car championship *and* a stock car championship. I've finally got one up on the old man."

That little moment—Stewart playfully ribbing cranky ol' A.J.—made the papers for the next couple of weeks. But what everybody in the media center missed was something that happened later on, at a casual party for the championship team beside Greg Zipadelli's motorhome in Homestead's VIP parking area. It was a gathering of comrades, of families, of a few old friends. Someone showed up with a couple of jars of white Carolina moonshine—one jar full of blueberries, the other strawberries—and both eventually worked their way around to the new NASCAR champion. Stewart, who rarely drinks, sampled a couple of swigs from each jar.

Maybe it was the 'shine. Maybe it was the euphoria of winning the title. Maybe Tony Stewart just wanted to bring his day, his *career*, full circle. Whatever it was, at 9:30 that night Stewart borrowed a cell phone from one friend, grabbed Foyt's number from another, and dialed Texas.

"Hey, big boy," Stewart said into the phone. "Check the record books."

Here Stewart laughed, and you could see from his face that Foyt must have been laughing, too, two hardass racers jabbing each other. But before long Stewart wandered away from his circle of friends, the phone still tight to his ear, and he and Foyt had a lengthy private chat.

Someday, historians might look back and say that in the long history of American automobile racing, no two drivers made more noise than Anthony Joseph Foyt and Anthony Wayne Stewart. But on this night, across all the miles and all their years, there was very little noise at all between them. It was clear that Stewart wasn't talking with the combative old warrior who had so tormented him in that Phoenix test, but rather with "the old man" he so admires, the grand hero who had hosted the kid at his Texas ranch in the weeks following that test in 1995. You could still picture the two of them tooling around Foyt's many acres, Stewart on a four-wheeler and A.J. on his tractor, clearing the land.

Remember Stewart's words about that visit? "We talked about racing, and about things that had nothing at all to do with the sport." In the darkness at Homestead, you got the sense that you were watching that same sort of conversation take place. Thirty years ago, the writers used to call Foyt "Terrible Tony." In 2002, they used the same name on Stewart. Funny, but on this night neither one of them seemed too terrible. The two loudest men in the sport, yesterday's champion and today's, just talked softly into the night.

Tony Stewart's world was quiet. For now.

December 2002

ACKNOWLEDGMENTS

TONY STEWART AND BONES BOURCIER WOULD LIKE TO THANK THE DOZENS OF teammates, fellow racers, family members, and friends who not only lent us the anecdotal memories scattered throughout these pages, but also provided invaluable background material. Without them, this story would have been less than complete. We also extend our gratitude to the photographers who dug into their archives to help illustrate this book.